SUBLIME COSMOS IN GRAECO-ROMAN LITERATURE AND ITS RECEPTION

Also available from Bloomsbury

ANAXIMANDER
by Andrew Gregory

EARLY GREEK PHILOSOPHIES OF NATURE
by Andrew Gregory

ECOLOGY AND THEOLOGY IN THE ANCIENT WORLD
edited by Ailsa Hunt and Hilary Marlow

THE ORIGINS OF MUSIC THEORY IN THE AGE OF PLATO
by Sean Alexander Gurd

SUBLIME COSMOS IN GRAECO-ROMAN LITERATURE AND ITS RECEPTION: INTERSECTIONS OF MYTH, SCIENCE AND HISTORY

ESSAYS IN HONOUR OF THOMAS D. WORTHEN

Edited by David Christenson and Cynthia White

BLOOMSBURY ACADEMIC
LONDON • NEW YORK • OXFORD • NEW DELHI • SYDNEY

BLOOMSBURY ACADEMIC
Bloomsbury Publishing Plc, 50 Bedford Square, London, WC1B 3DP, UK
Bloomsbury Publishing Inc, 1359 Broadway, 12th Floor, New York, NY 10018, USA
Bloomsbury Publishing Ireland, 29 Earlsfort Terrace, Dublin 2, D02 AY28, Ireland

BLOOMSBURY, BLOOMSBURY ACADEMIC and the Diana logo
are trademarks of Bloomsbury Publishing Plc

First published in Great Britain 2024
This paperback edition published 2025

Copyright © David Christenson, Cynthia White and Contributors, 2024

David Christenson and Cynthia White have asserted their right under the Copyright,
Designs and Patents Act, 1988, to be identified as Editors of this work.

For legal purposes the Acknowledgements on p. xii constitute an extension of
this copyright page.

Cover design: Terry Woodley
Cover image © Buena Vista Images/Getty

All rights reserved. No part of this publication may be: i) reproduced or transmitted in any form, electronic or mechanical, including photocopying, recording or by means of any information storage or retrieval system without prior permission in writing from the publishers; or ii) used or reproduced in any way for the training, development or operation of artificial intelligence (AI) technologies, including generative AI technologies. The rights holders expressly reserve this publication from the text and data mining exception as per Article 4(3) of the Digital Single Market Directive (EU) 2019/790.

Bloomsbury Publishing Inc does not have any control over, or responsibility for, any third-party websites referred to or in this book. All internet addresses given in this book were correct at the time of going to press. The author and publisher regret any inconvenience caused if addresses have changed or sites have ceased to exist, but can accept no responsibility for any such changes.

A catalogue record for this book is available from the British Library.
Library of Congress Cataloging-in-Publication Data
Names: Worthen, Thomas D., honoree. | Christenson, David M. (David Michael), editor. |
  White, Cynthia (Cynthia L. V. K.), editor.
Title: Sublime cosmos in Graeco-Roman literature and its reception : intersections
  of myth, science and history : essays in honour of Thomas D. Worthen /
  edited by David Christenson and Cynthia White.
Description: New York : Bloomsbury Publishing Plc, 2024. |
  Includes bibliographical references and index.
Identifiers: LCCN 2023039094 (print) | LCCN 2023039095 (ebook) |
  ISBN 9781350344679 (hardback) | ISBN 9781350344716 (paperback) |
  ISBN 9781350344686 (pdf) | ISBN 9781350344693 (ebook)
Subjects: LCSH: Religion in literature. | Classical literature–History and criticism. |
  Sublime, The, in literature. | Classical literature–Appreciation.
Classification: LCC PA3015.R4 S83 2024 (print) | LCC PA3015.R4 (ebook) |
  DDC 880.09—dc23/eng/20231103
LC record available at https://lccn.loc.gov/2023039094
LC ebook record available at https://lccn.loc.gov/2023039095.

ISBN: HB: 978-1-3503-4467-9
      PB: 978-1-3503-4471-6
   ePDF: 978-1-3503-4468-6
  eBook: 978-1-3503-4469-3

Typeset by RefineCatch Limited, Bungay, Suffolk

For product safety related questions contact productsafety@bloomsbury.com.

To find out more about our authors and books visit www.bloomsbury.com
and sign up for our newsletters.

THOMAS D. WORTHEN

philosopho ridenti

CONTENTS

Notes on Contributors		ix
Acknowledgements		xii
1	**Introduction** *David Christenson*	1

Part I Sublime Epic

2	**Homer's *Odyssey* and the Mystery of Time** *Norman Austin*	11
3	**Helen, Paris and the Philosophical ἔρως: Love, Strife and Sublime Contact from Homer to Plato** *Boris Shoshitaishvili*	29
4	**The Hard-Break at Hesiod, *Theogony* 200** *Frank Romer*	51
5	**Visions and Memories of Lucretius in Seneca's *Naturales Quaestiones*** *Christopher Trinacty*	67
6	**Vergil's *bougonia* Rite in *Georgics* 4: Its Nature, Sources, Origins and Possible Link to the Indo-European Myth of Creation** *Michael Teske*	89

Part II Celestial Drama

7	**An Early Morning Person? Aristophanes and His Star-Studded Comic Prologues** *Gonda Van Steen*	107
8	**Frighteningly Funny Gods: Comic and Cosmic Space in Plautus** *David Christenson*	133

Part III History, Historiography and the Cosmos

9	**Day Suddenly Became Night: Eclipses and the Sublime in Greek Historiography** *Philip Waddell*	159
10	**The Cosmic Barrier: The Isthmus of Corinth in Imperial Latin Poetry** *David J. Wright*	171

Contents

Part IV Reception

11 **Reading the Classics in Plague-Ridden England, 1629–1722**
    Thomas Willard 189

12 **'Solution Sweet' and Keats's Poetic Ideal: Erotic and Nuptial Imagery
    in *The Eve of St. Agnes*** *Cynthia White* 207

Index 227

CONTRIBUTORS

Norman Austin, born in China in 1937 as the child of missionaries, received his BA in Classics from the University of Toronto (1958), and his PhD from the University of California at Berkeley (1965). He joined the University of Arizona in 1980, where he twice served as Head of the Department of Classics and for one year as Acting Dean of the College of Humanities. He is the author of five books on classical topics and more than thirty essays in academic journals. He is currently working on two book-length projects, one on Plato's *Symposium*, the other on Vergil's *Aeneid*.

David Christenson is Professor of Classics at the University of Arizona, where his current teaching and research interests include reception, translation and trauma studies. He has published translations of ten Greek and Roman comedies and is the author of editions of, and commentaries on, Plautus' *Amphitruo* (2000), *Pseudolus* (2020) and *Rudens* (forthcoming in 2024). His Bloomsbury publications include *Plautus: Casina* (Bloomsbury Ancient Comedy Companions, 2019) and a forthcoming book on Roman Comedy. He has published chapters and journal articles on Aristophanes, Plautus, Terence, and other Greek and Latin authors.

Frank Romer is an ancient historian at East Carolina University who works with texts, language and material culture. He has published on aspects of Greek and Roman history, literature and religion, with current research focusing on ancient geography, mapping and ethnography. His *Pomponius Mela's Description of the World* provides a translation of, and introductory commentary on, Mela's *Chorographia*. He has analysed historical evidence in support of archaeological excavations at Lugnano in Teverina and Chianciano Terme, Italy. In addition to recent articles on Hesiod's ethnographic approach to Aphrodite, his interests include the cultural mix of Phoenician, Greek and Roman sites in North Africa.

Boris Shoshitaishvili is a University of Southern California and Berggruen Institute Fellow. His background is in ancient Greek poetry, comparative literature and evolutionary biology. His current project focuses on the relationship between the Earth sciences and collective identity. He has published in *Earth's Future*, *The Anthropocene Review* and *Bryn Mawr Classical Review*, and co-authored scientific papers in *Ageing Research Reviews* and *The Journal of Vertebrate Paleontology*. He completed a postdoctoral fellowship in the Anthropology Department at the University of California, Berkeley, after earning his PhD in Comparative Literature from Stanford and MA in Classics from the University of Arizona.

Until his untimely death, **Michael Teske** had taught at the University of Arizona for nearly two decades, interrupted by five years' teaching at East Carolina University. He

Contributors

was devoted to his students and encouraged their work in mythology, Indo-European linguistics and literature. His own interests in mythology spanned the whole range of theory and practice from prehistoric to modern times. As a graduate student at the University of North Carolina, Mike developed a linguistics-based etymology course that he brought with him and enhanced at both Arizona and East Carolina. A chapbook of his poems, *The Meow of Eclipse*, appeared in 2020.

Christopher Trinacty is Professor of Classics at Oberlin College. His primary research interests are the works of Seneca, both the tragedies and the philosophical works, Horace, and classical reception. His various publications include *Senecan Tragedy and the Reception of Augustan Poetry* (2014) and 'Fear and Healing: Seneca, Caecilius Iucundus and the Campanian Earthquake of 62/63 CE' (2019). He oversees the website www.oberlinclassics.com, which features commentaries on Seneca, *Naturales Quaestiones* 3 and Horace, *Epistles* 1.

Gonda Van Steen holds the position of Koraes Chair of Modern Greek and Byzantine History, Language and Literature in the Centre for Hellenic Studies and the Department of Classics at King's College London. She is the author of five books: *Venom in Verse: Aristophanes in Modern Greece* (2000); *Liberating Hellenism from the Ottoman Empire* (2010); *Theatre of the Condemned: Classical Tragedy on Greek Prison Islands* (2011); and *Stage of Emergency: Theater and Public Performance under the Greek Military Dictatorship of 1967–1974* (2015). Her latest book, *Adoption, Memory, and Cold War Greece: Kid pro quo?* (2019), takes the reader into the new, uncharted terrain of Greek adoption stories that become paradigmatic of Cold War politics and history.

Philip Waddell is Associate Professor of Classics at the University of Arizona. His research interests focus on ancient historiography, rhetoric and narratology. He has published on temporal shadowing in Appian and sudden transitions in Tacitus' *Annales*. His recent book, published by Bloomsbury, is *Tacitean Visual Narrative* (2020).

Cynthia White is Professor of Classics at the University of Arizona, where she teaches Latin language and literature as well as courses on the city of Rome and its reception and ancient Christianity – in Tucson and Rome. She has published on ancient, late antique and medieval marriage poems, early Christianity, Latin pedagogy and medieval bestiaries, including *From the Ark to the Pulpit*, an edition and translation of, and commentary on, the thirteenth-century Northumberland Bestiary, which has somewhat recently (in the life of a medieval manuscript) become one of the prized gems in the Getty Museum manuscript collection.

Thomas Willard is Emeritus Professor at the University of Arizona. His research covers esoteric aspects of English literature and their European sources. Recent publications include *Thomas Vaughan and the Rosicrucian Revival in Britain, 1648–1666* (2022) and book chapters on topics in Shakespeare and Paracelsus. He has also edited *Reading the Natural World in the Middle Ages and the Renaissance* (2020) and the alchemical writings of Jean d'Espagne (repr. 2018).

David J. Wright is Visiting Assistant Professor of Classics at Bowdoin College. He received his BA from Holy Cross, MA from the University of Arizona, and his PhD from Rutgers. His research interests include Augustan poetry, classical reception and monsters. He has published on a wide variety of topics, including Anna Perenna, images of Scylla on the coins of Sextus Pompey and the goddess Thetis. David also passionately uses ancient texts and material culture to encourage discussions about contemporary issues of social justice. His current book project examines Giants and Titans in Graeco-Roman literature.

ACKNOWLEDGEMENTS

This collection has happily found the light of day despite many difficulties and delays, including a global pandemic and the health challenges of some contributors. Michael Teske tragically died before its publication. Mike, a beloved teacher and colleague, was instrumental in launching this project to honour Thom Worthen, who taught Mike as an undergraduate and further stoked his passion for etymology and myth. We are most grateful to Aimee, Anna and Mary Worthen for their patience in the years since Thom's death. Finally, special thanks are owed to Alice Wright, Lily Mac Mahon and Zoe Osman at Bloomsbury for their encouragement and forbearance throughout this volume's production process.

CHAPTER 1
INTRODUCTION
David Christenson

Time's subjectivity; ontological insecurity; divine birth and the nature of divinity; (im)mortality and regenerative rites; metatheatricality and the notion that we are actors in a cosmic drama; the sublimely metaphysical power of erotic passion and what threatens it (e.g. strife, marriage); the impact of astronomical (ir)regularity and cosmic (dis)order; catastrophic epidemics; the play of reflection and distortion in our perception of the world; awesome technology and the suspicion it may overpower us in spite of, or because of, our self-interest: these phenomena, fears, thoughts and intimations that suggest human experience runs deeper than its mundane particulars make up the stuff of this volume. Since Graeco-Roman antiquity and no doubt much longer, human beings in moments of expansive thought and feeling have lived and laboured under the conviction, or delusion, that there is more to our biology-, time- and gravity-bound planetary experience than meets the eye, and that we respond profoundly to the vast, enveloping cosmos that dwarfs and awes us – or viewed differently, that human existence and thought open out to 'the sublime' (cf. Lat. *sublimis*, Grk. ὕψος). Sublimity in turn tenders the allure of consciousness beyond normalcy, conventionality and quotidian experience.

James Porter has persuasively argued for the prevalence of a more encompassing idea of sublimity in antiquity than that historically assumed by classicists, based primarily on their restrictive and misrepresentative readings of Longinus', or Pseudo-Longinus', *Peri hupsous*. This evocative first century CE (?) essay in fact constitutes an amalgam of collective Graeco-Roman reflection on the concept.[1] The sublime, as it seems to have been broadly perceived and experienced in antiquity, might be glimpsed not only in the unfamiliar and exuberant intensity of extreme circumstances (high or low, massive or miniscule, etc.), but through encounters with, for example, the immanence of (im)mortality, violent transitions and transformations, the collision of opposite forces, the expression of extraordinarily intense emotions, irregularities of time and season, shocking violations of nature or other jolting disruptions of regularity and cosmic order. Porter further suggests:

> Whatever the sublime is, it remains highly paradoxical to the core. Not fixed in objects *per se*, its assertion will always be the sign of a willed, if not willful, reading. But more than anything else, sublimity is a sign of the human propensity to locate great heights or depths of meaning in the surface of *all* things. Thus, if we have trouble putting our finger on the sublime whenever we try to catch it in the act, as though it were something else and more, this is because we are looking in the wrong places: the sublime, in the end, is nothing other than the very ecstasy of

language, thought, and experience in their day-to-day workings and in all their extraordinary contingency.

2016: 56

The sublime no less for us than for ancient Greeks and Romans may ultimately be, as Porter suggests, a vague, albeit powerful thought, feeling, sensation or intuition constructed and located entirely in our heads, often the product of art and language. Yet we cannot exclude the possibility that simply by conceiving of sublimity we may latch on to some Other outside and beyond ourselves, as is suggested in e.g. Platonic and other mystical or religious conceptualizations of reality.[2]

The eleven essays that here examine various manifestations of the cosmic sublime in ancient literature and its reception have been collected to honour Thomas D. Worthen, late Professor of Classics at the University of Arizona. Worthen, whose expansive curiosity and expertise spanned ancient science (especially astronomy), myth, philosophy and linguistics, plumbed the sublime cosmos throughout his career. His innovative study, *The Myth of Replacement: Stars, God, and Order in the Universe*, is an intricate interpretation of how global myths centred on changes in season, rulership, human fortune and their associated cycles of time reflect the irregularities of astronomical precession (a change in an astronomical body's rotational axis). Expanding on the work of Lévi-Strauss and others, Worthen analyses myths of various epochs from both related and independent traditions across the globe, in order to identify the structural elements of a bundle of complementary motifs ('the myth of replacement'), schematized as follows: '(A) replacement; (B) violations of sexual taboos; (C) symbols of female sexuality; (D) symbols of male sexuality; (C–D) male and female elements going together correctly in right running; (C/D) male and female elements dysfunctional in wrong running; (E) hiding; (F) disaster; (G) creation and re-creation; (H) etymological concurrence; and (I) cosmic significance' (1991: 69). Seemingly disparate, geographically and culturally discrete stories can thus be collectively understood as individualized, creative narrative responses to the destabilizing celestial anomalies arising from the cyclical wobbling of the earth on its axis, an irregularity that in recent history has been anthropogenically augmented.[3] Incorporating philological detail, astronomical phenomena and abstract theory, and sometimes illuminating complex linguistic and conceptual puzzles (as those involving mills, hammers and bowdrills), Worthen's study mirrors the rich scope of the Greek word κόσμος (*cosmos*) itself, whose range of meanings includes 'construct(ion)', 'order(liness)', 'adornment' (e.g. a piece of fine jewellery), as well as 'world' and 'universe'.

Worthen's challenging study did not reach many readers in classical studies nor gain the recognition it deserves, perhaps because few classicists possess the technical understanding of astronomy required to grasp fully all its arguments, and astronomers may not have been willing to follow its deep engagement with literature and myth. Those who have worked through *The Myth of Replacement* typically find it to be an original and insightful model of multidisciplinary scholarship on universal(izing) myth that sheds light on the cognitive processes activated in mythmaking. It may well become a book whose brilliance is not appreciated until decades after its author's death.

Introduction

A primary goal of this collection of essays in honour of the memory of Thomas D. Worthen is to revive interest in *The Myth of Replacement* (now regrettably out of print). Worthen's enduring influence on three generations of students and colleagues in the University of Arizona's Classics community is inestimable. His intellectual legacy may best be recognized by engaging with the kinds of profound cosmic questions that motivated his study of the ancient world. Lest its title create false expectations, this volume is not a systematic investigation (philosophical, philological, theological, etc.) of ancient conceptions of (the) *cosmos*, usually translated *mundus* in Lat.: readers should not look here for formal study of cosmology, cosmogony or cosmography, though individual essays range into these areas.[4] Here we use 'cosmos' in its modern English sense to refer generally to the universe,[5] and in close conjunction with an amorphous concept of sublimity. Nor are this collection's essays focused on particular aspects of ancient myth, science or history, but, rather, they all treat literary texts that operate within these conceptual fields. Across the four sections of *Sublime Cosmos*, the contributors investigate a wide array of brushes with the sublime, as these are situated either in the physical cosmos or in contemplation of it, in ancient Greek and Roman literature and its reception. No attempt is made to confine the Protean concept of the sublime to a singular manifestation, but the volume's essays together trace some of its manifold expressions in the logic, patterns of thought, rhetoric, ideas and imagery of texts. The individual chapters, which apply diverse critical methods and approaches, are instead united by their partial engagement with the sublime across the breadth of its aesthetic, agential and metaphysical aspects. The sections and essays are summarized as follows.

Sublime epic

Since antiquity, the *Iliad*, with its tragic focus on humanity's starkly limited (im)mortal prospects, has often been received as the more profound, sublime and cosmic of the Homeric epics. But as **Norman Austin** argues in 'Homer's *Odyssey* and the mystery of time', Odysseus on his journey home emerges as a transcendent figure closely identified with time itself. Odysseus' return to Ithaca significantly coincides with the end of the old year and the beginning of the new and is a matter of correct timing, crucially so in the remarkable convergence of Penelope's and Odysseus' divergent timelines for the previous twenty years, the approximate length required for synchronization of the solar and lunar calendars. This coincidence of time in the *Odyssey* is realized as light: the stranger returns as *Aithōn* to herald the genuine Odysseus' arrival between the old and new moons. In Austin's analysis, Homer's mythopoesis offers a meditation on the mysterious nature of cosmic time and human efforts to calibrate it. After Worthen's work, he finds in these numinous events a (localized) myth of replacement heralding a new order of justice and reverence in Ithaca.

Boris Shoshitaishvili's 'Helen, Paris and the Philosophical ἔρως: Love, Strife and Sublime Contact from Homer to Plato' also finds fundamental, cosmic tensions at work in Homeric epic. Embedded within the *Iliad*'s agonism is the love of Helen and Paris, a

3

passionate and transgressive case of *erōs* amid the poem's pervasive *eris* ('strife'), for which it is responsible. Shoshitaishvili sees in Paris a proto-philosopher of ethics, while Helen can be understood as a kind of divinely inspired metaphysician. Paris uniquely among Homer's warriors distances himself from the battlefield to abstractly analyse and compare the ethical types of lover and warrior. The self-effacing Helen of the *teichoscopia* shows a capacity for detached, quasi-transcendental reflection as she surveys the unfolding destruction that her desire and desirability have released. In the union of Paris and Helen, *erōs* can be glimpsed as the *Iliad*'s great subdued divine force, despite its eclipse by the poem's brilliant battles. Shoshitaishvili concludes by tracing the subsequent development in Greek thought – through Heraclitus' interplay of harmony and conflict and Empedocles' dichotomy of Love and Strife and culminating in Plato's *Symposium* – of the intuition that *philosophia* is an act born of *erōs*.

A pair of chapters examine mysterious births in didactic epics. In 'The Hard-Break at Hesiod, *Theogony* 200', **Frank Romer** explicates the function of this verse in reconciling the familiar problem of Aphrodite's single-birth from Ouranos' genitals and her two-parent birth in Homer. In Hesiod's *Theogony*, which describes the generation of the universe and the cosmic sexual conditions under which the Olympian gods came into being, Aphrodite appears as a paradoxical descendant of Earth and Sky. *Theogony* 200, Romer argues, pivotally summarizes the theogonic miracle of Aphrodite's spontaneous generation (188–200) and separates it from the myth's post-theogonic expansion (201–6). The post-theogonic elements and normalization of Aphrodite's motherless birth align her with the more recent Olympian generation of gods for an androcentric audience through a two-step process of Hellenization and Panhellenization. Romer concludes that, apart from Aphrodite's miraculous birth, all other references to her in *Theogony* are to a post-theogonic role that reflects a separate development outside the context of oral *mythos*. References to the paradoxical Aphrodite in *Theogony* are tied to her post-theogonic, Panhellenic development, a process that hierarchizes and divides the goddess's many powers into both epichoric and universally Hellenic spheres.

Michael Teske takes a fresh look at Vergil's strangely sublime account of 'ox-generation' – actually two distinct accounts, one apicultural (*G.* 4.295–314), the other ritualistic (4.537–58) – in 'Vergil's *bougonia* Rite in *Georgics* 4: Its Nature, Sources and Possible Link to the Indo-European Myth of Creation'. Teske begins by reviewing Vergil's likely sources (Greek, Roman, Egyptian), as well as what we can glean of the third-century CE Florentinus' account of *bougonia*, in order to identify the rite's fundamental features. In *Georgics* 4, Vergil's *bougonia* significantly falls within a series of allusions to Homeric cosmogony, much as it was later read by Porphyry at *De ant. Nymp.* 18.9–15. Teske further relates Vergil's Aristaeus and Orpheus to the divine twins *Manu and *Yemo in reconstructions of the IE creation myth (cf. its Roman incarnation in Romulus and Remus), so as to locate the *bougonia*'s conception in a Vergilian allegorical cosmogony.

Introduction

Christopher Trinacty's 'Visions and Memories of Lucretius in Seneca's *Naturales Quaestiones*' examines Seneca's redeployment of Lucretian epic in articulating, through complex intertextuality, his critical reception of Epicurean physics and ethics, especially Lucretius' assertions about the divine. While various scientific topics of *Natural Questions* necessarily recall Lucretius' sublime epic, Seneca's first book offers an extensive critique of Epicurean sense-perception by evoking *De Rerum Natura* 4. Seneca caps *Q Nat.* 1 with the notorious account of Hostius Quadra and his magnifying mirrors to showcase the deficiencies of Epicurean tenets. Appropriations of the Lucretian technical terms *simulacra* and *imago* in particular show Seneca rejecting Epicurean physics as he promotes his own view of the divine. Hostius, who feeds on distorted reflections knowingly, and only to spur unfulfillable desires, problematizes the Epicurean idea that all sense-perceptions are true, and is ultimately shown to be ludicrously ignorant of a Stoic universe in which god is pure *ratio*.

Celestial drama

In 'An Early Morning Person? Aristophanes and His Star-Studded Comic Prologues', **Gonda Van Steen** considers references to sky, stars and constellations in Aristophanes that brilliantly collapse real time, plot-time and cosmic time. Individual plays metatheatrically exploit the sky, immediately visible to spectators in the open-air theatre, as a virtual agent in performance. Comedies beginning with pre-dawn or dawn scenes demonstrate that both playwright and audiences were acutely aware of the particularities of the star field and their impact on the play's progression, the festival calendar and civic calendrical practice. Van Steen's approach unlocks an innovative vista for interpreting Athenian comedy through the confluence of play, sky and the surrounding physical environment of Athens spread out below the open-air Theatre of Dionysus. Rereading Aristophanes' comedies with an eye to the sky opens up alternative categories of space and time that in turn promote fresh interpretations diverging from dominant, text-centred readings of comedy.

David Christenson's 'Frighteningly Funny Gods: Comic and Cosmic Space in Plautus' explores the surprising vastness and complexity of the Roman playwright's comic universe through a reassessment of the boundary-crossing *Amphitruo*. In a performance-focused study of Plautus' self-described *tragicomoedia*, Christenson suggests that the persistently metatheatrical *Amphitruo*, in its striking collapse of the human and divine, presents its audience(s) with the sublimely frightening spectre of an unstable, unsettling and even hostile universe. Through its farcical yet dissonant representation of a polymorphic Jupiter – simultaneously ruler of the cosmos, top-ranking god of Roman cult and mythic philanderer – *Amphitruo* raises provocative cultural, theological and moral questions, especially related to themes of power, hierarchy and privilege. By projecting a freighted Roman cosmos as a deeply tragicomic construct, the play invites spectators and readers to contemplate its incongruities and inequities across a spectrum of emotional and dramatic modes.

History, historiography and the cosmos

In 'Day Suddenly Became Night: Eclipses and Characterization in Greek Historiography', **Philip Waddell** identifies ancient historiographers' persistent and pointed practice of combining portentous astronomical and religious phenomena with the dramatic characterization of their works' protagonists by assigning narrative functions to eclipses – specifically within Herodotus' account of Xerxes' invasion of Greece, Thucydides' depiction of Nicias in the Sicilian Expedition and Alexander's reactions to a lunar eclipse before the battle of Gaugamela as described in Arrian (and other writers). Waddell demonstrates how Greek historiographers, fully aware that the experience of an eclipse was a memorable, numinous and frightening moment for their audiences, powerfully mobilize this convenient or invented natural phenomenon as a narrative device to heighten dramatic interest in their protagonists and their sublimely fateful choices.

David J. Wright's 'The Cosmic Barrier: The Isthmus of Corinth in Imperial Latin Poetry' examines the Corinthian Isthmus as a compelling metonym, with both historical and literary resonances, for cosmic destruction in Seneca's tragedies and Lucan's *Pharsalia*. The storied Isthmus of Corinth, a topographical wonder in its own right, became an even greater source of wonder and anxiety in the ancient world when human beings attempted to transform it through technology, specifically through the (planned) construction of a canal connecting the two seas on its sides. Ancient scientific literature portends a disastrous outcome for such a project, including dire warnings that linking the Corinthian and Saronic Gulfs would result in catastrophic flooding. Early Imperial Latin poets, Wright argues, are keenly focused on the Isthmus because of grandiose imperial designs, most notably Nero's, to construct the canal. References to the Isthmus in Seneca and Lucan, framed in terms of boundary violations and even cosmic catastrophe, subtly reflect these poets' anxieties about imperial power generally and Nero in particular.

Reception

This volume concludes with two chapters on the classical reception of ideas central to its overall project. In 'Reading the Classics in Plague-Ridden England, 1629–1722', **Thomas Willard** discusses the intellectual climate in which the Longinian sublime was incorporated into the Neo-Classical criticism of England during the seventeenth and eighteenth centuries, specifically vis-à-vis the catastrophic plagues and fires of this period. As English writers became familiar with the conception of the sublime *c.* 1700, they realized that Milton's *Paradise Lost* was a sublime epic *par excellence* and that Dryden had anticipated this new critical theory as well. In this same light, Willard examines Thomas Sprat's *History of the Royal Society of London* (1668), which promotes scientific inquiry and discovery – including treatments of plague as Lucretius and Thucydides had before him – in illustrating that many of the recent horrors of war and fire and disease turn out to be subjects of the terrible sublime as Longinus presents it.

Introduction

Cynthia White in '"Solution Sweet" and Keats's Poetic Ideal: Erotic and Nuptial Imagery in *The Eve of St. Agnes*' explores the poem's rich appropriation of elements of Roman love-elegy, ancient epithalamia and martyr texts. Set amid pastoral landscapes beneath the poetic constellations of seasonal agricultural cycles, epithalamia exhort the newlywed couple to mimic nature in its regenerative fecundity. In sharp contrast, Roman elegy, a genre of thwarted erotic passion, rejects marriage and celebrates passion that is consuming yet unconsummated and irreconcilable with the civic institution of marriage. Keats's narrative poem, White demonstrates, sensuously and metapoetically blends genre conceits, superstition, religion, love, desire and marriage, along with their associated tensions and contradictions, into a 'Solution sweet' (322) that is mysteriously instantiated the moment Porphyro melts into Madeline's dream – a charged moment in which elegy yields to epithalamia and dream to reality to explicate a central tenet of Keats's poetic programme, the progress of the sublime to the beautiful.

Conclusion

It is our hope that these essays, in addition to inspiring renewed interest in their honorand's work, will resonate with a variety of readers. Fascination with our sublime cosmos has not abated today, though more diverse instances of experiencing it may have emerged, alongside fresh theories of sublimity and the cosmos's organization. While mountains, earthquakes, floods, pandemics, monsters, superheroes and imaginings of powerful gods still astonish us, science increasingly has become a source of overwhelming complexity, mystery and beauty in the gradually discovered sublime of particle physics, astrophysics, cold dark matter, Big Bang cosmology and the deep time traversed in the evolutionary history of life – as well as in wondrous advances in, for example, molecular neuroscience's mapping of the tiny neural networks supporting cognition and human consciousness. Less anthropocentric orientation towards the natural world continues to deepen our understanding of the communication, collaboration and consciousness of non-human animal species and of plants. The nightmarish political history of the twentieth century has also ushered in postmodern and peculiarly grim manifestations of the sublime: alienation, trauma and scepticism, loss of faith in the stability of language and meaning, *aporia* and suspicion of human reason (to name a few). Finally, awash in a catastrophic climate crisis, humankind in the Anthropocene now confronts the prodigious spectre of an Earth System disrupted and an entire biosphere decimated by the planetary impact of our own globalization. Given our contemporary, profound yet fraught relationship with the world around us, *Sublime Cosmos* will exceed the contributors' expectations if, beyond clarifying temporally and culturally distant moments in which myth, science, history and metaphysics communicated with one another, its essays lend nuanced perspective to ongoing expressions of wonder at our cosmos's sublime heights and depths.

Notes

1. See further Porter 2016, esp. 1–134. For a critical edition and translation of, and commentary on, Pseudo-Longinus, see now Halliwell 2022 (which appeared too late for contributors to incorporate here).
2. Shaw (2017) provides an insightful survey of the sublime in western thinking, ancient to postmodern. He begins by distinguishing between predominately older and non-secular notions of the sublime rooted in transcendence and (usually) postmodern ones emphasizing immanence (2–5).
3. Additional wobbling of the earth's axis observed in recent decades has been attributed to human causes (climate change, groundwater depletion): https://www.nytimes.com/2023/06/28/climate/groundwater-earth-spin-axis.html?smid=nytcore-android-share (with links to scientific literature), accessed 28 June 2023.
4. For the origins of the ancient cosmos, see for example Clay 2003 and Graham 2006. Philosophically inclined accounts of the nature of the universe include Horky 2019 and Salles 2009. Gagné 2021 describes his study of the Hyperborea (the world's northernmost extremes) in Greek cult and literature as cosmography, which he defines as 'the rhetoric of cosmology: the art of composing worlds' (3).
5. For the Greek concept's introduction and development in English, see Horky 2019: xv–xviii.

Works cited

Clay, J. S. (2003), *Hesiod's Cosmos*, Cambridge: Cambridge University Press.
Gagné, R. (2021), *Cosmography and the Idea of Hyperborea in Ancient Greece*, Cambridge: Cambridge University Press.
Graham, D. W. (2006), *Explaining the Cosmos: The Ionian Tradition of Scientific Philosophy*, Princeton: Princeton University Press.
Halliwell, S. (2022), *Pseudo-Longinus, On the Sublime*, Oxford: Oxford University Press.
Horky, P. S. (ed.) (2019), *Cosmos in the Ancient World*, Cambridge: Cambridge University Press.
Porter, J. I. (2016), *The Sublime in Antiquity*, Cambridge: Cambridge University Press.
Salles, R. (2009), *God and Cosmos in Stoicism*, Oxford: Oxford University Press.
Shaw, P. (2017), *The Sublime*, London and New York: Routledge.
Worthen, T. D. (1991), *The Myth of Replacement: Stars, Gods, and Order in the Universe*, Tucson: University of Arizona Press.

PART I
SUBLIME EPIC

CHAPTER 2
HOMER'S *ODYSSEY* AND THE MYSTERY OF TIME
Norman Austin

Introduction

Homer's *Odyssey* is a mystery narrative that abounds with elements of ancient mystery religions.[1] It is perhaps not as systematic a mystery as we might expect in those works of literature that can profitably be read through the lens of esotericism or hermeticism. But it satisfies two of Faivre's six components of works classified as hermetic:[2] first, the principle that everything – every phenomenon and every event – has significance; and second, true wisdom requires a study of this significance, and an understanding of the relations between, objects, events and persons.

Another element in the mystery religion and hermetic tradition is initiation. Initiation is the process whereby a person is led from a blandly superficial relationship with phenomena into a deeper significance that binds each phenomenon to every other.[3] The most obvious initiation in the *Odyssey* is the process that takes Telemachus, the son of Odysseus, from boyhood to manhood. The numinous symbol that marks this initiation is given to us when Odysseus and Telemachus are removing the weapons from the hall and stowing them in some secret place, where they will be secure and out of sight. Their action takes place after dark. Penelope's suitors have left the hall to return to their own homes for the night, and the women have been dismissed. Secrecy and invisibility are of preeminent concern. But who then is to carry a torch to provide the necessary light? In a word, 'Athena' (*Od.* 19.33–4). As the two men undertake this work, Athena goes before them bearing a golden torch, which casts a splendid illumination.

Telemachus experiences a moment of sublime amazement (*thauma*, 19.36): 'This is a great wonder', he says, 'The walls, the beams, the pillars appear as if lit up by a blazing fire. Surely here is one of the gods who hold the wide sky.'[4] To which Odysseus replies: 'Silence. Put this in your mind, and do not question it.[5] This is the custom of the gods.' The boy has just experienced his first epiphany.[6] This truly is his initiation.

The word here translated 'custom' is δίκη. *dikē* is used as 'custom' of both humans and gods, but scholars sometimes baulk at translating it as merely 'custom', when it is one of the words of deepest moral import ('justice', 'fairness') in ancient Greek.[7] The sublime illumination of the gods is surely more profound than mere custom. This is their very nature. This divine illumination marks the boy's initiation into manhood. The secret of the gods is now revealed to him, and his father enjoins his silence, which is the customary rule imposed on initiates.

In this hermetic tradition, all life is a mystery. At the risk of oversimplification, we might classify this mystery under four categories: first, the mystery of existence. Why do things exist? Second is the mystery of life itself. Third is the mystery of consciousness. And fourth is the mystery of time. All these mysteries are interconnected and interdependent. We cannot study the mystery of time without also studying the mystery of consciousness.

The question of time leads us at once into the mystery that has beset philosophy since Heraclitus and Parmenides opened Pandora's Box to find therein two inseparable enigmas, Being and Becoming. This enigma leads us directly into the phenomenology of time: how do we experience the enigma of time? Literary works that command our respect and attention perhaps treat all these mysteries, with a greater emphasis on one or another of the four as they are constructed in hermeticism.[8]

Epic mystery

The *Odyssey* makes clear at its outset that its theme is mystery. The hero of the epic has gone missing, and the teleology of the poem is to locate him and to bring him home. All the principal characters in this poem are mysteries. Certainly, Penelope is a mystery, Circe is a mystery, Calypso is a mystery, Helen is a mystery; even Menelaus,[9] her somewhat bland husband, is made a mystery. He will escape death and be transported to Elysium, thanks to his privilege of being the husband of Helen.

The poem itself begins with the mystery of time as it affects Penelope, the wife of Odysseus, and his son, Telemachus. Odysseus has been absent from his home for twenty years. Telemachus has now reached manhood, the time when an aristocratic young Greek male goes out into the world to make a name for himself. Instead, he is living a life of arrested time, almost an interloper in his own home, while his mother's suitors occupy the palace and squander its resources.[10] Instead of taking action against them as a heroic figure like his father would, Telemachus sobs among this invading horde, every one of them an enemy to him and his house, 'seeing his father in his mind, and hoping that he might return, and scatter the suitors, and so he might himself exercise his rule and be lord of his own house' (*Od*.1.114–17).

This is the picture of a youth arrested in his development. If only his father might return and with his father's power restore his son to his rightful place in this home. Time is proceeding at its inexorable pace; it does not wait for Telemachus, it is pressing on him, but Telemachus has no idea of how to manage time.[11] A human being who does not understand time becomes time's passive victim.

Penelope feels even more acutely the weight of time. For twenty years she has been a married woman but knowing only the burdens of marriage and not its potential joys or pleasures. Her husband has been absent for twenty years, and she has received no word from him. She knows not where he is, or even if he is alive. She is not a single woman, nor is she married; she is neither wife nor widow. For Penelope, too, time stands still. The trick that she plays on her importunate suitors, weaving a shroud for her father-in-law by day and unweaving it at night, in an excellent strategy for outwitting the house's unwanted intruders. It is also her strategy for marking time. My friend Bob Byars reminds me that Penelope is the timekeeper in this poem; her weaving and unweaving is like a metronome – tick tock, tick tock. She is a prisoner in her own home, and she marks time as a prisoner would, marking each passing day by scribbling on a prison wall. But Penelope's scheme has been discovered; that means her time is up. In her conversation with her own husband, when he is still in disguise, she says the gods destroyed both her excellence and her beauty when her husband Odysseus went with the other Greek warriors to Troy (19.124–6). This is a poignant expression of time's burden on a woman who is neither single nor married nor widowed in a society with no opportunities for women to build lives independent of men. Time passing for such a woman is time wasted. Penelope has been wasting time for twenty years, but not of her own volition.

The enigma of time is made most acute when we turn our attention to Odysseus. In his case, time itself becomes the most profound issue for his life. The first four books of the *Odyssey* are occupied primarily with Telemachus and his search for his father. Odysseus himself, whose whereabouts are a mystery to everyone who knew him, does not appear until book 5, when we find that he has been sequestered on Calypso's island, somewhere at the far edge of nowhere for the past seven years, to shield him from Poseidon's wrath. But the time has come for him to leave Calypso's protection and return to his own home. This island, called Ogygia, which means something like 'primordial' (West 1966: 378), is a place of exquisite beauty. Plants, birds, streams make it a paradise, and at its centre is Neumann's Mother Goddess herself, in one of her countless impersonations, whose name means, 'I shall conceal' (the future of καλύπτω, 'cover'). Her island is the womb, but a womb cannot become a permanent residence.[12]

In our first sighting of Odysseus, he is not in Calypso's cave, which has been his home for seven years, nor is he wandering around the prolific beauties of the island. Instead, we see him sitting on the rocky shore, staring out to sea, which the Homeric bards elsewhere call 'the barren sea' (*atrugetos*), and weeping copiously, and with his tears he weeps away his *aiōn*. Here is time given its most exact definition. αἰών in later Greek became 'a period of time' (Latin *aevum*), hence a person's 'lifetime'. Onians 1951: 200–9 has demonstrated that if we trace the word back to its earliest usage, it was not merely the abstract idea of time but something more specific: the spinal fluid. Each person is endowed with a certain supply of *aiōn* at birth. This *aiōn* cannot be replenished. It flows from our bodies in blood, sweat and tears; it is the fluid that sustains our life. Odysseus exists on Calypso's island, but none of her island's abundance can give him life. Instead, his life seeps from him drop by drop.

At their evening meal, Calypso, who has already promised that she will assist Odysseus in leaving her island, asks him if he would really prefer the hazards in store for him instead of the comforts and serenity of her island. And surely his wife Penelope can be no match for Calypso herself. Can a mortal woman compare with a goddess? Calypso can make Odysseus timeless and deathless. Who would not leap at such an opportunity? And what hero has ever been offered the transcendental gift of timelessness?[13]

Timelessness is the prerogative of the gods. They live lives much like humans but on a transcendental plane. They love to eat and listen to good music and at nightfall they retire to their beds, as we do. But their existence is a mere simulacrum of our lives (for comic inversion of this idea, see Christenson's chapter in this volume). They do not work, hence they never suffer the deterioration of time. They exist in the golden haze of perfection, but this haze is only our projection. They are as we might be if we could conserve all the delights of existence, with time subtracted from the equation. But Odysseus, offered this golden opportunity, declines. He wants, indeed he needs, to live in time. Time is what lends his *aiōn* meaning, intention, purpose. His life on Calypso's island is meaningless. Humans need meaning, and only time can give them that necessary meaning.

Reconstructing time

Once Odysseus has confronted this sublimely forbidding choice, to prefer time to timelessness (in *Od.* 5), the rest of the poem, which is to say most of the poem, is dedicated to his re-entry into time. First, he builds for himself a boat, and, with Calypso's blessing and cooperation, sets sail across the open sea, with the constellations of the night sky as his only guides across that barren waste, stars being his markers of both time and space (di Santillana 1969 and Worthen 1991 have devoted much research to this topic). These constellations give Odysseus his direction, but they are also his timepiece. They inform him as they inform us, that his voyage across the sea comes at the end of the sailing season. The constellations given in this passage indicate that Odysseus is sailing in October. The word for 'winter' in Greek (χεῖμα) also means 'storm'. The first storm in the autumn season marks the beginning of winter. When Odysseus barely arrives on Scheria after a storm, he, now naked, searches for a place where he can hide to find protection from the night frost.

He buries himself under a great heap of fallen leaves, a sure sign of winter, as a farmer buries a coal at the far edge of his property, which Homer calls 'the sperm of fire' (*sperma puros*, 5.490). Odysseus has re-entered time, and time is presented in its most brutal form. He is being born into time, or rather reborn.

The sea across which Odysseus sails in silence and solitude, in hermetic terms, can only be the Amniotic Sea. And Ino's veil, which protects him once his raft has been destroyed, but which he must throw back into the sea once he reaches land, that is, once he emerges from the sea, is then the placenta, which sustains the embryo until it (now a foetus) exits from the womb and can sustain life on its own.[14] Odysseus, re-entering time, must re-enact the universal experience of humans as they are born into time.

It heightens the drama to have Odysseus rediscover time in the winter season, since winter is time at its worst. The frost adds its threat to his survival, for he is nude with nothing to protect him from winter's threat. But there is another, more important reason for his arrival, which is slowly made apparent in the ensuing narrative. Odysseus is the harbinger of the new year. He is the herald of time. His final arrival in his own palace on

Ithaca, once he leaves Scheria, will mark the end of the old year and the beginning of the new.[15]

Once Odysseus has made landfall on Scheria, the land of the Phaeacians, another element comes into play: time is no longer merely extension or duration, but timing. Since time itself is a catastrophe, the only relief from time is when humans comprehend the nature of timing and how and when to exercise it. Odysseus has landed in a destitute condition on foreign soil. His survival is seriously threatened. Ergo, timing!

Athena enters the royal palace and addresses the princess Nausikaa. She chides the girl for her carelessness. The time has come for her to put aside her childish ways and ready herself to become a woman. What better paradigm could the poet find for the principle of timing than that moment of transition from child to adult? It is time for Nausikaa to gather up the men's clothes and take them down to the river to be laundered. The magic word here is γάμος ('marriage'). 'Your *gamos* is at hand, Athena tells the girl, when it's important for a girl to be well dressed, and to provide clean clothes for the men who will accompany her' (6.28–9). Having delivered her instructions, Athena vanishes and betakes herself to 'the timeless perfection of Olympus, where men say the seat of the gods is unshakeable, a place never troubled by wind or rain, or snow, but the air is cloudless, and everywhere is spread a radiance. This is what the gods enjoy permanently' (6.41–6). The pleasure of this eternal transcendental radiance and lucidity, suffused with omnipotence and omnitemporality, is what Odysseus declined when dining with Calypso.

When Nausikaa requests a wagon from her father, she is afraid to mention the word 'marriage' (Austin 2017: 14–17), but her father understands what is on her mind and has a wagon prepared to take Nausikaa and the laundry down to the river. Marriage is the single most important marker of time for an aristocratic Phaeacian girl, her initiation into adulthood.

Nausikaa (who is not wearing her traditional veil, 6.100) and her friends launder the clothes at the river, spread them on the rocks to dry, then amuse themselves with a ball game. Here is yet another instance of time. This would be, if Nausikaa were Greek, the last time she would play ball with her girlfriends. Once married, she would have new obligations on her mind besides playing ball with the girls.[16]

A girlish shout arouses the man buried under the autumn leaves. He then emerges from his hiding spot and, in still another marker of time, must find a branch to cover his genitals. Odysseus has arrived back in human society, where nakedness is an issue of considerable consequence. Here enters another element in our study of time: coincidence. Coincidence is the intersection of two timelines (or 'world lines', as physicists say). Such intersections happen by the thousands every day. Many coincidences we cast aside as mere flotsam and jetsam of our daily lives. But others we ignore at our own peril. Recognized and properly understood, they may determine the very structure of a life and give it meaning and consequence.

Coincidences abound here. A princess arrives at the river with men's clothing sufficiently elegant to be worthy of a royal prince. For Nausikaa's part, she, with a wagonload of fine raiment, has gone to the river now ready to meet her future husband.

Alas for Nausikaa, the man she meets is looking for a wife, not a new wedding. He is looking for the wife to whom he is already married.[17] If this episode were in the timeless zone where Calypso dwells, Odysseus might embark upon a brief affair with this beautiful princess. But he is now back in time, and time has meaning and consequence. Instead of consummating an affair, Odysseus must resort to his best alternative, flirtation. Many readers have felt that Nausikaa has been misused, by Homer if not by Odysseus. Rather than seeking flirtation with Odysseus, she is perfectly poised to marry, at the very peak of beauty and opportunity.[18] But we must put aside our grievances with the narrative's faults, such as they may be, and accept the terms of the narrative itself, which are to show us timing and coincidence as they affect Odysseus' re-entry into the world of time.

Meanwhile, back in Ithaca

Once Odysseus arrives in Ithaca, his own island home, we discover that time and timing are now of extreme urgency. Time is the central preoccupation of all the major characters in the last books of the poem. And now another element is added that bears directly on the calendar: light. First, the theme is adumbrated in the fire that is to keep the room warm for the conversation soon to take place between Odysseus and Penelope. A fire in the hearth *adumbrates*: it paradoxically disguises even as it illuminates. The nature of the light in this hearth, which encourages both Odysseus and Penelope to decipher the signs in all their ambiguity, is one of several symbols that govern the mechanics of this poem. In the flames flickering in the hearth, we discover symbolism and allegory.

As the evening comes on, Penelope's suitors, with help from Penelope's own maidservants, set up barriers in the great hall, with logs stacked behind each, and the women kindle the fires. But Odysseus needs to have the hall cleared so that he and his son can remove the arms and stow them in a secret place where they will be invisible and out of reach. Odysseus tells the women that they can leave the hall, and that he will be responsible for keeping the braziers burning. Odysseus himself has become the light in the hall. This provokes the suitor Eurymachus into a fit of laughter. 'Look,' he says, 'this man must be sent by the gods into this hall. His head, with not a single hair on it, is lit as if it were a torch itself' (18.353–5). It adds to our mirth to hear these hooligans spouting insults prompted by their mindlessness. How little they understand of time.[19]

One of Penelope's suitors is called Antinoos ('Anti-mind'). Mindlessness is the dominant characteristic of these lordly idiots, and nowhere do they exhibit greater mindlessness than in the matter of time. Yes, the light has by the gods' will returned to the house, but for this unruly crowd that profound event only provokes them to greater stupidity. These men are utterly ignorant of time's relentless progress, even as time silently bears down on them in the most forcible and obvious way.

As we have seen, once Penelope's suitors have vacated the hall and the maidservants have been dismissed, Odysseus and Telemachus begin to remove the arms from the hall, and Athena provides the light. She goes before them carrying a golden torch, which casts a splendid light. Telemachus is amazed. 'This is a great marvel,' he says, 'the walls and the rafters appear to my eyes as if lit by a blazing fire. Surely some god must be here' (19.36–40).

'This is the very nature of the gods' (19.43), Odysseus explains to his son, who is only just beginning to comprehend the complexity of the relations between humans and their gods. Telemachus has been vouchsafed his first sublime vision of transcendence. He and his father and the very walls of the house are lit by this transcendence. Light is the gods' very nature. And the light has now returned to this house, which has been shrouded in darkness for so many years. A vital element in the poem's structure is the return of the light which marks the calendar, the passing and coincidences of time, as the very foundation of the poem.

With the armour cleared from the room, and all Penelope's 'guests' gone home, Odysseus, disguised as an old and useless vagabond, and his suspicious but circumspect wife sit down for a private and intimate conversation. Some scholars have debated whether Penelope in fact recognizes this vagabond as her husband. It would certainly be in character for her to parry and thrust as he does, being his equal as a trickster. Odysseus chooses not to identify himself, and why should his wife, with all her antennae on the alert, expect any such precipitous disclosure?[20] The *Odyssey* asks us to enjoy the strategies and the manoeuvres of both husband and wife, each testing the other. This is a courtship. Why should we not enjoy a courtship that proceeds in the typical manner of courtships, with disclosures, revelations, guesses and half-guesses?

Here we are given to watch two timelines gradually converging, timelines which have been widely divergent for many years. Why not enjoy the poetic nuances of this convergence, so unlike anything else in literature, ancient or modern? The subject of the conversation between these two people is, of course, time, time being the theme around which this whole poem is constructed. We learn here how truly acute is the crisis of time at this point in both their lives. Penelope's method of marking time – weaving and unweaving a shroud for her ageing father-in-law – has been discovered.[21] With her strategy exposed, she is now compelled to complete her weaving and thus make herself available for a new marriage with one of her husband's detested rivals. Also, her son has now clearly passed from boyhood to manhood, and, before he left, her husband had told her that at this point she should remarry if he had not yet returned.

Time is of the essence here, but even more acute has become the issue of timing. Coincidences abound in this evening's conversation between Odysseus and Penelope, and Penelope takes each one up to scrutinize it as if it were a precious jewel, as of course it is. Imagine! This man knew her husband! He knew exactly what her husband was wearing twenty years ago. And to further the coincidences, this stranger goes on to say that her husband had found shelter from a storm in the harbour at Amnisos in Crete, where is a cave honouring Eileithyia, the goddess of childbirth (19.188–9). We, having long ago repudiated mythology, might take this coincidence as merely a poetic decoration, but those whose lives were cradled in myth would have registered this group of coincidences as cosmic timing.[22] Who was being born? Or perhaps reborn?

Penelope's task in this evening's conversation with this mysterious guest in her house is to study coincidence, which is one way in which people in antiquity studied time.

Scholarship has given considerable attention to Penelope's role in this poem and in this scene: see, in particular, Murnaghan 2011: 87–108. Like many modern scholars, Murnaghan is puzzled by Penelope's ignorance of the stranger's identity: 'Like the suitors, she is a participant in a plot from the knowledge of which she is excluded, even though, unlike them, she shares Odysseus' desire for what this plot effects' (2011: 92). The ambiguities of Penelope's behaviour are better understood when we realize that both Odysseus and Penelope are studying time and the pressure it exerts on human decisions. With both in disguise, each is focused on the idea of synchronicity. Penelope is an active participant in the plot, and the significance of her action is closely related to the significance of time in the poem's narrative. The two most important actions in the whole poem are centred on the issue of time: first, Penelope's decision to hold the contest of the bow on the night following her conversation with Odysseus; and second, Odysseus' stringing the bow and shooting the arrow through the twelve axes. The action of shooting the arrow through the axes falls to Odysseus, but this action requires two persons, both Odysseus and his wife Penelope. Without Penelope's decision to institute the contest, there would be no contest, hence no method by which Odysseus could assert and prove his identity. This contest requires synchronicity and Penelope is the human actor who shows that she understands synchronicity.[23] The decision reached by Penelope and Odysseus working together to institute the contest of the bow indicates that they both understand that the issue here is time. The exchange would be banal if they were not partners, if only Odysseus perceived that the issue impinging on his behaviour was the issue of time. The contest of the bow is a poetic device full of significance for an understanding of the critical moment to which time has brought both Odysseus and Penelope.

The second crucial action in the poem is the trick that Penelope plays on Odysseus with regard to their matrimonial bed to force him to disclose his identity (23.177–80). When she pretends to Odysseus that she has had their bed removed, Odysseus bursts into anger, and tells the story of his own making of that bed, thus unmistakably disclosing his identity. The narrative of the *Odyssey* tells of the return of Odysseus to his own home (his *nostos*), and that return requires two actions above all others – his aiming the arrow through the twelve axes, and the description of his building the matrimonial bed (key to his recognition).[24] Both these actions, if they are to be documented, require the collusion of his wife Penelope. Both are the means by which Odysseus establishes his identity. And both, to be successful, require the hand and mind of Penelope, working behind the scenes, as it were. When we readers of the *Odyssey* understand time's significance in the poem, and the essential value of synchronicity, we better appreciate Penelope's value in the poem, not just as the faithful wife, but as a co-inventor of the plot.

Odysseus, who is given to inventing names for himself, invents a new one for himself in this conversation with Penelope, and this fictive name is another signifier of time: *Aithōn*, 'Blaze' (cf. αἴθομαι/αἴθω, 'burn', and αἶθος, 'fire').[25] In the Cyclops' cave, he had exercised his wit by naming himself Nobody (*Outis*). But the circumstances are very different now and an entirely different name is called for. The dictionary translates *aithōn* as 'fiery', or if we like, 'aflame'. Here again we must consult our calendars if we are to appreciate the full significance of the information that the stranger shares with Penelope through his improvised name. This strange man, whose every aspect exudes mystery, swears a solemn oath that Odysseus will return between the old moon and the new, which means, for those paying attention to the calendar, tomorrow. That day, which we call the dark of the moon, held a special significance in the Athenian calendar, and no doubt in all Greek calendars. It is that night when the new moon is not yet visible; there is in effect no moon at all. An ominous night, the Athenians called this ἕνη καὶ νέα (sc. ἡμέρα), 'The Day of the Old and the New', when time ends and then begins again.[26] Odysseus, in calling himself 'Blaze' is announcing that he is about to be manifested as new light in the house. How artfully Odysseus has introduced this critical idea into the narrative.

Penelope, adding the coincidences one to another, makes a bold calculation. The time has come. Asserting her mathematical acumen, she announces that she will institute a contest for her new husband on the following day, using the bow of Odysseus, the instrument that has two functions here. It represents, first, Penelope's sense of timing, but Odysseus in his response assures her that he is in complete agreement with her sense of timing. Odysseus has just informed her that her husband will be back in his own house tomorrow, when, as we soon discover, there is to be a festival in honour of Apollo.[27] Whereupon Penelope proposes the contest of the bow. At every step in the progress of the narrative, we are reminded that the critical factor influencing both Odysseus and Penelope is time, registered in the poem as 'timing'. Penelope's decision to hold the contest of the bow, and to use it as her means to select a new husband, is an act of divination. How will the stranger respond to this daring proposal? The stranger in his response confirms that her divination is exactly on target. Now playing the part of a clairvoyant, the stranger prophesies that Penelope's husband will be home before her suitors can even string the bow. Has timing ever been more beautifully and majestically encoded?

The convergence of the twain

The agreement confirmed, the two clairvoyants retire for the night, Penelope to her room upstairs and Odysseus to his makeshift bed in the hall, using an animal hide as his floor covering, and fleeces heaped on him to be his coverlet. Each of these two masters of time spends a very troubled night, as would any person who had wagered life and happiness on such a daring gamble. Two lifelines have converged. Or have they? Only the bow, to be used the next night, will decide whether their hypothesis, jointly calculated, will prove accurate. Here is timing presented as the greatest threat to human happiness. Any miscalibration would spell disaster for both Odysseus and Penelope.

And now we reach one of the most sublime episodes in the poem, but in a poem studded with remarkable moments it is easy to glide past this episode without fully appreciating its value. It takes us to the very core of Greek religion (an omen will confirm the couple's cosmic synchronicity), and to the core of the poem's study of the mystery of time. Here is surely the most significant moment in the whole poem, except perhaps the moment in Calypso's cave when Odysseus repudiates the charm of timelessness for the hazards and hardships of human existence in time. Here Odysseus proves himself truly clairvoyant as he solicits proofs from the cosmos that he has made the correct decision when he entered into the complex mystery of time. Odysseus wakes in acute anxiety after a troubled night's sleep, and in his anxiety decides to solicit a double omen to affirm that he has not miscalculated, that he has not misread the signs. First, he takes his bedding and places the fleeces on a seat inside the hall. The hide he leaves on the ground outside. Nothing is said to explain this arrangement, but we might at least ponder the polarities here: earth and sky, inside and outside, up and down. Standing outside the palace, with his feet planted on the earth and his arms raised to heaven in prayer, positioned at the very axis of the cosmos, he might seem a prototype of Leonardo de Vinci's Vitruvian Man, a synthesis of balance and symmetry.

Poised like this, as the axis of earth and sky, Odysseus solicits two omens, and two different words are used to distinguish them. From Zeus he solicits a prodigy (τέρας) in the heavens, and from inside the house he needs to hear a human voice, to give him what he calls a 'word of omen' (φήμη), which will acknowledge that outward sign, and therefore recognize it as indeed a prophetic prodigy (20.100–1). This prayer is pregnant with religious meaning. Odysseus has become the pontifex maximus, practicing divination. He commands the heavenly powers not only to reveal themselves, but even to bend themselves to his will. How potent are these two words for omen, *teras* and *phēmē*, first an event in nature, but so implausible as to be a prodigy of nature, with nature itself expressing that Odysseus has been selected as the saviour. And the prodigy must be answered by human speech; nature and language are to be in exact correspondence.

Nature, thus commanded, responds with a thunderbolt in the heavens. And then, from within the building a human voice affirms that the prodigy of the thunder in a cloudless sky is indeed an omen. The voice comes from one of the women working the mills grinding the grain for the daily needs of the house. There were, the poet tells us, twelve women at the mills. Eleven had finished their work for the day, and only one remained, the twelfth, the weakest of them all, who had not yet finished her task. This woman, weak and tired, one of the lowliest of the household slaves, hearing the thunder sounding in a cloudless sky, speaks the word that translates that mere sound into an omen. May this be an omen, she says, to announce that this is the last day on which she will have to expend her weak energy milling grain for the palace's intruders.

Mills! How did mills make their appearance in the poem, and at this very moment when Odysseus needs to know if he is reading the calendar correctly? What can these mills be but time itself, a metaphor meticulously researched by di Santillana 1969 and Worthen 1991 (who prints and analyses 'The Mill Song', 40–50)? The twelve women working at their mills must be the twelve months of the year, and only one is left, the weakest of them all, which is to say the last month of the year, exhausted, almost finished. This is the last day of the old year. If we have any doubts as to whether the woman grinding grain at the mill represents time, these two studies can assure us that this is not a far-fetched modern interpretation of certain ideas expressed in the *Odyssey*. With time as the underlying theme of the poem, we now reach the most significant aspect of time, which is 'timing'. Odysseus knows that he must that very night string the bow that is his own property, though it has been stored safely out of sight ever since he left for Troy. Is his timing on the mark? In his prayer to Zeus, he solicits timing and coincidence; that is, he wants coincidence to manifest itself to confirm his intuition – one omen from the sky, and the other from the earth, the coincidence confirming that he is now at the centre, the most significant moment of his life. The voice of the woman at the mill is not merely 'coincidental', as we might use the word. This is the moment when coincidence is given its truly cosmic meaning. 'Grinding', as di Santillana 1969: 2 writes, 'stands, as the evidence develops, for an astronomical significance, the secular shifting of the sun through the signs of the zodiac, which determines world ages, each numbering thousands of years'. He adds, 'It (the Mill) must belong to the permanent equipment of the ancient universe' (91; note also his identification of the mill with heaven, 140). The woman grinding at the mill in her calendrical embodiment underscores this pivotal coincidence as it is superimposed upon the whole poem as a study of time. The woman grinding grain at the mill, though a human slave, speaks for time itself.

One other indication of the time is the thunderbolt of Zeus. It is expressive of his power as the greatest of the gods, but in particular as the Indo-European weather god, and the thunderbolt is the tool with which he apportions the seasons. One of the epithets used of Zeus in the *Odyssey* is τερπικέραυνος, 'he who takes pleasure in the thunderbolt' (14.268). The epithet as we have it results from metathesis; the prefix in the original formula was *trepo-*, meaning 'turn', rather than *terpi-*, the root for 'pleasure'. The formula thus would be more accurately translated as 'he who hurls the thunderbolt'. Some translators, made aware of the original meaning, translate 'he who wields the thunderbolt'.[28]

But such a translation misses the movement in this epithet, and movement is essential to its meaning. Zeus is 'He who turns the thunderbolt'. This meaning takes us again to Worthen's *The Myth of Replacement*. With Zeus whirling his thunderbolt in the sky, and a poor, exhausted woman milling the grain inside the house, everything makes clear that the cosmic and local replacement is at hand. The corrupt old order is about to be destroyed, to be replaced by a new order, based on justice and reverence for the gods.

The rest, as they say, is history, or rather, history about to be renewed. Penelope's suitors, dining gratuitously in her halls, fall into a fit of hysteria. 'They laughed', the poet says, 'with alien lips, their eyes were filled with tears (even as they laughed), and their spirits were set on wailing' (20.346–9), a graphic image of minds totally confused.[29]

Theoklymenos, the seer whom Telemachus has invited to his palace, analyses their grotesque behaviour, point for point, and sees in their hysteria utter destruction.[30] Heraclitus (*Quaestiones Homericae* 75) advances the hypothesis that this scene is an allegory of a solar eclipse, and modern scholars have added their support to this (e.g. Baikouzis and Magnasco 2008). All the elements in the narrative that express the movement of time also point in this same direction.

Amid the raucous hysterics, Penelope emerges to announce that the day has come for her to choose her new husband.[31] The axes are set in place for the archery contest, Penelope fetches the bow, that near-sacred instrument, from the storeroom, and all her suitors, each in his turn, have their try at this sacred experiment, but to no avail.[32] Finally, only Odysseus is left, and over their protests, is given his chance to shoot an arrow through the twelve axes and, *mirabile dictu*, shoots the arrow cleanly through all twelve axe-heads, thus confirming Penelope in her reading of the signs and in the accuracy of her timing. Two images given at this point in the poem are of sublime significance. First, when Odysseus strings the bow, the string gives off a sound like the sound of a lyre as when a singer, an *experienced* musician, fastens a new string to his instrument when he is about to begin his performance (21.404–10).[33] Here too is a register of time: the singer and his lyre announce that the time has come for celebration. Then, when Odysseus tests the string, 'the string sang out sweetly with the sound of a swallow' (21.409–10). Shortly thereafter, Athena darts up into the rafters taking the form of a swallow. The calendar has indeed come full circle. The first swallow in the house heralds the arrival of spring, and in springtime, other sources inform us, the Greeks would welcome swallows into the house.[34] There has been some discussion among scholars as to the significance of this bow. Ready 2010, for example, treats the bow as a significant cultural artefact, but does not discuss its function in the poem as it relates to time.[35] When Penelope institutes the contest of the bow, she in a daring move makes herself a master of time; and when Odysseus shoots the arrow through the twelve axes, he proves that he too is a master of time – and timing (*kairos*: n. 8 below).

Conclusion

There was in antiquity a cycle of nineteen years, now called the Metonic cycle, named after Meton who in the fifth century BCE calculated the mathematics of this cycle, though an understanding of it can be traced as far back as the Babylonian calendar. This cycle is the synchronizing of the solar and lunar calendars. The calendar of the *Odyssey* is (approximately) the twenty years of this cycle. Odysseus leaves Ithaca, tracing a course far distant from his home, and it requires a cycle of twenty years for the sum courses of the sun and moon to recur in exactly the same correspondence that marked them twenty years earlier.

And so draws to its conclusion this remarkable epic on the mystery of time, a study of time and timing scarcely equalled in European literature. Time is the greatest source of grief for humans, who are every minute subject to its damages. Ignored or misunderstood, time is a calamity. But with a proper study and with now and then a daring gamble, time can be a miracle. In fact, without time there would be no miracles. The Hallelujah Chorus would have no meaning except for those who know the meaning of time.

Notes

1. van Gennep [1909] 1960 argues that all life transitions as enacted through mystery religions may be understood through rituals of separation, liminality and incorporation. On the model of van Gennep's paradigm, Dodd and Faraone 2003 offer an excellent collection of essays on initiation in ancient Greek literature and society.

2. 1994: 10–15, summarized in Faivre and Voss 1995: 60–2. For a full discussion of mystery religions and esotericism, see Magee 2016: 1–23.

3. Cosmopoulos 2003 and Bremmer 2014 reconstruct the initiation rituals of various mystery religions.

4. All translations of Homer are my own.

5. For νόος ('mind') here, see Marcinkowska-Rosół and Sellmer 2021: 13: 'All terms denoting a mind-container are in some way specific: the Greek words φρένες, θυμός and στήθεα have their own physiological or anatomical meanings (whereas νόος lacks them)'. This passage has been interpreted as advising Telemachus to 'discipline his thoughts' (e.g. Wilson 2018: 40); in another reading, Telemachus' silence is commanded as a 'restraint of emotion' (e.g. Rutherford 1992: 138). In this context, involving a fraught confluence of timing and high stakes, when 'the mind-container transcends the sphere of actual consciousness' (Marcinkowska-Rosół and Sellmer 2021: 15), a better gloss of Odysseus' enjoinder might be, 'preserve and interiorize this knowledge, but keep it at the ready to use when necessary'.

6. For the epiphanic elements here, see de Jong 2001: 462.

7. It is cognate with δείκνυμι ('show'), and so *dikē* in this sense may refer to the customs, models, *et sim.*, the gods have revealed to human beings.

8. Time, as Augustine concludes in *Confessions* 11, is indefinable. We experience the effects of time every minute of our lives, yet we cannot define it. Augustine examined time from multiple angles but could find no adequate definition of something with no mass and escaping physical measurement. In his *aporia*, Augustine determines that time is a *distentionem ... animi*, 'a (dis)tension of the mind' (11.26.33), a much-discussed phrase that may suggest time is only a product of human consciousness: see further O'Donnell 1992 *ad loc*. The modern study of time in the Homeric poems must begin with the 1955 essay by Hermann Fränkel. Fränkel was the first scholar to note that the word for 'time' (χρόνος) is never used as the subject of a sentence, but only in an adverbial sense ('for a long time'). This was an astounding observation since time plays a crucial role in the *Iliad*, even more so in the *Odyssey*, which offers an especially deep study of time. Fränkel's observation prompted various studies on this subject, which have brought considerable nuance to the analysis of time in Homer. Zanker 2019 exhaustively examines the ways in which time in Homer is described in terms of space. He makes a significant observation that time can be expressed only in terms of action; hence, it requires narrative (see also Purves 2010: 65–96). These scholars have analysed the terms by which time is represented in the Homeric poems; my analysis is more subjective in that I examine how time affects the characters in the *Odyssey* and, in particular, how significant *timing* is for the poem's narrative. In this light, time becomes the energy that drives the whole poem. I am thus less focused on quantitative time (χρόνος/*chronos*) than on the qualitative experience of time, καιρός/*kairos* (not used in Homer), especially in the sense of 'right time', 'opportunity'. For the latter, more dynamic notion of time as a (largely) malleable construct and response to contingency, see further Onians 1951: 343–8 and Sipiora and Baumlin 2002; cf. Shoshitaishvili's chapter in this volume, pp. 45–6. Faure, Valli and Zucker 2022 is a collection of focused essays (none on Homer) in such areas as cyclicity and linearity, human time, time and language, and narrative time.

9. Castiglioni 2020 examines the nuanced complexity of Homer's representation of Menelaus, especially as a figure of grief poised between memory and forgetfulness of his past.

10. For the arrogant, violent and 'cannibalistic' (recalling the Cyclopes) suitors' occupation of Ithaca, see Dougherty 2001: 164–7.

11. Here Telemachus falls short of his father as is the case in other respects (Allan 2010).

12. Bergren 2008: 58–78 provides an excellent study of the symbolism of rebirth as it is configured in the *Odyssey*, especially book 5. However, she does not take time into consideration. Van Nortwick [2009] 2020: 13–19 contrasts the stasis of Odysseus' time on Ogygia with his impetus to leave, his irrepressible (human) desire for *kleos*.
13. Hall 2008: 147–60 argues that the *Odyssey* addresses still timely philosophical questions of ethics, ontology and epistemology, and that Odysseus' rejection of Calypso's offer of immortality sets him on a journey through physical space tantamount to an allegorical 'journey across time – the journey of consciousness (here, of his mortal existence) each of us embarks on at birth' (154).
14. Thus Holtsmark 1966: 208–10. Bergren 2008: 67 notes Ino's role as a midwife here and also sees the 'immortal veil' as a figural umbilical cord. Ino-Leukothea's veil is a polyvalent symbol, with a cluster of associations. For example, Rhyan Kardulias 2001 explores its connections with ritual transvestitism and social reintegration. West 2020 examines the veil-motif throughout Homer, which he argues is closely identified with the restoration of chastity and marriage.
15. Austin 1975: 241. The setting of the Pleiades marks the end of the sailing season, the beginning of winter, the end of the year.
16. As part of the preparations for their weddings, young girls made dedications to Artemis or Hera, often their playthings. Several Greek epigrams feature this motif, e.g. *Anth. Pal.* 6.133, 207, 276, 280.
17. For this encounter as a rehearsal of the initiatory rituals of marriage for Nausikaa and 'remarriage' for Odysseus and Penelope, see Ingalls 2000.
18. In a study of Homeric terms for beauty and the subjective responses they provoke, Shakeshaft 2019 examines Nausikaa's close association with Artemis, with whom she shares 'untamed' status, to elucidate her 'peculiar social position in the epic: unwed though ready for marriage' (16).
19. For the suitors' misdirected and mistimed laughter, see de Jong 2001: 440.
20. For the many and convoluted ways that Odysseus guards his (changing) identity, see Austin 1972.
21. Bergren 2008 analyses weaving in Homer as part of women's strategy for communicating in a world where all overt communication is by and between men. She emphasizes Helen's weaving of a robe in her own chambers in the *Iliad*, on which she embroiders her own story. On Penelope's literal weaving and her metaphorical weaving of *mētis*, see Clayton 2004: 21–52.
22. On the numinous associations of caves (with further references), see Rutherford 1992: 163.
23. Dougherty 2015: 134–9 analyses Odysseus' and Penelope's collusion here and elsewhere in the *Odyssey* in terms of skilful improvisation.
24. Hall 2008: 163–7 discusses Odysseus' *nostos* as reliant upon *noein* ('accurate mental perception') to overcome the challenges of a prolonged sea journey in the ancient Mediterranean. His acquisition of knowledge and successful return, then, is a psychic journey experienced literally and as a metaphor for the shared journey of humankind.
25. Levaniouk 2000 fruitfully examines the semantics of this *nomen loquens*, ultimately highlighting its figurative sense, *burning as longing* – in Odysseus' case 'for the lost household, vengeance, and return' (50). The suggestion is that Odysseus' repressed inner flame conceals an explosive potential to achieve all for which he burns.
26. Austin 1975: 244–6. The precise etymological significance of the time-marker given for Odysseus' return (τοῦδ' αὐτοῦ λυκάβαντος, 19.306 = 14.161) is contested. West 2013 argues

that λυκάβας describes the month 'going to the (day)light' and explains: 'As the moon wanes towards the end of the month and approaches the sun, it becomes progressively less visible at night, its time above the horizon coinciding more and more with the hours of daylight' (256–7).

27. For its possible reference to the festival of Apollo Neomenios ('Apollo of the New Moon') see Levaniouk 2011: 203–5.
28. See Stanford 1958: 227; cf. Bowie 2013: 202, who notes that τερπικέραυνος 'may suggest how Zeus created the panic'.
29. On the suitors' hysteria and the interpretation of Theoklymenos, see Rutherford 1992: 231–2; for the laughter of the suitors as a daemonic omen, see Colakis 1986.
30. On the temporal aspects of prophecies (analeptic, proleptic, etc.) in the *Odyssey*, see Gartziou-Tatti 2010.
31. See further Murnaghan 2011: 99–108 on the significance of this contest. She argues that in staging this contest, Penelope recognizes that she can no longer hold out against the ineluctable pressures of time. What we might add to her observations are the two issues by which time manifests itself in narrative: timing and synchronicity.
32. Unless we understand the manifestation of time through narrative, we are likely to miss the deeper significance of Penelope herself visiting the chamber where Odysseus has stowed his bow. How deeply we are reminded in this incident of timing and synchronicity.
33. See Mackenzie 2021 on Heraclitus' bow-lyre fragment and this scene in the *Odyssey*.
34. I elaborate at greater length on the tokens of Spring here in Austin 1975: 239–53.
35. For a summary (with further references) of scholarly theories regarding the type of poet with which Odysseus is being linked in the simile, see Ready 2011: 267. The conflation of bow and lyre here also recalls Apollo, who as archer-god and preserver of established order can be seen as overseeing Odysseus' exaction of revenge. Thalmann 1984: 176 comments, 'Song and battle should properly be kept distinct. Their mixture characterizes the ensuing action as well. Song typically accompanies the meal; but while the suitors eat, the bow will replace the *phorminx*.' Grethlein 2008: 42–3 notes the bow's past association with *xenia* (it is a gift from Odysseus' guest-friend Iphitos) and so its present relevance to the suitors. Cf. Thalmann 1998: 174–5.

Works cited

Allan, A. L. (2010), 'Generational Degeneration: The Case of Telemachus', *Scholia*, 19: 14–30.
Austin, N. (1972), 'Name Magic in the *Odyssey*', *California Studies in Classical Antiquity*, 5: 1–19.
Austin, N. (1975), *Archery at the Dark of the Moon*, Berkeley: The University of California Press.
Austin, N. (2017), Nausikaa and the Word That Must Not Be Spoken: A Reading of Homer's *Odyssey*, Book Six', *Arion*, 25: 5–36.
Baikouzis, C. and M. O. Magnasco (2008), 'Is an Eclipse Described in the *Odyssey*?', *Proceedings of the National Academy of Sciences*, 105: 8823–8.
Bergren, A. (2008), *Weaving Truth: Essays on Language and the Female in Greek Thought*, Cambridge, MA: Harvard University Press.
Bowie, A. M. (2013), *Homer: Odyssey Books XIII and XIV*, Cambridge: Cambridge University Press.
Bremmer, J. (2014), *Initiation into the Mysteries of the Ancient World*, Münchner Vorlesungen zu antiken Welt, Bd 1, Berlin: De Gruyter.

Castiglioni, B. (2020), 'Menelaus in the *Iliad* and in the *Odyssey*: The Anti-Hero of πένθος', *Commentaria Classica*, 7: 219–32.
Clayton, B. (2004), *A Penelopean Poetics: Reweaving the Feminine in Homer's* Odyssey, Lanham, MD: Lexington Books.
Colakis, M. (1986), 'The Laughter of the Suitors in *Odyssey* 20', *Classical World*, 7: 137–41.
Cosmopoulos, M. B. (2003), *Greek Mysteries: The Archaeology and Ritual of Ancient Greek Secret Cults*, London: Routledge.
de Jong, I. J. F. (2001), *A Narratological Commentary on the* Odyssey, Cambridge: Cambridge University Press.
di Santillana, G. (1969), *Hamlet's Mill: An Essay on Myth and the Frame of Time*, Boston: Gambit.
Dodd, D. and C. Faraone (eds) (2003), *Initiation in Ancient Greek Rituals and Narratives*, New York: Routledge.
Dougherty, C. (2001), *The Raft of Odysseus*, Oxford: Oxford University Press.
Dougherty, C. (2015), 'Nobody's Home: *Metis*, Improvisation and the Instability of Return in Homer's *Odyssey*', *Ramus*, 44: 115–40.
Faivre, A. (1994), *Access to Western Esotericism*, Albany: The State University of New York Press.
Faivre, A. and K.-C. Voss (1995), 'Esotericism and the Science of Religions', *Numen*, 42: 48–77.
Faure, R., S.-P. Valli and A. Zucker (eds) (2022), *Conceptions of Time in Greek and Roman Antiquity*, Berlin: De Gruyter.
Fränkel, H. (1955), *Wege und Formen frühgriechischen Denkens*, Munich: Beck.
Gartziou-Tatti, A. (2010), 'Prophecy and Time in the *Odyssey*', *Quaderni Urbinati di Cultura Classica*, 96: 11–28.
Grethlein, J. (2008), 'Memory and Material Objects in the *Iliad* and the *Odyssey*', *Journal of Hellenic Studies*, 128: 27–51.
Hall, E. (2008), *The Return of Ulysses: A Cultural History of Homer's* Odyssey, Baltimore: Johns Hopkins.
Holtsmark, E. B. (1966), 'Spiritual Rebirth of the Hero: *Odyssey* 5', *Classical Journal*, 61: 206–10.
Ingalls, W. (2000), 'Nausikaa, Penelope, and Initiation', *Echos du Monde Classique/Classical Views*, 44, n.s. 19: 1–18.
Levaniouk, O. (2000), '*Aithōn, Aithon*, and Odysseus', *Harvard Studies in Classical Philology*, 100: 25–51.
Levaniouk, O. (2011), *Eve of the Festival: Making Myth in Odyssey 19*, Hellenic Studies 46, Washington, DC: Center for Hellenic Studies.
Mackenzie, T. (2021), 'A Heraclitean Allusion to the *Odyssey*', *Classical Quarterly*, 71: 71–6.
Magee, G. A. (2016), *The Cambridge Handbook of Western Mysticism and Esotericism*, New York: Cambridge University Press.
Marcinkowska-Rosół, M. and S. Sellmer (2021), 'The Mind as Container: A Study of Metaphor in Homer and Hesiod with a Parallel Analysis of the Sanskrit Epics', *Mnemosyne*, 75: 1–25.
Murnaghan, S. (2011), *Disguise and Recognition in the* Odyssey, 2nd edn, London and New York: Roman and Littlefield.
O'Donnell, J. J. (1992), *The Confessions of Augustine: An Electronic Edition*: https://faculty.georgetown.edu/jod/conf (accessed 16 December 2022).
Onians, R. B. (1951), *The Origins of European Thought*, Cambridge: Cambridge University Press.
Purves, A. C. (2010), *Space and Time in Ancient Greek Narrative*, Cambridge: Cambridge University Press.
Ready, J. L. (2010), 'Why Odysseus Strings His Bow', *Greek, Roman, and Byzantine Studies*, 50: 133–57.
Ready, J. L. (2011), *Character, Narrator, and Simile in the* Iliad, Cambridge: Cambridge University Press.
Rhyan Kardulias, D. (2001), 'Odysseus in Ino's Veil: Feminine Headdress and the Hero in *Odyssey* 5', *Transactions and Proceedings of the American Philological Association*, 131: 23–51.

Ricoeur, P. (1984), *Time and Narrative*, trans. K. McLaughlin and D. Pellauer, vol. 1, Chicago: The University of Chicago Press.
Rutherford, R. B. (1992), *Homer:* Odyssey *Books XIX and XX*, Cambridge: Cambridge University Press.
Shakeshaft, H. (2019), 'The Terminology for Beauty in the *Iliad* and the *Odyssey*', *Classical Quarterly*, 69: 1–22.
Sipiora, P. and J. S. Baumlin (eds) (2002), *Rhetoric and Kairos: Essays in History, Theory, and Praxis*, Albany: The State University of New York Press.
Stanford, W. B. (1958), *The* Odyssey *of Homer*, 2nd edn, New York: MacMillan.
Thalmann, W. G. (1984), *Conventions of Form and Thought in Early Greek Epic Poetry*, Baltimore: Johns Hopkins University Press.
Thalmann, W. G. (1998), *The Swineherd and the Bow*, Ithaca: Cornell University Press.
van Gennep, A. ([1909] 1960), *The Rites of Passage*, trans. M. B. Vizedom and G. L. Caffee, Chicago: The University of Chicago Press, 2nd edn (2019), with new introduction by D. I. Kertzer.
Van Nortwick, T. ([2009] 2020), *The Unknown Odysseus: Alternate Worlds in Homer's* Odyssey, Ann Arbor: The University of Michigan Press.
West, D. (2020), 'Shipwrecked Spouses: Leukothea's Veil and Marital Reunion in the *Odyssey*', *New England Classical Journal*, 47: 1–14.
West, M. L. (1966), *Hesiod:* Theogony, Oxford: Oxford University Press.
West, M. L. (2013), 'λυκάβας, λυκηγενής, ἀμφιλύκη', *Glotta*, 89: 253–64.
Wilson, E. (2018), *The* Odyssey *of Homer*, New York: Norton.
Worthen, T. D. (1991), *The Myth of Replacement: Stars, Gods, and Order in the Universe*, Tucson: The University of Arizona Press.
Zanker, A. T. (2019), *Metaphor in Homer: Time, Speech, and Thought*, Cambridge: Cambridge University Press.

CHAPTER 3
HELEN, PARIS AND THE PHILOSOPHICAL ἔρως: LOVE, STRIFE AND SUBLIME CONTACT FROM HOMER TO PLATO
Boris Shoshitaishvili

> Let that be our defense for our review of poetry, since for good reason indeed we dismissed (the Muse of epic and tragedy) from our state earlier for being what (she) is ... But let us add, in case (the Muse) condemns us for some kind of harshness or boorishness, that there's been a long-standing dispute between philosophy and poetry.
>
> Plato, *Republic* 10.607b1–6[1]

> Do not cast in my teeth the desirable gifts of golden Aphrodite.
>
> Paris to Hector, *Il.* 3.64[2]

Introduction

The banishment of poets in *Republic* 10 is a touchstone for interpreting the relationship of Platonic philosophy to Homeric epic. Plato's Socrates appears to declare independence for the philosophical project, in the conviction that achieving the ideal *polis* and *psyche* requires a break with the Homeric past. Yet the degree to which Socrates leaves Homer behind is questionable. First, there is resonance between Socrates' own combative stance towards Homer's cultural authority and the centrality of combative agonism and strife in Homeric epic. The *Iliad* and *Odyssey* repeatedly prioritize rivalry, challenges to authority and moments of head-to-head striving.[3] While a substantive renunciation of Homer might entail disavowing the Homeric reliance on challenge and conflict, the Socrates of the *Republic* does the opposite, engaging Homer in a memorable *Kulturkampf*. Plato's antagonistic approach to epic suggests that philosophy may have remained more Homeric than Socrates lets on.[4]

Another factor complicating a surface reading of *Republic* 10 is the eristic nature of Socrates' philosophical ἔλεγχος ('refutation'). Commentators have pointed out how the Socratic method draws participants into a new kind of Greek ἀγών ('contest'), with Socrates himself deploying metaphors of contest and competitive athletics across the dialogues.[5] So Plato not only positions himself as Homer's great rival for cultural authority, but, more granularly, his model philosopher competes vigorously against numerous conversation partners. Given these macro- and micro-features of Plato's dialogues, the philosophical project seems to reimagine older eristic Homeric dynamics rather than radically depart from them.

The same passages of the *Republic*, however, can be read in the reverse direction: that Plato is working towards a basis for philosophy different from, and even opposite to, the ἔρις/*eris* ('strife') animating Homer. This alternate basis for the philosophical project, as indicated by the very term φιλοσοφία/*philosophia*, is ἔρως/*erōs* and φιλία/*philia*, i.e. forms of attraction rather than strife. From this point of view, Socrates' eristic challenge to Homer is a means for establishing a non-eristic end. There are multiple appearances of ἔρως and φιλία in *Republic* 10 that align with this reading:

> 'And I'm sure we'd grant (the Muse's) champions, not those who are actual poets, but lovers of poetry (φιλοποιηταί), the right to make a defense on her behalf in prose, on the grounds that she is not only pleasing but also beneficial to political systems and human life ... And yet if she isn't, my dear friend, like those who were once passionate about her (ἐρασθέντες), but nevertheless abstain from their passion (ἔρωτα), albeit by force, if they consider it's not useful, so we too, on account of our passion (ἔρωτα) for such poetry nurtured in us by the upbringing of our fine political systems, will be well disposed toward her, to have her appear the best and truest possible. Yet as long as she cannot defend herself, while we listen to her we will use the argument we are now making to charm ourselves against her spell, taking care not to fall back into our childish ways and the passion of the majority (τὸν παιδικόν τε καὶ τὸν τῶν πολλῶν ἔρωτα).
>
> ...
>
> But we must look elsewhere, Glaucon.' 'Where?' he asked. 'At (the soul's) love of wisdom (φιλοσοφίαν), and think about the things it latches on to and what associations it desires, as it's akin to the divine, the immortal, and the eternal.
>
> *607d6–611e3*

More than a locus of rivalry, the difference between poetry and philosophy is for Plato a progression and reorientation of love. Socrates urges those who had been lovers of poetry (φιλοποιηταί) dominated by childishness and the *erōs* of the masses (τῶν πολλῶν) to rediscover the soul's proper *love of wisdom* (φιλοσοφία), linked as it is to the divine, immortal and eternal.

So does Platonic philosophy successfully break with Homeric *eris* by embracing sublime forms of love and attraction? Or is Plato reconceiving Homeric strife on two levels of scale: of cultural authority and in the elenctic method? In other words, are epic poetry and Platonic philosophy both about war, or is epic about war while philosophy is ultimately about love?

In this chapter, I explore the question of philosophy's relationship to epic through analyses of exceptional ἔρως-oriented figures who pre-date and, as I will argue, set the stage for Plato. I begin with Homer and consider two unusual figures in the *Iliad*, Helen and Paris, who exemplify erotic dynamics amid the Trojan War's uninhibited *eris*. Helen and Paris' participation in *erōs* gives them distance from, and perspective on, their expansive eristic context, which allows them to proto-philosophically formulate concepts about themselves, their characters and their world. In the two lovers, Homeric epic gives an initial shape to the relationship between *erōs* and philosophical contemplation.

I then turn to Heraclitus and Empedocles, where I pursue conceptions of ἔρως and the related idea of the beautiful as the basis for philosophical contemplation and as the contrast for ἔρις. These two Presocratic thinkers supply genealogical and conceptual bridges that link Homeric and Platonic *erōs*. In the third section, I return to the ἔρως of Socrates, with a focus on Plato's *Symposium* and its elaboration of *erōs* (the most extensive such elaboration in Greek antiquity). I discuss how Diotima's union of τὰ ἐρωτικά/*ta erōtica* and philosophy resonates with, and enhances, earlier Presocratic and Homeric intuitions that the erotic and the contemplative are linked.

My conclusion presents a speculative reinterpretation of *erōs* and *eris* as antipodes of a single underlying Greek cultural mode that I call a 'metaphysics of contact'. Greek poets and thinkers were able to generate and organize ontologies using moments of extreme conflict (ἔρις) to explore differentiation as well as moments of intense attraction (ἔρως) to establish unities. Plato's achievement at the beginning of the Greek philosophical tradition lies in his reversal of the priority of *eris* over *erōs* while preserving the metaphysics of contact.[6]

The Iliadic lovers (and hence, proto-philosophers): Paris' even-handed judgement

The beginning of *Iliad* 3 is the one time in the poem that the two men intimately linked to the war's original grievance – the seduction of Helen – make contact. Yet what promises to be a definitive violent exchange tied to the cause of the war markedly fails to rise to the levels of decisive intensity, or even exhausted stalemate, of the poem's other conflicts. Paris and Menelaos cast their spears, both ineffectively (346–60). Paris is struck on the helmet and manhandled by Menelaos, but he neither resists nor suffers significant injury (361–70); finally, while dragged by his chinstrap to what is expected to be a humiliating death, the Trojan prince is spirited to safety by Aphrodite (371–82). A comparison with Hector and Ajax's duel (book 7), or Hector and Achilles' duel (book 22), or even the verbal clash of Agamemnon and Achilles in the first book, reveals how one-sidedly the battle of Helen's lovers progresses and how anti-climactically it ends.

This opening duel's ineffectiveness foreshadows the rest of book 3, which describes no other battles. Instead of the poem's great eristic warriors, this book's attention is given to Helen and Paris, the couple entangled in the dynamics of *erōs*. In fact, the distinction between eristic and erotic excellence begins to unfold before the duel, when Hector rebukes his brother for hesitating to accept Menelaos' challenge:

Accursed Paris, outstanding only in beauty, woman crazed, seducer –
(Δύσπαρι εἶδος ἄριστε γυναιμανὲς ἠπεροπευτὰ).

>   ...
>   Your appearance
> is beautiful, but there is no strength in your heart, nor courage.
>   ...
> You will not stand to face Menelaos, beloved by Ares?
> You would learn what kind of man was he whose luscious wife (θαλερὴ παράκοιτις)
>   you hold.
> Your lyre and the gifts of Aphrodite would be of no use to you,
> nor your hair and looks when you coupled with the dust.
>
>   *39–57*

Hector sets Paris' inadequacy as a warrior into striking juxtaposition with the younger man's erotic prowess. It is as if Hector sees two Parises and has trouble reconciling them: there is a beautiful Paris who achieved the great erotic triumph, the seduction of the most seductive woman. But the same man is superimposed onto the weakling Paris who shrinks from his challenger, the husband and fighter wronged by Paris' erotic success. Paris' beauty, disdained as useless in battle, is nevertheless repeatedly emphasized in Hector's speech. Its elements coalesce into a potent non-warrior panoply: Paris' 'locks' (κόμη), his 'lyre' (κίθαρις), his 'beauty' (εἶδος), the 'gifts of Aphrodite' (δῶρ' Ἀφροδίτης) and the 'blooming wife' (θαλερὴ παράκοιτις) he has because of them. Although he seeks to devalue his brother's erotic powers, Hector ends up sketching, against the overt goal of his speech, a portrait of a figure empowered in very different fashion from himself and other warriors.

In this regard, the first two lines of Hector's speech are emblematic, arriving as a cluster of rare words and *hapax legomena*. In order to gain semantic purchase on Paris' bewildering character, Hector deforms his brother's name; Paris becomes 'Dys-Paris' in a rare act of renaming that marks Paris' otherly character and Hector's difficulty understanding it from his eristic point of view (appearing one other time in 13.769, of Paris again by Hector).

The rest of the verse (39) is an extended attempt to explicate the strange power of Dys-Paris by presenting three vocatives in apposition, all rare: εἶδος ἄριστε ('beautiful' or 'best in form'), γυναιμανὲς ('woman-crazy') and ἠπεροπευτὰ ('seducer'). They bring Paris closer to mortal and divine female figures. The combination of εἶδος with the adjective ἄριστος appears eight times in the poem: five times of women ('loveliest of the daughters of Pelias/Priam/Agamemnon'),[7] twice of Paris (in identical lines, here and 13.769) and once of Hector when his courage is challenged by Glaucus (17.142). Being 'best in appearance' associates Dys-Paris with female forms of exceptionalness and lack of courage in warriors.

The second vocative, γυναιμανὲς, supplements εἶδος ἄριστε. This compound is reserved for Paris (here and in 13.769) and has two possible meanings: 'crazy for women' or 'making women crazy'. The second half of the word, -μανὲς, derives from the verb μαίνομαι ('to rage'), which refers in seventeen of twenty-three Iliadic occurrences to maddened warriors or the war-god himself. When used of male figures, μαίνομαι

Helen, Paris and the Philosophical ἔρως

typically signifies complete dedication to the rage of battle and its overwhelming agonistic frenzy. For Paris, by contrast, 'raging' is targeted at women. The implication is that only among, and in relation to, women does Paris' character intensify beyond its normal limit. Where εἶδος ἄριστε connects him to steady feminine beauty, γυναιμανὲς associates him with female intensity, a kind of 'berserk spirit' of/for the feminine.

In response to Hector's rebuke and struggle to acknowledge the difference between the eristic and the erotic man, Paris makes the distinction explicit:

> Hector, since you rebuke me fairly, and not beyond what is fair –
> your heart is ever unyielding, like an axe
> that goes through wood wielded by a man (διὰ δουρὸς ὑπ' ἀνέρος) who skillfully
> carves timber for a ship, and the axe increases the man's swing (ἀνδρὸς ἐρωήν);
> just so is the spirit in your breast relentless –
> do not cast in my teeth the desirable gifts of golden Aphrodite (δῶρ' ἐρατὰ ... χρυσῆς Ἀφροδίτης).
> Not to be thrown away are the glorious gifts of the gods (θεῶν ἐρικυδέα δῶρα),
> whatever it is they might give (δῶσιν); not at will can a man obtain them.
>
> 59–66

Paris' language, in contrast to Hector's invective and grasping disbelief, is crystalline. Hector's heart is likened to a ship-builder's axe in its direct driving force: 'an axe that goes through wood wielded by a man' and, a verse later, 'the axe increases the man's swing'. Paris' repetition of ὑπ' ἀνέρος and ἀνδρὸς across one line underscores the masculine quality of the axe's force.[8] Moreover, the simile goes beyond seeing in the older brother a male agonistic impulse; Paris also presents this impulse as a constructive form of activity. Instead of defensively criticizing the eristic man when under attack for not being one himself, Paris associates Hector's driving force with the creative act of shipbuilding.

At the same time, Paris remains clear-eyed about the power of his own qualities. He takes Hector's earlier mocking words, the δῶρ' Ἀφροδίτης ('gifts of Aphrodite', 39), and expands them into his δῶρ' ἐρατὰ ... χρυσῆς Ἀφροδίτης ('sweet/ἔρως-imbued gifts of golden Aphrodite', 64). He emphasizes that these gifts arrived to him through divine 'giving' ('glorious gifts of the gods, whatever it is they might give', 65–6). The unusually packed repetition of δίδωμι-derived ('giving') words – δῶρ' ἐρατὰ (64), ἐρικυδέα δῶρα (65), δῶσιν (66) – with Paris as recipient can be contrasted with the repeated use of ἀνήρ-forms for Hector just prior. Hector's eristic character may be the hallmark of a productive man worthy of respect, but it cannot negate Paris' erotic qualities, which are venerable in having been gifted by a god (δῶρ' ἐρατὰ).

In short, Paris succeeds in comprehending his and his brother's contrastive characters without the linguistic struggle Hector experienced. The younger man firmly and serenely describes two ways for a man to be exceptional: eristic and erotic. His controlled recognition of these contrastive ethical types, without privileging one over the other, is remarkable in the epic. Even Achilles' famous aside in 9.312–13 ('for hateful to me as the gates of Hades is that man, / who hides one thing in his mind, but says another'), with its ethical implications, is one-sidedly judgemental; whereas Paris, perhaps because he exists at a remove from the dominant Iliadic mode of the eristic warrior, is able to consider character types even-handedly, almost abstractly. His distanced stance in how he regards these two different kinds of human excellence, only one of which is his own, is philosophical (or proto-philosophical), and the calm measure of his words – an unusual equanimity in the face of public censure – is a performance of non-agonism. Hector may drive at him like an axe but Paris neither loses his cool nor drives back, abstaining from conflict even in direct confrontation.

Helen's encompassing vision

The ability to derive philosophical distance from entanglement in *erōs* connects Paris to Helen, his greater erotic counterpart. *Iliad* 3 is where both Helen and Paris appear most frequently and prominently in the poem. Helen's ἔρως-excellence is especially evident in the episode later called the *teichoscopia* ('the viewing from the wall'). As she ascends the ramparts to watch the duel between Menelaos and Paris, the Trojan elders, already seated on the wall, murmur to one another:

> No blame that the Trojans and strong-greaved Achaeans
> have suffered so long on account of such a woman;
> terribly (αἰνῶς) does she seem like the immortal goddesses to look on.
> But even so – such as she is, let her go back home in the ships,
> let her not stay as a bane to us and our children after.

3.156–60

The ambivalence in their speech recalls Hector's ambivalence as he grasped at words to capture his brother's character in 39–40 and 54–5. The elders emphasize the extraordinary power of Helen's beauty; in fact, they are the sole Iliadic figures who highlight her attractive force in more words than a single adjective. Yet just after prizing Helen's beauty as worth the suffering of war, trepidation enters their praise. They apply the adverb αἰνῶς ('terribly') to her likeness to the gods (158), a word appearing elsewhere in the poem only of negative states such as grief, dread or anger.[9] Initial praise of Helen's sublime beauty becomes tinged with fear, a shift made explicit when the elders end their speech hoping Troy loses her to the Achaeans and she is given up despite (or because of) her beauty. The possibility of destruction Helen brings, at first judged worthwhile on account of her beauty, is re-evaluated in the course of their short speech as too much to bear, a dangerous surplus.

The elders' ambivalent mixture of appreciation and fear reflect Helen's relationship to the city. Unlike Paris' more narrowly influential erotic gifts, Helen is the war's erotic focal point. While Paris attracted Helen to himself, Helen has attracted not only Paris to herself but the war-hungry Achaeans *en masse* to Troy. She is the organizing figure of Troy's perilous situation, the ἔρως-figure motivating the great *eris* and *polemos* ('war') that will devastate the towering city.

The elders' understanding of Helen as 'bane to (their) children' is significant. Even if Troy could survive the war their erotic bond causes, Paris and Helen do not contribute to the community's continuity. Though together for nine years, they do not have children, and Helen has left her only child behind in Sparta (375).[10] Their erotic excellence may be a beautiful adornment for Troy, and the war they cause may secure Troy a form of immortality in poetry, but these come at the cost of the city's physical endurance and the biological continuity of its ruling line, a stark contrast to the intergenerational promise of Hector, Andromache and Astyanax.

In the rest of book 3, Helen gives voice to an unrivalled lucidity regarding the circumstances besetting Troy and her role in creating them, a lucidity even more notable than Paris' clarity in his earlier exchange with Hector. While Paris holds the divine gifts of Aphrodite, Helen speaks with Aphrodite directly (389–420) and has the unusual ability to see through the goddess's mortal guise. Frustrated at being told by Aphrodite to go to Paris, after the goddess had just rescued him from his loss to Menelaos, Helen challenges the goddess to go off and herself become a lover dragged to far corners of the world. Her defiant challenge for the goddess to 'abandon the gods' way' and never again 'return to Olympus' (406–7) reveals the gulf between *erōs* as the goddess's sphere and Helen's own lived experience as an ἔρως-entangled human being. These lines addressed to Aphrodite are remarkable; their eristic equivalent would be Achilles' daring Athena to become mortal and risk dying in battle herself instead of shepherding mortals like himself into war.

Helen presents a similarly expansive view in her response to Priam, when Troy's king declares he blames not her but the gods for the war (3.164–5). Rather than accept absolution by allowing Priam to conflate her actions with the gods' will, she makes a point of condemning herself for succumbing to desire: 'would that evil death had pleased me at that time ... dog-faced as I am' (173–80). Again, she draws a distinction between her own experience and the gods' plans, maintaining space for self-understanding and agency (even when this means self-condemnation for calamity) amid the turbulence in which she is enmeshed.[11] She also expresses astonishment about the course her life has taken – 'if that ever happened' (180) – an abstracted amazement at her own transformation from the prized wife of an Achaean king to a semi-member of the Trojan royal family, and at how she exists not only at the centre of war, but oscillates between the war's two sides as well.

The impression Helen creates with these declarations is of a very different kind from other Homeric figures. On the one hand, she is more deeply entangled in the erotic dynamics of desire and desirability than any other human character. Yet she also remains barred from participating directly in the vast eristic situation of the *polemos* rooted in her *erōs*. From the strange combination of being the ultimate source and focus of the war but also having her excellence constrained primarily to its erotic basis, she achieves and maintains a comprehensive perspective on the complex whole at whose centre she stands. Against Priam's attempt at absolving her through the gods and against Aphrodite's attempt to coax or command her as a goddess, Helen asserts her own agency, culpability and suffering, as well as her proximity and distance from the divinity of ἔρως, experiencing in the process an almost sublimely detached contemplation of her life.

All this can be set in useful comparison with the perspective Paris gained through his eroticism. Paris departs significantly from the kind of excellence expected of him as a warrior while projecting the atypical excellence of the erotic man. Helen, by contrast, embodies the characteristic excellence of the alluring and desirable female figure more emphatically than any mortal peer. Yet she also acts on her own desire (not remaining solely the object or inspiration of desire) by choosing to leave Sparta for Paris and Troy. She refuses to renounce this act of agency, even when renouncing it would mean absolution. So, unlike Paris, she inhabits both positions within *erōs* fully: she is the most desirable figure *and* she makes the most destructive choice based on her own desire. At the same time, and also unlike Paris, she is alienated from activity in those contrastive dynamics that her ἔρως has enflamed: the eristic war. Paris may be at some distance from *eris* because he is a poor and disinterested warrior, but he still participates in battle to some extent. For Helen, the eristic role of warrior is unavailable.

Therefore, between the two, Helen holds the greater distance from the *Iliad*'s warworld, while also being implicated more immediately and agentially in its erotic underpinning. She holds simultaneous status as the war's greatest erotic subject and object. This mixture of distance from the *Iliad*'s primary martial dynamics and her profound identity with its underlying erotic dynamics afford her fuller appreciation of Homeric dimensionality. More precisely and in contemporary terms, Helen is closest to acting as the poem's 'metaphysician' – the philosopher attuned to the fundamental aspects of her Homeric world. She possesses a distanced view of the cosmic Trojan War's violent expressions, a view emerging from intimate engagement in the erotic nexus from which the war itself derives.[12] Paris' partial participation in the agonistic-eristic dimension and his significant – but less than Helen's – empowerment in the erotic result, by contrast, not in a view of the whole but in an unusually even-handed perspective of character types, including his own. This abstracted view of different forms of human excellence positions him as more an ethical than metaphysical proto-philosopher.[13]

Helen enacts her metaphysical stance poetically at two moments in book 3: the *teichoscopia* and the description of her weaving that precedes it. When Helen steps onto the walls of the citadel and identifies for the Trojan elders the key figures of the opposing side, she not only relies on her experience crossing the two clashing sides of ἔρις, but also demonstrates her comprehensive vantage over the whole. Her ability to serve as effective guide depends on the distanced vision she achieves through erotic entanglement with an Achaean as well as a Trojan man.

A different aspect of Helen's standpoint as proto-metaphysician shows itself in her first appearance in book 3 (and in the poem itself) when Iris arrives to urge her to the ramparts:

(The goddess) came on Helen in the chamber; she was weaving a great web,
a red folding robe, and working into it the numerous struggles

of Trojans, breakers of horses, and bronze-armoured Achaians,
struggles that they endured for her sake at the hands of the war god.

3.125–8

This first image of Helen at the loom has long inspired interpretations of her as the poet's icon within the poem. Early scholiasts sought to explain how Helen wove her 'great web' of the Trojan War in comparison to the poet singing the great epic of war. Yet there are fundamental differences between Helen's art and the poet's, the most significant of which is the nature of her working medium, as Kennedy argued decades ago (1986). The fixed nature of visual decorations in/on fabric limits its ability to depict the complex temporal dynamics that the poet conveys through sung verse. While Kennedy's critique resisted the impulse to equate Helen's weaving to poetic activity, his analysis stopped short of identifying the unique affordance of Helen's visual medium: Helen's weaving can express the distinctive quality of philosophical achievement.

Helen's creation of the robe is an act transforming the *Iliad*'s raging war into an integrated visual object. This unifying art comprehends a world in flux and riven by conflict as a stable structured whole. Unlike the singer's *post factum* song of war that unfolds in time, Helen exists at the immediate centre of the conflict, as war's final erotic subject and object – but also at unique distance, as neither Greek nor Trojan, nor as a warrior in the war her ἔρως helped spark. This position allows her to weave a great holistic web as if perched above, or outside, it. The *aoidos* ('bard') moves with the *Iliad*'s story while singing; by contrast, Helen comprehends and presents core aspects of the poem's divisive flux in atemporal imagery. In her first appearance in the poem, she is performing the creation of metaphysical rather than poetic art.[14]

Love, strife and beauty in the Presocratics: Heraclitus and Empedocles

These love-oriented, proto-philosophical themes first expressed in Homer's Helen and Paris can be traced through Heraclitus and Empedocles before their amplification by Plato. A well-known gesture among Presocratic thinkers was their positing a single basis or *archē* for the cosmos as a whole: a specific substance (such as water or fire), concept (e.g. the *apeirōn*), faculty (*nous*) or single set of principles (mathematics). Heraclitus and Empedocles stand out among their contemporaries in making dynamics such as love and/or strife cosmically fundamental.[15]

Heraclitus' war for beautiful ἁρμονία

A number of Heraclitus' surviving fragments emphasize the creative potential of strife and war, thus recalling the agonism prevalent in Homeric epic. Fragment D63 (B80) is one of the clearest, using a gnomic tricolon structure to emphasize the universality of the conflictual and eristic: εἰδέναι χρὴ τὸν πόλεμον ἐόντα ξυνόν, καὶ δίκην ἔριν, καὶ γίνομενα πάντα κατ' ἔριν καὶ χρεών ('One must know that war is in common, and justice is strife, and all things come about by strife and constraint'). This aphorism opens with the proposition that *polemos*, the most expansive and exaggerated expression of strife, division and violence in the human world, is implicated into what seems to be its opposite: the ξυνόν, or 'that which is shared in common'. The paradoxical assertion that war's violent division is linked to commonality opens up to at least two interpretations. It may refer to the community forged in war, the fact that war's violence knits the participants and victims of either side closer by cementing collective identity in us-them opposition. Or, and at the same time, people in war share experiences of intensity and extremity across the divisions of the warring parties. A sensitivity to this shared experience of war, regardless of which side one is on, may account for the sympathetic treatment received by Achaeans and Trojans alike in the Homeric poems. War's commonality is both divisive and unifying.

In the movement from its first to second part, fr. D63 shifts from a non-evaluative claim ('war is in common') to the normative sphere ('justice is strife'). The assertion that justice is a form of strife may invoke the elucidative results of controlled, non-physical conflict when two sides in a dispute each argue their case before arbiters (as in the depiction of the contestants and circle of judges in the 'city of peace' on the shield of Achilles in *Il.* 18.497–508). It may also reflect the conviction that in conflict the side with the greater claim on what is right would be vindicated in some ultimate reckoning, an intuition present in Hesiod's *Works and Days*, as well as the final books of the *Odyssey*.

But the aphorism's final colon expands war and strife into a generative force of universal metaphysical significance. Here in particular Heraclitus expresses the cosmic dimensions of Homeric agonism in formal terms – that war and strife clarify not only human relationships and belonging but also the coming into being of the more-than-human world. The exigencies, intensities and transgressions of war serve in Homeric epic to structure a narrative in which ontologies and hierarchies are revealed, such as how the gods relate to each other, as well as the semi-permeable boundaries distinguishing divine, human and animal beings (Shoshitaishvili 2019). Conflicts like the Titanomachy similarly serve to structure and texture the cosmos presented in the Hesiodic poems.[16]

This message of a profoundly generative strife is reinforced by the stylistic qualities of fr. D63. Heraclitus combines concepts which initially appear in tension with each other – war-commonality, justice-strife – to call to mind unexpected relationships. The same juxtapositional style appears in other aphorisms and fragments, e.g. fr. D53's etymological doubleness: 'The name of the bow (cf. βιός/*biós*) is life (βίος/*bíos*), but its work is death.'[17] In the *Nicomachean Ethics*, Aristotle relates this stylistic technique to Heraclitus' metaphysical commitments:

> Heraclitus says that what is opposed converges (συμφέρον) (cf. fr. D47), and that the most beautiful harmony (καλλίστην ἁρμονίαν) comes out of what diverges (cf. fr. D49), and that all things come about by strife (κατ' ἔριν) (cf. fr. D63).
>
> *1155b4–6*

Helen, Paris and the Philosophical ἔρως

Although Heraclitus emphasizes strife and war (and creates linguistic echoes of productive strife through jarring conceptual combinations), he does so, according to Aristotle, in service of ideas that exist in counter-distinction to strife: the emergence of harmony (ἁρμονία/*harmonia*) and commonality (συμφέρον). We may compare our descriptions of Homeric epic above: narrative poetry with extensive and sustained focus on conflict, war and strife, yet all rooted in the contrastive dynamics of *erōs*. The causality is reversed from Homer to Heraclitus: war and strife do not emerge from their counterpoint dynamics (such as ἔρως) but rather exist to generate their contrast (in ἁρμονία). Instead of the καλλίστη woman and her beautiful lover (Helen and Paris) sparking *polemos* and *eris* through *erōs*, *eris* in Heraclitus becomes the source of καλλίστη ἁρμονία ('the most beautiful harmony').[18] Despite the causal reversal, however, the conviction that strife exists in profound relationship to those dynamics that contrast with it (ἔρως, ἁρμονία, κάλλος) shapes both Homeric epic and Heraclitean thought.

Empedocles' dual cosmology and the culmination of love in the σφαῖρος

Empedocles theorizes the relationship between strife (Νεῖκος/*Neikos*) and its opposite (Φιλότης/Φιλία, *Philotēs*/*Philia*) in greater detail than Heraclitean suggestions of eristic contrasts generating ἁρμονία. In Empedocles' cosmology, Νεῖκος and Φιλότης alternate in bringing about two cosmic states: one where all things are separated and one where everything gathers together.

In fr. D73, Empedocles describes the dynamic interchange of these two forces with attention to the affective associations of each:

> And these (sc. the elements) incessantly exchange their places continually,
> Sometimes by Love (Φιλότητι) all coming together into one,
> Sometimes again each one carried off by the hatred (ἔχθει) of Strife (Νείκεος).
> ...
> And baleful (οὐλόμενον) Strife is separate from them, equivalent everywhere,
> And Love (Φιλότης) in them, equal in length and in breadth ...
> She who mortals too think is implanted in their joints,
> And by whom they have loving thoughts and perform deeds of union,
> Calling her 'Joy' (Γηθοσύνην) as byname and 'Aphrodite' (Ἀφροδίτην).
>
> 239–55

Strife, although a universal force in this cosmology, is also positioned in a semantic cluster of affect-laden terms including hatred (ἔχθει) and destruction (οὐλόμενον). Strife's cosmological counterpart, *Philotēs*, is placed in its own cluster with Joy (Γηθοσύνη) and Aphrodite, the goddess of desire and sexual pleasure. While Empedocles reworks the two concepts into fundamental metaphysical forces guiding the movement of all 'elements' in the cosmos, strife and love in his system continue to exhibit their wider emotional resonance in human experience.

Empedocles' shift to the cosmic scale and into the dual dynamics of strife and love on a discourse-level recalls the perspectives of Helen and Paris in the *Iliad*. Helen and Paris' erotic prominence distinguishes them from the poem's predominant strife and affords them more comprehensive views of a strife-riven cosmos. But while they speak with an unusually collected distance about different character types and about their world as a whole, their abstracted perspectives also never go so far as to eliminate their own personal experience of ἔρις and ἔρως. They hover in between the immediate experience of a turbulent world and the full outside-perspective on it, in a state of partial abstraction. Something similar unfolds in Empedocles' fragment, though much more formally. He abstracts Νεῖκος and Φιλότης into cosmic and eternal forces yet continues to underscore their activity as part of immanent and affective human experience.

In another fragment, Empedocles theorizes the specific form taken by the cosmos at the point when *Philia* comes to dominate and *Neikos* is minimized:

> For from [its] back two branches do not shoot forth,
> No feet, no swift knees, no generative organs,
> But (it) was Sphairos (a sphere), and <everywhere> equal to (itself).
>
> D93

The form of the cosmos brought about by Φιλία/Φιλότης at its peak completely departs from the state of substantial differentiation – where bodies are internally differentiated and differentiated from each other – familiar to human beings. Instead, at the hypothetical extreme of love, everything conglomerates and the whole cosmos transforms into the more conceptual perfection represented by a 'sphere, equal to itself from all sides', which (Ps.-)Hippolytus, the source of this Empedoclean fragment (cf. fr. 29 DK), glosses as a shape of ultimate beauty: κάλλιστον εἶδος τοῦ κόσμου ('the most beautiful form of the cosmos').

This emphasis on precisely the κάλλιστον εἶδος ('the most beautiful form') of the love-dominated cosmos echoes another theme of our analysis of Paris and Helen and the interaction of the eristic and erotic in Homer. The paradigmatic lovers are the two epic figures associated most closely with *erōs/philia/philotēs* and Aphrodite. And both are profoundly linked to beauty (καλ-) and form (εἶδος).[19] Exhibiting these qualities alongside their contemplative and distanced perspective, Paris and Helen stand out as Homeric predecessors to Empedocles' recasting of love as the force behind the creation of beautiful form.

The link from Homer to Empedocles becomes even stronger when we note that ἔρως and ἔρις are entangled in all these cases. Paris in his response to Hector insists on the value of both the eristic and erotic male types, juxtaposed by him without personal bias. Analogously, Empedocles sets up *Neikos* and *Philotēs* as parallel forces each vital to a dualistic vision of a dynamic cosmos. Meanwhile Helen, through exceptional agency in the midst of extreme erotic dynamics, has the capacity to perceive in unified form the primarily eristic world surrounding her. Her grasp of the Trojan War as a whole, and her knowledge of both sides, is available due to her centrality in the *erōs* and *philia* that teems behind and motivates the conflict. This metaphysically holistic vantage resulting from erotic power begins to approach Empedocles' theorization that *Philotēs*, at its full expression, can bind the world together (if only temporarily) into the unified form of a perfect sphere.

Comparing Heraclitus and Empedocles vis-à-vis Homer

Unlike Empedocles, Heraclitus does not present *erōs* or *philia* as a countervailing force to conflict. Even so, fragments from Heraclitus clarify that the creativity of eristic dynamics derives from the fact that conflict reveals or results in the beauty of harmonized form: what he describes as καλλίστη ἁρμονία. This Heraclitean idea that strife produces its 'most beautiful' opposite is not so far from Empedocles' vision of an interchanging strife and love, with love culminating in 'the most beautiful form of the cosmos' (κάλλιστον εἶδος τοῦ κόσμου) as a sphere 'everywhere equal to itself'. Such a treatment of strife and beautiful harmony approximates to some extent Homeric depictions of Helen and Paris' role in the Trojan War: in both Homeric epic and Heraclitus, strife is the pervasive and predominant dynamic but remains connected with its opposite, stemming from the union of beautiful, erotically charged bodies or producing beautiful harmony.

Nevertheless, it is Empedocles' dual cosmology that expands more directly on the specific Homeric dynamics at play around Paris and Helen, especially in *Iliad* 3, against the epic's overarching privileging of conflict. For Empedocles and for Paris and Helen, strife and love are coeval forces deserving of equal recognition, and ἔρως has the power of affording a cosmic view. In short, Heraclitus re-expresses in gnomic aphorism the dominant Homeric current of *eris* (and its intensified form in *polemos*), while maintaining that *eris* is connected to its opposite; but Empedocles, in his cosmology, enhances and formalizes the distinctive qualities of the *erōs* epitomized by the Homeric lovers, drawing them out from a subordinate role in epic and setting them on equal footing with strife. Plato's Socrates will continue on the Empedoclean trajectory, pushing his conceptual shift further by representing ἔρως as not only equal but primary in the philosophical enterprise, a change which entails making strife subordinate instead.

Platonic philosophy and the erotic sublime

Plato transforms the erotic-contemplative thread that originates in Helen and Paris and runs through Heraclitus and Empedocles into primary material for what would henceforward be called philosophy. Most obviously by the choice of the term itself, Plato's Socrates underscores that *philo*sophy has its basis not simply in the gaining of wisdom but in the love of it.

At the start of this chapter, I remarked on the oscillation in *Republic* 10 between the dynamics of conflict (between Socrates and Homer, or between Socrates and his elenctic partners) and those of attraction (the soul's love of wisdom) in regard to the role of poetry and philosophy in education. In the *Symposium*, we find an even clearer expression of the interplay of eristic and erotic dynamics, now building towards metaphysical claims and revelations. On the one hand, the *Symposium* has an eristic or, more precisely, agonistic structure. The set of speeches that make up most of the dialogue unfold competitively, a late-night ἀγών/*agōn* of encomiasts enlivening their celebration of the host's victory in a recent dramatic contest (Agathon's in the Dionysia of 416 BCE).

Yet Plato deploys this eristic form of verbal competition and duelling praise in an effort to clarify fundamentally erotic dynamics. The structure of the *Symposium* may be agonistic, but *erōs* is the shared thread of its encomia. In fact, Eryximachus explains that his choice of ἔρως as theme is aimed at achieving something more long-term than maximizing the evening's enjoyment. Rather, the entertainment of this *agōn* is meant to address a cultural lacuna:

> Isn't it strange ... that there are hymns and paeans composed by the poets to some of the other gods, but to Love, a god of such age and so great, not one of the great number of our poets that have ever been has ever yet written anything in his praise? But again, if you care to consider the worthy sophists, that they write eulogies of Heracles and others in prose, such as the excellent Prodicus – and that is not so very surprising, but a while ago I came across some book by a clever fellow in which salt was lauded in a remarkable way for its usefulness and you can see many other things like that extolled – to think that they have devoted much serious effort to such things, but no human being to this day has ever yet ventured to sing the praises of Love in worthy fashion! Yet this is how far such a great god has been neglected.[20]
>
> *177a5–c4*

Eryximachus' rationale is a recognition of *erōs* having been, for all its power, largely subordinate or subliminal in Greek culture – especially in comparison to the *eris* that saturates Homer and Hesiod – and clues us into Plato's project in this dialogue to reposition ἔρως as a primary force. Moreover, if erotic dynamics and the importance of beauty had in Presocratic thought and poetry afforded rare but remarkably comprehensive, contemplative perspectives (Helen and Paris in *Iliad* 3; Heraclitus' and Empedocles' fragments), by the end of the *Symposium* Socrates will make the links between *erōs*, the beautiful and sublime forms of contemplation systematic and pronounced.

The philosophical peak of the *Symposium* arrives in Socrates' famous final encomium of ἔρως. He delivers his praise of love in the form of a reported conversation he had long ago with his own mentor, the prophet Diotima, whom he credits for his knowledge of τὰ ἐρωτικά.[21] Socrates' description of Diotima educating his younger self about *erōs* and its relevance for wisdom, philosophy and the forms (εἴδεα/*eidea*) is one of the clearest accounts in Plato of how these ideas are connected. It comes at the point in the dialogue when the agonistic mode of the elenchus has also reached its peak – Diotima had just played the role of confrontational questioner typically played by Socrates, after Socrates himself had challenged and refuted Agathon's encomium of love. Her exposition of the

Helen, Paris and the Philosophical ἔρως

nature and birth of love, as well as the philosopher's ascent up the steps of love, lifts the reader from the symposium's playful verbal combat and elenctic grappling into a mystical discourse that treats ἔρως as pathway to the immutable divine.

By the logic that one desires only what one does not already possess (in this case, wisdom and goodness), Diotima recasts *erōs* as a cosmic intermediary (a δαίμων μέγας rather than a μέγας θεός) acting to bridge the distance between mortal and divine: 'being in the middle of both, he fills the gap between them, so that the whole is bound together into one' (202e6–7). She gives this bridging function more specificity through a mythic genealogy when she adds the story of Erōs as the child of two contrasting deified forces mingling at a wedding (Πόρος, 'Abundance', and Πενία, 'Lack', 203b6–c1), with the δαίμων continually expressing both parents in his activity.

This interpretation of *erōs* as a force helping to achieve wholeness by relating oppositions recalls some of the themes explored above: that Helen bridges the two sides of the Iliadic war, belonging among both Achaeans and Trojans, and is able to represent the whole of the conflict in weaving the 'two-folded' cloak depicting the war; that Paris' response to Hector juxtaposes and, to some extent, bridges the erotic and eristic male paradigms (himself moving between one type and the other, as lover and warrior); that *harmonia* balances opposites in Heraclitus' conflictual ontology; and that the *Sphairos* in Empedocles' cosmological doctrines is a shape of gathered wholeness arising from the greatest expression of *philia*. The idea that ἔρως/φιλία/φιλότης/ἁρμονία brings together distant domains exists in all of them, from the Homeric characters through the Presocratic thinkers and into the *Symposium*.

Diotima's account goes on to adopt and magnify the contemplative perspectives initially exhibited in Homeric and Presocratic figures. Arguing wisdom to be 'one of the most beautiful things' and establishing *erōs* as oriented towards beauty, Diotima concludes that ἔρως must be a 'lover of wisdom' or φιλόσοφος (204a1–2). Diotima then redefines the relationship of ἔρως, beauty and goodness further in connection to immortality:

> For love, Socrates, she said is not love of the beautiful, as you think ... It's of procreation and giving birth in the beautiful ... Because procreation is something eternal and immortal, as far as can be the case for a mortal. From what has been agreed there must be a desire for immortality along with the good, if love is always about possession of the good for oneself. Indeed from this argument love must also be love of the eternal ... a desire to possess the good forever'.
>
> *206e1–207a5*

Beauty becomes specified as the setting necessary for the lover to reach the ultimate goal, which is the everlasting possession of the good through the mortal means of procreation. This formulation of the lover's desire could have led easily to Diotima extolling physical beauty as well as biological procreation through physical offspring, but Diotima's account, while acknowledging the embodied world as one domain, pointedly swerves from this direction and orients her description of *erōs* towards the world of ideas instead. She describes how the higher-order initiate into τὰ ἐρωτικά ascends the steps of love by leaving behind physical bodies and physical procreation. In a final effort to reach the immortality of goodness, the lover leaves behind even attempts at immortality through ideational 'procreations,' such as poetry, law, fame and the virtues themselves. The peak of the lover's ascent is a turning to a 'great ocean of beauty':

> Having turned to the great ocean of beauty and contemplating it may engender many fine and indeed magnificent words and thoughts in an unlimited love of wisdom, until there, strengthened and increased in growth, he may catch sight of a single kind of knowledge which is of a sort of beauty I shall now describe... beauty will not appear to him like a face or hands or anything else that a body has a share of, nor like any discourse or piece of knowledge. Nor do I think it exists in anything else, such as in a living being either on the ground or in the sky, or in any other thing, but alone by itself with itself it is an eternal single form.
>
> *210d3–211b2*

Analysing Diotima's account in full is beyond our scope, yet we can unearth the important roots of her ideas in the Presocratic visions of *erōs* and *philia* explored above (pp. 31–7, 39–41). Like the ἔρως of Helen and Paris, the Platonic lover's ascent leads away from the world of beautiful bodies and physical reproduction into a world of sublime concepts and conceptual practices, and finally into a view of the forms and of beauty as a whole. Homer's Paris and Helen had some purchase on the higher steps in this ascent. Both left behind physical reproduction in their *erōs* (they had no children together). Paris through his erotic experience achieved the unique ability to abstract and appreciate different ethical types as though they constituted different Platonic forms; Helen's ἔρως opened for her sublimated conceptual views of the whole, i.e. of the conflict-driven totality in which she is embroiled.

But the 'eternal single form' (μονοειδὲς ἀεί) of the great ocean of beauty (τὸ πολὺ πέλαγος τετραμμένος τοῦ καλοῦ) and its appearance to the ideal lover as being neither 'like a face or hands or anything else that a body has a share of' (οὐδ' αὖ φαντασθήσεται αὐτῷ τὸ καλὸν οἷον πρόσωπόν τι οὐδὲ χεῖρες οὐδὲ ἄλλο οὐδὲν ὧν σῶμα μετέχει) perhaps come closest to recalling Empedocles' *Sphairos* (see p. 40 above), the product of *Philotēs* at its cosmological peak, which was similarly unified, beautiful (κάλλιστον), and non-anthropomorphic or -zoomorphic: 'For from [its] back two branches do not shoot forth, No feet, no swift knees, no generative organs, But (it) was *Sphairos* (a sphere), and <everywhere> equal to (itself).' Despite numerous differences between Empedocles' and Plato's bodies of thought, the impression that love leads to the creation of, or sublime access to, a complete and abstracted unity informs both.

Conclusion: ἔρις and ἔρως as antipodes in a Greek 'metaphysics of contact'

Epic figures and philosophical thinkers from Homer to Plato present erotic dynamics as emerging in relationship to eristic ones. That love and war are opposing yet deeply linked forces may sound like a cliché, but, when considering the origins of Greek philosophy, is a formulation that helps explain the development of a distanced, contemplative and self-deprecating practice out of predominantly strife-focused archaic Greek poetic and intellectual history.

The argument put forward in this chapter has been primarily structural. If *eris* was a nearly ubiquitous theme among the exceptionally agonistic communities of the early Greeks, then the erotic, by sheer difference from the eristic, could become the basis of distanced, slanted perspectives on the dominant culture. First, poetic-philosophical figures like Helen and Paris and early Greek thinkers like Empedocles – and Heraclitus, through his focus on beauty and harmony – developed some of the key affordances of erotic distance; following them, Plato was able to embellish, systematize and transform *erōs* into the sublime driving force of philosophy.

Yet why are *eris* and *erōs* in particular the focal points of how early Greek philosophy unfolded against its epic background instead of a different internally related and contrastive pair, such as war (πόλεμος) and peace (εἰρήνη)? To touch on this question of the duality of ἔρις and ἔρως and its special hold on early Greek poetics and thought, I conclude with the sketch of a theory of commonality between them, one that exists beneath the basic fact of their difference.

Rather than simple opposites, we might reconceptualize ἔρις and ἔρως as two poles in a broader 'metaphysics of contact'. Both conflict and attraction involve subjects coming into definitive contact with each other, whether contact of bodies, wills, ideas or a combination. On one extreme, intensified contact results in opposition and a clearer distinction of one subject from its other (eristic contact); on the other, intensified contact can mean an entity coming into closer identification with its other (erotic contact). Greek poetry and thought appear to have maintained a fascination with the revelatory potential at the locus where two sides encounter each other. This found form in two deified contrastive dynamics, i.e. in a dual orientation of contact towards differentiation as well as union, their commonality resonating even in the morphological and phonetic similarity of the words ἔρις and ἔρως, distinguished as they are by only a single vowel. By underpinning ontological distinction as well as identity, the poetics of contact in its eristic and erotic forms served a metaphysical function.

Alongside this spatial account of two sides meeting precipitously, the metaphysics of contact involves a temporal dimension that can shed light on the unusual concept of καιρός/*kairos*. Scholars have long recognized the qualitative distinctiveness of this Greek word – of the 'right time' or 'opportunity' or 'perfect timing'.[22] The deified *Kairos*, the god of the moment, was salient in agonistic or eristic events such as athletic contests, as Austin reminds us in his analysis of the altar dedicated to Καιρός at Olympia:

> The Greeks venerated the moment, not time in the abstract, but *timing*. *Kairos* is the moment of crisis. Out of a deep reverence, colored by a deep anxiety, for the significance of the moment in human life, they made Kairos a god. The *Oxford Classical Dictionary* calls this Kairos 'personified Opportunity'. Time for us may be stooped and old, but *timing* can never be old; it is always born anew in every new

crisis ... Every moment is a golden opportunity. Kairos too is also ageless, and for the same reason. He too is the god of the moment, the moment itself personified. In every one of the athletic contests held at the sacred site, Kairos would shine on one youth, and one alone – the victor.

2011: 82

Austin's description (cf. also his chapter in this volume) points to the nearly paradoxical temporal significance of *kairos* – the link between the shining moment as fleeting phenomenon and the potential agelessness that may obtain if this moment is seized, occupied and amplified. The same nexus of the ephemeral, the eternal and the agonistic informs the Greek concept of κλέος/*kleos*, the glory of one's moment(s) of personal greatness reverberating perpetually in social memory. By entering into intense rivalries that unlock kairotic moments of agonistic excellence, a person could secure immortal presence in performance, song and narrative.

The erotic form of contact also linked kairotic time to immortality, but differently. Agonistic κλέος depends on each participant of a conflict enhancing their own performance over and against their competitor until one or both might accomplish a feat worth remembering forever. In other words, a rival presses against the other in order to express a momentary yet externalizable, i.e. 'monumental', expression of their own self and effort. In erotic contact, by contrast, one seeks the opportune moment to merge with, rather than push against, the other. The beauty of the moment of union had the creative potential to allow the erotic subject to bring forth, and dissolve into, an emergent novelty that outlived the pre-union self.

Each mode of contact contains prospects of instability and destruction. Eristic contact involves the likelihood of one side destroying the other, both corporeally as well as in terms of status. This is shown in the charged exchanges of warriors like Achilles and Hector at Troy. Their *kleos* lives on yet their bodies perish at their acme: for Hector, his life is destroyed and his body is desecrated; for Achilles, his prospect of a life spanning multiple stages (beyond glorious youth) is lost at Troy. Eristic contact involves outward-directed aggression at the other, along with the possibility of destruction by the other in response, for the sake of immortal memory.

In erotic contact, the self is pulled to yield its own coherence to the other as part of an effort to fulfil the desire to merge and achieve novelty through union. Accordingly, the great early figures of ἔρως – Helen, Paris and Socrates – are noteworthy for their performances of self-deprecation,[23] and for their (relative) equanimity when challenged aggressively. This manner of readily yielding the self stands in contrast to eristic figures such as Achilles, Agamemnon or Hector, who remain steadfastly self-bolstering and hyper-sensitively attuned to conflict in word and deed.

By reconceptualizing the eristic and erotic as antipodes of contact, we might better understand the newfound prominence of *erōs* and *philia* at the origins of Greek philosophy. For a Hellenic thinker like Plato, shifting the weight from the eristic to the erotic pole of the underlying metaphysics of contact was a delicate manoeuvre that could be accomplished without exiting the cultural framework itself. Helen, Paris and

Helen, Paris and the Philosophical ἔρως

Empedocles began this process of rebalancing, providing the earliest examples of erotic, sublime and union-oriented contact, even as *erōs* in their case remained subsidiary or, at most, equal to an otherwise eristic environment. Plato went furthest in fashioning the philosopher as the self-deprecating *erōs*-invested pursuer of sublime vision, a figure oriented towards productive contact with the good and beautiful, and created a model that endures to this day. The tension with which this chapter began, that between Plato's agonistic attack on Homer and his insistence that philosophy is grounded in the dynamics of love, resolves when we see that *eris* and *erōs* alike belong to the metaphysics of contact.

Notes

1. Translations of Plato's *Republic* are from Emlyn-Jones and Preddy 2013.
2. Translations of the *Iliad* are Alexander's (2016).
3. See Arendt and Kohn 2005: 165–8, Barker 2009, Nietzsche and Acampora 1996, Wolfe 2015 for differing overviews of Homeric agonism.
4. Already in antiquity, Plato's agonistic stance was noticed and even celebrated: Longinus cast Plato as an ἀνταγωνιστὴς νέος ('a young antagonist') who was able to produce sublime verbal art precisely because he challenged Homer παντὶ θυμῷ ('with all his heart') in the 'good' form of ἔρις ('strife'; *Subl.* 13.4). See also the argument of Patterson 1997 that Plato envisioned the figure of the philosopher as an ἀγωνιστής ('competitor').
5. See Nietzsche and Large 2008: 14 and, especially, Zovko 2020.
6. I treat ἔρις/*eris*, νεῖκος/*neikos*, ἀγών/*agōn* and πόλεμος/*polemos* as belonging to a single semantic cluster (of strife/the eristic), and ἔρως/*erōs*, φιλία/*philia* and φιλότης/*philotēs* as belonging to a separate one (of love/attraction/the erotic). While differences and nuances exist between the terms in each set, they appear in close enough association in the texts analysed in this chapter that each can be taken as belonging exclusively to one or the other semantic sphere.
7. 2.715, 3.124, 6.252, 13.365, 378.
8. The two lines contain an unusually close juxtaposition of two morphologies of ἀνήρ/*anēr* ('man') for the same idea, with the word cycling between its two genitive forms, ἀνέρος and ἀνδρὸς. Paris emphasizes maleness but through oblique cases of the noun.
9. The closest use elsewhere in the poem is at 10.547, when Nestor wonders at the 'terrible' gleam of the horses Odysseus and Diomedes have just stolen from the Thracians and asks whether the horses are divine. Almost all the word's other eighteen appearances in the poem describe negative experiences: someone dreading or grieving or being angered 'terribly'.
10. Succumbing to *erōs* with Paris meant removing herself from renewing the family-city sphere in which she was a mother and queen. Sappho 16 highlights how Helen was neither mindful of her child nor parents when she left with Paris; the *eris-erōs* contrast frames the poem, with the speaker endorsing the beauty of the object of ἔρως (κάλλιστον ... ὄτ- / τω τις ἔραται, 3–4) over the eristic magnificence of war (ἰππήων στρότον ... δὲ πέσδων ... δὲ νάων, 1–2).
11. For insightful analysis of the complexity of Helen's agency in the *Iliad* in relation to her absolution and (self-) blame, see Blondell 2010.
12. We may recall Aristotle's description of poetry as 'more philosophical' (φιλοσοφώτερον) than history for conveying 'more aspects of the whole' (μᾶλλον τὰ καθόλου) over particulars (*Poet.*

1451b1–7). Helen, through holistic vision of the ἔρις-ἔρως dynamics of her world, becomes epic's φιλοσοφώτερον figure in this sense.

13. Paris' ethical orientation and equanimity align with the tradition of his selection to judge among Hera, Athena and Aphrodite when the apple of Ἔρις/*Eris*, a prize of the beauty of its possessor (περὶ κάλλους), brings the three goddesses into conflict (*Cypria* fr. 1; Ps. Apollodorus, *Bibliotheca Epit.* E 3). For the apple in antiquity as sign of love as well as strife, see McCartney 1925.

14. Helen's unique ability to transcend and represent the war and the *erōs* beneath it can be clarified by contrast with Andromache, her principal female peer in the city. Andromache is also presented weaving a 'red folding robe' at 22.437–44, a δίπλακα πορφυρέην like Helen's δίπλακα μαρμαρέην in 3.126, just before she learns of her husband's death. These are the only two folding robes in the poem. Andromache's experience at the loom is more humanly tragic, absent of divinity and metaphysical vision. The poetic focus falls not on what she weaves but where she weaves (the 'inner room of her high house', μυχῷ δόμου ὑψηλοῖο, 440); i.e. in the μυχός or most intimate part of the home, and for whom (Hector).

15. Translations of Heraclitus and Empedocles are from Laks and Most 2016a and 2016b, respectively.

16. For the broader cosmic background of opposition, conflict and replacement in Greek mythopoesis, see Worthen 1991: 121–55.

17. For a vivid pictorial distinction between *eros*/*eris* as 'bed and bow', see Austin in this volume, p. 18.

18. The extreme beauty (καλλίστη) of Heraclitean *harmonia* emerging from strife recalls the intersection of extreme beauty, love and strife in the Trojan War – both the terrible beauty of Helen and Paris who cause the war, and the story of the Judgement of Paris, with the apple meant to bring strife through competition over divine beauty.

19. Consider the repeated emphasis on Paris' εἶδος in Hector's rebuke in book 3: εἶδος ἄριστε (3.39); καλὸν εἶδος (3.39); οὐκ ἄν τοι χραίσμῃ ... τό τε εἶδος (3.54–5). Hector's rebuke emphasizes Helen's εἶδος as well: γυναῖκ' εὐειδέ' ἀνῆγες (3.48). His rebuke of Paris is remarkable for the sheer density of εἶδος-related words. Helen's exceptional beauty is emphasized elsewhere in the poem as well: the Trojan elder's αἰνῶς ἀθανάτῃσι θεῇς εἰς ὦπα ἔοικεν (3.158) discussed on pp. 34–5 above; and in Agamemnon's offer to Achilles: αἵ κε μετ' Ἀργείην Ἑλένην κάλλισται ἔωσιν (9.140).

20. Translations of Plato's *Symposium* are from Emlyn-Jones and Preddy 2022.

21. See Halperin 1990 for his landmark essay on why Diotima is a woman and what it has meant to ask this question. Another possible approach to Diotima's presence in the *Symposium*, in light of this chapter's argument, is that the Socrates-Diotima relationship reinterprets the Paris-Helen pair, with Diotima and Helen as the more philosophical and empowered figure in each erotic pair.

22. The temporal precision of *kairos* relates to a spatial precision signalled in cognate words such as the adjective *kairios* (*Il.* 4.185, 8.84). See Trédé-Boulmer 2015 for meticulous study of *kairos* and its conceptual-linguistic development through archaic and classical Greek. For the connection of *kairos* to the sublime, see Porter's list of the sublime's 'logical and thematic markers' (2016: 51–3); this chapter's discussions of ἔρις, ἔρως, philosophical vision and (p. 46 above) *kleos* also resonate with Porter's items.

23. The σφαῖρος Empedocles designates as the zenith of *philotēs* in the cosmic cycle is also self-effacing in its form, losing all distinguishing (anthropomorphic and zoomorphic) characteristics for the sake of a purely geometric shape of wholeness, symmetry and totality.

Works cited

Arendt, H. and J. Kohn (2005), *The Promise of Politics*, New York: Schocken Books.
Austin, N. (2011), *Sophocles' Philoctetes and the Great Soul Robbery*, Madison: The University of Wisconsin Press.
Barker, E. (2009), *Entering the Agon: Dissent and Authority in Homer, Historiography and Tragedy*, Oxford: Oxford University Press.
Blondell, R. (2010), '"Bitch that I Am": Self-Blame and Self-Assertion in the *Iliad*', *Transactions of the American Philological Association*, 140: 1–32.
Diels, H. and W. Kranz (1951), *Die Fragmente der Vorsokratiker*, 6th edn., Berlin: Weidmann.
Halperin, D. (1990), *One Hundred Years of Homosexuality: And Other Essays on Greek Love*, Abingdon-on-Thames: Routledge.
Homer (2016), *The Iliad: A New Translation by Caroline Alexander*, trans. C. Alexander, New York: Ecco.
Kennedy, G. A. (1986), 'Helen's Web Unraveled', *Arethusa*, 19: 5–14.
Laks, A. and G. Most (2016a), *Early Greek Philosophy, Volume III: Early Ionian Thinkers, Part 2*, Cambridge: Harvard University Press.
Laks, A. and G. Most (2016b), *Early Greek Philosophy, Volume V: Western Greek Thinkers, Part 2*, Cambridge: Harvard University Press.
McCartney, E. (1925), 'How the Apple Became the Token of Love', *Transactions and Proceedings of the American Philological Association*, 56: 70–81.
Nietzsche, F. and C. Acampora (1996), *Homer's Contest*, Urbana, IL: North American Nietzsche Society.
Nietzsche, F. and D. Large (2008), *Twilight of the Idols, or, How to Philosophize with a Hammer*, Oxford: Oxford University Press.
Patterson, R. (1997), '"Philosophos Agonistes": Imagery and Moral Psychology in Plato's *Republic*', *Journal of the History of Philosophy*, 35: 327–54.
Plato (2013), *Republic, Volume II: Books 6–10*, trans. C. Emlyn-Jones and W. Preddy, Cambridge: Harvard University Press.
Plato (2022), *Lysis. Symposium. Phaedrus*, trans. C. Emlyn-Jones and W. Preddy, Cambridge: Harvard University Press.
Porter, J. I. (2016), *The Sublime in Antiquity*, Cambridge: Cambridge University Press.
Shoshitaishvili, B. (2019), 'Homer's World at War: Cosmic Agonism in the *Iliad*', diss. Stanford: Palo Alto, CA.
Trédé-Boulmer, M. (2015), *Kairos, l'à-propos et l'occasion: Le mot et la notion, d'Homère à la fin du IVe siècle avant J.-C*, Paris: Les Belles Lettres.
Wolfe, J. (2015), *Homer and the Question of Strife from Erasmus to Hobbes*, Toronto: The University of Toronto Press.
Worthen, T. D. (1991), *The Myth of Replacement: Stars, Gods, and Order in the Universe*, Tucson: The University of Arizona Press.
Zovko, J. (2020), 'Agōn as Constituent of the Socratic Elenchos', in H. Reid, M. Ralkowski, C. Zoller (eds), *Athletics, Gymnastics, and Agon in Plato*, 173–84, Sioux City, IA: Parnassos Press.

CHAPTER 4
THE HARD-BREAK AT HESIOD, *THEOGONY* 200
Frank Romer

Preface

When I first arrived at the University of Arizona for the fall term of 1992, Thom, who recently had published *The Myth of Replacement*, welcomed me in a collegial and friendly way. He initiated a number of conversations about Hellenic myth since I was scheduled to teach a section of the large course on classical mythology that term. Thom liked to talk about the myths, the evidence for them and various interpretations of them, including his own. I do not think we ever talked about the Hesiodic birth-narrative of Aphrodite, but, in his memory, I offer the present discussion as a remote descendant of our early conversations.[1]

Introduction

In the familiar Hesiodic birth-story of Aphrodite, Kronos castrated his father Ouranos and threw his severed μήδεα ('genitals'[2]) into the sea; the seaborne genitals then travelled around for a long time until, in the *aphros* ('foam') emitted by them Aphrodite was conceived and nurtured (ἐθρέφθη in its fullest sense, 192), and she eventually was born on Kypros (199).[3]

Hesiod and Homer are 'the ones who created for the Hellenes the genealogy of the gods, gave the gods their eponyms, divided their honours and arts, and indicated their visible forms' (Hdt. 2.53.2).[4] In tandem, then, according to these famous words of Herodotus, Hesiod and Homer virtually created the Hellenic gods, presumably out of traditional materials. This process was not entirely seamless, however, and so it is not without its own hitches, one of which is well known and manifests itself in the early history of Aphrodite. For Hesiod, Aphrodite is generated spontaneously from Ouranos' castrated genitals, while Homer gives her a more familiarizing and familiar kind of lineage by making her the daughter of Zeus and his namesake nymph Dione.[5] In order of composition the Homeric epics probably preceded the Hesiodic *Theogony*,[6] but in mythical order the events narrated in *Theogony*, which treats the origin of both the cosmos and the gods, precede those described in the *Iliad* and *Odyssey*. *Theogony* knows the Homeric poems but presents a pointedly different version of Aphrodite's origin, which provides an informative point of comparison and contrast with the Homeric epics, particularly as they relate to her Panhellenic representation.

In Aphrodite's case, Homer's genealogy not only gives her new parents (she is distinctively motherless in the Hesiodic account) but also strips her of the cosmogonic status she had as a member of the previous generation of gods. According to the Hesiodic narrative, Aphrodite was born into a universe that was home to the Titans and overseen by Kronos. Her move to the more recent Olympian tier of gods also made her, like the other Olympians, subordinate to the will of Zeus. Aphrodite's reassignment reflects a major power play by Zeus, as described in the *Iliad*, to stabilize his regime (pp. 58–9 below), but this corrective also makes her birth more comprehensible in human terms. The present argument aims, then, to understand the Hesiodic account in its literary and historical settings, since it documents socio-culturally genuine archaic Hellenic thinking in an Aphrodisian context.

Supernatural beings, preternatural events

Supernatural beings and preternatural events exert a strong presence in myths, although either may operate only behind the scenes in any given myth.[7] It is no secret that in the most familiar narratives Hellenic gods are typically both anthropomorphic and anthropopathic. In remote times, however, in the primordial world in which myths first began to develop, divine powers pervaded all facets of human life,[8] and theogonic myths most probably were concerned with a variety of numinous powers (*ta deina*; cf. Lat. *numina*). As a general principle, the more anthropomorphic or anthropopathic these powers become in a given telling, the farther those individual performances or narratives stray from the primal form of an original mythos.[9]

Theogony also differentiates between, on the one hand, elements of Aphrodite's birth-story that are truly theogonic because they contribute to her own birth as literally spelled out in the poem, and, on the other hand, those elements that directly result from that birth. This distinction reflects an awareness that the mythos involving Ouranos and Aphrodite, having originated in the remote past, had been passed down through untold generations of unnamed oral performers.[10] Use implies change, and at the time of its composition the poem apparently was attempting, at least in this instance, to recover what was being lost from the primal theogonic mythos. (Paradoxically, additions to the primal narrative also constitute losses because they alter that narrative and take away from its original self-contained, self-referential completeness.) Likewise, events that defy reason and cannot be explained as part of the natural order are, by definition, miracles. The competing Homeric version of the Aphrodite myth seeks to normalize her birth in naturalistic terms, and commentators often appear to downplay the fact that in *Theogony* her birth is, by any standard, both unique and miraculous (sublimely so), that is, outside or beyond ordinary human understanding and therefore begging to be normalized in repeated performances over time.

The offspring of Gaia and Ouranos

'The "Succession Myth" is the backbone of the poem.'[11] That myth tells how Ouranos was toppled by Kronos, who ruled with his fellow Titans until Zeus brought him down. This succession story is told largely in eight episodic units dealing with the descendants of Gaia and threaded throughout the poem, each in a structure that is interlocking and balanced but asymmetrical.[12] For the sake of convenience, I begin here with the following chart, which breaks down the initial episode that is our focus:

	Children of Gaia and Ouranos, first episode (*Theog.* 126–210)	
126		First episode begins
126–53		Gaia's, and Gaia and Ouranos', children
	126–32	Introduction: Gaia's parthenogenic birthing – Ouranos, Mountains, Pontos
	132–8	Gaia and Ouranos' children: birth of the Titans (not yet so named as a group)
	139–53	Gaia and Ouranos' children: birth of the Cyclopes and the Hundred-handers
154–200		Ouranos' castration and its direct consequences
	154–87	Ouranos' unending copulation with Gaia, his castration
	188–200	Ouranos' daughter: *mēdea* of Ouranos at sea, her single-parent origin and the names of Aphrodite
200		Hard-break in the narrative
201–10		Conclusion: after-effects of the whole account
	201–6	Aphrodite's single-parent birth, first steps and *timē/moira*
	207–10	Naming of the Titans as a group
210		First episode ends

Structurally, this first episode of the Succession Myth (126–210) opens with almost seven hexameters (126–32) addressing Gaia's parthenogenic birthing of Ouranos (Sky), Mountains (haunts of the Nymphs) and Pontos (Sea). Gaia dominates the introductory lines of this episode with her self-produced offspring before introducing individual Titans as the first of her and Ouranos' children, while Ouranos dominates its concluding ten verses (201–10) with his self-produced and last-born child Aphrodite and the group-naming of his and Gaia's first-born children, the Titans. This last juxtaposition is motivated and asymmetrically linked by the naming of both Aphrodite and the Titans but involves an entirely different order of explanation from that of Aphrodite's birth-process itself.

In between, we get the continuous story of Ouranos' genitals, which (a) begins (implicitly) with the obstructed birth of the Titans (129–38), (b) is marked explicitly by the *mēdea* of Ouranos and highlighted by Aphrodite's miraculous birth-story and the explanation of her names (154–200), and (c) is topped off by her first steps and the listing of her *timē/moira* (201–6),[13] and which ends, as indicated, by explaining the group name of the Titans (207–10). Ouranos' *mēdea* are indispensable to Aphrodite's being as also to her miraculous birth itself, but the Titans, too, have a specific connection to Ouranos' genitals through his obstructive role in the Titans' own two-parent birth. Ouranos' struggle with the Titans, because of his fear and hatred of them, results in an oblique prediction of future retribution (*tisis*), which points ahead to the Titans' defeat by Zeus (perhaps on Ouranos' and Gaia's advice[14]) and their consequent banishment to Tartarus

(617–720). This whole episode starts with the primacy of Gaia's solo role in parthenogenesis and ends with Ouranos' solo part in an act of spontaneous generation and his own negative interaction with the Titans, which motivated his eventual castration.

Reclaiming the Aphrodite-mythos

Aphrodite is a strong and complex divinity, a divine power; in fact, her primary function is human sex and sexuality, which appears first as a generalized (vegetal) fertility; as she steps ashore, full-grown, on Kypros, that fertility is marked by the free-sprouting grass beneath her feet, an obvious statement of abundance and power in the world of nature.[15] Outside the poem, she has an enticing ethnographic history of her own, and the Hellenization of her birth-story is documented in *Theogony*, which denies programatically (but wrongly) any historical connection to the Near East[16] and attempts to distinguish in purely Hellenized terms between elements of a primal mythos and elements added to it in the course of telling and expatiating on it.[17] The word-for-word description of her actual birthing in *Theogony* breaks into two main parts, the literal theogonic narrative (188–200) and the immediate consequences of her miraculous birth (201–6), which highlight her *timē/moira* (203–6) and are more in keeping with heroic epos and other poetic genres. There is a marked difference, then, between theogonic and non-theogonic – or, better, post-theogonic – aspects of the story in Hesiod, a difference that is enforced at 200, which both summarizes Aphrodite's birth-story and clarifies its literal meaning.

The major textual question is which accusative singular is to be read in 200, *philommēdea* ('to whom the male genitals belong'; 'penis-loving') or *philommeidea* ('smile-loving'). Heubeck and Burkert make it clear both linguistically and religiously that *philommēdēs* is the operative word,[18] and I argue that since it bears the semantic load of this sentence in oral performance, the accusative *philommēdea* passes for authorial and should appear in modern printed texts.[19] *Philommēdēs* is the last in a series of explanations for Aphrodite's familiar names, and so in 195 and 197–200 the goddess is identified as Aphrodite 'because she was conceived in foam', Kythereian 'since she had drawn near (προσέκυρσε) to Kythera', Kypros-born 'since she was born on sea-girt Kypros', as well as 'Penis-loving because she appeared out of male genitals': ἠδὲ φιλομμηδέα ὅτι μηδέων ἐξεφαάνθη. The first-level, literal meaning of this line is indisputable as far as concerns the active role and the relevance of Ouranos' *mēdea* in the poem.

In her miraculous birth, Aphrodite emerges full-grown from Ouranos' genitals in a precisely framed narrative, which is, oddly, not always appreciated for its preciseness. For example, Kirk restricts the 'relevance' of Ouranos' phallus to the earlier period before Aphrodite's conception when Ouranos' continuous intercourse trapped his children in Gaia's womb.[20] His view of the relevance of the *mēdea* is short-sighted since the activity, and therefore the relevance, of those genitals obviously extends into Aphrodite's procreation in the birth-story proper; in addition, after her birth, the characteristic property of the *mēdea* shapes Aphrodite's *timē/moira*, an effect depending only in part on

The Hard-Break at Hesiod, *Theogony* 200

whether she is *philommēdēs* ('penis-loving') or its (virtual) homonym *philommeidēs* ('smile-loving') 'because she appeared out of male genitals'. For Kirk, however, the relevance of Ouranos' genitals ended at 188, but their relevance is best measured, first and foremost, by their direct action in the narrative, which continues into the birthing and naming process all the way to 200, and, secondarily, by their underlying, indirect manifestation in Aphrodite, as Ouranos' excessive sexual potency reappears as Aphrodite's own excessive sexual potency, which is sketched in the first part of the conclusion (201–6).[21]

Theog. 200 closes the literal theogonic narrative of Aphrodite (188–200), which is fully integrated into the long account of Ouranos' genitals (154–200) and is effectively co-extensive with it. That story, in turn, is part and parcel of the story of Gaia, who produced Ouranos by parthenogenesis, then mated incestuously with him and finally produced with him the line of offspring described in the poem.[22] The theogonic process in this first episode culminates in Aphrodite's birth, and what follows requires a different order of explanation.

The function of *Theog.* 200

In word-processing, a hard break marks the end of one paragraph and signals the beginning of another, a clear shift in the narrative, a new wrinkle in the argument. *Theog.* 200 functions in just that way in this poem. However, it is most commonly read simply as the end of the birth-story of Aphrodite, which it certainly functions as. At the same time it is summative as it also terminates the active and relevant role of Ouranos' genitals in the narrative, and it creates the opportunity to move towards a new and different but related topic, the goddess's attributes. The conclusion, which immediately follows 200 is a coda of ten lines, a tail to the story, the content of which is in important ways formally different from what preceded it. This coda gives point to the climax of the birth-narrative by illustrating the power of Ouranos' genitals as that power now is transformed and embodied in Aphrodite and by pointing obliquely to a future stage in the Succession Myth.

This verse is so explicit and assertive, however, in its most literal rendering, given above (p. 54), that it feels confrontational, even polemical, as it terminates the birth-narrative and the seaborne meandering of Ouranos' castrated *mēdea*, and at the same time suggests that something else is to come now. Ouranos' story culminates in the birth of Aphrodite because his *mēdea* are both the cause and the means of her miraculous single-parent gestation and birth. Her birth completes the direct action of the *mēdea* in the narrative but, *pace* Kirk, does not fully account for their relevance, which implicitly reaches into the coda as well. In this view, the hard break bounds, and attempts to stake out, a theogonic narrative tradition that already had become blurred over time in the course of numerous performances and was likely to be blurred further by other new developments, both literary and socio-cultural (p. 60 below).

In contrast to the Homeric genealogy, the theogonic mythos proper presents the least anthropomorphic and least anthropopathic manifestation of the goddess that the Hesiodic poem could fashion in this context. The coda focuses on Aphrodite's *timē/moira* and then, by comparison and contrast through both Aphrodite and the Titans, connects the coda first with the beginning of the episode and Gaia's parthenogenic procreation, second with Gaia and Ouranos' copulation and their offspring, and third with the end of the episode and Ouranos' miraculously engendered daughter and the first-born Titans. In that way, the coda seals in and unifies the two-part episode as a necessary building block for the poem as a whole.

In the end, the decisive feature for recognizing a hard break at *Theog.* 200 must be the simple fact that Aphrodite's birth marks a major departure in the poem: she is the first anthropomorphic deity to be born (*kourē*, 192; *aidoiē kalē theos*, 194). Her theogonic moment in the poem ends with her birth as a young woman, which is summarized in 200 and leaves the discussion of her anthropic character to be treated in the coda.

The attributes of Aphrodite

Aphrodite's attributes (*timē/moira*) are her inherent characteristics, that is, her seductive behaviours, all of which reflect the extreme sexual potency she inherited from her father. Her sexual behaviours and seductive power are set out in understandably human terms in what is, after all, an androcentric social and poetic environment (205–6): παρθενίους τ' ὀάρους μειδήματά τ' ἐξαπάτας τε / τέρψίν τε γλυκερὴν φιλότητά τε μειλιχίην τε ('girlish whisperings and smiles and deception and sweet delight and lovemaking[23] and graciousness'). These characteristics, however, were explored and exploited outside the theogonic context per se, and therefore are technically non-theogonic or post-theogonic elaborations that begin for us with Homer but also are seen here where the poem overlaps with, or alludes to, Homeric epos.

The remote cause of Aphrodite's attributes is the copulation of Gaia and Ouranos, which linked the long line of their individual and joint offspring, but their immediate cause lay apart from Gaia and in Ouranos' excessive sexual power and the miraculous act of spontaneous generation. 'Creative energy is a fundamental attribute of power, and, in Hesiod's myth-language, is manifested in procreation; likewise, in Hesiod's myth-language, the character of a divine power is revealed in his children'.[24] Thus, the attributes of Aphrodite are undeniably connected through the *mēdea* to Aphrodite's theogony and specifically to her inherited sexual power. Her birth-story connects both Aphrodite and that power to the sky (her father), the sea (the seaborne genitals) and the earth (her first step on Kypros) and is thus universalizing and all-inclusive, and yet not all her Hellenized mythological and cultic connections to any one of these three elements earn their way into her Panhellenic image.

How Aphrodite evolved

The development of Aphrodite outside the theogonic tradition has notable differences and problematic consequences. To start with, as already noted, Homer gives Aphrodite a mother (the nymph Dione: *Il.* 5.370–1) – she does not have one at all in *Theogony* – and a different father, Zeus (*Il.* 5.131 *et passim*). In *Theogony*, Aphrodite originates as a cosmogonic divinity insofar as she belongs to the generation prior to Zeus, but the *Iliad* moves her to a different, younger generation with the other Olympian gods and makes her subject to Zeus. Likewise, Eros began as a cosmogonic god, with little mythology and no cult of his own, and he even comes into existence before Aphrodite (116–22) and, with Himeros ('Desire'), welcomes her as she is born on Kypros (201–2).[25] At this mythic moment, both Eros' and Aphrodite's roles are in flux. As a primordial force of sexuality, Eros is replaced over time by Aphrodite in the Olympian pantheon, and inscriptions and sculpture came to represent him as her son at least from the mid-fifth century on, though that relationship does not appear in literature until the Hellenistic era.[26] Finally, there is even the trace of an alternate theogony, when Hera tells Aphrodite that the gods had their genesis from Okeanos, information that, curiously enough, is elicited from Hera in the *Dios Apatê* scene as she seeks erotic help from Aphrodite (*Il.* 14.200–1).[27]

In Homer, the most conspicuous of Aphrodite's attributes are smiling, deception and lovemaking, while others such as girlish whispering are developed only outside heroic epos. The essential characteristics of Aphrodite's sexual power, as given in her *timē/moira*, reflect both the anthropomorphism and the anthropopathism that typify the Homeric Aphrodite, but not the Aphrodite of the primitive theogonic account. The hard break, then, separates the content of two different traditions. In this way, as indicated earlier (pp. 55–6), the poem is reclaiming an older tradition, for which it now is named.

Further, the fact that some behaviours listed in Aphrodite's *timê/moira* are not reflected in the Homeric epics, but are illustrated outside theogonic narrative altogether, suggests that her characteristic behaviours – her personality, as some critics now call it – owe their origin to the development of the goddess in various social and religious practices and in other strains of heroic tradition and new or inchoate literary modes of expression. The principle at stake is similar to the one Telemachus expresses: 'for people (*anthrōpoi*) admire more a song that most recently resonates for those listening' (τὴν γὰρ ἀοιδὴν μᾶλλον ἐπικλείουσ' ἄνθρωποι, / ἥ τις ἀκουόντεσσι νεωτάτη ἀμφιπέληται, *Od.* 1.351–2). New is better. At the time *Theogony* was being composed, Aphrodite's listed behaviours were being identified and expanded both in heroic epos and in other genres like the imitatively-Homeric hymns and, quite possibly, even in proto-lyric poetry. All these characteristic behaviours were delineated sharply and magnified as they spread more widely both at that time and later. In contrast, the coda in the poem reflects not only the Homeric elaboration of the goddess's attributes in antithesis to the purely theogonic account, but also the simultaneous and subsequent embellishment of her sexual roles as proclaimed in an androcentric social and poetic milieu.

Hesiod's account of Aphrodite's birthing is cast as an airtight Hellenic phenomenon (which does not reflect historical reality), and it is not only airtight but emphatic in demonstrating that she had no mother, while Homer's account, as we have seen, gives her a mother and also changes her procreation to a more biologically comprehensible and socially intelligible arrangement with Zeus and Dione. The Hesiodic description of the new-born Aphrodite as *aidoiē kalē theos* marks the end of the gestation period, and her *timē/moira* belongs to a post-theogonic period as well as to a post-theogonic poetic tradition, which for us is epico-heroic in origin. Thus begins the Homeric attempt to subdue Aphrodite and redirect her inherited sexual powers; but the Homeric content already had spread beyond its Homeric confines, for example, in the Homeric *Hymn to Aphrodite*, which is nearly contemporary with *Theogony*, and explores and expands on Aphrodite's behaviours.[28] *Theogony* documents, then, what it represents as an original, pre-Homeric ethnographic understanding of Aphrodite's birth, which is modified in the Homeric poems, and thereby brings up the question of her Hellenization and Panhellenization amid the subsequent elaboration of her *timê/moira* and its applications (p. 60 below).

Aphrodite and the rule of Zeus

The Succession Myth in *Theogony* describes an evolutionary process, which is treated as factual and historical. 'The regime of Zeus, which is the final outcome of the historical process, is not only patriarchal but also political. Zeus is not only "the father of gods and men," but also "the king".'[29] In 617–720, Zeus is elected king of the gods and distributes to them their *timai*, and he also tries to put the world in order and stabilize his regime. Eventually he devours the pregnant Mētis, an act which both usurps the female role in procreation and puts a stop to the cycle of the Succession Myth (881–929). In recounting three generations of the Succession Myth, *Theogony* makes Zeus, the leader of the third generation, the survivor who governs the world as the audience knows it, and who, to all appearances, is expected to do so on a permanent basis.

Theogony is the victory song of Zeus (cf. 402–3, 506, 613–16, 881–5), but a careful reading of the *Iliad* shows that in this mythical construct his regime was still new, unfamiliar and open to challenge. It is therefore wrong to assume that at this particular juncture his victory was necessarily secure or permanent, as is sometimes too easily done. True, in the *Iliad* Zeus is 'the mightiest of all the gods' and 'greatly superior to gods and men,' as he claims (8.17–27), and as Athene quickly acknowledges (8.31–2), but initially, Zeus' rule was not without its pitfalls and challenges. It takes the following events to verify his claim. At 1.396–496, Hera, Poseidon, Athene and other Olympians had plotted to put Zeus in chains, but Thetis and the Hundred-hander Briareus intervened in order to aid Zeus in putting down the rebellion. Later, at 8.198–211, Hera floats the idea of rebellion against Zeus, but gives it up when Poseidon objects. Still later Poseidon himself threatens to go after Zeus if the latter fails to deliver on his promise to destroy Troy (15.133–41). On two subsequent occasions, Zeus similarly sparks resentful opposition, thereby endangering his own regime, by proposing first to save Sarpedon (16.431–61) and then Hektor (22.167–81). Thus, there were still clear and present dangers posed by the other gods, and Aphrodite was singled out for special treatment. As Jackson argues, 'Homer ... uses Aphrodite, particularly during her interactions with Zeus and Athena, to highlight an even greater conflict: that between Zeus and the rest of the gods.'[30] Athene, the favourite of Zeus, is verbally and physically antagonistic to Aphrodite (5.131–2, 427–30; 21.423–33). Most importantly, an ongoing rivalry pitted the two goddesses against one another, and they notoriously supported opposite sides in the Trojan War. In general, 'Zeus displays clear favouritism toward Athena, while taking pains . . . to subvert and control Aphrodite's power.'[31]

Aphrodite's Near Eastern predecessor was, among other things, a goddess of war, and war was certainly within the original capabilities of Aphrodite, as evidenced by her abundant epichoric military and naval associations,[32] but a well-known, if still problematic, episode in Homer shows the mortal Diomedes, buoyed by Athene (cf. 5.129–32, 256, 260–1), wounding Aphrodite and 'recognizing that she was a weakling god (*analkis theos*), not one of those goddesses (*theaōn*) who take charge in a war of men – neither an Athene, then, nor a city-sacking Enyo' (5.331–3). Because of her ineptitude, Aphrodite seeks refuge with her Iliadic father and mother, and she is mocked again and emphatically disrespected in Zeus' consolation, when he favours the marital over the martial in her assigned sphere of activity (5.428–30): 'οὔ τοι, τέκνον ἐμόν, δέδοται πολεμήϊα ἔργα, / ἀλλὰ σύ γ' ἱμερόεντα μετέρχεο ἔργα γάμοιο, / ταῦτα δ' Ἄρηϊ θοῷ καὶ Ἀθήνῃ πάντα μελήσει' ('Not to you, my child, are works (*erga*) of war given, but you attend to the love-inspiring works (*erga*) of marriage, and all these things (you ask) are concerns for swift Ares and Athene'). However else this passage may be understood, it illustrates Zeus' power to assign *timai* and to restrict or limit them in some way that makes Aphrodite conform to his will.[33] Aphrodite's refuge with Zeus and Dione is the hallmark of the ethnographic – and Panhellenic – Aphrodite as it developed in Homer: she is reduced to whining to her father and mother, curtailed in her military powers and relegated to the status of fertility deity and patron of human sexuality.[34] The important point here is that Aphrodite originally had the capacity for a variety of *erga* that are denied to her through the Homeric and other poems, all of which create and highlight her now-emerging, post-theogonic image. As a result, she becomes increasingly a Panhellenic goddess of love and desire, and while love can have terrible consequences, ordinarily they are substantially different in kind, if not metaphorically, from the terrible consequences of warfare unless the war results from the *erga* of Aphrodite. In the Hellenic world, Aphrodite does retain significant military cult associations, as evidenced by her various epiphanic names, but on the epichoric, not the Panhellenic level.

An important example of the spreading of the Homeric Aphrodite and of Zeus' undercutting her comes from another significant poem nearly contemporary with *Theogony*, the Homeric *Hymn to Aphrodite*. Tired of hearing her boast and tease[35] about making gods and goddesses mate with mortals and produce human offspring, Zeus turns the tables on Aphrodite and causes her to fall in love with Anchises (*Hom. Hymn Aphr.* 5.33–57), with what results is well-known. 'Aphrodite bows tacitly to the will of Zeus, with the concession that she will no longer force immortals to mate with mortals. The hymn celebrates the power of Aphrodite, while at the same time reinforcing her subordination to Zeus in the divine sphere and confirming the natural distinction between mortals and immortals.'[36] If so, then mythically the cosmic power of Eros has not yet shifted fully to Aphrodite, whose characteristic behaviours are, likewise, still in a developmental stage.[37]

Hellenization and Panhellenization

Aphrodite not only is differentiated by the process that is first documented in our written record by the Homeric epics, but tamed as well. The point of giving Zeus to Aphrodite as her father and one of Zeus' many lovers as her mother is to make Aphrodite similar to other Olympians and to bring her under Zeus' control. But in so doing, the *Iliad* also makes Aphrodite increasingly anthropomorphic and anthropopathic. She therefore ceases to be cosmogonic, and her sublimely difficult-to-understand birth as the incarnation of Ouranos' genitals fades and ultimately becomes a secondary, alternative mythic explanation instead of the primary one it functioned as in *Theogony*. As her spontaneous generation that over time is less intuitively appreciated by the poem's audience, her birth is made more palatable to an audience that is less ready and willing to accept the original mythos on its own terms. Again, use implies change, and change in myth reflects the uses to which society puts it. This process of change both defines Aphrodite and demarcates her powers in an androcentric society.

As one of many stories contained in the *Iliad*, Zeus' taming of Aphrodite stands out. Her great power is undercut and redirected. *Theogony* creates and highlights a meaningful ethnographic moment early in both the Hellenization and Panhellenization of the Aphrodite-mythos. As is well known, Hellenic culture is not a single homogeneous entity, and local and regional differences are often distinctively marked. Hellenization is generally a 'centripetal and separative' process, a first step that is local or regional and *polis*-oriented; and Panhellenization is a 'centrifugal and unifying' process that transcends local and regional concerns, finds some things that are common and connects the broader Hellenic world of competing *poleis*.[38]

The Panhellenization phenomenon appeared in the eighth century and continued well into the fifth century. It created broad cultural and social institutions and fostered communication among those competing *poleis*. As a result, aspects of Aphrodite, which were established at the local level, and which were viewed as regional and separative remained epichoric, while elements seen as more broadly shared throughout the Hellenic world were taken up and emphasized in her broader Panhellenic image. Both Hesiod and Homer work at the Panhellenic cultural level in which all Hellenes can participate. Aspects of Aphrodite that are well established on the local plane are not all taken up at the Panhellenic level. Some Hellenized aspects of her various epiphanies may even be specialized and relatively widespread in different localities, but that fact alone does not warrant their being included in the universal Panhellenic image of the goddess.

Conclusion

'The direction of the cosmic evolution is not only from a natural to an anthropocentric order, but also from the primacy of the female to the primacy of the male.'[39] Over time, in a larger androcentric cultural setting, Aphrodite's Panhellenic reflex became even more widespread and more exaggeratedly seductive and feminized in cult, art and literature. That is a marked pattern in antiquity, and it overshadows the Hesiodic account about Aphrodite's miraculous birth from Ouranos' severed genitals. That pattern is the main underlying reason why popular audiences today too narrowly think of Aphrodite almost exclusively as the goddess of love and beauty instead of recognizing her broad powers and multiple functions, some of which apply only to her local Hellenized epiphanies, others to her Panhellenic ones.

Although this is not the place for a full discussion of Aphrodite in art, it is, nevertheless, appropriate to note the following. First, a terracotta plaque, found in the shrine of Hera Limenaia at Perachora in the Korinthia, and dated to 675–650, shows a bearded female figure apparently emerging from what has been identified as a genital sac.[40] Needless to say, she has been identified as Aphrodite Ourania. Second, at the other end of a long timeline, in Roman times on Kypros, a statue showed the goddess as bearded, garbed in women's clothing, but with male genitals (Macrob., *Sat.* 3.8.1–3), while, in general, her typical portrayals otherwise showed her in her familiar anthropomorphic femininity. In both instances, the bearded portrayal of Aphrodite addressed the goddess's so-called bisexuality, which resulted from her miraculous Ouranic birth, and her Hellenized local character at Perachora and on Kypros in contrast to the more numerous and widespread representations produced from her Panhellenized, post-theogonic character and imposed retroactively on Aphrodite Ourania.[41]

The birth-narrative of Aphrodite shows the ability of myth to integrate polar opposites. The fundamental paradox of Aphrodite is expressed by her gendering. Her 'feminine' wiles include deceit, and yet, because of her transformative gestation, her own body is a deception. Aphrodite literally embodies Ouranos' genitalia; yet paradoxically her feminine wiles are irresistible to males.[42] Her seductive cunning is the biological inheritance (*moira*) from her father's *mēdea*. Thus, Aphrodite authorizes all aspects of sexual behaviour,[43] both male and female, as Pausanias in Plato's *Symposium* (180c–185c) correctly estimated but then explained presumptuously and in a haphazard and lopsided manner that is distinctly ahistorical.[44]

Notes

1. There is another personal connection as well. The first part of this argument (Romer 2020) appeared in a memorial volume for Diskin Clay. Thom and Diskin were roommates for a time during their graduate studies in Classics at the University of Washington. The stories they shared with me from those days, however, mostly concerned only their mischievous foundling dog, Πέλωρ, a beast himself now of mythological proportions.

2. In this usage, *mēdea* refers explicitly to male genitals. It is unclear whether *mēdea*, 'thought', is the same word or a homonym. Based on Aphrodite's and Athene's births, Zeitlin 1978: 169 suggests the possibility that 'male generative capacity is displaced from phallos to head, or rather, put somewhat differently, phallos and head are associated together'.

3. In a future article I will address misconceptions about the role of *aphros* and *aphrogenēs* in relation to Aphrodite's spontaneous generation, and attend to niggling questions raised by the work of Pironti 2007 and that of various authors in Smith and Pickup 2010.

4. οὗτοι δὲ εἰσὶ οἱ ποιήσαντες θεογονίην Ἕλλησι καὶ τοῖσι θεοῖσι τὰς ἐπωνυμίας δόντες καὶ τιμάς τε καὶ τέχνας διελόντες καὶ εἴδεα αὐτῶν σημήναντες. All translations of Greek texts here are my own.

5. In the *Iliad*, she is formulaically 'daughter of Zeus Aphrodite' (Διὸς θυγάτηρ Ἀφροδίτη) eight times (3.374, 5.131, 312, 829; 14.193, 224, 21.416, 23.185), and in the *Odyssey* once (8.308); and only once in extant epic is Dione called Aphrodite's mother (*Il.* 5.370–1). In the *Iliad*, Aphrodite only once is 'daughter of Zeus' (Διὸς κούρης, 20.105).

6. The prevailing scholarly view continues to be that the Homeric epics were composed prior to *Theogony*; *contra* West 1966: 46, who leaned in the opposite direction: 'The *Theogony* may well be the oldest Greek poem we have.'

7. This phenomenon is evident even in myths that centre on mortal heroes.

8. Cf. MacLachlan 2002: 368: 'In the ancient world, particularly as early as the Bronze Age, it is safer to assume that all aspects of life were permeated by divine forces'; in support (374n.4), she cites the mot of Thales, 'all things are full of gods' (πάντα πλήρη θεῶν εἶναι).

9. I distinguish between an original mythos, now lost and therefore theoretical, and individual myths that descend directly or indirectly from it.

10. See Nagy 1982: 49–57 (esp.) for *Theogony*, and Lamberton 1988: 1–37 for the basic issues. But see also Koning 2018: 17–29, Bakker 2018: 143–56 and Griffith 1983: 37–65.

11. West 1966: 18, echoing Solmsen 1949: 20. For Greek mythic themes of succession and replacement in broader cosmic terms, see Worthen 1991: 121–55 *et passim*.

12. The episodes involving the children of Gaia are divided as follows: (1) 126–210, (2) 233–69, (3) 270–336, (4) 337–452, (5) 453–506, (6) 507–616, (7) 820–80 and (8) 881–962.

13. West 1966: 320 (n. ad 544), defines *moira* simply as 'portion' or 'helping'; and at 180 (n. ad 74), he defines *timē* as a 'province' or 'sphere of influence', which is assigned typically at the beginning of Zeus' regime; but *timē* also has the meaning 'honour' or 'reverence' that is earned and deserved. In ordinary usage, then, *moira* is the basis on which *timē* is accrued, and that sequence also turns out to be the arrangement in Aphrodite's case, as borne out by the tenses of the two verbs in 203. In the Hesiodic construct her *moira* manifests itself at birth, i.e. in Kronos' universe before Zeus' rule, and her *timē* is awarded by Zeus on his accession to power, although for Aphrodite it is awarded on the basis of what had been acquired earlier (cf. 112, 393–4, 425–8 and 881–5). In 203 the terms *moira* and *timē* are virtually synonymous, redundant and therefore interchangeable. When referring specifically to the content of lines 201–6 exactly as it appears in the text, I use the locution *timē/moira*, but I separate the two terms when talking about either if it applies individually in my argument.

14. Gaia eventually is implicated in Ouranos' conflict with the Titans. She gives her own prophetic advice on Zeus' future (624–8), and West 1966: 226 (n. ad 210) observes that Ouranos assists in the overthrow of the Titans and their banishment to Tartarus 'to the extent that it is his and Gaia's advice which saves Zeus from the fate of his brothers and sisters (470)'.

15. It is natural for a goddess whose first characteristic is vegetal fertility to have that power extended to all forms of animate life. Hesiod, however, portrays Aphrodite's power for sex and sexuality only as it applies to the human sphere, but see the roughly contemporary *Hom. Hymn Aphr.* 5.1–6 and 69–74 for her influence on non-human animals. The historical question raised by the existence of this hymn is whether it gives genuine theogonic information or additional post-theogonic information about Aphrodite.

16. Näsström 1998: 32: 'The love goddess of the Classical Greeks was probably a synthesis of a Mesopotamian-Phoenician fertility goddess and an Indo-European goddess of Heaven, in

close association to the Great Goddess of Asia Minor.' See also Boedeker 1974: 1–17. Indo-European studies continue to provide important background for Greek and Roman studies (cf. Teske's chapter in this volume).

17. Romer 2020 argues (a) that *philommēdēs* ('to whom (the) male genitals belong'; 'penis-loving') has logical, semantic and historical priority over the virtually homonymous *philommeidēs* ('smile-loving') as the correct reading to be printed in modern texts at 200, and (b) that the narrative is framed in such strongly ethnographic terms that it precludes, and therefore denies (wrongly and polemically), the actual Near Eastern background in the historical development of this goddess.

18. Heubeck 1965: 204–6, Burkert 1985: 154–5, 409n.29, citing Heubeck; see also Romer 2020: 186–95 (esp. 193–4) on the force of φιλο- in the compound *philommēdēs*; *contra* West 1966: 119 and Most 2006: 18, who both print *philommeidea* in 200. Bouchard 2015 reads 200 very differently from the way I do.

19. See Romer 2020: 186–91 on the meaning of 'authorial' for a text that originated in oral performance and what to print at line 200.

20. 1970: 219: 'in all this (*sc.* the Hurrian story of Kumarbi) the phallus is all important, whereas in the Greek version its relevance was entirely confined to the preceding episode in which Ouranos blocked Gaia'; Kirk 1990: 99 claims that Homer 'wished to gloss over the savage old tale of her birth in the sea from Ouranos' genitals'.

21. Statistically, the Aphrodisian conclusion (201–6), joined only with the birth-story of Aphrodite (188–200), declines from being one third of the combined narrative (188–206) to being about 12 per cent of the combined narrative when joined with the story of Ouranos' genitals (154–206). The difference in percentage illustrates the relative biological importance of her *moira* to Aphrodite and its relative biological distance from Ouranos' genitals, the defining element in both considerations. It also balances the presentation of the story more proportionally.

22. All cosmogonic myths must accept or circumvent the problem of an original incestuous act.

23. Pironti 2007: 38–41 (esp. 40n.89) on the meaning of *philotēs*: 'Dans la suite de cette étude, la preference sera accordée à "union, relation intime" afin de respecter, dans les traductions, la sphère sémantique du mot φιλότης et le register linguistique choisi par les auteurs grecs. Le lecteur est invitée à entendre dans cette traduction le sens d'"union sexuelle"'.

24. Brown 1953: 8.

25. Eros' cosmogonic origin is indispensable in understanding him: Breitenberger 2007: 137–69 on Eros' origins.

26. Pirenne-Delforge 1994: 72–3, citing the work of Oscar Broneer, reports in a subsection on 'Éros, Aphrodite et l'iconographie': 'Les inscriptions retrouvées dans le sanctuaire rupestre du flanc nord de l'Acropole indiquent qu'Éros y était honoré, en compagnie de celle qu'on lui attribue le plus souvent comme mère, depuis la moitié du Ve siècle avant J.-c. au moins.' Mark 1984: 295–302 observes about the east frieze of the Parthenon: 'That Aphrodite and Eros appear on the frieze as mother and son has often been noted' (295); see also Rosenzweig 2007: 92–5. Breitenberger 2007: 2 asserts, 'The popular image of the mother Aphrodite and her little son Eros ... does not occur before the Hellenistic period, being first presented in Apollonius Rhodius' version of Medea's love for Jason in *Argonautica* book 3.'

27. There are, of course, alternate theogonies apart from this reference in Homer. Among the more noteworthy is the Orphic version: see West 1983 and especially Edmonds 2018: 225–42.

28. Effectively, although these scholars might not see it exactly as I do, the individual works of Rosenzweig 2004, Breitenberger 2007 and Bouchard 2015 document pathways by which to trace and outline how Aphrodite's sexual roles grew, deepened and changed – and, in some

instances, were enacted and defined more fully – as post-Hesiodic poetic settings in the mythic construct, while new social and religious venues also absorbed, reinforced, elaborated on Aphrodite's post-theogonic behaviours.

29. Brown 1953: 19. By 'the historical process' Brown refers to the procession of events detailing the emergence of Zeus in the poem.
30. 2010: 151, citing Grube 1951: 64, who makes similar observations on some of these incidents.
31. Jackson 2010: 151. For the sake of completeness, add to this resumé the humiliation Aphrodite is made to suffer when Hephaistos catches her in bed with Ares (*Od.* 8.266–366), which magnifies her reduced status on Olympus.
32. Cf. Budin 2010: 79–112, Flemberg 1991.
33. On this passage, see Pironti 2007: 209–12 (esp. 12): 'Sans nier ces oppositions (sc. between the domain of Aphrodite and that of Ares) soient parfois àl'oeuvre dans le poème et que les rôles respectifs du masculine et feminine contribuent à structure les valeurs de la sociêtê homêrique, cette grille n'est pas pour autant applicable telle quelle au monde de dieux.' I am concerned here with how the audience perceives the values of the Homeric world as expressed in this passage.
34. Cf. Flemberg 1991: 114, but see Pironti 2007: 106.
35. *Hom. Hymn Aphr.* 5.49, a new wrinkle on *philommeidēs*: ἡδὺ γελοιήσασα φιλομμειδὴς Ἀφροδίτη ('smile-loving Aphrodite, laughing teasingly').
36. Shelmerdine 1995: 124.
37. Cf. Shelmerdine 1995, who adds, 'The story of Aphrodite's birth in Hesiod (*Th.* 188–200) and its allusions in the Aphrodite hymn provide a good example of the aetiological connection between myth and cult.' One objective of Breitenberger 2007 is to examine the relationship between myth and cult in the case of both Aphrodite and Eros.
38. I have adapted this terminology from Tsagalis 2006: 141. See also Nagy 1990: 52–115.
39. Brown 1953: 17.
40. The Perachora plaque was put into discussion by Payne 1940: 232, with parallel figures from Sparta; taken up by Sale 1961: 508–21; noted by West 1966: 211–13 (n. ad 154–210); and referenced by MacLachlan 2002: 371, who also specifies that the bearded image attests 'to the fact that the goddess, as she emerged from the primordial severing of the whole, embodied the dual features necessary for her to assume creative powers'.
41. Aphrodite's beard unmistakably marks the biological heritance from her father's genitals, and her bisexuality is not a surprise in this context. MacLachlan 2002 also addresses bisexuality in the imagery of Eros. See below, notes 43–5.
42. See Romer 2020: 206–8 for conclusions about male genital narcissism and Aphrodite's literal colonization by the patriarchy.
43. MacLachlan 2002: 365 'attempts to shed some light . . . by exploring the extent of a dual-gendered divinity on Cyprus who eventually went by the name of Aphrodite and to propose some explanation for this phenomenon, looking at textual and archaeological evidence that establishes, beyond a doubt, that bisexuality was an important feature of her cult'.
44. Parker 1983: 94 on *LSCG* (Sokolowski 1969) 151 A42: 'A Coan law cited earlier shows, if correctly restored, that on the ritual level no distinction is drawn between heterosexual and homosexual contact'; and 94n.81: 'this text apart, the possibility of homosexual contact seems not even to be envisaged in early ritual rules'. In Hellenistic times sexual morality became more important; previously, sexuality was almost exclusively the subject of cult regulations, not sexual morality.

Works cited

Bakker, E. J. (2018), 'Hesiod in Performance', in A. C. Loney and S. Scully (eds), *The Oxford Handbook of Hesiod*, 143–56, Oxford: Oxford University Press.
Boedeker, D. (1974), *Aphrodite's Entry into Greek Epic*, Mnemosyne Supplementum 32, Leiden: Brill.
Bouchard, E. (2015), 'Aphrodite Philommēdēs in the Theogony', *The Journal of Hellenic Studies*, 138: 8–18.
Breitenberger, B. M. (2007), *Aphrodite and Eros: The Development of Erotic Mythology in Early Greek Poetry and Cult*, Routledge: New York and London.
Brown, N. O. (1953), *Hesiod's Theogony*, Pearson: London.
Budin S. L. (2010), 'Aphrodite Enoplion', in A. C. Smith and S. Pickup (eds), *Brill's Companion to Aphrodite*, 79–112, Leiden: Brill.
Burkert, W. (1985), *Greek Religion*, Cambridge, MA: Harvard University Press.
Edmonds III, R. G. (2018), 'Deviant Origins: Hesiod's *Theogony* and the Orphica', in A. C. Loney and S. Scully (eds), *The Oxford Handbook of Hesiod*, 225–42, Oxford: Oxford University Press.
Flemberg, J. (1991), *Venus Armata: Studien zur bewaffneten Aphrodite in der griechischrömischen Kunst*, Stockholm: Paul Åström.
Griffith, M. (1983), 'The Personality of Hesiod', *Classical Antiquity*, 2: 37–65.
Grube, G. M. A. (1951), 'The Gods of Homer', *Phoenix*, 5: 62–78.
Heubeck, A. (1965), 'Ἀφροδίτη φιλομμηδής,' *Beiträge zur Namenforschung*, 16: 204–6.
Jackson, K. (2010), 'Father-Daughter Dynamics in the *Iliad*: The Role of Aphrodite in Defining Zeus' Regime', in A. C. Smith and S. Pickup (eds), *Brill's Companion to Aphrodite*, 151–63, Leiden: Brill.
Kirk, G. S. (1970), *Myth: Its Meaning and Function in Ancient and Other Cultures*, Cambridge and Berkeley: The University of California Press.
Kirk, G. S. (1990), *The Iliad: A Commentary*, vol. 2: *Books 5–8*, Cambridge: Cambridge University Press.
Koning, H. H. (2018), 'The Hesiodic Question', in A. C. Loney and S. Scully (eds), *The Oxford Handbook of Hesiod*, 17–29, Oxford: Oxford University Press.
Lamberton, R. (1988), *Hesiod*, New Haven: Yale University Press.
Larsson Lovén, L. and A. Strőmberg (eds), *Aspects of Women in Antiquity: Proceedings of the First Nordic Symposium on Women's Lives in Antiquity, Gőteborg, 12–15 June 1997*, 29–43, Jonsered: Paul Åström.
MacLachlan, B. (2002), 'The Ungendering of Aphrodite', in D. L. Bolger and N. Serwint (eds), *Engendering Aphrodite: Women and Society in Ancient Cyprus*, 365–78, Boston: American Schools of Oriental Research.
Mark, I. S. (1984), 'The Gods on the East Frieze of the Parthenon', *Hesperia*, 53: 289–342.
Martin, R. P. (2018), 'Hesiodic Theology', in A. C. Loney and S. Scully (eds), *The Oxford Handbook of Hesiod*, 125–41, Oxford: Oxford University Press.
Most, G. (ed. and trans.) (2006), *Hesiod: Theogony, Works and Days, Testimonia*, Cambridge, MA: Harvard University Press.
Nagy, G. (1982), 'Hesiod', in T. J. Luce (ed.), *Ancient Writers: Greece and Rome*, vol. 1, New York: Scribner's.
Nagy, G. (1990), *Greek Mythology and Poetics*, Ithaca: Cornell University Press.
Näsström, B.-M. (1998), 'Cybele and Aphrodite: Two Aspects of the Great Goddess', in L. Larsson Lovén and A. Strömberg (eds), *Aspects of Women in Antiquity*, 29–43, Jonsered: Paul Åström.
Parker, R. (1983), *Miasma: Pollution and Purification in Early Greek Religion*, Oxford: Oxford University Press.
Payne, H. (1940), *Perachora*, vol. 1, Oxford: Clarendon Press.

Pirenne-Delforge, V. (1994), *L'Aphrodite grecque*, Kernos Supplément 4, Athènes-Liège: Centre International d'Étude de la Religion Grecque Antique.
Pironti, G. (2007), *Entre ciel et guerre: Figures d'Aphrodite en Grèce ancienne*, Kernos Supplément 18, Liège: Centre International d'Étude de la Religion Grecque Antique.
Romer, F. E. (2020), 'Aphrodite φιλομμηδής and Radical Gender Differentiation in an Ethnographic Myth', in P. Burian, J. S. Clay and G. Davis (eds), *Euphrosyne: Studies in Ancient Philosophy, History, and Literature in Memory of Diskin Clay*, Beiträge zur Altertumskunde 370, 183–208, Berlin: De Gruyter.
Rosenzweig, R. (2004), *Worshipping Aphrodite: Art, and Cult in Classical Athens*, Ann Arbor: The University of Michigan Press.
Sale, W. (1961), 'Aphrodite in the *Theogony*', *Transactions and Proceedings of the American Philological Association*, 92: 508–21.
Shelmerdine, S. (trans.) (1995), *The Homeric Hymns*, Newburyport, MA: Focus.
Smith, A. C. and S. Pickup (eds) (2010), *Brill's Companion to Aphrodite*, Leiden: Brill.
Sokolowski, F. (ed.) (1969), *Lois sacrées des Cités grecques*, Paris: E. de Boccard.
Solmsen, F. (1949), *Hesiod and Aeschylus*, Ithaca: Cornell University Press.
Tsagalis, C. C. (2006) 'Ποίηση και Ποιητική στη Θεογονία και στα ˝Εργα καὶ Ἡμέραι', in N. P. Bezantakos and C. C. Tsagalis (eds), Μουσάων ἀρχώμεθα: Ο Ησίοδος και η αρχαική επική ποίηση, 139–255, Athens: Patakis.
West, M. L. (1966), *Hesiod: Theogony, Edited with Prolegomena and Commentary*, Oxford: Clarendon Press.
West, M. L. (1983), *The Orphic Poems*, Oxford: Clarendon Press.
Worthen, T. D. (1991), *The Myth of Replacement: Stars, Gods, and Order in the Universe*, Tucson: The University of Arizona Press.
Zeitlin, F. I. (1978), 'The Dynamics of Misogyny: Myth and Mythmaking in the *Oresteia*', *Arethusa*, 11: 149–84.

CHAPTER 5
VISIONS AND MEMORIES OF LUCRETIUS IN SENECA'S *NATURALES QUAESTIONES*
Christopher Trinacty

Introduction

Seneca knew Lucretius' *De Rerum Natura* well.[1] Quotations of *DRN* appear at a number of moments in Seneca's prose works (e.g. *Ep.* 95.11, 106.8, 110.6, *Q Nat.* 4b.3.4), and certain scenes from his tragedies clearly recall Lucretius' poem.[2] For instance, Lucretius is quoted at *Tranq.* 2.14 (*hoc se quisque modo semper fugit*, 'In this way each man is constantly fleeing himself', *DRN* 3.1068) when Seneca discusses the bored day trippers who flit from countryside to shore in vain attempts to alleviate their ennui, not realizing that the problem lies within.[3] This sentiment stuck with Seneca and we see him returning to it late in his career when he allusively writes to Lucilius, 'Are you surprised that it does no good to run away [from vice]? The things you flee are with you' (*tecum sunt, quae fugis*, *Ep.* 104.20).[4] Seneca validates the self-alienation that Lucretius explored in *DRN* 3,[5] but fights against it in different ways: by wielding Stoic *exempla* in the letter with Socrates and Cato (*Ep.* 104.22–34), or by urging devotion to one's duties as citizen and *proficiens* in the *Dialogues* (*Tranq.* 3.1). This is typical of Seneca – a Lucretian quotation or intertextual nod is coupled with a response that seeks to repurpose the Lucretian passage in the larger, often Stoic philosophical context.

Quotation and intertext are the primary ways in which Seneca engages with Lucretius,[6] and Lucretian ideas of the sublime lurk behind many of Seneca's references. For instance, when Seneca writes about the loftier (*altius*) aspirations of philosophy, he does so by quoting Lucretius (*Ep.* 95.11 ~ *DRN* 1.54–7), who sheds light on the 'mighty ... and heavenly matters above you' (*magna ... supraque vos posita*, *Ep.* 95.10). Lucretius' sublime poetics and his poetry of the sublime have been a focus of scholars since Kant, and Lucretius was identified as a sublime figure in antiquity.[7] His attempts as *vates* to explain the secrets of the universe and to see what is infinitesimal (atoms and atomic motion), to comprehend the abyss (void) and to describe the magnificent works of nature and the cosmos (especially in books 5 and 6) show a poet working to convey sublime topics in moving poetic language.[8] Thus his sublime poetics are marshalled to understand sublime subject matter. While confronting such profound topics can lead to horror or dismay, Lucretius aims to inspire the reader to contend with the difficult substrata of the sublime through an understanding of Epicurean physics. Williams remarks on the 'positive sublimity' of Epicurean philosophy by which 'Lucretius asserts a superiority over fearsome nature that finds important parallels in Seneca' (2016: 174); this essay will stress how Seneca finds ways to delineate his approach to *natura* in all its sublimity through selective intertexts with Lucretius.[9]

Lucretius offers Seneca a rival *exemplum* of a philosopher-poet from a competing philosophical school. In his works, Seneca actively reinterprets the precepts that Lucretius promotes by finding different connotations in the language of Lucretius' poetry. His most thorough and creative retorts to Lucretius can be found in his *Naturales Quaestiones*. An audience that appreciates this dialogue between Seneca and Lucretius will recognize how Seneca acknowledges his Epicurean interlocutor by repeating key terms from *DRN*, only to question their validity. In *Q Nat.*, Seneca refashions Lucretius' didactic epic in a variety of ways. This chapter investigates both small-scale intertextual echoes as well as larger, book-length responses to suggest that Seneca critiques not so much the ethical goals of Lucretius as his larger conclusions about the divine.[10] Lucretius' sublime vision of *natura*, ranging from the microscopic interactions of atoms to larger meteorological and astronomical phenomena, is placed within a larger Stoic framework that stresses divine order, not random chance. Seneca finds those who rely on, and take pleasure in, their senses inclining towards moral depravity, in contrast with those who employ true *ratio*, which Seneca figures as divine in *Q Nat.*

It is not surprising that Lucretius looms behind sections of *Naturales Quaestiones*. Earthquakes, lightning, rainbows and the flooding of the Nile constitute just a sampling of the subjects that Seneca takes up from Lucretius and the larger meteorological tradition. Graver has hypothesized that the theological and epistemological questions raised by meteorology would, by Seneca's time, have a markedly Epicurean flavour.[11] If so, Seneca is engaging with Lucretius on Epicurean ground, and with similar didactic techniques, but with an underlying Stoic purpose. Both works rely on linguistic repetitions, analogies, digressions or 'purple passages', appeals to their addressees (Memmius and Lucilius), and vivid imagery in order to teach the secrets of nature.[12] If Lucretius' work explains the natural world in order to deliver the reader from anxiety and fear of death and the gods and to recognize that happiness is within her grasp, Seneca often ties his own teachings about *natura* to the moral improvement of the reader as well as to the cultural and societal evils lurking everywhere (esp. *luxuria*, the decline of philosophical schools, perverted sexual *mores*). In doing so, Seneca often draws connections between physics and ethics:

> The study of physics inevitably implicates ethics, not least because the rational functioning of the physical world that Seneca charts in the *Natural Questions* establishes a paradigm of normative behavior that is overthrown by the human excesses that he features in his moral excursuses.
>
> Williams 2014a: 188

By bridging the divide between ethics and physics, Seneca covers ground that was previously explored in *DRN*.[13] While for Lucretius death should mean nothing to us because we are merely atoms and void, such materialistic cold comfort is transformed in Seneca to a 'cosmic viewpoint' in which mankind is part of the larger natural world, a world under the care of a providential god, who can be identified with *natura* itself.[14] In contrast to Lucretius, Seneca argues that bodies are not composed of atoms and void (*Q*

Nat. 2.6-7), and that the world is controlled by fate (i.e. god, 2.36.1–38.4) and not merely the result of chance (1.pr.14–15; cf. *DRN* 2.1058-63).[15] In addition, the senses, the Epicurean epistemological basis for understanding the world, are found to be fallible in Seneca's work:

> Epicurean science is based on the reliability of sense, especially sight (cf. frr. 36, 247, 251 Us). In pointed contrast, Seneca repeatedly emphasizes the fallacy of sight ... The most important of the five senses, the very foundation of scientific knowledge, is subject to error and deception, both because of its intrinsic limitations and because of reflected and refracted images, optical illusions that, for instance, explain the rainbow (I.4.1).
>
> Berno 2015: 87

Even if his therapeutic goals are similar, Seneca is careful to note the differing routes to gaining the necessary wisdom – indeed part of Seneca's appeals to *ratio* includes studying the results of previous attempts to explain the natural world by others (including Lucretius, albeit intertextually), not just accepting Epicurus' pronouncements.[16] The dogmatism that Lucretius favours is contrasted with Seneca's willingness to weigh eclectic philosophical points of view impartially. Nevertheless, both authors are striving, in part, to demystify the world and address anxieties that the reader may have, such as the fear of death and the question of what is most important in life. It seems that Seneca at this point in his career is revisiting Epicurean works and ideas and trying to ascertain and distinguish commonalities and differences in thought.[17] By tracing the intertexts in *Naturales Quaestiones* we can understand how Seneca read Lucretius' treatise, how he reinterpreted Lucretius' treatment of sublime topics in the service of Stoic philosophy, and what he felt was problematic about the vision of nature promulgated in *DRN*.

Intertextual differentiation: downplaying or heightening the sublime

Seneca's work, like Lucretius', begins in a rather expansive manner that might have surprised a reader picking up a work on investigations into nature. After forefronting his desire to 'travel around the cosmos' (*mundum circumire*) and unearth its secrets (3.pr.1), he complains of the years he wasted on 'vain studies' (3.pr.2–4), lambasts historians (3.pr. 5–6) and delves into the problem of *Fortuna* (3.pr. 7–9), before turning to the question: *quid praecipuum in rebus humanis est?* ('What is most important in human life?', 3.pr.10). Seneca's first response to this question (others include tolerating adversity, maintaining a virtuous mind, being willing to commit suicide if necessary) is the following:

> non classibus maria complesse, nec in Rubri maris litore signa fixisse, nec deficiente ad iniurias terra errasse in oceano ignota quaerentem, sed **animo omne** vidisse et, qua maior nulla **victoria** est, vitia domuisse. innumerabiles sunt qui populos, qui urbes habuerunt in **potestate**, paucissimi qui se. (3.pr.10)

Not filling the seas with fleets, nor setting up standards on the shore of the Red Sea, nor, when the earth runs out of sources of harm, wandering the ocean to seek the unknown; rather it is seeing everything with one's mind, and conquering one's faults, which is the greatest victory possible. There are countless people who have been in control of nations and cities, very few who have been in control of themselves.[18]

This opening salvo has been seen as the goal of the *Naturales Quaestiones* as a whole.[19] As Gunderson observes, 'What one sees with the mind's eyes is ... that everything is itself but a single, unitary thing, an *omne*. When the lot of it has been seen *qua* lot, then the revolution takes place' (2015: 68). Roman imperial expansion and military glory are shown to constitute a less important victory than the victory over one's own vices, which can be achieved with the proper understanding and perspective.[20] This section also restates Lucretius' initial portrayal of Epicurus.[21] In the opening book of *DRN*, Lucretius praises Epicurus in language that Seneca is cleverly reprising:

ergo vivida vis animi pervicit, et extra
processit longe flammantia moenia mundi
atque **omne** immensum peragravit mente **animo**que,
unde refert nobis victor quid possit oriri,
quid nequeat, finita **potestas** denique cuique
quanam sit ratione atque alte terminus haerens.
quare religio pedibus subiecta vicissim
obteritur, nos exaequat **victoria** caelo. (1.72–9)

> The vital force
> Of his intelligence prevailed, and he advanced his course
> Far past the blazing bulwarks of the world, and roamed the whole
> Immeasurable Cosmos in his mind and in his soul.
> In triumph he returns to us, and brings us back this prize:
> To know what things can come about, and what cannot arise,
> And what law limits the power of each, with deep-set boundary stone.
> Therefore it is the turn of Superstition to lie prone,
> Trod underfoot, while by his victory we reach the heavens.
>
> *trans. A. E. Stallings 2007*

Seneca restates the language of Epicurus' journey (***omne** immensum peragravit mente **animo**que*) and his movement beyond the flaming boundaries of the cosmos.[22] This sublime vision of an Epicurus who can transcend the known world and make his way to the heavens is also the goal for the reader of the *Naturales Quaestiones,* who will have seen 'everything with one's mind' – one should not discount the way Seneca may encourage this identification.[23] However, the results of such exploration and insight differ, as the surrounding context makes clear.[24] There is real subtlety and craft on display in Seneca's intertextual rhetoric. For Lucretius, Epicurean knowledge will lead to a victory in which 'we reach the heavens' (*nos exaequat **victoria** caelo*, 1.79) and deny the workings of *religio*, while Seneca posits a resulting self-knowledge and trampling of vice (*qua maior nulla **victoria** est, vitia domuisse*, 3.pr.10). Lucretius' martial imagery is made even more explicit by Seneca, as he debunks Epicurus' status as a Lucretian epic hero.[25] In fact Seneca's *victoria* is 'greater' (*maior*): he elevates his scientific/philosophical prose above the hexametrical *De Rerum Natura* in a conscious effort to outstrip Lucretius' work.[26] That *victoria*, however, is framed personally, not ideologically. The antagonism between Epicurus and *religio* is anathema to Seneca's view, in which god can be identified with the very workings of the *omne* (i.e. *natura*) and one's *animus* is divine.[27] In fact, the elision of *animo omne* in Seneca's text may indicate the close connection between these two concepts (the soul as part of divine *natura*) in this passage. Elsewhere Seneca intimates that in the sublime landscapes of the natural world one can discover god (e.g. when looking at a spacious cavern 'it will impress upon your mind an intimation of religious awe', *animum tuum quadam **religionis** suspicione percutiet*, *Ep.* 41.2–4). Seneca draws a stronger connection between ethics and physics for the individual, using Lucretius' attack against religion to highlight how such understanding will aid one in day-to-day philosophical progress. Following Williams's structural argument about the movement of *Q Nat.* from the terrestrial to the celestial and sublime, this is the proper 'terrestrial' conclusion to make at this moment, fitting for the opening of the *Q Nat.* and the subsequent investigation into terrestrial waters of book 3.[28] Seneca concludes this in his preface to this book:

> For these reasons it will be useful for us to investigate nature: first, we shall leave behind what is sordid; next, we shall keep our mind, which needs to be elevated and great, separated from the body; next, when our critical faculty has been exercised on hidden matters, it will be no worse at dealing with visible ones. And nothing is more visible than these remedies which are learned in order to counter our wickedness and madness, things we condemn but do not forsake.[29]
>
> 3.pr.18

It is a first step, and as the work continues, Seneca will consider topics and muse upon *caelestia* and *sublimia* when he investigates divinity more fully. For Seneca there is a sense that this contemplation and these actions will bring one closer to god, whereas for Lucretius and the Epicureans in general, there was no 'intelligent, divine, and philanthropic creation and government of this world'[30] and religion only led one astray from the conception of the divine.

This initial intertext establishes a connection with Lucretius that is continued throughout *Naturales Quaestiones*. Some feature brief intertextual nods as in the preface of book 3, but others are more extensive. Let me give one more example of a passing intertextual link before I focus on larger correspondences. At the conclusion of *Q Nat.*

3, Seneca writes about the flood that will destroy the earth, a literary and rhetorical tour-de-force that highlights the power and plan of *Natura* should she decide to destroy the human race (*ad exitium humani generis*, *Q Nat.* 3.27.1).[31] *Natura* is anthropomorphized as an agent of annihilation because of the moral depravity of humankind, and the flood becomes 'an ideal opportunity for consistent reassertion of the centrality to Stoic physics of the relationship of god (or nature) to man' (Inwood 2005: 170). Seneca writes, 'one day will destroy the human race' (***unus*** *humanum genus condet* ***dies***, *Q Nat.* 3.29.9), just as Lucretius had described the end of the world ('one day will cause its destruction', ***una dies*** *dabit* ***exitio***, 5.95). Both writers believe in the mortality of the world (*Q Nat.* 6.2.6, *DRN* 5.91–415), but Seneca lavishes more detail on its destruction in a way that Lucretius hints at (fires, earthquakes, floods, 5.338–50), but fears he is unable to prove (5.97–109).[32] Thus, Seneca can be seen to be both competing with, and completing, what Lucretius only suggested in his sublime description of the world overwhelmed by the flood. Moreover, this intertext further stands out because Ovid incorporates the Lucretian line when describing Lucretius' sublime poetry, and Seneca directly criticizes Ovid's flood description in his own flood passage.[33] For Ovid, Lucretius' fame will live on, as long as the world remains ('the poems of sublime Lucretius are destined to die / when a single day brings destruction to the earth', *carmina sublimis tunc sunt* ***peritura*** *Lucreti,* / ***exitio*** *terras cum dabit* ***una dies***, *Am.* 1.15.23–4).[34] Ovid highlights Lucretius' sublimity (*sublimis . . . Lucreti*), and Seneca here clearly aims to create a passage that underscores his own rhetorical sublimity in undertaking a subject that transcends the normal bounds of the human world. His elevated prose is a better medium for a sublime event. Porter has found Lucretius' predilection for describing fearful feats of destruction a fundamental tenet of his own sublime metaphysics: 'this fear is in turn based on a deeper metaphysical fear that the world is not quite the way it is commonly known and experienced (as something more or less solid, permanent and secure), a fear which expresses itself psychologically as, one might say, a pervading *horror vacui*' (2007: 171, citing *DRN* 6.565-7). Seneca is acknowledging the influence of Ovid and Lucretius even as his own flood works to destroy all their stories (*omnes novum mare fabulas obruet*, *Q Nat.* 3.29.7), the names of seas (***peribunt*** *tot nomina*, *Q Nat.* 3.29.8) and all boundaries in general (***peribit*** *omne discrimen*, *Q Nat.* 3.29.8). Seneca's double allusion to Lucretius' single apocalyptic day and to Ovid's clever refiguring of Lucretius' 'poetry destined to die' (*carmina . . . peritura*) reveals how Seneca's 'literary flood' reacts to, subsumes and transcends his poetic predecessors. The metaliterary ramifications are clear – Seneca takes inspiration from Lucretius (and Ovid) to construct his flood narrative, a massive conglomeration of his own literary and philosophical influences that will overwhelm and submerge previous accounts (i.e. the *novum mare* is the literary 'sea' he has created).[35] Worthen has fruitfully illustrated how flood narratives figure in his larger 'myth of replacement', and Seneca's flood can be seen as an instantiation of such a moment.[36] The sublimity that Lucretius hinted at and that Ovid touched upon is surmounted by Seneca's truly sublime account of a world wiped out by cataclysm; his intertextual engagement with his predecessors illustrates Longinus' observation that such *aemulatio* encourages sublimity.[37]

Hostius Quadra as Lucretian *monstrum*

Lucretius continues as an intertextual presence throughout the *Naturales Quaestiones*. Famous images such as the Lucretian dust motes reappear (5.1.2, to prove that air is always moving), as does a quotation, 'the fall of a drop hollows out a stone' (*stillicidi casus lapidem cavat, DRN* 1.313 ~ *Q Nat.* 4b.3.4).[38] Often these are distorted to fit Seneca's purpose, as Seneca builds, book upon book, his own rival *De Rerum Natura*, in which Lucretian lines are artfully repurposed in Seneca's philosophical rhetoric.[39] Certain sublime topics of *Naturales Quaestiones* correspond to those of Lucretius (e.g. earthquakes in book 6,[40] in book 2 lightning[41]), and some scholars have found these points of convergence to be useful stepping-stones to Seneca's larger thematic and philosophical concerns. *Q Nat.* 6 even aligns with some fundamental beliefs of Epicureanism and Lucretius, since Seneca agrees with Epicurus (broadly) that the fundamental cause of earthquakes is 'air/breath' (20.5). In other instances, Seneca's ideas about the sublime as well as the elements vie with Lucretius' views.[42] If we take these connections as fruitful indicators of Seneca's reception of Lucretius, then we can read *Q Nat.* 1 – in its investigation of atmospheric fires – as a critique of Epicurean sense-perception (evoking *DRN* 4).

Distortion is key for Seneca and reflections are often faulty (Seneca's atmospheric fires are themselves distorted reflections of celestial light), so the very subject matter does not map in quite the one-to-one manner as some subjects of other books.[43] In this section, I argue that in *Q Nat.* 1 Seneca intertextually references *DRN* 4 in order to critique the Lucretian/Epicurean reliance on sense perception found therein, and to suggest a superior Stoic understanding of the world, one based on *ratio*.[44] Structurally, Seneca emphatically looks back to Lucretius in this book when he offers examples of optical illusions: the colonnade of *Q Nat.* 1.3.9 ~ *DRN* 4.426–31, the movement of the sun at *Q Nat.* 1.3.10 ~ *DRN* 4.391–6, the image of the oar underwater at *Q Nat.* 1.3.9 ~ *DRN* 4.438–42, and, especially, how mirrors work (*Q Nat.* 1.3.5–14, 1.17.1–10 ~ *DRN* 4.98–344).[45] While Lucretius passes over the rainbow briefly (*DRN* 6.524–6), Seneca devotes a long section to its explanation (replete with an Ovidian quotation) that features language important for the moral and physical investigations of the book (*Q. Nat.* 1.3.1–14, with a quotation of Ovid *Met.* 6.65–7).[46] The structure of *DRN* 4, especially its concluding 'purple passage' that parodies *res veneriae* and deluded lovers, inspires Seneca's own construction of *Naturales Quaestiones* 1. Lucretius attacks lovers for their faulty attachment and beliefs, and Seneca parallels this attack but now against an Epicurean surrogate, Hostius Quadra. While *DRN* 4 ultimately posits passionate love as yet another optical/mental illusion, Seneca concludes *Naturales Quaestiones* 1 with Hostius Quadra's faulty epistemology and his multiple magnifying mirrors to illustrate and exaggerate the drawbacks of Epicurean tenets concerning perception, pleasure and the divine.[47]

The preface of *Q Nat.* 1 concludes with unequivocal objections to Epicurean ideas about the cosmos, both its randomness and the relationship posed between man and god. Seneca encourages the reader to move beyond what can be perceived by the eyes (*philosophia . . . non fuit oculis contenta*) because *natura* has placed her secrets beyond the reach of the visible (*extra conspectum*, *Q Nat*. 1.pr.1).[48] For Seneca, the investigation of nature through *ratio*, and not the senses, leads directly to god, as he claims: 'I give thanks to nature not whenever I look upon the part of her that all can see, but when I have entered into her more secluded regions' (*tunc rerum naturae gratias ago cum illam non ab hac parte video qua publica est, sed cum secretiora eius intravi*, *Q Nat*. 1.pr.3).[49] While Seneca uses the phrase *rerum natura* often in this work to stand for 'nature', the resonance with the title of Lucretius' didactic poem is significant because Seneca is arguing against Epicurean thought in this context. This section asks 'what is god' (*quid sit deus?*, 1.pr.3) and debates whether god is completely divorced from human activities. Seneca is quick to demolish the Epicurean premise of divine carelessness later in the preface, indicating that the mind's delight in exploring the heavens and questioning the divine is the very proof of its own divine nature ('It has this proof of its own divinity, that it takes delight in the divine and enjoys it not as someone else's possession but as its own', *hoc habet argumentum divinitatis suae quod illum divina delectant, nec ut alienis sed ut suis interest*, 1.pr.12). The soul is divine ('The mind is the superior part of us; in him [sc. god] there is nothing apart from mind. He is nothing but reason', *nostri melior pars animus est, in illo nulla pars extra animum est. totus est ratio*, 1.pr.14) and god has control over the world that is his creation. Seneca develops the idea of the soul as a spectator (*curiosus spectator*, 1.pr.12), but one that knows there is more to the universe than meets the eye. It is not merely seeing what is *publica*, but entering the very secrets of the universe, a process that can only be accomplished through the imagination and *ratio*. In such contemplation one will discern the Epicurean idea that the universe is vulnerable to chance to be hogwash (*fortuitum et casu volubile*, 1.pr.14; *temeritate*, 1.pr.15; cf. *DRN* 2.1060). In addition, it is absurd that individuals would recognize their own potential for thought and foresight (*animum . . . providum*, 1.pr.15), but deny it to the universe, as if 'nature does not know what it is doing' (*natura nesciente quid faciat*, 1.pr.15). In fact, doing the very work of natural philosophy and exercising one's *ratio* is what brings one closer to the gods: 'Seneca equates nature and the gods. These are rational gods whose "worship" requires that we use the methods of rational investigation to go deep beneath the surface world of our ordinary observational experience' (Inwood 2005: 182).

Lucretius lurks behind the structure, subject matter and language of this book – pointed references to Lucretian terms like *simulacra* and *imago* show how Seneca critically appraises Epicurean physics in order to promote his view of the divine.[50] An echo of Lucretius occurs early in the doxography of this book, when Seneca writes that shooting stars happen during the day: 'Just as they [stars] are hidden and occluded by the brightness of the sun, so too torches shoot across in the daytime as well, the intensity of the daylight conceals them' (*quemadmodum illae latent et solis fulgore obumbrantur, sic faces quoque transcurrunt et interdiu, sed abscondit illas* **diurni luminis** *claritas*, *Q Nat*. 1.1.11). The phrase for daylight comes from *DRN* 4.457, where Lucretius writes about dreams and what we think we see when asleep: 'We believe we see the sun and the daylight' (*cernere censemus solem* **lumenque diurnum**).[51] The senses can be fooled, awake or asleep (from a Lucretian standpoint both states receive *simulacra*), and Seneca leads the reader to understand that such impressions can be faulty (i.e. 'torches' exist both night and day, and dream images are merely flimsy *simulacra*). Seneca recalls Lucretius again when he argues that 'nothing is more deceiving than our eyesight' (*nihil esse acie nostra fallacius, Q Nat.* 1.3.9), evoking the Lucretian examples of the colonnade, the 'broken' oar and Epicurus' idea that the sun is the size of a foot (*Q Nat.* 1.3.9–10). These examples remind the reader of their previous appearances in Lucretius and foster an identification between *DRN* 4 and the current subject, and may help explain why Seneca belabours his discussions of various optical illusions and mirrors in this book. If the senses are conduits to grappling with the sublime, they can also be fallible guides to such experiences.

Seneca builds his argument about such celestial fires against the criticism of his interlocutor, who sometimes seems to espouse an Epicurean point of view.[52] Aside from his brief (correct) discussion of eclipses, all the examples given of such atmospheric phenomena lead to the conclusion:

simulacra ista sunt et **inanis** verorum corporum imitatio, quae ipsa a quibusdam ita conpositis ut hoc possint detorquentur in **pravum**.

They are semblances, an empty imitation of real bodies that themselves are corruptly distorted by things so constituted as to have that effect.

Q Nat. *1.15.8*

This quotation features a number of Lucretian 'buzz-words', from *simulacra* to *inanis* (often of the void), as well as a notable repetition of *pravus*, which Lucretius exploits in his discussion of the senses (cf. *DRN* 4.513, 517, 520, 1155; *Q Nat.* 1.pr.16). Seneca concentrates these terms at this moment to suggest the Epicurean overtones of his subsequent *fabella* about Hostius Quadra. Hostius becomes a satiric stand-in for the Epicurean who believes in Epicurean self-fulfilment via pleasure (especially visual), not the ethical self-fulfilment of Seneca's ideal reader. Lucretius' own discussion of passionate desire was amplified by his satiric rhetoric and parody of lovers' language that make up a large part of the conclusion of *DRN* 4 (1058–1191). Seneca places the Hostius episode in a similar position in *Naturales Quaestiones* 1 to show his response to *DRN* 4 as a whole in this book. Both books ultimately deal with sense perception, especially sight, and the final critiques of delusional individuals underscore how Seneca employs *aemulatio* on a large-scale to disparage Lucretian ideas.

Many aspects of the Hostius story relate broadly to Lucretius' language, imagery and subject matter. Hostius feeds on his own images like Mars feeding on Venus' love in the preface to *DRN* 1; he incites his own *furor* (as Lucretius describes passion), and does it all for the sake of *voluptas*.[53] Seneca relates the story of Hostius Quadra in order to illustrate how 'lust (*libido*) does not disdain any means of stimulating pleasure (*inritandae voluptatis*) and applies its ingenuity (*ingeniosa*) to encouraging its own madness' (*Q Nat.* 1.16.1). He outfits his bedroom with magnifying mirrors that allow him to take pleasure in, from all angles (*opus sibi suum per imagines offerebat, Q Nat.* 1.16.4),[54] the depraved acts he engages in, and Seneca gives him a speech in which he expresses his outlook:

'simul' inquit 'et virum et feminam patior. Nihilominus illa quoque supervacua mihi parte alicuius contumelia marem exerceo. Omnia membra stupris occupata sunt: oculi quoque in partem libidinis veniant et testes eius exactoresque sint. Etiam ea quae a conspectus corporis nostri positio submovit arte visantur, ne quis me putet nescire quid faciam. Nil egit natura quod humanae libidini ministeria tam maligne dedit, quod aliorum animalium concubitus melius instruxit. Inveniam quemadmodum morbo meo et imponam et satisfaciam. Quo nequitiam meam, si ad naturae modum pecco? Id genus speculorum circumponam mihi quod incredibilem magnitudinem imaginum reddat. Si liceret mihi, ad verum ista perducerem; quia non licet, mendacio pascar.

Q Nat. *1.16.7–9*

'I submit,' he said, 'to a man and a woman at the same time. Nevertheless even with the part of me that is so far redundant I act the man for someone's humiliation. All my members are occupied in acts of debauchery: let my eyes have a share in my lust as well and be its witnesses and inspectors. Even the things that are kept out of sight by the structure of our bodies should be made visible by technology, so that no one can think I do not know what I am doing. Nature wasted her time, being so mean with the assistance she gave to human lust and organizing the coupling of other animals better. I shall find a way of both deceiving and satisfying my obsession. What use is my wickedness if my wrongdoing keeps within nature's limits? I shall surround myself with the kind of mirror that gives off incredibly large images. If I could, I would make them real; since I cannot, I shall feed on the illusion.'

In Seneca's over-the-top prosopopoeia, Hostius becomes a parody of the sage, using mirrors not to understand more about the natural world (*Q Nat.* 1.17.2–3), but rather to try to surpass nature (*Quo nequitiam meam, si ad naturae modum pecco*). Williams has shown how the language of the Hostius episode reflects (imperfectly) some of the themes of this *fabella*: Hostius is a *hostia*, he is a 'slave to his fortune' killed by his slaves, his *obscenitas* is represented on the *scaena*.[55] In this passage, Hostius highlights the strong connection between his eyes and his testicles as *loci* of libidinous impulses.[56] Seneca stresses throughout that what makes Hostius particularly notable/immoral is the way he manipulates his gaze to see all these degenerate acts (*Q Nat.* 1.16.3: *ipse flagitiorum suorum spectator*, 1.16.4: *oculos suos ad illa advocabit*, 1.16.5: cf. the repetitions of *spectabat, passim*).

This stress on vision and the passive nature of Epicurean sense-perception, in which *simulacra* penetrate the eyes in a manner suggestive of Hostius' own passivity,[57] helps identify him with the problematic nature of *simulacra* in love. As Lucretius explains, 'love is unique: the more we have of it, the more it's not enough, and the more calamitous desire sets the heart aflame' (*unique res haec est, cuius quam plurima habemus, / tam magis ardescit dira cuppedine pectus*, 4.1089–90). Lucretius further describes such images:

ex hominis vero facie pulchroque colore
nil datur in corpus praeter simulacra fruendum
tenuia; quae vento spes raptast saepe misella
ut bibere in somnis sitiens quom quaerit, ut umor
non datur, ardorem qui membris stinguere possit,
sed laticum simulacra petit frustraque laborat
in medioque sitit torrenti flumine potans,
sic in amore Venus simulacris ludit amantis,
nec satiare queunt spectando corpora coram,
nec manibus quicquam teneris abradere membris
possunt errantes incerti corpore toto. (4.1094–1104)[58]

But of a human face's bloom and beauty, what comes in
For the body to enjoy? Just images, flimsy and thin,
And the wind often snatches even this scrap of hope away.
As in a dream, when a man drinks, trying to allay
His thirst, but gets no real liquid to douse his body's fire,
And struggles pointlessly after mere images of water,
And though he gulps and gulps from a gushing stream, his throat is dry,
So Venus teases with images – lovers can't satisfy
The flesh however they devour each other with the eye,
Nor with hungry hands roving the body can they reap
Anything from the supple limbs that they can take and keep.

trans. A. E. Stallings

This is the nature of Hostius' *insatiabile malum* (*Q Nat.* 1.16.3 ~ *nec satiare queunt, DRN* 4.1102), one that Seneca places within the fun house distortions of his bedroom (as well as in the new context of the *Naturales Quaestiones*) to prove how feeding on such *simulacra* leads to a grotesque viewpoint, one in which Hostius aims to know 'whatever he is doing' while denying nature's ability to do the same (1.pr.15). If we read Hostius Quadra as the extreme Senecan version of Lucretius' misguided lovers, we can see how his misguided use of one of nature's gifts, mirrors (*Q Nat.* 1.17.1), leads to problematic ideas of self-control and self-knowledge within the larger cosmic context.[59] Seneca has been striving in this book to show how the soul's natural curiosity (*curiosus spectator*, 1.pr.12) and predilections will lead ultimately to the knowledge of god (*illic incipit deum nosse*, 1.pr.13).[60] For Hostius, and consequently an Epicurean epistemology that privileges the sense of sight, the self-spectatorship (*ipse flagitiorum suorum spectator*, 1.16.3) and warped sense of self-knowledge (*ne quis me putet nescire quid faciam*, 1.16.8) constitute an indictment of how narcissistic, pleasure-seeking Epicureans are deceived into favouring the senses disproportionately.[61] False epistemology leads to false ideas of true knowledge.

Lucretius already pointed out some of the ways in which love can cause a distorted sense of reality at the conclusion of *DRN* 4, and Seneca aims to cap Lucretius' parody with his *aemulatio* of it in the Hostius Quadra episode. Both Lucretius and Seneca attack their false lovers with gusto but Seneca turns Lucretius' vitriol against Epicurean principles per se, as embodied in Hostius Quadra.[62] Hostius' strange fusion of pseudo-Stoicism and Epicurean epistemology creates a distorted justification of mere pleasure for pleasure's sake with mirrors that do not lead to ethical self-knowledge (*inventa sunt specula ut homo ipse se nosset*, 1.17.4), but only reproductions and replications of crude actions that spur an unquenchable desire for more.[63] Hostius' *voluptas* will never be sated because it is based on false premises and is made of distorted, ephemeral *simulacra*.[64] The cosmic knowledge that could be gained from mirrors (*Q Nat*. 1.17.2–3 argues for using mirrors to understand the shape of the sun and eclipses) has been perverted by an abuse that undermines any sense of sublimity. Both Lucretius and Seneca explain the proper attitudes towards love and mirrors, respectively, but their correctives pale in comparison with their satiric *exempla*. In this parody of Epicurean tenets, we see how Seneca has posited a counter-pleasure to the *voluptas* of Lucretius' poem, namely, the pleasure that attends the contemplation of nature and the resulting greatness of the soul.[65] That is true sublimity; the moral message of Seneca's denunciation of Hostius Quadra ultimately parallels Longinus' own ideas about the sublime author, as Shaw summarizes them: 'As the echo of a noble mind, the sublime elevates man above the tawdry concern with wealth and status . . . The implication of Longinus' observation is, therefore, that the true sublime is on the side of morality' (2017: 25). Hostius' immorality is anything but sublime, and the larger intertextual mapping onto *DRN* 4 shows how Seneca derides Epicurean sense-perception as a false conduit to conceiving the divine.

Conclusion

If Seneca's true goal is to teach about the divine,[66] then his careful repudiation of Epicurean theology is done in part through pointed intertextual recollection of Lucretius' language.[67] His emulation of Lucretius in itself is indicative of a sublime mentality, as Shaw notes: 'Longinus conceives literary production as a form of competition in which aspirant poets battle with established poets for literary prestige' (2017: 35). Lucretius' descriptions of nature may result in a grandeur of things (*maiestas rerum*, 5.7), but Seneca wants his sublime moments to lead one to god. Inwood has stressed that for the Stoics theology is the culmination of physics and 'epistemological themes need to be given equal or greater weight' (2005: 161n.14) in our analysis of Seneca's *Naturales Quaestiones*.[68] Lucretian intertexts show how Seneca creatively recasts aspects of Lucretius' teachings about Epicurean ideas of the gods and sense-perception. Initial intertexts found in the opening of Seneca's *Naturales Quaestiones* may appear to equate the Senecan reader with Epicurus, but Seneca is careful to distinguish what sort of *victoria* is more important to a Stoic *proficiens*. Earthly vices must first be conquered, and one should not view the universe as mere happenstance or *religio* as an adversary. As the work continues, Epicurean ideas are interpreted as part of the doxographical work that Seneca sees as a proper use of one's *ratio*.[69] Seneca posits Lucretius as an author of the sublime, but his own sublime destruction of the world overwhelms the poetic versions of

Lucretius. Lucretius' valuation of *ratio* is shown to be hollow when compared with a *ratio* that is the very essence of the divine.[70] In addition, Lucretius' jeremiad against love is transformed into a satiric view of Epicurean epistemology and found at a similar location in its corresponding book. By equating Epicurean *voluptas* with sexual desire and the acts of Venus with *simulacra* (*sic in amore Venus simulacris ludit amantis*, 4.1101), Seneca makes Hostius Quadra an Epicurean embodiment of sense perception, as this figures in *DRN* 4, and a figure worthy of censure. The Epicurean idea that all sense-perceptions are true is shown to be problematic for one like Hostius who feeds on distorted reflections knowingly (only to spur further unfulfillable desires). Sense-perception is all-too-fallible when compared to the Stoic rational universe in which god is pure *ratio*. Seneca clearly is inspired by the sublime impulse he finds in Lucretius and aims to redirect it towards his own epistemological and theological goals. While the honey at the rim of Lucretius' cup is sweet, Seneca stresses that the bitter medicine must be spat out.[71]

Notes

1. At *Ep*. 95.11 he even has personified philosophy speak through a quotation of Lucretius (1.54–7). For more on the relationship between Seneca and Lucretius, see Lana 1955: 12–19, Mazzoli 1970: 206–7 and Gatzemeier 2013: 59–83. Williams 2016 stresses the manner in which Seneca's 'sublime *sapiens*' is indebted to Lucretius' idea of the sublime. Seneca's decision to write letters may have been influenced by the Epicurean tradition: cf. Inwood 2007 and Schiesaro 2015. Wildberger 2014: 447n.52 calls attention to a 'clear allusion' to an idea found in *DRN* 3.935–8 at *Ep*. 99.5.

2. E.g. the plague of *Oedipus* responds to the conclusion of *DRN* 6, the *sacer ignis* that Phaedra endures is Lucretian (6.660), and the *extispicium* of *Oedipus* mimics Lucretian language (*mutatus ordo est*, *Oed*. 366 ~ *DRN* 1.677).

3. As Seneca will go on to say, 'What is the point of fleeing if he doesn't escape himself? He is his own escort and drives himself on, the most burdensome of companions' (*Tranq*. 2.14, trans. Fantham 2014). This idea is also Horatian (cf. *Epist*. 1.11.25–7).

4. Sentiment and context are very similar, with the primary change being from third person to second (as we may expect in a letter); cf. *Q Nat*. 1.pr.6: *multa* (*sc. vitia animi*) *effugisti, te nondum* and *Ep*. 28.2: *quaeris quare te fuga ista non adiuvet? tecum fugis*.

5. See further Asmis 2008: 152 for this 'altogether new view of human distress . . . a multifaceted picture of self-alienation'.

6. Although he does humorously include Lucretius the man in a larger discussion of *genus* and *species* at *Ep*. 58.12 ('For *homo* comprises species: by nation, Greek, Roman, Parthian . . . and individuals also: Cato, Cicero, Lucretius'). Seneca recognizes Lucretius as a sublime poet, as Williams 2016 illuminates.

7. For an overview of the sublime in Lucretius, see Conte 1994, Porter 2007 and Hardie 2009: 67–228. Authors such as Ovid (p. 72 above) and Statius (*docti furor arduus Lucreti*, *Sil*. 2.7.76) clearly regarded Lucretius as sublime.

8. Conte 1994 shows how Lucretius appropriates the persona of a mantic *vates*.

9. Shearin 2019 investigates models of the sublime in Lucretius and Seneca and finds 'the sublime . . . is deeply imbricated in both what we know (or can know) about the *kosmos* as well as in how we come to that knowledge' (249).

10. In essence, I am trying to expand the discussion between Inwood 2000 and Graver 2000 about meteorology in the *Naturales Quaestiones* and the way that Seneca responds to the Epicurean tradition. Late in his life, Seneca seems to be more amenable to utilizing Epicurean or other non-Stoic sources, which appear often in *Epistulae Morales*: e.g. 'whatever is well-said by another I claim as my own' (*quidquid bene dictum est ab ullo, meum est, Ep.* 16.7). The difference between a single intertext and a book-length response may map onto Seneca's own suggested reading techniques expounded in the opening books of *Epistulae Morales*, in which he moves from consideration of maxims (e.g. *Ep.* 2.5–6, 4.10) to understanding the whole (*Ep.* 33).
11. 2000: 50–4. For more on Seneca's general reception of Epicurus, see Graver 2020.
12. This could be expanded to include the quasi-missionary zeal of both philosophers at heightened moments (for the blend of 'hot' passionate rhetoric and 'cool' scientific discourse, see Williams 2017), and the metaphor of the journey for the learning process (as well as one's progress through the text); cf. Volk 2002: 88–93 for this latter feature in Lucretius.
13. For ethical connections in Epicureanism, see Mitsis 1988: 129–66 (tracing back to Epicurus), Packman 1976 (ethics in *DRN* 5), Asmis 2008: 149, 'To my mind the differences are so radical as to transform a physical text into an ethical text.'
14. See further Williams 2012; Hine 2006 for the Roman context of philosophical learning.
15. Seneca is hostile to Epicurean ideas of god: *Ben.* 4.4.1, 4.19.1–4, 7.31.3.
16. Seneca's doxography provides the hypotheses of a variety of philosophers, but he avoids naming Lucretius in the *Q Nat*.
17. As one can see from the preponderance of Epicurean material in the opening books of the *Epistulae Morales*, which are being written concurrently with the *Naturales Quaestiones*; cf. Williams 2014b.
18. This surely is thinly veiled criticism of Nero. All translations of the *Q Nat*. come from Hine 2010.
19. Cf. Williams 2012: 135.
20. Cf. Hine 2006: 44–7. Also note how Seneca employs Lucretius at this point in the preface to double-down on his own (current) lack of political engagement and his view that historical figures and history as a genre are worthless in comparison with ethical betterment. This use of Epicurean quotation and intertexts to signal an anti-political stance also can be seen as a compositional strategy in the first letters of the *Epistulae Morales* written at this time (see Wilson 2015).
21. Schiesaro 2015: 250 and Williams 2016: 175–6 have seen the Lucretian sublime lurking behind this phrase and point out that *Otio* 5.6 also alludes to this passage of Lucretius, which shows Seneca's broad knowledge of this section of *DRN*.
22. The *omne immensum* may evoke Epicurus' idea that 'the All was and always will be as it now exists' (Clay 1983: 153; cf. *DRN* 2.294–307). If *omne* has this connotation, then Seneca is giving it his own spin in his preface. *Q Nat*. stresses the importance of 'measuring' god for proper perspective: 'I shall know that everything is puny when I have measured god' (*sciam omnia angusta esse mensus deum*, 1.pr.17). Garani 2020 finds this description of Epicurus resonates with Seneca's sublime version of Phaethon as expressed earlier in the preface of *Q Nat*. 3.
23. This bait-and-switch technique creates some of the dramatic surprise when Seneca explains what *victoria* might be for the reader.
24. I am sensitive to the way that Stoic and Epicurean ideas here swerve close together, as Graver 2000 elucidates, 'we should be aware that its (*Q Nat*.'s) emphases on the nature of divinity and

on the limits of human knowledge are not his alone ... It is, in fact, entirely possible that in devoting portions of his own work to such reflections, Seneca is consciously adapting a hallmark of the competing system' (51).

25. Cf. Hardie 1986: 194–200 and Penwill 2009: 80, 'The whole of book 1 of the *De Rerum Natura* is structured as a rival triumphal procession, celebrating the victory over *religio* by parading the victor in his chariot.'

26. We will see a similar impulse for *aemulatio* in the flood passage below. Seneca's appropriation of Lucretian passages, especially programmatic passages such as this one, indicates his close reading of *DRN* and his desire to surpass Lucretius' text.

27. 'To live according to our experience of what happens by nature is our goal not just because it helps to free us from fear, but also because we are naturally contemplative creatures, fellow-citizens of the gods in the cosmic state and born to contemplate as well as to imitate the cosmos, being imperfect parts of the whole' (Inwood 2000: 35). Cf. *Q Nat.* 2.45.1–2 and Algra 2009 for how Stoic foundationalist epistemology offered 'a secure basis for their theology' (228).

28. I am swayed by William's (2012) structural argument about the movement of the *Q Nat.* from terrestrial to celestial and sublime. I assume, with Williams and Hine, that the original order of the *Q Nat.* was book 3, 4a, 4b, 5, 6, 7, 1, 2.

29. Cf. Inwood's comments about the way the preface moves into the investigation of terrestrial waters (*quaeramus* **ergo** *de terrestribus aquis*, 3.1.1) and how this transition stresses the continuity between physics, ethics and even the divine (2005: 167, esp. n.31).

30. Clay 1983: 151, citing *DRN* 2.167–83 and the support offered at 5.156–234. For Epicurus and Lucretius, the gods do exist, but they reside *intermundia* (*DRN* 3.18–22, Cic. *Fin.*2.75.5, *Nat. D.* 1.18.3) and are not interested in the world, humanity or the affairs of the world which they did not create. Seneca strongly identifies god as the *mundus* in *Q Nat.*

31. The term *exitium* is repeated in this section, e.g. 3.27.3, 3.28.9, 3.30.5, 7.

32. The flooding of great rivers or 'the boundless ocean rising with rebellious force' (Kant 1952: 28) are traditional expressions of sublimity (cf. *DRN* 6.608–737) and Porter 2016: 450–4. For cataclysmic flooding in connection with Nero's plan for an Isthmian canal, see Wright's chapter in this volume.

33. For the flood see *Met.* 1.294–312. Seneca's literary criticism in this passage has been well-analysed by Morgan 2003 and Williams 2012: 130–2. At times, Ovid does not handle this impressive material (*pro magnitudine rei*, 3.27.13) with the elevated diction and tonality it demands.

34. This features in Ovid's book-concluding poem heralding his own immortality (*ergo etiam cum me supremus adederit ignis, / vivam, parsque mei multa superstes erit, Am.* 1.15.41–2).

35. Cf. the way Seneca writes about literary fame: 'Deep is the flood of time that will close over us. A few talented minds will raise their heads above it, and although they too must eventually depart into silence, yet for long will they resist oblivion and assert their freedom' (*profunda super nos altitudo temporis veniet, pauca ingenia caput exerent et in idem quandoque silentium abitura oblivioni resistent ac se diu vindicabunt, Ep.* 21.5; cf. *Q Nat.* 3.27.11: *omnis tumulus in profundo latet et immensa ubique altitudo est*). Star 2021: 153 also identifies Lucretius' insistence on the mortality of the world in book 5 as a primary intertext in this section of Seneca's work.

36. Worthen 1991: 102–3 discusses Phaethon's connections with the flood and Seneca ties his version to Phaethon by quoting from Ovid's version of the Phaethon myth during the flood passage (*Q Nat.* 3.27.13~*Met.* 2.264).

37. See Hardie 2009: 109 on intertextual sublimity in Vergil and Lucretius, and Longinus 13 (cf.

38. For the quotation (which is paired with a quotation of Ovid), cf. Williams 2012: 154–5, 'Seneca's distortion of their original illustrative point is immediately striking: it is the shape of the attrition, not the time it takes or the atomic depletion that it causes, that now matters above all'. In another example (*DRN* 2.1026-38 ~ *Q Nat*. 7.1.1-4), the wonder evoked by contemplating the night sky is contrasted with novel ideas (of Epicurus) or rare phenomena (comets).

39. In his discussion of the sublime in *DRN*, Porter 2007 posits another echo: 'A clue that these texts point to the right vein, so to speak, is a passage from Seneca's *Natural Questions* (5.15.1–2), citing Asclepiodotus, a pupil of Posidonius and the author of a treatise on natural phenomena, on how men sent by Philip II of Macedon to explore an abandoned mine discovered not the riches he had hoped for, but something far more breath-taking: vast reservoirs of subterranean water, held in the generous embrace of the earth, which greeted the visitors "not without a thrill of awe/horror" (*non sine horrore*). Seneca reads this "with great pleasure" (*cum magna . . . voluptate*) – evidently a smiling glance at *DRN* 3.28-9' (175). See further Gunderson 2015, Williams 2016 and Littlewood 2017 on the sublime in Seneca.

40. Cf. DeVivo 1992: 77–109, Williams 2012: 219–25 and Althoff 2005.

41. Williams 2012: 328–30.

42. E.g. *Q Nat*. 6.3.1–3, 29.1; Tutrone 2017.

43. I.e. although specific passages are appropriated from *DRN* 4, *Q Nat*. 1 is not a direct response to *all* its topics (e.g. the other senses are not mentioned by Seneca), but rather an indirect reproduction (as per the subject matter and his critique of the *simulacra* and optic methodology of *DRN* 4). For Seneca, 'we may consider both the reflection itself and the perception of it flawed, and we may do so because the nature of lights observable on earth is bound up inextricably with man's morally and physically fallen existence on earth. The distorted reflections characteristic of haloes and other atmospheric lights, then, are both a by-product and an emblem of the human condition' (Leitão 1998: 132).

44. Not to denigrate the importance of *naturae species ratioque* (1.148, *passim*) that Lucretius espouses; cf. Williams 2012: 219 for the way Lucretius' *ratio* concerning earthquakes is enhanced by Seneca. Stoic *ratio* in its quasi-divine form (e.g. *Q Nat*. 1.pr.13–17) seems to be qualitatively different from that of Epicurean materialistic images (*DRN* 3.13–16; cf. Clay 1983: 133–4). See Lehoux 2013 for Lucretius' tendency to invoke vision in his scientific investigation. Epicurus believed the senses were infallible, but that men judged incorrectly.

45. M. Graver (*per litteras*) cautions that many of these optical illusions are part of a larger tradition, but what is especially important is their appearance together in a single book of Lucretius as well as in a single book of Seneca's *Q Nat*.

46. See Leitão 1998: 132–3 for language in this passage that has both moral and physical connotations. One can see a similar expansion of Lucretian material as in the flood (p. 72 above).

47. For more on Hostius Quadra, see Leitão 1998, Bartsch 2006: 106–14, Berno 2003: 31–62, Toohey 2004: 261–82, Williams 2005, Limburg 2008 and LeBlay 2013. None of these scholars discusses possible Epicurean/Lucretian parallels with the Hostius episode, although Lehoux 2012: 101 points out 'the number of times Seneca flags inappropriate vision as being at the centre of the moral problem with Hostius'.

48. As scholars such as Berno 2003 and Leitão 1998 have noted, many of these terms are then repurposed in the Hostius Quadra section. I think Seneca's Hostius, as an Epicurean stand-in, can be an attractive figure (cf. Leitão 1998: 146, 'the question becomes how to explain the dissenting voice which makes the debauched Hostius a philosopher if not a god') and a rival

type of 'philosopher' but the larger context points to a satirical treatment.

49. For this section as a direct response to *DRN* 5.200–34, see Schiesaro 2015: 249. Cf. Inwood 2009: 222, 'So we need to do physics to learn to navigate in the moral world and we want to do physics because, well, it is in us to do so, to explore and savour the body of knowledge which reflects our best selves and our kinship with the gods.'

50. *simulacra*: *Q Nat.* 1.5.1, 1.13.1, 1.13.2, 1.15.8, 1.17.1; *imago*: *passim*.

51. Admittedly a passing link, but it is not a common expression in Latin.

52. Cf. Williams 2005: 159.

53. Cf. *pascit amore avidos inhians in te, dea, visus, DRN* 1.36, and *mendacio pascar, Q Nat.* 1.16.9; *inque dies gliscit furor, DRN* 4.1069, and *ingeniosa sit ad incitandum furorem suum, Q Nat.* 1.16.1; *DRN* 1.1, 2.3, *passim* and *inritandae voluptatis, Q Nat.* 1.16.1.

54. See Gunderson 2015: 71 for the way Hostius' *opus* connects with both Seneca's and god's; McCarty 1989: 170 on how Lucretius' mirror metaphor (like peering out of a house) applies to Hostius Quadra's use of mirrors: 'It may not be merely fortuitous that Lucretius' metaphor also reproduces the circumstance of the individual self-consciousness, peering out through the eyes from the bony house of the skull into a world reachable only through the senses. Thus, paradoxically, the metaphor suggests not only access to the interior world of essences but also entrapment within the limits of the self.'

55. Williams 2005: 142, 146, who highlights the resemblances to mime in this story by citing *Q Nat.* 1.16.1: *Hostius fuit Quadra obscenitatis in scaenam usque perductae*. Others have wondered about connections between Hostius and Horace (*Horatius*), who is reported to have had a bedroom full of mirrors (cf. Suet. *Vita Horatii*). This sort of distorted etymological play may also evoke Lucretius' anagrams and puns such as the famous *lignis/ignis* of *DRN* 1.901. 'Quadra' may also hint at Seneca's target for this passage, namely *DRN* **4** (*quadr-*, 'four' as a prefix). Books are sometimes referred to by number in ancient commentaries, e.g. Serv. *ad Aen.* 1.3.

56. This pun is as old as Plautus, *Cur.* 31; see Berno 2003: 49 for its use here.

57. As Seneca stresses repeatedly through forms of *patior* (*Q Nat.* 1.16.2, 5, 6); earlier in the book Seneca describes myopic men who seem to run into themselves and see their own image everywhere (*Q Nat.* 1.3.7); cf. Leitão 1998: 140, 'How well this description of a man with exceptionally weak vision matches the blindness of Hostius Quadra!' Lucretius stresses that the lover's eyes are penetrated by *simulacra* and this subverts Roman masculinity, 'leaving him violated and wounded (4.1048–9) not by human violence, but by physics. Since nearly every man sees, the nature of miniscule atoms, it turns out, proves to be revolutionary at a personal and social level' (Pope 2018: 209).

58. Lucretius gives much attention to the mouths of lovers (4.1080–1, 1108–10); cf. Seneca's own emphasis on Hostius Quadra's mouth (*os*) and the Latin connections of *os* as 'implying the gaze' (*OLD* 10a).

59. Seneca first identifies mirrors as a way to view the sun and celestial phenomena before moving on to ethical self-betterment (1.17.2–4). Physics comes before ethics for the proper use of a mirror and, in a sense, that preference is posited throughout *Q Nat.* 1 in particular (cf. 1.pr.1–2). Of course, Ovid's tale of Narcissus also lurks behind much of the erotic self-love in this passage: cf. *Met.* 3.339–510 and McCarty 1989: 176–82.

60. This builds upon earlier calls to look beyond the senses in the investigation of earthquakes, which will produce 'the greatest possible benefit, the knowledge of nature (*nosse naturam*). The investigation of this subject has many benefits, but none is finer than the fact that it captivates people with its own magnificence, and their motives for studying it are not gain

but wonder' (*Q Nat.* 6.4.2).

61. Cf. Williams 2016: 178–9 for the 'system of optics overturned in Hostius' grotesque style of penetration and energetic quest . . . in contrast to an enduring, authentic, and fully internalised greatness of soul, the reflected *magnitudo* that Hostius delights in is purely external, unreal, and ephemeral – a greatness of gland, not mind'.
62. Seneca's creative 'misreading' equates Lucretius' deluded lover with Epicureanism proper, as opposed to the figure of mockery that Lucretius lambasts (4.1073–1170).
63. It is not surprising that Seneca alludes to Ovid's story of Erysichthon (*Met.* 8.877–8) at *Q Nat.* 1.16.3; cf. Parroni 2002 *ad loc.*
64. Hostius' viewing is often connected with consumption (*Q Nat.* 1.16.4, 9) and so, like hunger, it is impossible to be satisfied permanently, but arises soon again.
65. *Q Nat.* 1.pr.12 asserts that the divine pleases the soul because it recognizes its own divinity (*hoc habet argumentum divinitatis suae quod illum divina delectant, nec ut alienis, sed ut suis interest*); cf. *humanissima completur animus voluptate*, Cic. *Luc.* 41.127, Sen. *Q Nat.* 3.pr.18 and Hadot 2006: 184–5.
66. Cf. *Q Nat.* 1.pr.1–2.
67. Shearin 2019: 264 also sees a 'differing valuation of knowledge' as distinguishing Lucretian and Senecan conceptions of the sublime.
68. Seneca will state that part of the goal of studying the natural world is to realize that the gods are not 'outside the world' (*Ep.* 90.35), as the Epicureans maintained.
69. See his comments on human/scientific progress at *Q Nat.* 6.5.2–3, 7.25.3–5; Hadot 2006: 166–81 and Foucault 2005: 278, 'Whereas the role and function of Epicurean analysis, of the Epicurean need for a knowledge of physics, was basically to free us from the fears, apprehensions, and myths that have encumbered us from birth, the Stoic need to know nature, the need to know nature in Seneca, is not so much . . . in order to dispel these fears . . . Above all, this form of knowledge involves grasping ourselves again here where we are . . . within a wholly rational and reassuring world, which is the world of a divine Providence.'
70. As Schiesaro 2015: 248 clarifies, 'The *NQ* display a strong tendency towards a "totalizing worldview" (Williams 2012: 3–4) that in its import and outlook is directly comparable to the Epicurean unification of all natural phenomena under a very limited number of general laws, but, unlike Epicurus' and Lucretius' *ratio*, these are ultimately guaranteed by divine authority.'
71. Margaret Graver read an earlier version of this paper and offered extensive criticism. The editors provided helpful feedback and caught many errors. I thank them for the opportunity to write this paper in honour of Thom Worthen, who first introduced me to Lucretius. Any remaining errors are my own.

Works cited

Algra, K. (2009), 'Stoic Philosophical Theology and Graeco-Roman Religion', in R. Salles (ed.), *God and Cosmos in Stoicism*, 224–51, Oxford: Oxford University Press.

Althoff, J. (2005), 'Senecas Naturales quaestiones, Buch 2, und Lukrez', in T. Baier, G. Manuwald and B. Zimmermann (eds), *Seneca: philosophus et magister. Festschrift für Eckard Lefèvre zum 70 Geburtstag*, 9–34, Freiburg im Br./Berlin: Rombach Verlag.

Asmis, E. (2008), 'Lucretius' New World Order: Making a Pact with Nature', *Classical Quarterly*, 58: 141–57.

Bartsch, S. (2006), *The Mirror of the Self: Sexuality, Self-Knowledge, and the Gaze in the Early*

Roman Empire, Chicago: The University of Chicago Press.
Berno, F. R. (2003), *Lo specchio, il vizio e la virtù: Studio sulle Naturales Quaestiones di Seneca*, Bologna: Pàtron Editore.
Berno, F. R. (2015), 'Exploring Appearances: Seneca's Scientific Works', in S. Bartsch and A. Schiesaro (eds), *The Cambridge Companion to Seneca*, 82–92, Cambridge: Cambridge University Press.
Clay, D. (1983), *Lucretius and Epicurus*, Ithaca and London: Cornell University Press.
Conte, G. B. (1994), *Genres and Readers: Lucretius, Love Elegy, Pliny's Encyclopedia*, Baltimore and London: The Johns Hopkins University Press.
DeVivo, A. (1992), *Le parole della scienza: sul trattato de terrae motu di Seneca*, Salerno: Pietro Laveglia Editore.
Fantham, E., H. M. Hine, J. Ker and G. D. Williams (eds) (2014), *Lucius Annaeus Seneca: Hardship and Happiness*, Chicago: The University of Chicago Press.
Foucault, M. (2005), *The Hermeneutics of the Subject: Lectures at the Collège de France 1981-1982*, trans. G. Burchell, New York: Picador.
Garani, M. (2020), 'Seneca as Lucretius' Sublime Reader (*Naturales Quaestiones 3 praef.*)', in P. Hardie, V. Prosperi and D. Zucca (eds), *Lucretius: Poet and Philosopher. Backgrounds and Fortunes of De Rerum Natura*, 105–26, Berlin: De Gruyter.
Gatzemeier, S. (2013), *Ut ait Lucretius: Die Lukrezrezeption in der lateinischen Prosa bis Laktanz*, Göttengen: Vandenhoeck & Ruprecht.
Graver, M. (2000), 'Commentary on Inwood', in J. J. Cleary and G. M. Gurtler (eds), *Proceedings of the Boston Area Colloquium in Ancient Philosophy*, 15, 44–56, Leiden, Boston and Köln: Brill.
Graver, M. (2020), 'Seneca's Reception of Epicureanism', in P. Mitsis (ed.), *Oxford Handbook of Epicurus and Epicureanism*, 487–506, Oxford: Oxford University Press.
Gunderson, E. (2015), *The Sublime Seneca: Ethics, Literature, Metaphysics*, Cambridge: Cambridge University Press.
Hadot, P. (2006), *The Veil of Isis: An Essay on the History of the Idea of Nature*, trans. M. Chase, Cambridge, MA: Harvard University Press.
Hardie, P. (1986), *Virgil's Aeneid: Cosmos and Imperium*, Oxford: Oxford University Press.
Hardie, P. (2009), *Lucretian Receptions: History, the Sublime, Knowledge*, Cambridge: Cambridge University Press.
Hine, H. M. (2006), 'Rome, the Cosmos, and the Emperor in Seneca's *Natural Questions*', *Journal of Roman Studies*, 96: 42–72.
Hine, H. M. (2010), *Natural Questions*, Chicago: The University of Chicago Press.
Inwood, B. (2000), 'God and Human Knowledge in Seneca's *Natural Questions*', in J. J. Cleary and G. M. Gurtler (eds), *Proceedings of the Boston Area Colloquium in Ancient Philosophy*, 15, 23–43, Leiden, Boston and Köln: Brill.
Inwood, B. (2005), *Reading Seneca*, Oxford: Oxford University Press.
Inwood, B. (2007), 'The Importance of Form in Seneca's Philosophical Letters', in R. Morello and A. D. Morrison (eds), *Ancient Letters: Classical and Late Antique Epistolography*, 133–48, Oxford: Oxford University Press.
Inwood, B. (2009), 'Why Physics?', in R. Salles (ed.), *God and Cosmos in Stoicism*, 201–23, Oxford: Oxford University Press.
Kant, I. (1952), *The Critique of Judgement*, trans. J. C. Meredith, Oxford: Oxford University Press.
Lana, I. (1955), *Lucio Anneo Seneca*, Turin: Loescher.
LeBlay, F. (2013), 'Une version pervertie de la connaissance de soi: le cas d'Hostius Quadra', *Pallas*, 92: 305–13.
Lehoux, D. (2012), *What Did the Romans Know? An Inquiry into Science and Worldmaking*, Chicago: The University of Chicago Press.
Lehoux, D. (2013), 'Seeing and Unseeing, Seen and Unseen', in D. Lehoux, A. Morrison and A. Sharrock (eds), *Lucretius: Poetry, Philosophy, Science*, 131–51, Oxford: Oxford University

Press.
Leitão, D. D. (1998), 'Senecan Catoptrics and the Passion of Hostius Quadra (Sen. *Nat.* 1)', *Materiali e discussioni per l'analisi dei testi classici*, 41: 127–60.
Limburg, F. (2008), 'The Representation and Role of Badness in Seneca's Moral Teaching: A Case from the *Naturales Quaestiones* (*NQ* 1.16)', in I. Sluiter and R. M. Rosen (eds), *KAKOS: Badness and Anti-Value in Classical Antiquity*, 433–50, Leiden: Brill.
Littlewood, C. (2017), '*Hercules Furens* and the Senecan Sublime', *Ramus*, 46: 153–74.
Mazzoli, G. (1970), *Seneca e La Poesia*, Milan: Casa Editrice Ceschina.
McCarty, W. (1989), 'The Shape of the Mirror: Metaphorical Catoptrics in Classical Literature', *Arethusa*, 22: 161–95.
Mitsis, P. (1988), *Epicurus' Ethical Theory: The Pleasures of Invulnerability*, Ithaca and London: Cornell University Press.
Morgan, L. (2003), 'Child's Play: Ovid and His Critics', *Journal of Roman Studies*, 93: 66–91.
Packman, Z. M. (1976), 'Ethics and Allegory in the Proem of the Fifth Book of Lucretius' *De Rerum Natura*', *Classical Journal*, 71: 206–12.
Parroni, P. (2002), *Seneca: ricerche sulla natura*, Milan: Fondazione Lorenzo Valla.
Penwill, J. L. (2009), 'Lucretius and the First Triumvirate', in W. J. Dominik, J. Garthwaite and P. Roche (eds), *Writing Politics in Imperial Rome*, 63–88, Leiden and Boston: Brill.
Pope, M. (2018), 'Ocular Penetration, Grammatical Objectivity, and an Indecent Proposal in *De Rerum Natura*', *Classical Philology*, 113: 206–11.
Porter, J. I. (2007), 'Lucretius and the Sublime', in S. Gillespie and P. Hardie (eds), *The Cambridge Companion to Lucretius*, 167–84, Cambridge: Cambridge University Press.
Porter, J. I. (2016), *The Sublime in Antiquity*, Cambridge: Cambridge University Press.
Schiesaro, A. (2015), 'Seneca and Epicurus: The Allure of the Other', in S. Bartsch and A. Schiesaro (eds), *The Cambridge Companion to Seneca*, 239–51, Cambridge: Cambridge University Press.
Shaw, P. (2017), *The Sublime*, 2nd edn, London: Routledge.
Shearin, W. H. (2019), '"The Deep-Sticking Boundary Stone": Cosmology, Sublimity, and Knowledge in Lucretius' *De Rerum Natura* and Seneca's *Naturales Quaestiones*', in P. S. Horky (ed.), *Cosmos in the Ancient World*, 247–69, Cambridge: Cambridge University Press.
Stallings, A. E. (trans.) (2007), *Lucretius: The Nature of Things*, London and New York: Penguin Books.
Star, C. (2021), *Apocalypse and Golden Age: The End of the World in Greek and Roman Thought*, Baltimore: Johns Hopkins University Press.
Toohey, P. (2004), *Melancholy, Love and Time: Boundaries of the Self in Ancient Literature*, Ann Arbor: The University of Michigan Press.
Tutrone, S. (2017), 'Seneca on the Nature of Things: Moral Concerns and Theories of Matter in *Natural Questions* 6', *Latomus*, 76: 765–89.
Volk, K. (2002), *The Poetics of Latin Didactic: Lucretius, Vergil, Ovid, Manilius*, Oxford: Oxford University Press.
Wildberger, J. (2014), 'The Epicurus Trope and the Construction of a "Letter Writer" in Seneca's *Epistulae Morales*', in J. Wildberger and M. L. Colish (eds), *Seneca Philosophus*, 431–65, Berlin: Walter de Gruyter.
Williams, G. (2005), 'Interactions: Physics, Morality, and Narrative in Seneca *Natural Questions* 1', *Classical Philology*, 100: 142–65.
Williams, G. (2012), *The Cosmic Viewpoint: A Study of Seneca's Natural Questions*, Oxford: Oxford University Press.
Williams, G. (2014a), '*Naturales Quaestiones*', in G. Damschen, G. and A. Heil (eds), *Brill's Companion to Seneca: Philosopher and Dramatist*, 181–90, Leiden and Boston: Brill.
Williams, G. (2014b), 'Double Vision and Cross-Reading in Seneca's *Epistulae Morales* and *Naturales Quaestiones*', in J. Wildberger and M. L. Colish (eds), *Seneca Philosophus*, 135–66,

Berlin: De Gruyter.
Williams, G. (2016), 'Minding the Gap: Seneca, the Self, and the Sublime', in G. Williams and K. Volk (eds), *Roman Reflections: Studies in Latin Philosophy*, 172–91, Oxford: Oxford University Press.
Williams, G. (2017), 'A Passion for Nature: Seneca's *Natural Questions* and Hippolytus in his *Phaedra*', *Maia*, 69: 312–25.
Wilson, M. (2015), '*Quae quis fugit damnat*: Outspoken Silence in Seneca's *Epistles*', in H. Baltussen and P. J. Davis (eds), *The Art of Veiled Speech: Self-Censorship from Aristophanes to Hobbes*, 137–56, Philadelphia: The University of Pennsylvania Press.
Worthen, T. D. (1991), *The Myth of Replacement: Stars, Gods, and Order in the Universe*, Tucson: The University of Arizona Press.

CHAPTER 6
VERGIL'S *BOUGONIA* RITE IN *GEORGICS* 4: ITS NATURE, SOURCES, ORIGINS AND POSSIBLE LINK TO THE INDO-EUROPEAN MYTH OF CREATION
Michael Teske

Introduction

Vergil's didactic verse treatise on agricultural pursuits, the *Georgics*, serves as a poetic, if not practical guide to farming, planting, cattle-raising and beekeeping.[1] In *Georgics* 4, he discusses the characteristics of bees and their communal life at length, and ends the work with a detailed and bizarre sacrificial rite whereby a swarm of bees is supposedly engendered from the rotting carcass of a slain bull, or ox,[2] in a process often designated by the Greek term *bougonia* (βουγονία; Lat. *bugonia*), literally 'bovine-generation', which can indicate generation by a cow, bull, bullock or ox,[3] but is generally understood as 'ox-generation'.[4] The odd nature of the ritual immediately raises questions about its origins and relation to other rites within Graeco-Roman religious tradition, its precise literary function in the *Georgics*, and its multiplicity of symbolic associations emphasized by the poet's innovative linking of Aristaeus and Orpheus to it. By investigating Vergil's sources and analysing the evidence for the rite itself,[5] I aim not only to establish the uniqueness of the religious ritual in the Graeco-Roman world, but also to suggest its extremely archaic nature by noting striking parallels between Vergil's ritual *bougonia* and the Indo-European myth of creation.

Vergil's two descriptions of *bougonia*

Vergil does not use the word *bougonia* (n. 2 below), but *Georgics* 4 nevertheless contains two contrasting accounts of the practice (295–314, 538–58), which I designate simply as Vergil's first and second descriptions, respectively. Both descriptions are didactic, of course, but Vergil's first description lacks religious language and reads like an instructional pamphlet for an apiarist to foster a natural apicultural process, while, in contrast, Vergil's second description is cast in the express form of guidance for performing a religious rite.

In roughly the first three-fifths of book 4 (8–314), Vergil details the human construction of a hive and discusses the method of sprinkling herbs around the hive to entice a swarm to inhabit it. He follows these details with an imaginative, anthropomorphic description (not scientifically accurate) of the bees engaging in a tiny civil war to determine the superiority of one of the two so-called king bees.[6] Vergil later relates the activities of bees and gives an elaborate account of the divisions of labour within the bee community, which is both compared to, and conflated with, human society. Finally, he speaks of death and decay in a hive beleaguered by disease.

It is at this point that the poet begins to recount the myth of Aristaeus, traditionally the first beekeeper, whose hives, Vergil claims, all died out from sickness and hunger. The poet prefaces the story by giving his first description of the *bougonia*. An epyllion (4.315–558) follows, as Aristaeus commences his search for what caused the death of his hive and for a means of restoring his bees (315–58). He immediately invokes his mother, the water-nymph Cyrene. After he journeys beneath the waters of the river to implore her divine aid, Aristaeus discovers that he must capture the shape-shifting Proteus and compel him to explain the loss of the bees. Under duress, Proteus reminds Aristaeus of his attempt to rape the fleeing Eurydice, who was killed by the bite of a venomous snake. Proteus then relates a cautionary tale of Orpheus' journey to the underworld, his abortive attempt to bring his wife back to life and his return to the upper air. Orpheus is ultimately torn apart by maenads, and his parts strewn over the fields in a fertility rite (*sparagmos*). At the close, Proteus dives beneath the waters and Cyrene tells her son Aristaeus how to propitiate the wood-nymphs who loved Eurydice and, by implication, how to appease the soul of Orpheus.[7] Vergil's second description of the *bougonia* ritual follows this episode.

In this way, Vergil's first and second descriptions of *bougonia*, which are quite distinct in their details, frame the Aristaeus-Orpheus epyllion of human suffering and loss. His first description is devoid of religious language and gives the impression of a straightforward, instructional account. First, a small and narrow place is chosen for the generation of bees. Then, on this spot, a hut is constructed with a narrow roof of tiles and close walls. Four windows with slanting light are added, each facing one of the four winds. Next, a two-year-old bull is found with newly curving horns. Then his nostrils and mouth are plugged up by force, and he is beaten to death. His innards are then pounded to a pulp through his intact skin, *integram ... pellem* (302). This process occurs in early spring when 'moisture, warming in the soft bones, starts to seethe' (*teneris tepefactus in ossibus umor / aestuat*, 308–9) and causes marvellous creatures to rise into view (*visenda modis animalia miris*, 309), namely bees.[8] At first, the animals are footless (*trunca pedum primo*, 310),[9] but soon they are buzzing with wings and keep increasing in number until they burst forth like a rain shower pouring from summer clouds.

Vergil's second description of the *bougonia*, which assumes the definitive form of a religious rite, proceeds in the following manner. Aristaeus is told to choose four exceptional bulls which are surpassingly beautiful and four heifers of untouched, that is, unyoked (*intacta*, 540) neck from among his herds. Then he is bidden to set up four altars at the lofty shrines of the goddesses (the wood nymphs), drain the sacred blood from their throats and leave the bodies of the animals within the leafy grove. On the ninth day, he is supposed to send funeral offerings of Lethean poppies to Orpheus, slay a black sheep and revisit the grove. Finally, he is to placate Eurydice by slaughtering a calf. But on returning to the grove, he sees a miraculous portent, *dictu mirabile monstrum* (4.554):

arising from the liquefied flesh of the oxen are bees, buzzing and surging forth from the stomachs and ruptured sides. The bees, streaming out in vast clouds, settle together on a tree-top and 'hang from its pliant branches in grape-like cluster', *lentis uvam demittere ramis* (4.558).

Vergil's sources

For the first part of the book (4.8–314), the two main extant sources for Vergil's bee lore appear to be Varro and Aristotle.[10] Varro's agricultural treatise, *De re rustica*, was published in 37 BCE, approximately eight years before the completion of the *Georgics*. The influence of this work is apparent throughout Vergil's bee account. For example, the poet closely follows Varro (*Rust.* 3.16.6) in describing the fragrant herbs planted around the hive (*G.* 4.30–2), the need to find a hive location free from any startling echoes (4.50), and the peculiar notion of drawing an unruly swarm back to its hive with balm and by beating cymbals (4.64). Varro observes that bees obey their leaders at a trumpet-like sound (*Rust.* 3.16.9): *iique duces conficiunt quaedam ad vocem ut imitatio tubae*. Vergil echoes Varro's language (*G.* 4.72),[11] which he adapts for the description of the sound (*vox*) as *fractos vox sonitus imitata tubarum* ('a sound imitating the broken blasts of trumpets'). Elsewhere Vergil relates how the beekeeper can easily quell the battle of the bees 'by throwing a little dust' (*pulveris exigui iactu*, 4.87) to settle the swarm, which is a conscious transformation of Varro's phrase *pulvere in eas iaciundo* (*Rust.* 3.16.30).

Many specific bee details found in Aristotle also surface in Vergil (*G.* 4.194–6), who follows the naturalist-philosopher, for instance, in maintaining that bees raise up tiny stones as ballast to steady themselves in storms (*Hist. an.* 626b29).[12] Both authors also refer to the divine nature of bees, the guard duty of the older bees and the silence of the hive as the bees drift off to sleep. Vergil sticks closely to Varro and Aristotle in minor details, although his poetic imagination organizes, and transforms the overall effect of, the source material.[13]

Vergil's sources for the *bougonia* are otherwise much more obscure about salient details. Varro twice claims that bees can spring from oxen (*Rust.* 2.5.5, 3.16.4), but he supplies no details of the process. Aristotle, too, though he believes in spontaneous generation (*Hist. an.* 5.1.13, 17 *et passim*),[14] does not describe *bougonia* as one of the ways bees are produced. He does, however, report that some think bees gather their young from the flower of the *kallyntron*, the 'broom' or 'brush' (*Hist. an.* 5.21). Vergil again follows Aristotle on this point and emphasizes the sexless nature of bees (4.200).

The Greek poet Nicander (second century BCE) is widely believed to have been Vergil's primary source for the end of *Georgics* 4.[15] His lost *Mellisurgica* dealt exclusively with bees, while a reference in his *Theriaca* (741–2) not only asserts that bees are engendered in the rotting carcasses of bulls, but that wasps arise from horses.[16] Ovid also writes of hornets arising from horses, but states specifically that in *bougonia* choice bulls slain in sacrifice are to be buried in a ditch: *in scrobe delectos mactatos obrue tauros* (*Met.* 15.364). Here Ovid describes a well-known practice, *cognita res usu* (365), yet he introduces this burial detail not present in Vergil, which suggests the existence of a variant (ritual) form of *bougonia*.

Egyptian considerations

Scholars generally have postulated an Egyptian origin for the belief in ox-sprung bees.[17] When he introduces the rite in his narrative, Vergil himself traces the practice to Egypt (G. 4.285–94).[18] The Old Testament story of Samson immediately comes to mind (Judges 14:14), in which honey is found in the carcass of a lion. Some think this tale may provide a key to the *bougonia* myth. If the notion originated in Egypt, where excessive heat quickly desiccates carcasses, a wandering swarm may sometimes have been observed inhabiting a corpse.[19] The *Historiae mirabiles*, once attributed to Antigonus of Carystus in the third century BCE but now more problematically dated,[20] had located the practice in Egypt; and, in what would be a forerunner of Ovid's description, the author relates how bulls are buried with only their horns exposed (19.1). Subsequently, once the horns are sawed off, bees allegedly arise, presumably from the interred head of the bull.[21] Columella (first century CE) uses the Carthaginian writer Mago (second century BCE), whose works were translated from Punic into Latin by order of the senate and later into Greek but are now lost in all three languages.[22] Mago like Vergil records how bees can be generated in springtime from a slain bull (*Rust.* 9.14.6). But Mago also apparently told how ox paunches could be used by themselves for the process of *bougonia*. Pliny seems to elaborate on this tradition when he relates how ox bellies covered with mud could engender bees (*HN* 11.23).

This variant *bougonia* may be connected to the Egyptian practice of the burial of the bull god Apis. Although there is a long tradition of beekeeping in Egypt (for example, horizontal hives are depicted on stone bas-reliefs as early as 2400 BCE),[23] no pre-Alexandrian link exists between bull sacrifice and the generation of bees. Perhaps the connection arose from equating Latin *apis*, 'bee', with the name of the Egyptian bull god Apis.[24] By Hellenistic times, 'ox-born' had become a common poetic epithet of bees, as evidenced by references in Meleager, Bianor, Erycias, Strato and possibly even Callimachus.[25] The fact that Aristotle does not mention *bougonia* as a means of engendering bees suggests that he did not know of the process. Indeed, before Aristotle there is only tenuous evidence for this practice. The Corinthian poet Eumelus is said to have written a now lost *Bougonia* in the eighth century BCE (n. 2 above), but it may only have detailed aspects of cattle procreation and made no reference to bees at all.[26] In the same place, Columella also reports that a certain Democritus, like Mago and Vergil, described a *bougonia*, but Columella does not set out the process. He may be referring to the Democritus who wrote a treatise on the *Causes of Animals* (Αἰτίαι περὶ ζῴων) in the fifth century BCE, yet there is no mention of bees in its surviving fragments.[27] In fact, this Democritus may be the well-known Egyptian author Bolus of Mendes, who wrote in the third century BCE (cf. Columella, *Rust.* 7.5). The only other pre-Aristotelian evidence for the *bougonia* concerns an Archelaus who is named in the work attributed to Antigonus of Carystus (*Hist. mirab.* 19.4) and the treatise of Varro (*Rust.* 3.16.4). This Archelaus is apparently not the fifth-century BCE Macedonian king.[28] Referring to *bougonia*-related phenomena, Antigonus says that Archelaus of Egypt spoke to Ptolemy about scorpions arising from crocodiles. This Archelaus should probably be identified, then, as the third-century BCE poet who wrote on natural wonders, including an *Idiophyê* ('Strange Creatures').[29] In Varro, the Archelaus who maintains that bees are 'the roaming children of a dead cow' (βοὸς φθιμένης πεπλανημένα τέκνα) is most likely the same writer. If these early sources are discounted, then, it is more plausible to believe that Aristotle was ignorant of *bougonia*.

The idea of *bougonia* involving burial either emerged or became popular at Alexandria during the third century BCE. At that time, the cult of Serapis (Osiris-Apis) was established and promoted there by Ptolemy Soter, and the god came to be worshipped primarily by Greeks.[30] Furthermore, through religious syncretism the Greeks began to equate Dionysus with Osiris, largely because of the similarities between the story of the infant Dionysus' mutilation by the Titans and his subsequent rebirth, on the one hand, and the saga of Osiris' dismemberment and eventual resurrection (Plut., *De Is. et Os.* 364F), on the other. This tradition of Dionysus' violent death and rebirth is central to Orphic beliefs and the Orphic theogony.[31] Connections were also made between Apis and Dionysus, since Bacchic-like fawnskins and thyrsoi were used by the participants in the bull's burial (Plut., *De Is. et Os.* 364E). In addition, the Greeks called Dionysus 'born of a bull', βουγενής (Plut., *De Is. et Os.* 364 F).[32] As a result, the hybrid deity Serapis inevitably became associated with Dionysus and, presumably, also with the Orphic cult, since the belief existed that Orpheus had brought the rites of Dionysus (as a manifestation of Osiris) from Egypt to Greece (Diod. Sic. 1.23.1-2). The variant burial practice (or myth) of the *bougonia*, then, may have developed in Egypt during the third century BCE with complex associations evolving among Serapis, Dionysus and the Orphic cult. The connection between bees and Orphic ideas will be treated further below (pp. 96-7).

Vergil's *bougonia*

Later evidence elucidates both Vergil's first and second descriptions of the *bougonia*. A millennium after Vergil, the anonymous *Geoponica*, an eclectic Byzantine agricultural collection produced for Emperor Constantine VII Porphyrogenitus, contains the most elaborate surviving account of the *bougonia*, which had been written by Florentinus in the third century CE. Most importantly, Florentinus' description is the only one whose general details correspond with Vergil's first description. Whether he is borrowing from an independent ancient source or merely recounting a later modified version of Vergil's description is unknown. The passage presents the practice of *bougonia* as an ongoing apicultural procedure, not as a religious ritual. Florentinus also claims, for instance, that clean white cloths dipped in pitch are used to close the bull's apertures and that the door and window of the hut are covered with strong clay to keep out the wind and air.[33] He adds that on the eleventh day, when the hut is reopened, bee clusters will be found and only the horns, bones and hair of the bull will remain. Finally, he explains the belief that so-called king bees are produced from the bull's brain, while the other bees arise from the flesh. Florentinus' details, then, appear to be post-Vergilian embellishments attempting to rationalize an ancient practice.

The question is whether Vergil's first account of the rite, though much more complex and detailed than previous descriptions, may be simply an intermediate stage in the evolution of the Egyptian burial *bougonia* that culminates in Florentinus' grand treatment.[34] Perhaps, but only if immuring a bull within an enclosure amounts to a symbolic entombment, and even then, the case is weak. The lack of earlier accounts, even fragmentary ones, prevents us from seeing a linear connection and systematic development of a single rite, complete with vestiges indicating the cudgelling of the bull, the construction of the building and other important details. In the absence of such clues, Vergil appears to preserve an independent tradition, presumably from an entirely different source that later merged with an account of the Egyptian *bougonia*.

Vergil's first description

Vergil's first description of the *bougonia* must now be considered in detail. The selection of a suitable site for the structure (*G*. 4.295) recalls the process of locating a good home for one's bees, described earlier in the book (8–32). The instructions for building the enclosure (nowhere in this passage called an altar) parallel the earlier stipulations for furnishing an ideal hive (33–6). This analogy is appropriate, since the hut eventually serves as a temporary home for the bees, and the strewing of the flowers and herbs around the slain bull becomes, then, yet another step towards creating conditions desirable for a hive.

A just-maturing bull is selected for the slaying, presumably because of the vitality of its life-force (cf. Hor. *Od* 3.13). The insistence on plugging up the animal's orifices before bludgeoning it to death is probably an attempt to preserve the soul within the carcass, as the importance of keeping the hide intact emphasizes. Eventually, the soul of the slaughtered bull is transformed into the soul of the bees. Ovid saw this connection when he writes of the *bougonia, fervent examina putri / de bove: mille animas una necata dedit* ('swarms [of bees] issue from the putrid bull: one life snuffed out gave forth a thousand souls', *Fast*. 1.379–8).

Earlier in *Georgics* 4, Vergil describes the divine nature of bees and notes that they share in the universal life-spirit, the *anima mundi* (219–27). The ancient belief that winged creatures not only resembled human souls but in fact were human souls is reflected in Greek ψυχή, both 'soul' and 'butterfly'. The souls on their way to rebirth, however, were called μέλισσαι, 'bees',[35] as were the priestesses of Persephone and Demeter,[36] which in turn reinforces the idea that the *bougonia* is a twofold rite of both death and regeneration.[37]

In *Aeneid* 6, Vergil espouses Pythagorean philosophy and the Orphic mysteries in which metempsychosis, the transmigration of souls, is developed as a means by which a spirit can return to life on earth after an underworld journey. The *bougonia* itself, then, giving rise to a myriad of bee-souls, underscores Orpheus' possibilities for renewal in a future life. The Lethean poppies offered to Orpheus at the end of *Georgics* 4 also support this conclusion. Their soporific qualities are similar to those of the waters of the river Lethe from which souls drink to forget their past existences before being reborn.

In Vergil's first description, we must consider the pounding of the bull apart from the need to ensure the proper entrapment of the soul because continuing the beating after death appears to aim at hastening the process of decay, which will engender the swarm. Though the pounding of the bull has no exact parallels in Graeco-Roman religious tradition, physical striking is an aspect of the festival of the Lupercalia, in which the whipping of participants was thought to ensure their fertility and drive off hostile influence.[38] Interestingly, Vergil's description of the molten flesh of the bull battered by the violence of man is analogous to his conjured images of nature's violence at the end of *Georgics* 3, where a plague dissolves the viscera of animals (3.484). The symptoms of the plague-stricken bull prefigure those of the bull prepared for the *bougonia* – the breath (*spiritus*) of the diseased bull is blocked by its own parched tongue, its nostrils gush blood in being denied their normal function and eventually its innermost bones begin to liquefy as fever courses through its body. These same conditions of heat and moisture will give rise to life in the *bougonia*.

Vergil's second description

Vergil's second description of *bougonia* differs significantly from his first. In the second description, the practice is ceremonial and ritualistic. The details about building the structures, here called altars (*G.* 4.541), are omitted. The procedure involving one bull is transformed into a multiple animal sacrifice in which no bludgeoning is included. In fact, the draining of blood from the beasts' throats seems antithetical to the first version's insistence on keeping the body intact. Collecting the sacrificial animal's blood in bowls, though, is a common feature of Greek and Roman rituals, notably Homeric burial rites, with which this ceremony appears to be closely allied.[39] In a requisite part of the burial rite, the funeral feast, many animals are slaughtered, just as in Vergil's account.

The graphic description of such a sacrifice may be related to the notion that the deceased person vicariously partook of the meal.[40] However, no feast occurs here, since the flesh of the bull needs to putrefy, and since, as Servius says, the sacrifice is an *animalis hostia* ('animate sacrificial victim') where the god receives only the *anima*.[41] The fact that nine animals are involved in Vergil's sacrifice (the tenth is slain on returning to the grove) may relate to the giving of funeral offerings to Orpheus on the ninth day. The rite may also be akin to the Ninth Day Feast, *cena Novemdialis*, celebrated after the occurrence of unusual prodigies.[42] Vergil's rite, then, anticipates the *monstrum* of the *bougonia*, and it is important to observe that the word *monstrum* can describe a portent that guides men to sites in order to found cities.[43]

Though the sacrifices are offered at the shrines of the goddesses (the wood-nymphs), the bulls presumably are used to pacify the male divinities, while the heifers of 'unyoked' neck (*intacta*, that is, untainted by labour) propitiate the female divinities; the sacrifice of the black sheep is intended for Orpheus and/or the god of the underworld.[44] Here the modified rite takes place after the rising of the Dog-star, that is, around the summer solstice (4.425). This timing contrasts with Vergil's first description, which insists on its taking place in early spring and points to the *bougonia* as, ultimately, a fertility rite in which life arises out of death. Nonetheless, Vergil's second description maintains the harmony of life and death through its language: the rite's fatal instruction, *demitte cruorem* ('drain the blood', 542), is echoed by the life-affirming image, *uvam demittere* ('to hang in a cluster', 558). This final image of the bees hanging from the trees in grape-like clusters appears to derive from Varro, who contends that bees exhibit this behaviour, but only just before sending out a new swarm to colonize (*Rust.* 3.16.29). Here another foundation association emerges.

It remains to explain why Vergil creates a twinning effect by deliberately linking Aristaeus and Orpheus in novel ways and by then framing them with the two descriptions of the *bougonia*. Both Aristaeus and Orpheus have Apollo as their father, which makes them half-brothers.[45] Both exhibit an excessive desire for Eurydice that eventuates in tragedy. Aristaeus' sexual crime, his lubricious pursuit of the maiden that causes her death, is related only by Vergil.[46] This outrage leads to the contagion that destroys all his bees. The sexless nature and purity of the bees cannot tolerate their master's turpitude.[47] Orpheus' uncontrollable passion, his madness (*furor*) as Eurydice calls it (G. 4.495), compels him to violate Proserpina's condition by looking back at his wife. Aristaeus' actions lead to Eurydice's first death and Orpheus' to her second. Aristaeus' journey to his mother's underwater realm, also unique to Vergil, establishes a parallel to Orpheus' underworld adventure.[48] Both tales, then, feature the 'conquest of death' theme. Aristaeus finally asserts his mastery of death by performing the *bougonia*, while Orpheus fails first to resurrect his wife and then to ward off the fatal blows of the maenads; yet he achieves a brief afterlife on earth as his disembodied head continues to lament as it floats down the Hebrus River.

Both are culture heroes, benefactors of mankind. The civilizing Aristaeus is credited with the development of beekeeping,[49] while Orpheus is honoured for refining music and song to a high art capable of even controlling nature. So, too, both are linked to fertility rites. Orpheus is incorporated into one, the *sparagmos*, as his body parts are scattered through the fields: *discerptum latos iuvenem sparsere per agros* (G. 4.522).[50] Aristaeus, on the other hand, is responsible for the life-giving *bougonia*.[51] As the originator of a kind of sacrificial practice, Aristaeus becomes a Prometheus figure, re-establishing the relationship between gods and men.[52] The fertility aspects of *sparagmos* and *bougonia* are now emphasized in a myth which fuses both rites. Commenting on *Aen.* 1.430, Servius relates how 'Melissa', a priestess of Ceres, had learned the goddess's mysteries. When Melissa refused to reveal them to a group of probing women, she was brutally torn to pieces. In punishment, Ceres besieged the women with a plague, and then made bees arise from Melissa's dismembered parts. This aetiological myth, or a similar one, apparently motivated Vergil's decision to construct parallel accounts of the two heroes.

Vergil at work

The ending of the *Georgics* has puzzled critics: what purpose is served by ending the poem with the *bougonia*? Farrell 1991: 262–70 argues convincingly that Vergil's Aristaeus epyllion is based on Homeric episodes that introduce myths or descriptions, which were interpreted by ancient commentators as allegorical cosmogonies. For example, Vergil's interview between Aristaeus and Cyrene is modelled on both of Thetis' meetings with Achilles in the *Iliad* (1.357–427, 18.65–137). The first meeting includes a speech (1.396–406) in which Achilles encourages his mother to speak to Zeus on his behalf. This passage also refers to an earlier rebellion against Zeus by Hera, Athena and Poseidon, which Thetis and Briareus had helped Zeus put down, a rebellion that threatened the cosmic order (cf. Romer's chapter, p. 58, in this volume). The grammarian and rhetorician Heraclitus (first century CE), an allegorist, associates the five gods (Zeus, Thetis, Hera, Athena, Poseidon) and Briareus with cosmic elements and elemental forces, and he reads the rebellion as an allegorical cosmogony (*QH* 25). In due course, the second meeting between Achilles and Thetis motivates the sublime description of Achilles' shield (*Il.* 18.478–613), which already was interpreted in antiquity as a representation of the cosmos. If the shield does represent the cosmos, then the creation of the shield is a cosmogony. In both cases, Homeric scholiasts – likely known to Vergil[53] – treated related events, which followed in the narrative structure, as allegorical cosmogonies.[54]

Vergil recognized how these two interviews with Thetis functioned in the narrative structure of the *Iliad*. They introduce episodes of allegorical cosmogony, and Vergil then used the meeting between Aristaeus and Cyrene in the same way to introduce the encounter with Proteus (*G.* 4.387–529). That encounter, in fact, is based on *Od.* 4.351–572, which the scholiasts also read as an elemental cosmogony. Proteus' 'very name suggests the primordial, particularly the primordial matter out of which the organized universe was ultimately composed',[55] and the rhetorician Heraclitus read the various forms of the Homeric Proteus as representing symbolically the four Empedoclean elements that combine to create primordial matter and the principle of mind, which carry over to Vergil's account. Since Vergil's abundant pattern of Homeric allusion in the latter part of *Georgics* 4 is heavily skewed towards allegorical readings of cosmogony, it is likely that the *bougonia* ritual itself was designed originally as an allegorical cosmogony, much as it was read centuries later by Porphyry (*De antr. nymph.* 18.9–15): 'ox-born bees are souls descending to genesis'.[56]

The Indo-European myth of creation

The parallels between Vergil's *bougonia* rite and the IE myth of creation can now be set out. Lincoln reconstructs an IE version (accepted by Polome and Puhvel), which involves a set of divine twins *Manu, 'Man', and *Yemo, 'Twin'.[57] *Manu sacrifices *Yemo and fashions the heavens and earth and the three social classes from his brother's body. At this point, two mythic variants appear. The Indo-Iranian version has an ox, or bull, which is also sacrificed, and from this beast all the species of the plant and animal world arise. In this myth, we encounter an original, grand version of a central feature of the *bougonia* ritual, which becomes reduced and localized in individual cultures that independently adapt the IE myth for their own purposes. It is this unusual feature of plant and animal generation that suggests the myth of the *bougonia* may be a pared-down reflection of the IE creation myth, in which a primordial blood sacrifice is offered to generate life throughout the world. And, interestingly, the Indo-Iranian account also contains *sparagmos*, as Yima 'Twin'[58] is brutally dismembered by his brother. Although precise parallels probably should not be insisted on, Aristaeus, who first performed the *bougonia* can be interpreted as a *Manu figure, and Orpheus can be viewed as the first victim, with his *sparagmos* mirroring Yima's mutilation in the Indo-Iranian account.

In the European version, however, a cow appears and nurtures the twins before the act of creation. Lincoln has postulated that Romulus and Remus are a reflex of these IE divine twins.[59] The Romans merely substituted the truculent she-wolf for the cow to underscore their own military might. Romulus assumes the role of the first sacrificer, *Manu. Etymologically, Romulus' name is a back-formation from the city of Roma (once Ruma) and thus is not cognate with *Manu. But Remus' name is derived from PIE *Yemo, where 'the initial *y- has changed to r- under the influence of Ruma, Roma, and Romulus'.[60] Remus is, then, the twin that serves as the first sacrificial victim. And as the founding of the city is an act of creation, he is sacrificed, in effect, so that the city of Rome might be established.[61] No animal sacrifice, however, occurs in this version.[62] Practices change over time, and 'human-animal sacrifice gave way to animal sacrifice, which again yielded to vegetable or liquid offerings in some locales'.[63] There appear to be two linked reflexes of the original IE cosmic creation myth, one of the *bougonia*, which descends directly from it, and the other of Romulus and Remus, which, with every related act of sacrifice, transforms that same myth into a city foundation myth.

Conclusion

Unlike the Egyptian burial *bougonia*, Vergil's first and second descriptions of the *bougonia* may have deep roots in Indo-European culture. Vergil's first description appears to portray an apicultural practice, which is accompanied by a narrative myth (the Aristaeus-Orpheus epyllion) and concludes with Vergil's second description. At the very least, his two descriptions strongly suggest a connection with the Indo-European creation myth.

Vergil's careful use of bee sources also indicates that his first description is not simply a poetic construct but a detailed account reflecting a traditional practice in ancient apiculture, even though the tradition scarcely survives and derives from barely uncoverable evidence. Vergil's first description is a didactic, mainly secular account of the practice of *bougonia*, while his second description has a markedly religious character:

not only does he require altars to be set up at the shrines of the wood nymphs, but he also recasts his first description to include religious elements of fertility, conciliation and funerary ritual.

What Vergil could not know, however, is that the *bougonia* ritual, as described by him, also re-enacted, on every occasion of the related sacrifice, the re-founding of the Roman people, essentially as a sublimely allegorical cosmogony. At the same time, he also preserved the reminiscence of an IE ritual, which, in a parallel reflex, was later transformed and historicized into the Romulus and Remus legend. In this way, the myth behind the *bougonia* ritual can be read as the ultimate foundation myth.[64]

Notes

1. Otis 1964: 146 asserts that the *Georgics* is a serious tribute to rural life but not to be considered an actual guide to farmers. In his view, the agricultural subject matter is generally accurate, but the poem's higher purpose is concerned with man's relation to nature and with cycles of life, death and rebirth. Conte 2001 by contrast sees in Orpheus and Aristaeus a rejection of elegiac poetry in favour of the *Georgics*'s *durus labor* in the service of the new Augustan cultural-literary program.

2. Although scholars commonly use the term *bougonia* to refer to this rite, the word does not occur in classical Greek literature and occurs only twice in Latin sources. The title *Bugonia* is cited by Varro *Rust.* 2.5.5 for an anonymous work, which is attributed to Eumelus (eighth century BCE) in Jerome's Latin translation of Eusebius' *Chronicle* 1255. See Mosshammer 1979: 198.

3. All these animals play a role in one version or another of related myths that have descended from an original shared PIE myth.

4. Osten-Sacken 1894 championed the now often cited notion that drone-flies (*Eristalis tenax*), which supposedly lay their eggs in carrion, were mistaken for honeybees because of their similar appearance. Nonetheless, Osten-Sacken's theory about mis-observation giving rise to the myth of *bougonia* assumes that the absence of honey and the behavioural differences between drone-flies and bees went undetected by the ancients. For a refutation of his ideas, see Kitchell 1989: apparently, drone-flies do not lay their eggs in animal flesh but 'in stagnant water rich in organic matter' (197). Still, *bougonia* could be accounted for by a double confusion in ancient times between bee larvae and blow-fly maggots (which do inhabit carrion) and between bees and droneflies; see Davies and Kathirithamby 1986: 65.

5. Osorio 2020a–b appeared too late to be given full consideration here. His title shows, however, that his focus differs from mine. Osorio 2020a explains the scientific credibility of *bougonia* for Vergil and his audience: 'I propose that Vergil's descriptions of *bugonia* in *Georgics* 4 (308–11 and 554–8) draw on Stoic theories of generation, according to which the heating properties of *pneuma* are responsible for any development of life'. We also hold different views about the evidence of the Egyptian *bougonia*.

6. Ancient authors generally refer to the leader of the hive as the king. The sex of the queen bee was not definitively determined until the seventeenth century by the Dutch naturalist Jan Swammerdam. On the 'mock-heroic' battle of the bees as a literary invention, see Wilkinson 1969: 101–2.

7. Cyrene's crucial role in the story is highlighted in Wallace 2003.

8. All translations here are my own.
9. There is play on the idea of 'footlessness' and the nominative plural *apēs* ('bees'), perhaps even a nominative singular *apes* (used by [Quint.], *Decl.* 13.16), since vowel lengths may be mismatched in such folk etymologies (n. 24 below).
10. For a discussion of Varro and Aristotle as primary sources for *Georgics* 4, see Williams 1979: 201–2, Thomas 1988b: 146–7; cf. Hardie 2020.
11. On specific Varronian echoes in Vergil's bee language, see Whitfield 1956: 111.
12. Kitchell 1988: 36–43 concentrates on how mistaken ideas about bees, as this one, were perpetuated in ancient times.
13. See Horsfall 2010 for a discussion of the nexus of interconnected imagery bees evoke in Vergil's works and in ancient texts more generally (religious, metapoetic, metaphorical, portentous, etc.).
14. On ancient sources for spontaneous generation, see Osorio (2020b: 35–40), and for Vergil as a possible reader of those sources, see ibid. 40–2.
15. Gow and Scholfield 1953: 215, Fraser 1951: 102.
16. The *Historiae memorabiles* (possibly containing evidence from the third century BCE), attributed to Antigonus of Carystus, notes that wasps come from horses and scorpions from crocodiles (19.3).
17. E.g. Gow 1944: 15, Shipley 1915: 97–100 and Williams 1979: 211. Kitchell 1989: 199–206 claims a Minoan origin for *bougonia*. Yet his arguments are based on the independent prominence of bees and bulls in Cretan culture (i.e. there is no link between bees and bull sacrifice in his evidence), and so his conclusions seem speculative and untenable.
18. Many modern scholars have even questioned whether the whole Aristaeus epyllion and the two *bougonia* descriptions were part of the first version of the poem. The short Egyptian passage, according to Servius, is a remnant of a completely different ending to *Georgics* 4. In the original version, says Servius, Vergil sang the praises of Gallus, prefect of Egypt at that time. That ending was later censored by Augustus when Gallus died a dishonourable death, in 27 BCE. On the accuracy of Servius' claim, see the survey of scholarly debate in Wilkinson 1969: 325–6, Thomas 1988a: 13–16, Mynors 1990: 296.
19. For a discussion of the rapid mummification of animal corpses in arid climates and their possible conversion into hives, see Shipley 1915: 98–100. Cf. Herodotus' account of bees inhabiting the decapitated head of Onesilaus (5.114).
20. Dorandi 1999: xiv–xvii asserts that the work is an anonymous Byzantine compilation, but his argument has not yet won the day.
21. Although Herodotus does not mention *bougonia*, he relates how the Egyptians disposed of dead bulls by burying them with their horns protruding to mark the spot (2.41).
22. For the significance of Mago's text in the Roman translation project, see Feeney 2016: 51, 203–5.
23. The earliest clear evidence of beekeeping comes from Egypt, based on scenes depicting horizontal hives. Two of the oldest are a stone bas-relief in the sun-temple of Niuserre, dated to 2400 BCE, and a wall-painting in a tomb in the Valley of the Nobles from *c.* 1450 BCE. Both are sufficiently similar to suggest that beekeeping was a well-developed craft from very early times. See Crane 1983: 36.
24. The equation of Latin *apis* with the Egyptian Apis was made despite the difference in the initial vowel quantity: Chouliara-Raios 1989: 46.
25. The bee epithets that occur include 'ox-born', βουγενής; 'child of the ox', βούπαις; and 'ox-made', βουποίητος. See *Anthologia Graeca*: Meleager 9.363.13, Bianor 9.548.2, Erycias

7.363 and Strato 12.249.1. Callimachus frag. 383.4 Trypanis βουγενέων likely refers to bees, since that is its ordinary meaning in Hellenistic poetry.

26. Varro seems to refer to an anonymous *Bugonia* (*Rust.* 2.5.5) after he calls bees *bugenes*. No author is stated, and its content is not discussed. Furthermore, Varro's overall concern in the passage is with cattle generation. Eusebius (via Jerome) refers to Eumelus' *Bugonia* (*Chron.* 1255), but again the work's subject can only be guessed at. Kitchell 1989: 194 nonetheless connects the two references and insists that Eumelus' is our earliest evidence of the bee-generating ritual.

27. Florentinus, like Columella, cites Democritus as a *bougonia* source (*Geop.* 15.2). But modern scholars have generally regarded the attribution in both authors as suspect. See Richter 1957: 370, Osten-Sacken 1894: 40n.2, 73 and Gow 1944: 15. Kitchell 1989: 194, however, accepts the ancient evidence as pointing to the fifth-century natural philosopher.

28. Kitchell 1989: 194, with references.

29. The *Historiae memorabiles* also quotes Philetas, a possible contemporary of Archelaus, as an authority on 'ox-born' bees (19.2). He is apparently referring to Philetas of Cos, the scholar and elegiac poet who was the teacher of Ptolemy Philadelphus during his reign (285–247 BCE).

30. Griffiths 1974: 40–1. Griffiths 1974: 394 notes that Ptolemy Soter gave national patronage to the existing cult of Osiris-Apis at the Serapeum of Memphis and broadened its appeal considerably. Plutarch *De Is. et Os.* 362C–E asserts that the majority of priests explained the combined deity of Serapis by regarding Apis as the corporeal image of Osiris' soul.

31. For a brief, comprehensive summary of Orphic theogony studies, see Gantz 1993: 741–3.

32. On the tauric nature of Dionysus, see Eur., *Bacch.* 100 where 'bull-horned' is his epithet. See also the descriptions of Bacchus appearing like a bull to Pentheus (*Bacch.* 618–19, 920–2). 'Sprung from a bull' is applied to the god in Orph. fr. 297a7 Kern.

33. For the Greek text of Florentinus' *Geoponica*, see Shipley 1915: 100–1; for an English translation, Fraser 1951: 8–10.

34. On the interpretation of Vergil's first *bougonia* account as a 'perfected version' of the Egyptian one, see Habinek 1990: 210 and Wilkinson 1969: 268–9.

35. The Neoplatonist Porphyry of Tyre (third century CE) claims that only virtuous souls on the way to rebirth were called μέλισσαι (*De antr. nymph.* 19.1), and he quotes Sophocles in linking bees with souls: βομβεῖ δὲ νεκρῶν σμῆνος ἔρχεταί τ' ἄνω (*De antr. nymph.* 18.5 / fr. 795 Nauck). Cf. also Vergil's simile at *Aen.* 6.706–9, in which the souls massing at the River Lethe are compared to bees.

36. Porphyry, *De antr. nymph.* 18.6. A scholiast on Pindar says that the term μέλισσαι was usually applied to Demeter's priestesses but sometimes generalized improperly to all priestesses. See Cook 1895: 14. For the possible influence of Philetas' (lost) *Demeter* on *Georgics* 4, see Marinčič 2007: 28–38.

37. The myth of Demeter and Persephone and the *bougonia* share the core theme of rejuvenation as outlined in Worthen 1991: 8–9.

38. Fowler 1925: 262.

39. Mylonas 1948: 57.

40. Cf. *Il.* 23.34: 'All around the corpse of Patroclus the blood ran in flowing cupfuls'.

41. Servius, *ad G.* 4.540.

42. Anderson 1954: 132.

43. For example, the future site of Alba is revealed to Aeneas by a *mirabile monstrum*, a white sow with thirty piglets (Verg., *Aen.* 8.81).

44. Ogilvie 1969: 43.
45. Vergil does not explicitly say that Apollo is Orpheus' father. In fact, *Oeagrius Hebrus* (*G.* 4.524) suggests that he is the son of the river god. See Gantz 1993: 725 on the traditional ambiguity of Orpheus' parentage. The close link between the master musician Apollo and Orpheus is obvious.
46. Gantz 1993: 723.
47. For a discussion of the association of bees with purity, see Davies and Kathirithamby 1986: 69–70, and Bettini 1991: 199–202.
48. On the possible influence on Vergil of Theseus' *katapontismos* in Bacchylides 17, see Bettini 1991: 237–8.
49. Glauthier 2020 argues further that Aristaeus' story provides an aetiology for the genre of didactic poetry itself.
50. On the significance of *sparagmos* and its connection to Dionysiac cult, see Dodds 1960: xvi–xx.
51. Aristaeus has strong connections with *sparagmos*. His conjugal tie to Autonoe conjures up images of Pentheus' dismemberment. Autonoe helps lead the bacchants in ripping him limb from limb. In the Orphic theogony, Dionysus, Aristaeus' nephew, is torn asunder and devoured by the Titans. By marriage, then, Aristaeus is linked intimately to the *sparagmos* of Pentheus and Dionysus, and by blood to the fate of Orpheus.
52. On Aristaeus as a Promethean figure and on the Hesiodic/Orphic cosmogonic tension developed by contrasting Orpheus and Aristaeus, see Habinek 1990.
53. Farrell 1991: 264–5 thinks Vergil was guided by the tradition of allegorical commentary on the *Iliad* and the *Odyssey*. In antiquity, Vergil already had earned a deserved reputation for broad learning, detailed scholarship and conscientious artistry, while *Georgics* was singled out for careful writing (*Vita Verg.* 23–46).
54. In the first episode, Zeus represents the dominant element fire which is assailed by air (Hera), earth (Athena) and water (Poseidon). In the second, Achilles' shield is viewed as the image of the universe, and so its construction is the creation of the cosmos. For a detailed interpretation of these Homeric passages, see Farrell 1991: 267–9.
55. Farrell 1991: 266, with references. For a hermetic reading of time in Homer's *Odyssey*, see Austin's chapter in this volume.
56. In late Republican times, the cult of Mithras, which originated in Persia (Iran), was spreading rapidly in the Roman Empire. It is important to note that a central tenet of Mithraic beliefs held that the sacrifice of a bull recreated the cosmic act of creation. Common images show the god Mithras plunging a dagger into the side of a bull while the wound sprouts ears of grain and its tail transforms into stalks of wheat. After 67 BCE, Pompey's soldiers apparently introduced the cult to Rome when they returned from Cilicia in the east. On the astronomical and astrological significance of bull sacrifice in Mithraism, see Ullansey 1989 *passim*.
57. Lincoln 1975: 139 and Puhvel 1975: 153 appear to accept each other's conclusions on this matter; Polome 1980: 163 accepts the reconstruction by Lincoln (whose work he used).
58. The older figure of Avestan Yima = Sanskrit Yama, 'Twin': so Lincoln 1975: 129.
59. Lincoln 1975: 137–3 and Puhvel 1975: 152–5.
60. Lincoln 1975: 138, with n.73.
61. In one version of Romulus' death, the *sparagmos* tradition has been reapplied secondarily from Remus to him. He is cut up by irate senators who abscond with body parts hidden under their robes. See Puhvel 1975: 155.

62. Curiously, in the third century CE Solinus (*Coll. rer. mem.*1.18–19), who does not even name Remus, claims blood sacrifice was proscribed the very first time the Romans made their foundation sacrifice. Vanggaard 1971: 102–3 argues that because the founding myth of Rome alluded to the killing of Remus, the impiety of that act would have been recalled symbolically by a blood sacrifice. For the same reason, Romer 2014: 79–83 suggests that the original foundation sacrifice for Rome grew out of an earlier shepherds' ritual that, in all probability, did involve the sacrifice of a sheep, an act which was then suppressed both to avoid recalling the fratricide of Remus and to preserve ritual piety.
63. Lincoln 1975: 144–5, with n.89.
64. On bees as portents of city foundations see Griffin 1979 and Horsfall 2000: 64–70.

Works cited

Anderson, F. B. (1954), 'Cycles of Nine', *Classical Journal*, 50: 131–9.
Bettini, M. (1991), *Kinship, Time, Images of the Soul*, trans. J. Van Sickle, Baltimore: Johns Hopkins University Press.
Chouliara-Raios, H. (1989), *L'Abeille et le miel en Égypte d'après les papyrus grecs*, Ioannina: The University of Ioannina.
Conte, G. B. (2001), 'Aristaeus, Orpheus, and the *Georgics* Once Again', in Sarah Spence (ed.), *Poets and Critics Read Virgil*, 44–63, New Haven: Yale University Press.
Cook, A. B. (1895), 'The Bee in Greek Mythology', *Journal of Hellenic Studies*, 15: 1–24.
Crane, Eva (1983), *The Archaeology of Beekeeping*, Ithaca: Cornell University Press.
Davies, M. and J. Kathirithamby (1986), *Greek Insects*, Oxford: Oxford University Press.
Dodds, E. R. (1960), *Euripides: Bacchae*, Oxford: Clarendon Press.
Dorandi, T. (1999), *Antigone de Caryste: Fragments*, Paris: Les Belles Lettres.
Farrell, J. (1991), *Vergil's* Georgics *and the Traditions of Ancient Epic*, New York: Oxford University Press.
Feeney, D. (2016), *Beyond Greek: The Beginnings of Latin Literature*, Cambridge, MA: Harvard University Press.
Fowler, W. W. (1925), *The Roman Festivals of the Period of the Republic*, London: MacMillan and Co.
Fraser, H. M. (1951), *Beekeeping in Antiquity*, London: The University of London Press.
Gantz, T. (1993), *Early Greek Myth: A Guide to Literary and Artistic Sources*, Baltimore: Johns Hopkins University Press.
Glauthier, P. (2020), '*Bugonia* and the Aetiology of Didactic Poetry in Virgil, *Georgics* 4', *Classical Quarterly*, 69: 745–63.
Gow, A. S. F. (1944), 'BOUGONIA in *Geoponica* xv.2', *Classical Review*, 58: 14–15.
Gow, A. S. F. and A. F. Scholfield (1953), *Nicander, the Poems and Poetical Fragments*, Cambridge: Cambridge University Press.
Griffin, J. (1979), 'The Fourth *Georgic*, Virgil, and Rome', *Greece & Rome*, 26: 61–80.
Griffiths, J. G. (1974), *Plutarch's De Iside et Osiride*, Cardiff: The University of Wales Press.
Habinek, T. N. (1990), 'Sacrifice, Society, and Vergil's Ox-Born Bees', in M. Griffith and D. J. Mastronarde (eds), *Cabinet of the Muses: Essays on Classical and Comparative Literature in Honor of Thomas G. Rosenmeyer*, 209–24, Atlanta: Scholars Press.
Hardie, A. (2020), '*Vergilius philosophus*: Bees, the Divine, and the Roman Reception of Aristotle (*Georgics* 4.149–227)', *American Journal of Philology*, 141: 381–419.
Horsfall, N. (2000), *Virgil*, Aeneid 7: *A Commentary*, Mnemosyne Supplementum 198, Leiden: Brill.
Horsfall, N. (2010), 'Bees in Elysium', *Vergilius*, 56: 39–45.

Kitchell, K. (1988), 'Virgil's Ballasting Bees', *Vergilius*, 34: 36–43.
Kitchell, K. (1989), 'The Origin of Vergil's Myth of the Bugonia', in R. F. Sutton, Jr. (ed.), *Daidalikon: Studies in Memory of Raymond V. Schoder, S.J.*, 193–206, Wauconda, IL: Bolchazy-Carducci.
Lincoln, B. (1975), 'The Indo-European Myth of Creation', *History of Religion*, 15: 121–45.
Marinčič, M. (2007), 'Back to Alexandria: The Bees of Demeter in Virgil's *Georgics*', *Vergilius*, 53: 17–51.
Mosshammer, A. (1979), *The Chronicle of Eusebius and Greek Chronographic Tradition*, Lewisburg, PA: Bucknell University Press.
Mylonas, G. E. (1948), 'Homeric and Mycenaean Burial Customs', *American Journal of Archaeology*, 52: 56–81.
Mynors, R. A. B. (1990), *Virgil: Georgics*, Oxford: Clarendon Press.
Ogilvie, R. M. (1969), *The Romans and Their Gods*, London: Chatto and Windus.
Osorio, Peter (2020a), 'Stoic Physics in the *Bugonia* of Vergil', Abstract, Session 68: Ritual and Magic, paper 3, Annual Meeting, Society for Classical Studies, Washington DC, 3–5 January.
Osorio, Peter (2020b), 'Vergil's Physics of *Bougonia* in *Georgics* 4', *Classical Philology*, 115: 27–46.
Osten-Sacken, C. R. (1894), *On the Oxen-Born Bees of the Ancients*, Heidelberg: J. Hoeming.
Otis, Brooks (1964), *Virgil: A Study in Civilized Poetry*, Oxford: Clarendon Press.
Polome, E. C. (1980), 'The Gods of the Indo-Europeans', *Mankind Quarterly*, 21: 151–64.
Puhvel, J. (1975), 'Remus et Frater', *History of Religion*, 15: 146–57.
Richter, W. (1957), *Vergil, Georgica: Das Wort der Antike*, Munich: Huber.
Romer, F. (2014), 'Reading the Myth(s) of Empire: Paradoxography and Geographic Writing in the *Collectanea*', in K. Broderson (ed.), *Solinus – New Studies*, 75–89, Heidelberg: Verlag Antike.
Shipley, A. E. (1915), 'The "Bugonia" Myth', *Journal of Philology*, 36: 97–105.
Thomas, R. F. (1988a), *Virgil: Georgics*, vol. 1: *Books I–II*, Cambridge: Cambridge University Press.
Thomas, R. F. (1988b), *Virgil: Georgics*, vol. 2: *Books III–IV*, Cambridge: Cambridge University Press.
Ullansey, D. (1989), *The Origins of the Mithraic Mysteries*, Oxford: Oxford University Press.
Vanggaard, J. H. (1971), 'On Parilia', *Temenos*, 7: 91–103.
Wallace, A. (2003) 'Placement, Gender, Pedagogy: Virgil's Fourth *Georgic* in Print', *Renaissance Quarterly*, 56: 377–407.
Whitfield, B. G. (1956), 'Virgil and the Bees: A Study in Ancient Apical Lore', *Greece & Rome*, 25: 99–117.
Wilkinson, L. P. (1969), *The Georgics of Virgil: A Critical Survey*, Cambridge: University Press.
Williams, R. D., (1979), *Virgil: The Eclogues and Georgics*, New York: St. Martin's Press.
Worthen, T. D. (1991), *The Myth of Replacement: Stars, Gods, and Order in the Universe*, Tucson: The University of Arizona Press.

PART II
CELESTIAL DRAMA

CHAPTER 7
AN EARLY MORNING PERSON? ARISTOPHANES AND HIS STAR-STUDDED COMIC PROLOGUES
Gonda Van Steen

Introduction: Aristophanes' *Ecclesiazusae* and early morning divine performance

'Don't act like dishonest courtesans, who only remember their latest companions,' Aristophanes warns his public as his *Ecclesiazusae* draws to a close (μηδὲ ταῖς κακαῖς ἑταίραις τὸν τρόπον προσεικέναι, αἳ μόνον μνήμην ἔχουσι τῶν τελευταίων ἀεί, chorus speaking, 1161–2).[1] 'And don't hold it against me that the luck of the draw has put me onstage first' (μηδὲ τὸν κλῆρον γενέσθαι μηδὲν ἡμῖν αἴτιον, ὅτι προείληχ᾽, 1158–9). Read at face value, these lines voice Aristophanes' concern that the audience might favour one of his fellow contenders at the comic festival: the competitor's play, which will come on after his own *Ecclesiazusae*, may sway the easily swayed Athenians with the roar of its good laughs still fresh in their recollection at the time of the vote. At the beginning of the same *Ecclesiazusae*, however, Aristophanes revels in the early morning setting, when he describes Praxagora and her female neighbours preparing to depart for the assembly meeting in the wee hours of a new and promising day. The early morning setting works so effectively for Aristophanes that he lingers over it for nearly one third of the entire play. In a mirror-image scene intended to depict the Athenian men's rude awakening to new realities, Blepyrus, Praxagora's unwitting husband, is left to stumble around in the dark – in women's clothes – to take care of pressing business (311–73). Both the metatheatrical comment on the draw for position on the programme and the length of the prologue may indicate that the draw by lot took place at least a few days prior to the festival.[2]

Praxagora opens with an elaborate comic address to the lamp that she holds up high and introduces as a much-valued accomplice in her favourite night-time or other 'illicit' activities (illicit for women, that is, 1–18, such as sneaking wine or initiating sexual encounters). This lamp becomes unnecessary as the sun slowly rises. The varying indications of time with which Aristophanes has infused the script of his *Ec.* would have worked best theatrically and metatheatrically if the timing of their delivery coincided with the real-time daybreak at the morning performances of the festival day, whether at the City Dionysia or the Lenaea. This hypothesis must be subjected to closer scrutiny in the light of the early morning opening scene that is the hallmark of other Aristophanic comedies as well. *Acharnians*, *Clouds*, *Wasps* and *Lysistrata* are among those plays in which the situational 'logic' of the opening scene is much enhanced by the theatrical integration of the celestial phenomena that coincided with the actual performance time and experience.[3]

Not all scholars agree that in classical Athens a sequence of plays started at dawn proper.[4] Eric Csapo and William Slater have drawn attention to some of the lingering unknowns: the order of the dramatic contests and the number of days devoted to these contests. The conventional view is that the date of 11 Elaphebolion featured the five comedies of the Dionysia (though fewer in wartime). Three days then followed, with each day devoted to the production of a selected tragedian's three tragedies and satyr play (Csapo and Slater 1995: 107). Aristotle observed that tragedy tended to fall within 'a single revolution of the sun' (ὑπὸ μίαν περίοδον ἡλίου, *Poet*. 1449b13). Thus, the spectators' experience of a full day of attending plays coincided with the conventional stage representation of passing time (Wiles 2000: 123).[5] A basic synchronization of real time and performance time – and with it the theatrical integration of celestial or seasonal phenomena – was an attractive option available to the playwright. Revermann characterizes such a synchronization or temporalization as a 'degree of "naturalism" [that] strikes any audience as something artificial, superimposed, and manifestly linked to a playwright's "message"' (2006: 110).[6] Nonetheless, such characterizations of an otherwise theatrically viable and appealing choice should not deter us from testing the potential of performance time staying in sync with real time, or of the deployment of celestial bodies as natural props.

Clifford Ashby is one of the most vociferous scholars to rule out dawn-set performances. In his 1999 study, he devotes an entire chapter (118–27) to debunking the feasibility of plays beginning at the crack of dawn. Ashby's guiding comparison of the City Dionysia to Mardi Gras is hardly convincing, nor is his fanciful depiction of what is and what is not 'the Greek way':

> To follow a late night of drinking, singing, revelry, and lovemaking with a before-dawn walk to a chilly theatre is hardly the Greek way … This version fits the almost-universal pattern of sleeping-in on holidays … Given the comfort-loving, even hedonistic, traits of the Classical Athenians, this account better fits the occasion than does the more rigorous early-rising version. The latter would require a sleep-ridden, slightly hung-over citizenry to leave their warm beds in the predawn hours, perform an elaborate toilet, don their holiday finery – and then walk some distance to the theatre, where they would sit shivering in the gray dawn as they waited for the sun's rays to warm a wooden but stone-cold theatre.
>
> *118–20*[7]

Ashby asserts that 'it makes better sense' for the playwright 'to comment upon stage time only when it is markedly different from actual time' (121). But he mainly takes into account the light and heat of the sun at the exclusion of other markers of real time, and he deals with Aristophanes' comedies in only a single line, which is half-accurate:

An Early Morning Person?

'Aristophanes has three of his plays, *Wasps*, *Lysistrata*, and *Clouds*, begin at dawn' (121). How about *Acharnians*? And *Ecclesiazusae*? I will return to the latter, after restating the synchronizing option from a positive perspective.

The very real possibility of temporal overlap between the early morning scene depicted onstage and the start of a new festival day at sunrise prompts reflection on the relationship between Aristophanes' text and its historical performance, on the one hand, and phenomena visible in the skies above, on the other. As the Athenians and occasional foreign visitors settle in to watch the day's first play in the order determined by lot, they become an audience to an unknown comedy set in motion, but also to known celestial phenomena that are always – most of the time, reliably – in motion. Moreover, the predictable routine of thousands of people noisily arriving and settling down within a short span of morning offered the comic playwright ample scope to engage in metatheatrical comments. The preliminaries to the assembly meeting comically depicted in *Ecclesiazusae*, for instance, can be interpreted as a meta-reflection of the spectators taking their time to come together as a theatre audience, which was, in comical or imaginary circumstances, identical to the public of attendees at the assembly on the nearby hill of the Pnyx.[8] The connection is easily made because the theatre's seating area and arrangements and the layout of the Pnyx resemble each other. The audience *qua* voting body in the theatre largely overlapped with the ecclesiasts, the voting public of the institutional assembly. Moreover, once a year in the Athenian political calendar, the assembly met in the theatre instead of in its usual locale on the Pnyx. Aristophanes effectively drew on the overlapping identities of the Athenian citizenry in his *Ecclesiazusae* and, even more directly, in his *Acharnians*.[9] He makes these identifications explicit in a passage of *Knights* (163–5), in which the sausage-seller is promised political power over the Athenians in the audience, who are the same as the Athenians of the market, the harbour and the assembly (Redfield 1990: 317; Van Steen 1994: 217). Thus, the relationship between the *demos* gathering in physical theatre space, as it did in the seating area of the Pnyx, and its instant opportunity to act as an audience to early morning phenomena in the celestial theatre above invites new interpretive conclusions about some of Aristophanes' comedies.

I intend to search Aristophanes' eleven preserved comedies for dispersed and largely overlooked cues of stage time as cosmic time and to deduce new meanings from the (pre)dawn settings and other references that some of the plays share. It is especially in the realm of the comedies' reception and their history of reperformance that those cues and references have been ignored, even though they often affect the ways in which modern directors produce the ancient plays. Moreover, those vital constituents of some of the comedies have been underexplored both in text-focused studies and in performance-sensitive treatments of Aristophanes' work. To make a modest start, I aim to provide evidence of the Athenians' awareness of, and fascination with, phenomena visible in the vast open skies above the performance spaces that housed Aristophanes' comedies. I also point to added levels of signification that these phenomena lent to the historical performance. We may in this way uncover some remnants of a scripted role for the sky as co-actor, co-spectator and even co-director of the plays. If we admit the sky as an integral part of the *mise en scène*, we may also unveil an Aristophanes willing and eager to participate in a complex scheme of role-sharing on a cosmic, even sublime level.

Play within the play, stars among the stars

Ecclesiazusae was first performed near the end of Aristophanes' long and successful career. By its approximate date of 392 or 391 BCE,[10] the playwright had experimented with early morning opening scenes on at least four prior occasions. Up until *Ec.*, however, he had not yet stated (at least not in any of the nine previous extant comedies) the putative risk involved in coming on first, or the perceived advantage of presenting one's work later in the festival day. Nor had he commented upon the random draw that fixed the competing plays' scheduling. Here is a tease, then, for all students of Aristophanes: did he or did he not prefer to come on first, to exploit the comic potential and near-guaranteed humour in the *topoi* of Athenian tardiness and obsessive behaviour? Half of the preserved comedies' prologues point to the playwright relishing concrete depictions of the Athenians' busybody behaviour (*polypragmosyne*), their drive to get a piece of the action, or even of fellow-citizens' defecatory and other relief efforts.

His seeming predilection for predawn opening scenes renders Aristophanes' complaint in the finale of *Ec.* comically specious. Viewers, he warns, should not forget his excellent play just because it was performed first (*Ec.* 1158–9). To be assigned the day's first slot held distinct advantages, of which Aristophanes was undoubtedly aware, especially near the end of his three-decades-long career. Some plays that Aristophanes must have finalized well before the draw by lot took place might reveal some wishful thinking on his part, that is, a wish for his comedy to open the festival at dawn and so to reify the scripted early morning opening scene. The plays' comic prologues situate the unravelling plot in time and space – and take a few extra lines to do so while the theatregoers get situated. While establishing the conditions of the plot's time and space is one of the prologue's intrinsic functions, Aristophanes comes close to overusing it or (self-referentially) mocking it in *Ec.* If the playwright got his way, however, and had his comedy start before daybreak, then he alone could be sure about the timing of the opening lines' delivery and of the anticipated sunrise, as well as a metatheatrically charged interaction between the two. The possibility to play out the coincidence of real time, plot-time and cosmic time is the kind of advantage or *tour de force* that would appeal to many a stage producer. But what are we to make of Aristophanes' comedies that deploy the predawn opening formula but whose order in the festival day is not known?

Some Aristophanic plays make explicit theatrical and/or metatheatrical use of the predawn setting but, unlike *Ec.*, they do not suggest that they were assigned the day's earliest slot: *Acharnians, Clouds, Wasps, Lysistrata* and probably also *Peace*. All except *Clouds*, which represents Aristophanes' revised text of a lost script that won only third prize at the City Dionysia of 423 BCE, were staged at the festival of the Lenaea, which fell in the lunar month of Gamelion (usually equivalent to January/February of our solar calendar). By 440 BCE, the Lenaea, likely in origin a local event (though its site remains undiscovered), was transferred to the Theatre of Dionysus. Both *Lysistrata* and *Thesmophoriazusae* were performed in 411 BCE, but their productions' time of year is not firmly established. Most scholars position the *Lysistrata* performance at the Lenaea, in which case they reserve a slot at the City Dionysia of the same year for *Thesmophoriazusae*.[11] The two productions most probably would not have run in competition with each other. A brief investigation of the celestial constellations that accompanied the two comedies lends support to the traditional view (see pp. 113-14).

The main festival of the City Dionysia, for which the Theatre of Dionysus was the designated stage venue, started on the tenth of the Elaphebolion month (which usually corresponded with mid-February through the first week of April). The internal timing of *Peace* and especially of *Thesmophoriazusae* and *Plutus* is to be derived from very subtle and far from decisive allusions. *Peace*, which was performed at the City Dionysia of 421 BCE, constructs an implicit time frame for the action's progress. References to time are minimal, however, in both of the later plays, with *Ec.* being the most notable late exception. Overall, when indications of time are specific, they denote early morning hours, though not necessarily the play's first-in-line presentation time. The reverse might hold true, too: those comedies without an early morning setting to constitute their prologue, such as *Knights*, *Birds* and *Frogs*, also lack specific pointers to time of day or indicators of seasons or signs in the sky. The prolonged comic *praeteritio* (1–20) of *Frogs* (405 BCE), for instance, centres on trite opening jokes that reputedly lambaste the work of rivals, whose plays may or may not follow in the course of the same day. Nonetheless, the many uncertainties that plague the general performance record do not prevent us from accepting the following working hypothesis: Aristophanes repeatedly worked with his favourite opening, the early morning scene, in comedies that he planned to present at the mid- to late-winter Lenaea festival. He did so even when composing the bulk of any given work well before he knew the precise order in which it was to appear. I will return to this preliminary conclusion and address its importance shortly, after we sketch out some of those plays' opening scenes and their characteristic performative invocations.

Invocations and acts of swearing by Zeus are frequent occurrences in *Ec.*, as in all the comedies, except for the early *Acharnians*. They gain special meaning, however, by the end of the opening scene, which runs well beyond the prologue and into the first epeisodion. The extended opening scene lasts until Chremes, Blepyrus' neighbour, invokes Zeus at *Ec.* 377 and 378, and complains that he arrived too late at the assembly to collect his three-obol payment (380–1).[12] At this point of transition, the number of invocations of Zeus increases: Blepyrus calls it done, 'by Zeus' (μὰ τὸν Δί', 373) and Chremes calls on Zeus again at 382 and 390. Chremes' mid-scene arrival may not help to accentuate the formal opening of the first epeisodion, but it does effectively coincide with Zeus' prominent presence in the text and in the sky. We do not know whether *Ec.* was presented at the Lenaea or at the City Dionysia. The celestial position of Zeus/Jupiter by the inferred, possible date of 392 or 391 BCE may invite a different approach both to the question and to the answer. Jupiter had become a morning star in mid-October of 392/1 and remained visible as such through April. This meant that the planet was slowly rising in the sky while the audience was taking its seats. Measurements indicate that the shadow of Mount Hymettus to the east did not interfere with Jupiter's visibility for the masses seated in the southern-oriented Theatre of Dionysus.[13] Jupiter would have been more prominent (as a morning star) at the time of the Lenaea than at the Dionysia (cf. Sommerstein 1998: 7 and n.33).

Our analysis assumes a process of contextualization that is heavily invested in the Greeks' identification of individual Olympian gods with individual planets. The equation of Zeus with the planet Jupiter, for one, may strike some critics as problematic. Many scholars doubt whether the Greeks had already identified the major planets with their divine counterparts by Aristophanes' time. Standard scholarship insists that the connections between the planets and the gods commence with the mid-fourth-century BCE pseudo-Platonic dialogue *Epinomis* (987b–c), in which such formal connections are made explicitly, i.e. Jupiter = Zeus, Saturn = Cronus, Mars = Ares, Venus = Aphrodite and Mercury = Hermes (Dicks 1985: 146). The *Epinomis*, attributed to Philip of Opus, turns tract-like when introducing these important identifications, which are intended to prompt the Greeks, newly exposed to this real knowledge, to become better worshippers of the gods. Peter Green comments: 'The ... *Epinomis* virtually assumes a religion of the heavenly bodies: the stars are not only gods but overseers of mankind, living and provident' (2004: 246). But the lack of extant attestations prior to this forcibly constructed *terminus post quem* does not rule out that fifth-century BCE Athenians had already made the planet-deity identifications, and that these identifications pre-date the publication of the *Epinomis* or the mid-fourth century BCE. If Greek literary sources from the decades prior to the *Epinomis* that firmly posited the planets as avatars of the gods were extant, then the scholarly objections and reservations would instantly lose their force. And yet, given how much of ancient literature is lost, the chances are substantial that such written sources did exist but do not survive. Their author(s) may have influenced or may have communicated with perceptive playwrights such as Aristophanes. And it is even more likely that star-gazing Greeks identified the planets they knew well with familiar divinities long before writers codified the practice.[14]

Alan Sommerstein returns to the 'list' and meaning of what he calls the 'early-attested "catasterisms"' on two occasions in his commentary on Aristophanes' *Peace* 832–3: 'we become stars in the sky' (κατὰ τὸν ἀέρα ὡς ἀστέρες γιγνόμεθ᾽) ([1985] 2005: 173 [his translation], 206 [quotations]). Sommerstein considers the latter tenet to be a 'popular belief (not otherwise attested at so early a date)' that pivots on the idea that 'certain star-groups and constellations were originally men, women or animals to whom the gods had granted immortality'. He succinctly traces this belief from the beginnings of Greek literature down through the fifth century BCE, with the examples of Orion, the Pleiades, the Hyades, Ursa Major (= Callisto) and probably also Virgo and Bootes ([1985] 2005: 173 [quotations], 206). Of course, the sun and the moon were regarded as deities by most Greeks in the classical period.[15]

Peter Green opens up a broader perspective when he posits the question: 'What ... did catasterism, the translation to heaven of mythical figures – heroes, or later, human aspirants – actually *mean*?' (2004: 245, his italics):

An Early Morning Person?

The night sky was comfortingly familiar, and a reassuring help in need to sailors and farmers, as both Hesiod and Aratus remind us. Here, too, anthropomorphism and theriomorphism had been at work, reducing planets, constellations, the zodiac to familiar entities: Jupiter, Mars, Venus, Perseus, the Charioteer, Andromeda, Orion the Hunter, and various swans, bears, dogs . . . But how did an ancient viewer conceive these phenomena? . . . The moment we pose questions like this, we realize that there is no answer in visual terms.

2004: 245

Aristophanes might have been one to deliver such an 'answer in visual terms'. The passages from his extant comedies discussed here suggest that those identifications occurred early and that they modulated and even mediated theatrical and metatheatrical play. For some scholars, the late attestation of the identifications in the *Epinomis* will remain an insurmountable hurdle. But it pays to think past this hurdle, to let go of the preoccupation with the strict timing of written sources only, and to try to comprehend more fully Aristophanes' prologues and their cosmic effects. If we are to consider the comic and cosmic use of divinities anew, we will occasionally need to reiterate the ways in which the traditional readings of the plays have bolstered their own authoritative position, at the expense of a richer conception of a divinely interconnected cosmos.

Invoking the stars – the theatre of catasterism

A minimal but important invocation in the opening lines of Aristophanes' *Thesmophoriazusae*, which was staged at the City Dionysia of 411 BCE, provides comparative material. In the comedy's very first line, Euripides' kinsman calls on Zeus and wonders if the swallow, the harbinger of spring, is ever going to appear. This reference may point to a festival date that was closer to early March than to early April. In his first slightly longer repartee, then, Euripides draws an analogy between the eye and the solar disc (*Th.* 17). Jupiter, who in late February through early April of 411 BCE was apparent as a morning star, was about to vanish as the first light brightened. The planet would have remained visible up until a few minutes before sunrise. These movements of the sun and the stars, or, more specifically, Jupiter's heliacal rise, may have formed the real-world celestial background to the opening lines of *Thesmophoriazusae*, but only if this play was the one selected to kick off the new festival day.[16] Alternatively, Aristophanes could have used this later comedy as an opportunity to demonstrate his skill at 'plotting' a cosmic prologue and deftly orchestrating the parts of his celestial players. The poet's latest and longest early morning scene, that of his *Ec.*, generates self-referential and metatheatrical humour, but is also the final (preserved) show of his mastery of the conventions. Apart from the initial invocation, there is, admittedly, no further language to set up an elaborate early morning scene for *Thesmophoriazusae*. Nor is there a need for such, because Aristophanes had used that pattern in his *Lysistrata*, performed (in all likelihood) only a few weeks earlier. All Jupiter and the sun had left to do in *Thesmophoriazusae*, then, was to burn off some of the morning chill that made the kinsman express his longing for the first signs of spring with references that were of meteorological and seasonal interest but did not expand on the celestial markers. As in his later *Ecclesiazusae*, Aristophanes parodies an early morning assembly-style meeting fictitiously scheduled and attended by the women celebrating the Thesmophoria, but this meeting contributes less to set up a dawn scene. After all, it takes Euripides and his kinsman a long span of comic time (about a quarter of the play) to prepare for the latter's appearance at the meeting, which has just started when he finally arrives (*Th*. 279).

The role of seemingly casual invocations and acts of swearing by the gods' names also plays out in interesting ways in Aristophanes' *Lysistrata*, another comedy to open with an early morning scene (1–77). When the conversation topic of the women's 'typical' tardiness has run its course, the Spartan Lampito swears by the Twin Gods, that is, by the Dioscuri or Castor and Pollux, the brothers of Helen and special patrons of the Spartans (81; see also 206, 988, 1300). The cosmic dimensions become manifest when the spectator looks up and sees – and when the reader realizes – that in early January, Castor and Pollux appear prominently in the morning sky to the north-west; in 411 BCE, they showed beside the planet Saturn. If the argument for placing Aristophanes' *Lysistrata* at the Lenaea festival of 411 BCE needs further corroboration, this may be found in the play's internal reference to characteristic celestial phenomena of January.

A special kind of extended invocation may be detected in Aristophanes' *Plutus* (388 BCE). Although the performance date and time of this late play remain uncertain (Sommerstein 2001b: 1, 28–33), the protracted opening conversation between Chremylus and his slave Cario supplies some general cues: Chremylus has just returned from Apollo's oracle at Delphi and repeatedly names the god in his capacity as Phoebus, the sun-god (e.g. 39–40, 81). Throughout the question-and-answer exchange with Cario, Apollo shines his light on the characters' doddering minds as well as on the better part of the prologue. But these references to Apollo merely suggest that the sun was out in full and that, therefore, *Plutus* may not have been the first play of the day.

The opening scene of the first-prize-winning *Acharnians*, staged at the Lenaea of 425 BCE, takes up full forty lines: the protagonist Dicaeopolis vents his frustration as he sits waiting on the Pnyx for the assembly meeting to open. He complains that, as always, the apolitical mass does not show up on time and needs to be dragged away from the commercial distractions of the *agora*. When the self-important officials or the *prytaneis* finally show up, VIP-style late, Dicaeopolis cannot refrain from commenting: 'Well, here are the Presidents – at noon!' (ἀλλ᾽ οἱ πρυτάνεις γὰρ οὑτοὶ μεσημβρινοί, 40). But since the meeting has not yet formally opened, his choice of the adjective *mesembrinoi* to describe the 'Presidents' as 'noon-day *prytaneis*' must be read as hyperbole intended to reinforce the imperative that *all* attendees arrive early in the morning.[17] The jostling 'noon-day' *prytaneis* of the imaginary assembly might even be the same latecomers and troublemakers in the comedy's audience, arriving at the very moment that they are mentioned. Such a staged coincidence, based on the predictability of the behaviour of the high and mighty, would give Dicaeopolis and Aristophanes a first opportunity that day to poke fun at politicians in attendance (Van Steen 1994: 216).

An Early Morning Person?

The assembly meetings held at the beginning of *Acharnians* and again as a constitutive comical part of *Thesmophoriazusae* and *Ecclesiazusae* make for veritable caricatures of what a serious democratic assembly was supposed to be. Or perhaps the slow start that the assembly took on early winter or spring mornings was enough of a tradition to invite parody. Aristophanes' openings that enact early morning scenes may comically undermine the famous opening scene of Aeschylus' *Agamemnon* of 458 BCE. This level of tragedy-comedy dialogue and/or parody is accentuated by Dicaeopolis' portrayal of himself as an audience member waiting for a performance of Aeschylus to begin (*Ach.* 10). Dicaeopolis deliberately confounds his role as ecclesiast with that of spectator and the comedy's anticipated prolonged opening scene with a well-known one from Aeschylean tragedy, that of the watchman's speech in *Agamemnon* (1–39). Such layers of theatrical and metatheatrical interplay suggest that the speech's resonance in tragedy influenced comedy as well. Part of the speech's memorable success was, no doubt, its conflation of beacon light with the sunlight rising from behind the summit of Mount Hymettus to the east and also with the appearance of the appropriate (for the script) celestial bodies aka divinities in the Athenian sky (Worthen, unpub. a, b).

Aeschylus' *Agamemnon* was the key play for Bieber to establish a dawn opening time for tragedy, but she did not flesh out her arguments ([1939] 1961: 53; cf. Ashby 1999: 120). Instead, she referred to an older article by Allen 1938, in which he reviewed the scant evidence and the many diverging views and posited a compromise solution regarding the festival programme of the City Dionysia. Both studies are very dated, yet they have done much to perpetuate the following programme outline for the Dionysia: beginning in 487/6 BCE, the five competing comedies were allocated a festival day of their own, with one of them kicking off the sequence in the early morning. During the Peloponnesian War, this big day for comedy was cancelled and each one of the three remaining days of dramatic contests featured, in order, three tragedies, a satyr play and one comedy. Again, studies of time in Greek drama and of the theatrical processing of literal and notional time are much needed.[18] Of course, in our approach, this theatrical time is never severed from the actual performance space from which planets and constellations are visible depending on the time of day, the seasons and the passing of years. Aristophanic comedy may pose additional challenges to the tight links between theatre time and space, but it also solidifies those links for an audience in the know. With the unflattering comment about the 'noon-day *prytaneis*' in *Acharnians*, then, the poet deploys time to measure audience involvement as he comically tracks the temporal progression of the play. Thus, known facts about Aristophanes' prologues pose a variety of complications that take the plays well beyond conventional perceptions of, and restrictions on, performance time and space.

In *Wasps*, which won second prize in 422 BCE, Aristophanes revels in a long comic prologue while it is still dark outside and the main characters are sound asleep (1–137; cf. 365–6).[19] The slave and 'night watch' Xanthias describes his master Philocleon's restless sleeping habits, as he lives – and sleeps – in fear of missing his chance to convict the accused in the early morning meetings of the Athenian lawcourts (2, 4, 87–102). It would have been dramatically very effective if, in the course of Xanthias' detailed description, a sleepwalking Philocleon acted out some of the most graphic, 'nightmarish' scenes. According to Xanthias, the court-addicted Philocleon may just get up again with his first three fingers pressed together, as if he is already holding a voting pebble, 'by Zeus' (νὴ Δί', 97). In this first instance, Xanthias might even gesture towards the sky. The name of Zeus is repeated many times as the prologue draws to a close and the play makes the transition to the first epeisodion (134, 146, 169, 173, 181, 184, 186, 193, 205, 209, 217, 231, 254). This invocation may again have been more than a standard or casual way of addressing Zeus, since Jupiter was visible in the sky as an evening star in January of 422 BCE, when *Wasps* was produced at the Lenaea. Perhaps Xanthias' allusion to the new moon, or dark moon, is to remind the audience of Jupiter's night-time appearance. Because no new moon can occur during the Dionysia, which is a festival of early mid-month, this lunar reference subtly confirms the production's scheduling at that year's earlier festival. By the time of the Lenaea of 422 BCE, the twelfth to the fifteenth day of the lunar month of Gamelion, the moon had already passed its quarter phase and was waxing to become a full moon on the fourteenth to fifteenth.

Peace earned Aristophanes a second prize at the City Dionysia of 421 BCE.[20] At *Peace* 80, Trygaeus' spectacular early morning take-off on his dung-beetle proves successful. His destination is the realm of Zeus itself. Aristophanes carefully prepares his audience for a possible appearance of Jupiter (56–9, 62–3, 68–70, 77, 80–1, 104, 128, 132, 161). This is understandable, given that Jupiter was normally visible during the days of the Dionysia. In 421 BCE, however, the festival must have fallen on the unusually late date of 29 April. This date marks a time when the phase of the moon met the requirements of the festival, and the newly risen Jupiter was far enough away from the sun to be visible. A festival date in late March would have found the sky devoid of Jupiter. Upon Trygaeus' arrival, then, it is Hermes who answers the door (177–80). After all the anticipation about meeting Zeus, this plot twist makes for a perfect comic incongruity. In the initial conversation that leads to the key question of the whereabouts of the Olympian gods, Trygaeus learns that Zeus and the other divinities are not 'at home', where he expected to find them:

Trygaeus Now go and call Zeus for me.

Hermes Haw haw haw! You aren't even going to get near the gods. They're gone; they moved out yesterday.

Trygaeus Where on earth to?

Hermes 'Earth'?

Trygaeus All right, where?

Hermes Far, far away, right under the very verge of heaven.

Τρυγαῖος ἴθι νυν κάλεσόν μοι τὸν Δί'.

Ἑρμῆς ἰὴ ἰὴ ἰή,
ὅτι οὐδὲ μέλλεις ἐγγὺς εἶναι τῶν θεῶν·

An Early Morning Person?

φροῦδοι γὰρ ἐχθές εἰσιν ἐξῳκισμένοι.

Τρυγαῖος   ποῖ γῆς;

Ἑρμῆς   ἰδοὺ γῆς.

Τρυγαῖος   ἀλλὰ ποῖ;

Ἑρμῆς   πόρρω πάνυ;
ὑπ' αὐτὸν ἀτεχνῶς τοὐρανοῦ τὸν κύτταρον.

195–9

Zeus is not in the expected location at the expected time, since the festival event takes place on an equally unusual date in the Athenian calendar. A human being would not normally make the trip to Olympus; the Athenian public would only exceptionally find itself in the Theatre of Dionysus at such a late time in the season. Irregularities up above have repercussions below. Such abnormalities, which constitute a recurring theme in Aristophanes' *Peace* and *Clouds*, then symbolize the warped or strained conditions under war versus those of peace.

From a celestial perspective, the choice of κύτταρος (LSJ: 'cell of a honey-comb') in 199 is highly effective, in that the term metaphorically denotes the concave vault, dome or canopy of heaven and also evokes the colour of the light at dawn. The word οὐρανός, in turn, does not only mean 'heaven' generally, but also denotes the morning and the evening sky when they are coloured by the sun as it sits low on the horizon. In this sense, οὐρανός here reinforces κύτταρος: Jupiter, who has recently come down from Olympus, is gloriously appearing in the honey-coloured οὐρανός as the sun rises over Mount Hymettus (known to this day for its honey). Saturn/Cronus, too, is visible in the vast star field. Mercury/Hermes, however, is absent, that is, the planet has sunk below the horizon after an abortive spring apparition (when the planet was dimly visible low on the horizon, where it would have been noticed only by watchful observers). Indeed, Mercury/Hermes greets Trygaeus up on Mount Olympus, a realm invisible to the earth-bound audience. Venus and Mars have moved out of view. The disappearance of Mars/Ares from the evening sky around the first of February may have provided a peculiar celestial endorsement to those advocating the Peace of Nicias, which the Athenians and the Spartans negotiated during the winter of 422/1 BCE and agreed upon in the same spring in which Aristophanes presented *Peace*. Mars' absence leaves him out of the traditional celestial dynasty governing the stars and planets – that of Mars, Cronus and Zeus, present with or in Ouranos as Sky, the father of them all.[21]

The impact of the invisible Mars, however, is everywhere present through the lingering effects of war. The conversation between Trygaeus and Hermes continues on the topic of ubiquitous war and the apparent impossibility of retrieving Peace, with Polemos himself making a first, terrifying appearance (*Peace* 236–7). Trygaeus grabs Hermes' attention again when he insinuates that all the Olympian gods might be threatened by some evil (404). He readily clarifies: 'Well, the Moon and that nefarious Sun have been plotting against you for some time now and mean to betray Greece to the barbarians' (406–8). But the unknowing Hermes and spectator require further explanation:

Hermes What do they hope to accomplish by that?

Trygaeus Simple: we sacrifice to you and the barbarians sacrifice to them; so naturally they'd want us all annihilated, so they could take over the rites of the gods themselves.

Hermes So that's why they've long been clipping days and taking bites out of the year: pure chicanery.

Ἑρμῆς ἵνα δὴ τί τοῦτο δρᾶτον;

Τρυγαῖος ὁτιὴ νὴ Δία
ἡμεῖς μὲν ὑμῖν θύομεν, τούτοισι δὲ
οἱ βάρβαροι θύουσι. διὰ τοῦτ᾽ εἰκότως
βούλοιντ᾽ ἂν ἡμᾶς πάντας ἐξολωλέναι,
ἵνα τὰς τελετὰς λάβοιεν αὐτοὶ τῶν θεῶν.

Ἑρμῆς ταῦτ᾽ ἄρα πάλαι τῶν ἡμερῶν παρεκλεπτέτην
καὶ τοῦ κύκλου παρέτρωγον ὑφ᾽ ἁμαρτωλίας.

409–15

Jeffrey Henderson (1998: 481) clarifies the allusion with a reference to *Clouds* 615–26: 'the moon blames … calendar tampering on the Athenians'. The excerpt from *Peace*, however, comically denounces the thievishness and the treacherous behaviour of the moon and the sun, who 'have been engaged in filching for a long time now' and 'have been nibbling off (some) of their circle' (trans. Olson 1998: 159). Either the moon's monthly 'cycle' and the sun's annual 'cycle' (κύκλος) have been disturbed and/or an unusual series of prior lunar eclipses (or eclipses of the moon's 'disk') left the moon feeling short-changed and deprived of sacrificial goods.[22] Celestial phenomena, broadly conceived, might have generated popular as well as intellectual debate in Athens on the politicized subject of calendar reform. This discussion may be reflected in Trygaeus' comic presentation of a conspiring moon and sun, who may choose the side of the barbarians (among them, the Persians) hostile to the Greeks *and* to the Olympian gods.[23] Such a revolt might subvert not only the time-hallowed religious rites but also the very hierarchy of the gods. It might equal the nefarious effects that the disarray resulting from the Athenians' 'calendar tampering' is already causing. Sommerstein concludes: 'the irregularities [in the Athenian calendar] are regarded as offensive by the [Olympian] gods, who apparently do not realize that it is the Athenians who are responsible for them and instead blame them on the heavenly bodies' ([1985] 2005: 152).

Clouds, moon and sun

Aristophanes' *Clouds* features repeated allusions to lunar eclipses. Various jokes relate to the moon and to other celestial and meteorological phenomena. They comically shed light on the observation, acceptance or rejection of such phenomena in Socrates' theory and practice. In *Clouds* 584–6, the chorus leader warns the Athenians against provoking further heavenly disapproval of their political support of Cleon, one of Aristophanes' stock arch-enemies: 'the moon deserted her orbit, and the sun forthwith withdrew his wick and refused to shine for you if Cleon became general' (ἡ σελήνη δ' ἐξέλειπε τὰς ὁδούς, ὁ δ' ἥλιος / τὴν θρυαλλίδ' εἰς ἑαυτὸν εὐθέως ξυνελκύσας / οὐ φανεῖν ἔφασκεν ὑμῖν, εἰ στρατηγήσει Κλέων). The resentment of the celestial bodies has manifested itself in both a lunar and a solar eclipse, the poet asserts.

In *Clouds* 607–26, the chorus leader engages in another sustained reference to ominous eclipses, stated proofs of cosmic displeasure and the Athenians' lax – or, in reality, challenged – use of the lunar calendar (i.e. the civic or solar calendar's lack of accordance with the moon's phases). The moon's gripes in particular may thus originate in the contemporary conflict between the lunar calendar espoused by the archon and the solar calendar upheld by the council of Athens (Dunn 2007: 25–6). The concerned chorus leader is played by a male actor dressed as a female cloud, which comically claims direct access to, and expertise about, the moon (607). The chorus responds to the first reference of the lunar eclipse with an invocation of Apollo, the sun-god (595–6), to sustain the idea of complicity between moon and sun. Then the chorus leader picks up with a comic rationale on the moon's behalf, explaining why 'she' is angrily withholding her light from the Athenians:

> When we [i.e. the chorus of clouds] were ready to set forth on our trip here, the Moon happened to run into us and told us first to say hello to the Athenians and their allies, but then she expressed her annoyance at the awful way she has been treated, after helping you all not with mere talk but with plain action.
>
> She says that though she does you other favours too, you don't keep track of your dates correctly, but scramble them topsy-turvy.
>
> As a result, Hyperbolus, allotted this year to be Holy Recorder, was stripped of his chaplet by us gods. That way he will better understand that the days of his life should be reckoned by the Moon.

ἡνίχ' ἡμεῖς δεῦρ' ἀφορμᾶσθαι παρεσκευάσμεθα,

ἡ σελήνη συντυχοῦσ' ἡμῖν ἐπέστειλεν φράσαι,

πρῶτα μὲν χαίρειν Ἀθηναίοισι καὶ τοῖς ξυμμάχοις·

εἶτα θυμαίνειν ἔφασκε· δεινὰ γὰρ πεπονθέναι

ὠφελοῦσ' ὑμᾶς ἅπαντας οὐ λόγοις ἀλλ' ἐμφανῶς.

ἄλλα τ' εὖ δρᾶν φησιν, ὑμᾶς δ' οὐκ ἄγειν τὰς ἡμέρας
οὐδὲν ὀρθῶς, ἀλλ' ἄνω τε καὶ κάτω κυδοιδοπᾶν.

ἀνθ' ὧν λαχὼν Ὑπέρβολος
τῆτες ἱερομνημονεῖν, κἄπειθ' ὑφ' ἡμῶν τῶν θεῶν
τὸν στέφανον ἀφῃρέθη: μᾶλλον γὰρ οὕτως εἴσεται
κατὰ σελήνην ὡς ἄγειν χρὴ τοῦ βίου τὰς ἡμέρας.

607–11, 615–16, 623–6

The moon naturally advocates for the lunar calendar, which has traditionally borne the authority to regulate religious observances and, in particular, sacrifices. Instead of reciprocating that kindness, Athens adopted a solar calendar to the detriment of the moon's prestige and the regularity with which religious practices were observed and safeguarded from the council's intrusive civil business (Dunn 2007: 26). The chorus leader also hints that the discrepancies or shifts in the lunar calendar may be affected less by the Athenians' tampering with the calendar and its scheduled festivals, sacrifices and court dates, than by the city's negligent failure to appoint a competent record-keeper, responsible for making the necessary intercalations of extra days into the lunar calendar (615–23). On the former complaint, Hannah notes: 'An odd feature of this interpretation, however, is the fact that it ignores the reference earlier in *Clouds* (16–18) to the expectation that when the moon has reached its "twenties", the month is nearing its end and with it the due date for the interest on loans. So if there was a difference between the phase of the moon and the date of the lunar month, it cannot have been great' (2005: 50).[24] The latter grievance, then, leaves Aristophanes with an ideal occasion to take a personal stab at a contemporary politician, Hyperbolus (623–6).

As soon as the chorus leader concludes her comic tirade in apparent support of the moon's revenge, Socrates makes a new appearance by stepping out of the Thinkery. In the ensuing quibble between a frustrated Socrates and the dim-witted Strepsiades, there is more talk about making the moon disappear. This time the allusion takes the form of Strepsiades' scheme to dodge the demands of his creditors: the maturation date of the loans they have granted to him follows the regular schedule based on the rising of the moon:

Strepsiades Suppose I bought a Thessalian witch and had her pull down the moon at night, and then locked it up in a round case, like a mirror, and then stood guard over it.

Socrates And how would that help you?

Strepsiades How? If the moon never again rose anywhere, I'd never pay my interest.

Socrates And why not?

Strepsiades Because money is loaned out by the month!

Στρεψιάδης γυναῖκα φαρμακίδ᾽ εἰ πριάμενος Θετταλὴν
καθέλοιμι νύκτωρ τὴν σελήνην, εἶτα δὴ
αὐτὴν καθείρξαιμ᾽ ἐς λοφεῖον στρογγύλον,
ὥσπερ κάτοπτρον, κᾆτα τηροίην ἔχων–

Σωκράτης τί δῆτα τοῦτ᾽ ἂν ὠφελήσειέν σ᾽;

Στρεψιάδης ὅ τι;
εἰ μηκέτ᾽ ἀνατέλλοι σελήνη μηδαμοῦ,
οὐκ ἂν ἀποδοίην τοὺς τόκους.

Σωκράτης ὁτιὴ τί δή;

Στρεψιάδης ὁτιὴ κατὰ μῆνα τἀργύριον δανείζεται.

749–56

The moon appears once more in the finale of *Clouds*, where Strepsiades lashes out at Socrates and his disciples: 'Then what was the idea of outraging the gods and peering at the backside of the Moon?' (τί γὰρ μαθόντες τοὺς θεοὺς ὑβρίζετε, / καὶ τῆς σελήνης ἐσκοπεῖσθε τὴν ἕδραν; 1506–7). What does it mean, then, for Aristophanes to have the 'outrageous' Socrates deny the existence of Zeus (367: 'Zeus doesn't even exist!', οὐδ᾽ ἔστι Ζεύς)? Jupiter would long have been visible as an evening star until the time of setting in early January of 423 BCE, when it disappeared into the bright light of the sun. Our *Clouds* represents a revised version that the playwright projected back to the original production time at the City Dionysia of 423 BCE; nonetheless, the January disappearance or setting of Jupiter, after the planet's conjunction with Saturn, was for the audience a matter of widely known and well-remembered fact. Therefore, Socrates' emphatic denial of the existence of Zeus/Jupiter coincides with the mass public's distinct and recent memory. The celestial counter-evidence to the philosopher's statement was the reappearance of Jupiter as a morning star by the time of the Dionysia (mid-March 423 BCE). Socrates juggled the evidence speciously only to be refuted by Jupiter's resurgence. This incongruity delivers more humour to the scene and renders the comic attack on Socrates all the more powerful.

Clouds is, of course, a special case, which needs to be treated with circumspection. The preserved text is not the one staged at the City Dionysia of 423 BCE, where the original comedy 'lost' badly when it took third prize. But because Aristophanes made the effort to revise the original *Clouds*, he could emphasize certain subjects and include jokes of greater complexity or based on a pattern of repetition and expansion. Thus, *Clouds* proves to be the ideal comedy to analyse as an example of Aristophanes' fascination with eclipses and celestial phenomena. He might have presumed that many in his audience shared this fascination, if indeed his revised play was to appeal to that idealized audience that would also wholeheartedly reward his ingenuity. The Athenian public could relate to cosmic and meteorological phenomena, especially when these functioned as parts of the plot of a comedy with the telling title of *Clouds*.[25] Unfortunately, we cannot be sure whether Aristophanes revised his *Clouds* for a reading public or for an actual theatre audience. In his overview of the 'ever-contentious' problem posed by the revision of *Clouds*, Revermann deems it 'the most plausible assumption' that the playwright intended the revised text for reperformance in 'some theatre' and not merely for the reading pleasure of a limited audience (2006: appendix C, 326–32 and 331 [quotations]). But would a contender keen to win not have revised the celestial references in his script to suit the conditions at the time of reperformance? Eager though Aristophanes might have been to wipe out the humiliation of his prior defeat, he did *not* change the celestial allusions in his *Clouds*: he left them to continue to reflect the sky of March 423 BCE. This *lack* of revision as far as the poet's complex but effective engagement with the star field was concerned may point to a more limited overhaul of the text for the merely literary enjoyment of a sophisticated reading public.

In the early morning opening scene of *Clouds* (1–80), Strepsiades observes the symptoms of the hippomania of his sleeping and tossing son. The scene reminds the reader of the slaves featured in the prologue of Aristophanes' *Wasps*, who observed the dreams and nightmares that manifested themselves in the bodily contortions of their sleeping master Philocleon. The known fact that the revised *Clouds* would probably not be performed in the near future renders the case made by the preserved text even more convincing: Aristophanes created another predawn setting, though not under the pressure of an impending performance, but because such opening scenes spotlighted some of his strongest comedy-writing. If the success of such scenes was a near-guarantee, then the coincidence of actual performance, celestial play and power play likely contributed to that achievement.

Revermann (n. 6 below) concedes that Aristophanes' act of theatrically integrating the sun greatly enhanced the performance experience of *Clouds* for both ancient actors and spectators. He confirms that the playwright tried to make the scene of Socrates' 'airwalk' and inspection of the sun (225) 'as memorable as possible'. 'This way the scene immensely gains point and humour', he concludes, because 'the sun becomes a prop, on a par with the other objects of inquiry in the Thinkery and subject to similarly absurd, and funny, examination' (2006: 112). Among 'other responses to the visible sun [that] would also make excellent sense', Revermann (112) includes the invocation of the sun in which Plutus engages once he has regained his eyesight (*Plutus* 771).[26]

Conclusion: diva stars in universal studios

A preliminary investigation of the dramatic role of the stars in Athenian comedy prompts us to rethink some of the interpretive practices through which we have traditionally engaged with classical Greek theatre and, in particular, with the comic prologues of nearly half of Aristophanes' plays. The modern reader, informed by the astronomical background that the ancients possessed, will find his or her reading of the plays and their performances much enhanced. The use of astronomical knowledge may also shed new light on some old conundrums, such as the dating of certain plays or the status of the revised *Clouds*. Even if not all these new insights are entirely convincing, they enrich our reading of the comedies, of their comic and metatheatrical potential, and also of the level of knowledge of their receptive audiences. The German *Sternstunde* means 'sidereal hour', but modulated by the wishful thinking that, for a particular duration of time (*Stunde*, 'hour'), the stars (*Sterne-*) would collaborate to achieve a hoped-for result. Taken as a non-technical term, the word may capture the nature of Aristophanes' prologues that publicly rely on the stars' cooperation to create memorable and award-winning opening scenes.

In later Greek literature, Aristophanes' skilful deployment of celestial phenomena resurfaces (in)famously in Plato's representation of his speech on the subject of Eros in the *Symposium* (cf. Shoshitaishvili's chapter in this volume, pp. 42-3). The playwright – always the comedian – tells of spherical human beings that originally resembled their parents: the male beings were the offspring of the sun, the females of the earth and the androgynous ones of the moon (*Symp.* 190b). The moon was of a dual sexual nature for the ancients, as also for the poet turned philosopher. Unfortunately, the limited textual evidence for New Comedy does not allow us to assess the true impact of Aristophanes' astronomical interest and his – apparently – pioneering and often winning combination of brilliant stars in the sky and stellar comic performances. In the more cosmopolitan New Comedy, the overlap of assembly and theatre performance as well as the favourite predawn opening scenes appear to be absent, at least based on preserved evidence. Perhaps only Menander's *Misoumenos* could fit the Aristophanic pattern. However, its opening scene, which is preserved on papyrus, is set closer to midnight (8) than to early morning, and the very opening words form an address to Nyx, or Night (1-3).[27]

Rehm observes that '[t]he openness of the Athenian theatre to the natural and civic environment worked a sympathetic magic that other theatres must struggle to achieve' (2003: 26-7). He illustrates his claim by citing a choral passage from the first stasimon of Sophocles' *Antigone* (100-5):

> Hail the sun! Brightest
> of all that ever dawned
> on the seven gates of Thebes,
> great eye of golden day,
> sending light across
> the rippling waters of Dirce.

The Athenian audience gathered at the Theatre of Dionysus did not need to expend much effort to imagine the scene of the sun rising over Thebes: it had seen the sun rise from behind the mountain peaks of Hymettus to the east numerous times, as on that very morning of the historical first performance of Sophocles' *Antigone*. Rehm asserts that the Athenian theatregoers who watched this performance also saw the morning sunlight brilliantly reflect off the Ilissus River south of the Theatre of Dionysus, perhaps at the moment when Sophocles' chorus evoked the glistening of the waters of the Theban Dirce. Rehm further associates the sun's rise, its zenith and its heat which causes Polyneices' corpse to putrefy (410-17) with its 'racing' to complete 'many laps' (πολλοὺς ... /

τρόχους ἁμιλλητῆρας ἡλίου τελεῖν, 1064–5). He concludes that the (incidences of the) sun's movements signal crucial stages and turning points in the tragedy's plot development, while they also mark how actual time progresses during the course of the performance (2003: 27). Rehm does not, however, touch upon any further celestial allusions that Sophocles may have intended when he describes the morning light's rise and play over the waters of Thebes.[28]

Further evidence from Athenian tragedy may help to extend traditional performance theory when we, as perennial students of ancient drama, consider how the panoramic, overarching sky with its celestial bodies or denizens serves as a co-actor, co-spectator and even co-director setting the city-stage, the sky-scape and the city-scape. The imposition of time of a different order or different contingencies involves attempts to express visibility, presence and agency and to alter the conventions that shape the comic plot, its humour and its eventual success. The play, the skies (relatively unpolluted when compared to the modern Athenian smog) and the physical environment of Athens as it spreads out below the open-air Theatre of Dionysus meet each other in the course of a performance's actualization in space as well as in time. They open up alternative categories of space and time that allow for alternative interpretations diverging from dominant, text-centred readings of things comical.

The Athenian contemporaries of the dramatists customarily gather as an audience to a scheduled play, but as an audience also to the city playing itself in real life, in that part of Athens that lies beneath the theatre. The large area that is visible from the seating space of the Theatre of Dionysus stretches as far as the confines of Hymettus' mountain ridges in the remote distance. The totality of the theatre's open-view setting combined with real life's acting space in front of the theatre forms a massive natural open-air stage and a vast natural *orchestra* to which the mountains and the skies form the backdrop. Frames of performance, spectating and surrounding environment intersect in ways seldom experienced in modern theatre. An infinitely renewable and metatheatrical fusion of the play's imaginary world and the physical space enveloping the theatre is thus shaped by Athens' urban as well as natural and celestial landscape. This sublime architecture of the city within nature lends additional authority to the overseeing signs and stars high up in the Athenian skies – and enhanced credence to the perceived sympathy of the cosmos's celestial bodies.

Notes

1. The ancient Greek text is taken from the OCT edition of Aristophanes by Wilson. All translations here (with occasional slight modifications) are from Henderson's Loeb edition.
2. Sommerstein 1998: 236–7. Russo, however, reiterates that there is no solid evidence to support that a *proagon* was held for comedy but, if there was one, it was likely scheduled 'a few days prior to staging, as it undoubtedly was for tragedy' ([1962] 1994: 39 [quotation], 253n.4). Russo further asserts that, during the first rehearsals, 'the poet could not have known

in what order the comedy was to be performed' ([1962] 1994: 219). But he does allow for 'a last-minute addition' at *Ec.* 1154–62 ('at the last moment nine lines were added to *Assemblywomen*, after a draw unfavourable to the author', [1962] 1994: 3). Such evidence strongly suggests that Aristophanes knew in which order his plays would be put on at the festivals, and that he likely learned this after he had submitted the drafts or outlines of proposed comedies. This may apply at least to the later stages of his long career as a playwright.

3. The concept of time has received relatively little attention in the scholarly literature on Greek drama, especially when compared to the notion of space, in its theatrical and metatheatrical dimensions. On space in Greek drama, see e.g. Rehm 2002 and Wiles 1997. On time as a powerful organizational and political notion in the Roman world, see Feeney 2007.

4. For more on the festival context of classical Athenian drama, see Csapo and Slater, who collect the relevant testimonia (1995: 103–38). Revermann rejects the possibility that the dramatic competitions began at the crack of dawn, mainly because spectators would have been too cold sitting still at that time of day (2006: 113, 335; similarly Ashby 1999: 107–8, 113, 119, 120, 126). Revermann further concurs with Ashby 109–10 in his rationale that the low-standing sun would have impeded the audience's viewing early in the morning or late in the day in the southern-oriented Theatre of Dionysus (335–6). Revermann's argument is implausible in the case of a Dionysia festival that fell on or around the spring equinox (25 March), because the sun rose due east and set due west. In the early morning hours, the height of Mount Hymettus, which blocks out the horizon to the east, alleviated the problem of the sun's glare. At noon, the sun's culmination was at 51 degrees, and this precise position offered some protection for viewers' eyes as they looked down at the stage. The Lenaea festival was not transferred to the Theatre of Dionysus until *c.* 440 BCE. In the new location, however, the Lenaea-goers would have had to face an occasionally blinding sun: the sun's rising point was then near Hymettus' southern end at 118 degrees azimuth south of east by south-east; at noon, the sun did not rise above 35 degrees. Typically, however, the Lenaea attracted fewer spectators than the grander Dionysia, and these spectators could therefore pick the better seats, wear some sort of head covering during the performances, etc. Perhaps those who travel to Greece only during the high summer months tend to forget that January and February seldom bring out the sun in full force over Athens and Attica. The many overcast days and other vagaries of weather at the time of the Lenaea should therefore not be discounted.

5. I do not believe that consecutive performances went on until late in the day. Theatre directors who produce classical drama in open-air settings in Greece tend to agree that the average-length play seldom lasted longer than one and a half hours (Arthur Beer, communication with the author). In that case, a one-day sequence of performances that began at 6:30 a.m. (on the spring equinox) could come to completion by 2:30 p.m., even including a few necessary breaks in between performances. Sunrise on 15 January, or around the Lenaea, occurred at 7:50 a.m. (by our clocks set to indicate solar time). Thus, the better part of a day's sequence at the Lenaea would have been finished before the sun, if it was out, started shining directly into the spectators' eyes.

6. Revermann does concede that such a synchronization might have enhanced spectators' experience of *Clouds*, especially the scene of Socrates' airborne inspection (225; p. 122 above; cf. 2006: 111–12, 188).

7. Ashby's portrayal of the ancient Athenians as Mardi Gras revellers continues, but he never delivers any hard evidence: 'This was a holiday crowd numbering in the tens of thousands' (1999: 121); 'a mass audience in a partying mood' (123). Ashby concludes that festival activities probably started at 9:30 a.m. (123). He then discredits some of the older scholarship

in support of dawn performances (123–5, with further bibliographical references). Of course, Athenian citizens got up early to participate in sessions of the courts and in regular assembly meetings, even if in the waning years of the democracy for many only the enticement of the obol-payment helped to increase early morning attendance (see n.12 below).

8. Historically, however, the Athenian assembly was open exclusively to adult male citizens, whereas theatre audiences included foreigners, slaves, children and (most plausibly) women. The presence of women in the classical theatre has long been contested but is now virtually certain. The evidence has been reviewed by Henderson 1991, among many others. See Connelly for an easily accessible overview of some of the testimonia and the scholarship (2007: 210–13, 345n.96). Cf. Austin and Olson 2004: 179; Dunbar 1995: 326; Olson 1998: 254–5.

9. Goldhill 1991: 186. See also Demosthenes, *Against Meidias* 8–10.

10. Sommerstein 1998: 1–8; Ussher 1973: xx–xxv. Cf. Russo [1962] 1994: 219, 268n.1.

11. See e.g. Henderson 1987: xv–xvi, xxv; Sommerstein 1990: 1; 1994: 1–3. Again, the leads given by scholars who are also theatre practitioners are of interest to us. Michael Walton comes to a different conclusion on the relative dating of *Lysistrata* versus *Thesmophoriazusae*, based on the former's more general appeal, which he sees as more suitable for the City Dionysia. Conversely, the sustained inside jokes on Euripides of *Thesmophoriazusae* would have been more appropriate for the 'parochial' festival of the Lenaea (1987: 199). By 411 BCE, however, Euripides and his tragedies had gained fame – and comic notoriety – well beyond Athens. For a detailed discussion of the problem of dating *Thesmophoriazusae* in conjunction with *Lysistrata*, see Austin and Olson 2004: xxxiii–xxxvi, xli–xliv. On the dating of *Lysistrata* in the light of contemporary political events, see also Wenskus 1998. On both plays, see further Russo [1962] 1994: 165, 193–4.

12. Athenian citizens had to be among the first six thousand ecclesiasts to attend, if they wanted to receive the compensation of a few obols, belaboured also at *Ec.* 83–5, 282–4, 290–2c, 392. The scene thus conveys the comic characters' strong sense of urgency to make it in time for the assembly to open and for them to receive their pay – an urgency that weighed more heavily on poorer Athenians and to which, no doubt, many of the spectators could relate personally. See also Ussher 1973: 117, 140.

13. For more details on the orientation of Greek theatres, see Ashby's chapter 7 (1999: 97–117). Ashby concludes that a southern orientation was by far the preferred direction in the construction of ancient outdoor theatres (107).

14. Admittedly, a type of 'what if?' scenario is at work here, which, however, is not a counterfactual, virtual reality but an alternative working hypothesis. 'What if?' scenarios may not yet have earned broad acceptance in the field of classical philology, but they have opened up new perspectives in history (see, for instance, Tetlock et al. 2006). Some critics find such hypothetical scenarios unacceptable. The comments of a reader of an earlier version of this chapter are telling: 'much of the paper depends on the unlikely claim that individual Olympian gods were identified with individual planets already in the 5th century ... [T]he assertion that "the chances are substantial that" lost sources argued this, and that they influenced Aristophanes and his audience, will convince no one'. On astronomical allusions and identifications in fifth-century BCE tragedy, see Worthen (unpub. a, b). In conversation with him, Worthen insisted that celestial activity might impose a certain order on terrestrial life. But he also agreed that Aristophanes' integration of planetary laws into theatre and performance was more often about challenging conventions than about bestowing a satisfying cyclical calm. For additional insightful applications of astronomical knowledge to Greek and Latin literary texts, see the articles and books by Hannah 1993a,b;

2002; 2005; 2009 and the older study by Fraenkel 1942. See, more recently, Stern's 2012 comprehensive volume on calendars in antiquity. A study of sources that pre-date the *Epinomis* will further corroborate the case for the Greeks' early identification of their gods with the planets.

15. For a brief discussion with references to the relevant testimonia, see Olson 1998: 157–8. Florence and Kenneth Wood 1999 adduce many examples to demonstrate how the *Iliad* embraces a terrestrial geography, whose formal and mythical conceptions are predicated on the highly visible celestial geography. The instantiations of this celestial geography repeat the land masses and sea lanes depicted in the *Iliad*, and some of those lands stand in a direct relationship to their various ancestral heroes (hence the connection between Ithaca, Odysseus and Bootes). The description of Achilles' shield at *Iliad* 18.478–617 is a key text in the broader argument and quest for earlier, oftentimes 'folkloric' evidence of the Greeks' perception of intertwined terrestrial and celestial geographies and for the identification of warriors as stars and constellations. For Odysseus' calibration with celestial time and season on Ithaca, see Austin's chapter in this volume.

16. Austin and Olson confirm that the play's time of day is early morning. They further note that, if the day of action is to be the third day of the Thesmophoria (as per *Th.* 80), then the audience 'would have expected it to be set in October-November', when the festival was normally held (2004: 51). Therefore, both commentators bestow a metaphorical meaning on the opening question regarding the swallow's arrival: 'since the second verse immediately converts the image into a metaphor ("Will this long period of misery ever come to an end?") in order to begin the process of introducing the plot, it may be that the idea of the swallow's arrival was already proverbial by this period and could be used at any time of year' (51).

17. See also Olson 2002: 64, 72, 80.

18. Nor do books such as Green's (1994: 6–9) deliver definitive answers.

19. For a detailed and insightful discussion of the prologue of *Wasps*, see Russo [1962] 1994: 124–7.

20. On the historical background to *Peace*, see Olson 1998: xxv–xxxi.

21. This paragraph is heavily indebted to Worthen 1988: 16–17, on the connection between Olympus and Ouranos. Worthen explains further, 'That Olympus, home of the gods, is Ouranos, and that the Olympian gods sometimes appear as stars would imply . . . that one avatar of the archaic Olympian deities was as astral gods, planets, meteors or stars' (18n.36). Worthen 1991 offers a broader, comparative mythological and astronomical study that contextualizes and strengthens such connections.

22. See also Stern 2012: 35. Hannah interprets the passage differently, arguing that the lunar phase and lunar month were, in Aristophanes' time, still coordinated (2009: 41–2, 161n.39). A significant, near-full lunar eclipse occurred on 28 September 424 BCE. For the spectators of *Peace* in 421 BCE, this most recent eclipse was preceded by lunar eclipses on 15 April and 9 October 425 BCE. A lunar eclipse on 25 March 424 BCE was a penumbral eclipse, which was probably not detectable by the naked eye. These eclipses were all the more memorable because the year 426 BCE had passed without any lunar eclipses. On 10 March 423 BCE, the moon and the sun were nearly in conjunction – or became co-conspirators. The solar eclipse of 10 March was visible from the Arabian Sea but not visible in Greece. These eclipses have thus far remained understudied, even though they can now readily be ascertained via computerized planispherical projections that are accessible online. Online astronomical tools (such as CyberSky4 by www.cybersky.com and Voyager 4.5 by Carina Software) allow for reconstructions of the ancient sky on particular days. In antiquity, devices such as the Antikythera Mechanism would have fulfilled similar functions, but we cannot know the extent of the poet's exposure to them. Sometimes the

dates cited by the modern programmes vary depending on whether they follow the Gregorian or the Julian calendar. The dates given above follow the latter.

23. Olson characterizes the co-conspirators as 'Sun and Moon – corrupt like almost everyone else entrusted with a position of public responsibility in Ar.' (1998: 159–60).

24. See further Hannah 2009: 20–1, 41. See also Sommerstein 1982: 193–4. On the 'calendar shock' reflected in this passage, see further Dunn 2007: 25 [quotation], 26. On the strengths and weaknesses of various proposed theories, see, more comprehensively, Dunn 1998: 47–50 and Stern 2012: 35–7, 44–6, 67. Porter presents *Clouds* as a popular example of the 'material sublime' and of the 'demystification of Olympus' that leads to a '(re)mystification of nature' (2016: 51–6, 390–4, 551 [latter quotations]). See also Shaw 2017, for a historical overview of the concept of the sublime, ancient to postmodern.

25. A point argued by Hannah 2002: 19 and Evans 1998: 183, and colourfully proven also by Anderson, who argues that there is more to the joke of *Clouds* 171–3 than meets the eye (1998: 49–50). Most scholars have traditionally suggested that the passage ridicules Socrates' astronomical research interests by presenting another scatological joke (as earlier in *Clouds* 156–68), but now a literalized one: a gecko is reported to have dropped his bodily waste right into Socrates' open mouth as he was gazing/gaping up at the stars. Also, this account by one of Socrates' students parodies the well-known tale about Thales of Miletus (mentioned by name at *Clouds* 180), who, as the story goes, was so absorbed in astronomical observations that he fell into a well (Pl. *Tht.* 174a). Anderson goes a step further in identifying the notorious gecko as the so-called Turkish gecko: its back, speckled with light spots, resembles a field of stars (with ancient testimony to this, the animal's most striking feature, from Ovid *Met.* 5.460–1). He then claims that Aristophanes' ancient audience, like Strepsiades (*Clouds* 174), would have appreciated the more complex joke: Socrates confused the starry gecko's back with a patch of the starry night in the background skies; his 'seemingly brilliant observation of a new constellation is nothing more than the inability to recognize a gecko when he sees one, and to get out of the way of its falling excrement' (Anderson 1998: 50). For an interpretation that places Socrates' astronomical investigations *indoors*, see Sommerstein 2001a: 253–4. On the figure of Meton as an intrusive astronomer and geometer in Aristophanes' *Birds* (992–1020), see Dunbar 1998: 371–80; 1995: 550–62; Sommerstein 1987: 263–7.

26. Sommerstein elaborates on what he regards as Wealth's modification of the ritual of making obeisance to earth and heaven: 'he (Wealth) substitutes the Sun (source of the light so long denied him and now restored) for the sky (too closely connected with his persecutor Zeus)' (2001b: 185).

27. The evidence of morning starts in New Comedy is scant, but I owe the following observations to David Christenson. He notes that the prologue of Plautus' *Rudens* (an adaptation of an unknown play by Diphilus) brings on Arcturus, who makes a clever joke about his dual status as a brilliant star/constellation and as a 'celebrity' on the Roman stage (as a famous actor or stage producer?). Arcturus puns on his celebrity status (3, *splendens stella candida*) as he, the 'star', 'appears' (4, *exoritur*). The latter pun, of appearing in the sky and onstage, is supported by a fragmentary epigram of Q. Lutatius Catulus celebrating the renowned actor Roscius: *constiteram exorientem Auroram forte salutans / cum subito a laeua Roscius exoritur*, 'I'd by chance stood still greeting Dawn as she rose when Roscius suddenly appears from the left (stage-wing)' (Courtney 1993: 2.1–2; see Christenson (forthcoming) for further discussion of the *Rudens*' opening). Cf. also Mercury (*Am.* 26–31) and Jupiter (*Am.* 863–4), who engage in similar metatheatrical play with their divine and acting status.

28. On those allusions in Sophoclean tragedy, see Worthen unpub. a, b.

Works cited

Allen, J. T. (1938), 'On the Program of the City Dionysia during the Peloponnesian War', *University of California Publications in Classical Philology*, 12: 35–42.
Anderson, C. A. (1998), 'An Unnoticed Gecko Joke in Aristophanes' *Clouds* 169-74', *Classical Philology*, 93: 49–50.
Ashby, C. (1999), *Classical Greek Theatre: New Views of an Old Subject*, Iowa City: The University of Iowa Press.
Austin, C. and S. D. Olson (2004), *Aristophanes Thesmophoriazusae, Edited with Introduction and Commentary*, Oxford and New York: Oxford University Press.
Bieber, M. ([1939] 1961), *The History of Greek and Roman Theater*, 2nd edn, Princeton, NJ: Princeton University Press and London: Oxford University Press.
Christenson, D. (forthcoming), *Plautus: Rudens*, Cambridge: Cambridge University Press.
Connelly, J. B. (2007), *Portrait of a Priestess: Women and Ritual in Ancient Greece*, Princeton and Oxford: Princeton University Press.
Courtney, E. (1993), *The Fragmentary Latin Poets*, Oxford: Oxford University Press.
Csapo, E. and W. J. Slater (1995), *The Context of Ancient Drama*, Ann Arbor: The University of Michigan Press.
Dicks, D. R. (1985), *Early Greek Astronomy to Aristotle*, Ithaca, NY: Cornell University Press.
Dunbar, N. (1995), *Aristophanes Birds, Edited with Introduction and Commentary*, Oxford: Oxford University Press.
Dunbar, N. (1998), *Aristophanes Birds, Edited with Introduction and Commentary. Student Edition*, Oxford: Oxford University Press.
Dunn, F. M. (1998), 'The Uses of Time in Fifth-Century Athens', *The Ancient World*, 29: 37–52.
Dunn, F. M. (2007), *Present Shock in Late Fifth-Century Greece*, Ann Arbor: The University of Michigan Press.
Evans, J. (1998), *The History and Practice of Ancient Astronomy*, New York and Oxford: Oxford University Press.
Feeney, D. (2007), *Caesar's Calendar: Ancient Time and the Beginnings of History*, Berkeley, Los Angeles and London: The University of California Press.
Fraenkel, E. (1942), 'The Stars in the Prologue of the *Rudens*', *Classical Quarterly*, 36: 10–14.
Goldhill, S. (1991), 'Comic Inversion and Inverted Commas: Aristophanes and Parody', in *The Poet's Voice: Essays on Poetics and Greek Literature*, 167–222, Cambridge: Cambridge University Press.
Green, J. R. (1994), *Theatre in Ancient Greek Society*, London and New York: Routledge.
Green, P. (2004), *From Ikaria to the Stars: Classical Mythification, Ancient and Modern*, Austin: The University of Texas Press.
Hannah, R. (1993a), 'Alcumena's Long Night: Plautus, *Amphitruo* 273–276', *Latomus*, 52: 65–74.
Hannah, R. (1993b), 'The Stars of Iopas and Palinurus', *American Journal of Philology*, 114: 123–35.
Hannah, R. (2002), 'Imaging the Cosmos: Astronomical Ekphraseis in Euripides', *Ramus*, 31: 19–32.
Hannah, R. (2005), *Greek and Roman Calendars: Constructions of Time in the Classical World*, London: Duckworth.
Hannah, R. (2009), *Time in Antiquity*, London and New York: Routledge.
Henderson, J. J. (1987), *Aristophanes Lysistrata, Edited with Introduction and Commentary*, Oxford: Oxford University Press.
Henderson, J. J. (1991), 'Women and the Athenian Dramatic Festivals', *Transactions of the American Philological Association*, 121: 133–7.
Henderson, J. J. (ed.) (1998–2007), *Aristophanes*, 5 vols, Loeb Classical Library, Cambridge, MA: Harvard University Press.

Olson, S. D. (1998), *Aristophanes Peace, Edited with Introduction and Commentary*, Oxford and New York: Oxford University Press.
Olson, S. D. (2002), *Aristophanes Acharnians, Edited with Introduction and Commentary,* Oxford and New York: Oxford University Press.
Porter, J. I. (2016), *The Sublime in Antiquity*, Cambridge: Cambridge University Press.
Redfield, J. (1990), 'Drama and Community: Aristophanes and Some of His Rivals', in J. J. Winkler and F. I. Zeitlin (eds), *Nothing to Do with Dionysos? Athenian Drama in Its Social Context*, 314–35, Princeton: Princeton University Press.
Rehm, R. (2002), *The Play of Space: Spatial Transformation in Greek Tragedy*, Princeton and Oxford: Princeton University Press.
Rehm, R. (2003), *Radical Theatre: Greek Tragedy and the Modern World*, London: Duckworth.
Revermann, M. (2006), *Comic Business: Theatricality, Dramatic Technique, and Performance Contexts of Aristophanic Comedy*, New York: Oxford University Press.
Russo, C. F. ([1962] 1994), *Aristophanes: An Author for the Stage*, trans. K. Wren, London and New York: Routledge.
Shaw, P. ([2006] 2017), *The Sublime*, London and New York: Routledge.
Sommerstein, A. H. (1982), *The Comedies of Aristophanes: Vol. 3 Clouds, Edited with Translation and Notes*, Warminster, UK: Aris and Phillips.
Sommerstein, A. H. ([1985] 2005), *The Comedies of Aristophanes: Vol. 5 Peace, Edited with Translation and Notes*, Warminster, UK: Aris and Phillips.
Sommerstein, A. H. (1987), *The Comedies of Aristophanes: Vol. 6 Birds, Edited with Translation and Notes*, Warminster, UK: Aris and Phillips.
Sommerstein, A. H. (1990), *The Comedies of Aristophanes: Vol. 7 Lysistrata, Edited with Translation and Notes*, Warminster, UK: Aris and Phillips.
Sommerstein, A. H. (1994), *The Comedies of Aristophanes: Vol. 8 Thesmophoriazusae, Edited with Translation and Notes*, Warminster, UK: Aris and Phillips.
Sommerstein, A. H. (1998), *The Comedies of Aristophanes: Vol. 10 Ecclesiazusae, Edited with Translation and Commentary*, Warminster, UK: Aris and Phillips.
Sommerstein, A. H. (2001a), 'Addenda: Clouds', in *The Comedies of Aristophanes: Vol. 11 Wealth, Edited with Translation and Commentary*, 250–63, Warminster, UK: Aris and Phillips.
Sommerstein, A. H. (2001b), *The Comedies of Aristophanes: Vol. 11 Wealth, Edited with Translation and Commentary*, Warminster, UK: Aris and Phillips.
Stern, S. (2012), *Calendars in Antiquity: Empires, States, and Societies*, Oxford: Oxford University Press.
Tetlock, P. E., R. N. Lebow and G. Parker (eds) (2006), *Unmaking the West: 'What-if?' Scenarios That Rewrite World History*, Ann Arbor: The University of Michigan Press.
Ussher, R. G. (1973), *Aristophanes Ecclesiazusae, Edited with Introduction and Commentary*, Oxford: Oxford University Press.
Van Steen, G. (1994), 'Aspects of "Public Performance" in Aristophanes' *Acharnians*', *L'Antiquité Classique*, 63: 211–24.
Walton, J. M. (1987), *Living Greek Theatre: A Handbook of Classical Performance and Modern Production*, Westport, CT: Greenwood Press.
Wenskus, O. (1998), 'Zur Datierung der *Lysistrata*', *Hermes*, 126: 383–5.
Wiles, D. (1997), *Tragedy in Athens: Performance Space and Theatrical Meaning*, Cambridge: Cambridge University Press.
Wiles, D. (2000), *Greek Theatre Performance: An Introduction*, Cambridge: Cambridge University Press.
Wilson, N. G. (ed.) (2007), *Aristophanis fabulae*, 2 vols, Oxford and New York: Oxford University Press.
Wood, F. and K. Wood (1999), *Homer's Secret Iliad: The Epic of the Night Skies Decoded*, London: John Murray.

Worthen, T. D. (1988), 'The Idea of "Sky" in Archaic Greek Poetry', *Glotta*, 66: 1–19.
Worthen, T. D. (1991), *The Myth of Replacement: Stars, Gods, and Order in the Universe*, Tucson: The University of Arizona Press.
Worthen, T. D. (unpub. a), 'Aspects of Time in Greek Tragedy'.
Worthen, T. D. (unpub. b), 'The Gods and the Stars in the Speech of Aeschylus's Watchman'.

CHAPTER 8
FRIGHTENINGLY FUNNY GODS: COMIC AND COSMIC SPACE IN PLAUTUS
David Christenson

Introduction: mapping a Plautine cosmos[1]

The cosmos projected by Plautus' comedies appears structurally stable: earth and the underworld, sea and sky, home to gods and celestial bodies. Plautus' universe extends below and above its hybridized Graeco-Roman setting[2] – usually 'Athens', the cosmopolitan abode of mortals – to encompass the realms of the *inferi* ('the dead') and *superi/immortales* ('the gods'/'non-dying'). Cult deities such as Apollo, Jupiter and the Magna Mater were felt to be physically present for theatrical performances associated with their festivals and temples (their civic 'homes'). A god's altar stood before one of the houses represented on the stage's backdrop.[3] Gods of the sky were never far away in that Plautus' characters frequently name, thank, comment on, swear and curse by, or pray to them in various situations. The Plautine stage is verbally suffused with divinity, especially 'divine qualities' (e.g. *Fides, Salus, Spes*),[4] including some created in lively moments of comic contingency (e.g. *Suauisauiatio*, 'Erotikissia',[5] *Bac.* 115), and human characters who are temporarily deified or imaginatively elevated to Olympus.[6] Plautus' underworld is a vivid comic projection, frequently associated with consuming, antisocial characters, especially the *senex amator*, portrayed as navigating a fast-track to hell because his bad behaviour poses a threat to his identity and to his household's stability and prosperity (Christenson 2016: 219–20). A complementary conceptualization of the underworld, compellingly argued by Connors 2020, attaches to Plautus' independent prostitutes, whose brothels are represented as karst sinkholes that serve as portals to the underworld, and whose clients are cast as doomed figures of a parodic *katabasis*.

Plautus thus creates dynamic sites for engagement with cosmic sublimity. As an extended social, civic and ideological locus, the Plautine cosmos is neither simple nor inert. Its ordered divisions prove to be permeable, its boundaries fluid; in and between its various regions, discourse – cultural, ethical, metaphysical, theological, metapoetic – is conducted. This chapter focuses on the Plautine corpus's most provocative instance of cosmic boundary-crossing: that of *Amphitruo*'s Jupiter and Mercury, who team up as disruptive gods of tragedy and comedy, respectively, in a sublimely terrifying play in which up and down, high and low, illusion and reality, just and unjust, and even tragic and comic are confused.

This divine *tragicomoedia* (*Am.* 59–63) significantly unfolds on the occasion of a state-sponsored religious festival. However secularized one imagines Roman festivals to be, the performance of *Am.* constitutes a ritual offering to a god.[7] Although *Am.*'s satirical presentation of Jupiter is undeniable, scholars have hesitated to identify in it any serious critique of divinity or the (human) system of power underlying *Am*.'s representation of divinity. Retreat from such claims is anchored in the standard dogma that what mattered most in the elite state enterprise of Roman religion was orthopraxy, the proper conduct of rituals. One may then compartmentalize *Am*.'s irreverent treatment of Jupiter as merely a frivolous caricature of his anthropomorphic and anthropopathic representation in myth, with little at stake for playwright and audiences beyond (expected) laughter.[8] Without engaging issues of Roman religion beyond the scope of this chapter (and my expertise), I note that there now seems to be growing scholarly consensus that even within Roman institutional orthopraxy, as also in mythopoesis, much space for theological interpretation, interrogation and critique existed.[9] Sorting out views of cult, belief,[10] myth, divinity (e.g. its immanence, transcendence) and their dramatic mimesis among segments of Plautus' diverse audience,[11] gathered together for a religious occasion (variously as viewers, officials or servants), is an impossible task. But it is rash to characterize *Am*. and its manifold reception by ancient spectators as only a mythological spoof free of further implications, especially since *Am*. represents a polymorphic Jupiter as, simultaneously, ruler of the cosmos, the *Iuppiter Optimus Maximus* of Capitoline cult and storied lecher. Plautus' presentation of Mercury is no less complex, and his and Jupiter's roles in *Am*. together reflect and reveal much about Roman power structure and its cognate construct of cosmic governance. This strange tragicomedy thus unavoidably participates in Roman and cosmic dialogues about the nature of power, hierarchy and privilege. Even if such broader discourse in Plautus' hands often takes farcical form, and lacks an interlocutor or specific cultural-historical point of reference (*Am*. obviously is not a religious tract), the play discursively engages with Roman religious thinking and views of cosmic justice.[12] In particular, *Am*. offers a dramatic representation, for a broad audience, of what absolute power looks like if left unchecked, a situation reified within a fictional comic household at a particular moment of festival performance. By examining the play in performance and its possible receptions by both ancient spectators and modern readers, I suggest that *Am*., in some respects a precursor to (post)modern theatricalized conceptions of the world, is a *tragicomoedia* that frighteningly resonates today.[13]

Crossing boundaries: divinity on the boards

We begin with a plot summary of this New Comedy that uniquely collapses lofty and low in recasting the myth of Jupiter's impersonation of Amphitryon and rape of Alcmena for the Roman stage. As we learn from Mercury's prologue (1–152), Jupiter has descended from the sky to Romanized Thebes to have sex with Alcmena, fashioned as the ideally virtuous, devoted and patriotic *matrona* (641a–53, 839–42). Jupiter has impersonated her husband Amphitryon while the Theban general is off at war.[14] To maximize his pleasure, the sky god has supernaturally lengthened the night (113–14), which spectators in the open-air theatre constructed for the festival are to imagine as the play's temporal setting until Jupiter banishes *Nox* and summons the day, disrupted by the god's libidinous urges (546–50).[15] Alcmena is fast nearing the term of her pregnancy with Amphitryon, and by superfetation will bear Jupiter's son Hercules along with his human twin offstage (1088–1124). Mercury's prolix opening introduces Jupiter as supreme master of the cosmos (*deorum regnator, architectust omnibus*, 45) and as serial philanderer (104–6) and unapologetic adulterer (*moecho*, 135).[16] Reflections of the Jupiter of Roman cult (e.g. *summo Iove*, 111) coexist with the portrait of a sexual opportunist, a figure of supersized lust (104–6) who has claimed Alcmena's body by *usucapio* (Roman 'squatter's rights', 107–8): Jupiter by deception sexually enslaves Alcmena by expropriating her body in her husband's absence.[17] Disguised as Amphitryon, Jupiter also purloins the victorious general's glorious *nostos*, one worthy of a Roman triumph,[18] by relating details of his mortal counterpart's campaign in pillow talk with Alcmena, who unknowingly engages in extramarital sex (135–9). Jupiter can effect all this because 'he easily does what he wants' (139), his will is tantamount to action. As a *vorsipellis* ('shape-shifter', 123), Jupiter can metamorphose as he pleases; the god is an actor with unlimited costumes and a fluid capacity to assume any role.

Mercury, a traveler and boundary-crosser in myth and cult, has stolen the identity of Amphitryon's slave Sosia to assist his father-now-master and sow further confusion in the Theban household. Now wearing a grotesque slave's mask and costume,[19] he describes his role as that of Jove's and the play's *orator* or 'ambassador' (20, 34), a reflection of Hermes' cosmic status as messenger of the gods, and a function he reprises at 463–98 and 984–1008. In light of the appearance of the gods and characters of Theban myth alongside a slave's part, Mercury characterizes *Am.* with a notoriously indeterminate neologism: *tragicomoedia* or 'mythical travesty' (60–3).[20] The gods' costumes are distinguished from their mortal doubles' only by their iconographically appropriate headgear (wings for Mercury, a golden tassel for Jupiter, 142–5), unnecessary since the performance context and the characters' words leave no doubt as to who's who in the comedy of errors that ensues. These arbitrary signs do little to distinguish the gods' physical forms from those of their mortal counterparts, but mainly highlight that deception and disguise are to be Mercury's and Jupiter's primary devices in the play. These distinguishing props also implicate spectators in the gods' ruse: they share privileged information and see what *Am.*'s human characters cannot. Once all misunderstandings and confusions of identity ostensibly are resolved, the play closes with a similarly artificial theatrical construct when an undisguised (i.e. as Amphitryon) Jupiter makes his onstage epiphany as he is raised aloft Amphitryon's palace by a mechanical device (*ego in caelum migro*, 1143). In this way we are implicated in the manufacture of the play's world and discouraged from being lulled into passive spectatorship of yet another formulaic New Comedy (which *Amphitruo* is not!).

As this abstract alone suggests, *Am.* activates a dizzying array of mimetic representations, transgressions and disjunctions. Critical to any assessment of *Am.*'s reception is an account of the gods' comic performances in *Am.*: if we laugh, do we laugh *with* – as Mercury and Jupiter clearly want us to where their treatment of the mortals is concerned – or *at* the gods? Is our laughter unrestrained, uncomplicated, deferred, nervous, hesitant or even painful? Do we view the action asymmetrically, 'with one weeping and one laughing eye' (Johann Adolf Schlegel apud Guthke 1966: 43–4)? Is the play especially disorienting to spectators in that tragedy seems to arise from comedy?

Mediating worlds, expanding gaps: Mercury

Mercury's main function in *Am.* is to mediate between gods and spectators, most often as Jupiter's publicist/apologist, in which role he speaks directly to the audience, most often in musically unaccompanied iambic trimeters.[21] Hermes/Mercury, the glib divine trickster, is well-suited for both 'spinning' public relations and convincingly impersonating Sosia, the would-be crafty comic slave: as an actor, Mercury essentially can play himself.[22] In his elaborate prologue-opening (1–16), Mercury assumes the persona of Roman god of commerce and negotiation. Crafting an inverse *do ut des* prayer, Mercury promises to support spectators' ventures in exchange for their giving the play a fair hearing, even though his father could simply use his power (*pro imperio*, 21) to compel spectators to do so, given their cultic obligation to 'fear and revere' Jupiter (*vereri . . . metuere*, 23). In his prologue, Mercury playfully conflates Jupiter's dual identity as a powerless actor (who, like himself, must win spectators over through flattering theatrical craft) and as an all-powerful god. In accordance with the core elite social value of *gratia* ('mutual benefaction'), spectators, as Romans, owe Jupiter for his past services (39–49), a clear indication that this Jupiter is more transactional mobster than benevolent figure of cosmic justice, and that Jupiter's justice is contingent.[23] Mercury's dazzling *praeteritio* (*quid ego memorem* (*ut alios in tragoediis / vidi*?), 41–2) links Jupiter's request for a favour with similar pitches allegedly made by Neptune, Virtus, Victoria, Mars and Bellona in (lost to us) *tragedies*, our first hint that *Am.* is an atypical comedy. In this roll call of deities who promote Roman military success (each had a temple in Plautus' Rome), Neptune, unless he is to be narrowly associated with naval victory, is the odd one out. Apropos of *Am.*, he is Jupiter's cosmic brother, ruler of the sea. And like his more powerful, sky-dwelling brother, Neptune is an inveterate rapist of mortal women, a shape-shifting master of deception, as Ovid's Arachne jointly characterizes the two brothers on her subversive tapestry (*Met.* 6.103–22).[24] At any rate, Mercury continues, 'the boss' won't browbeat spectators about his benevolence (*exprobraret quod bonis faceret boni*, 47) and knows he can count on their loyalty (48–9). Mercury's solicitousness suggests he's building to a request for significant indulgence.

Mercury also weighs in on the prospect of claques being planted among the audience to promote individual actors and the possible bribery of the sponsoring *aediles* in awarding actors' prizes (64–85). Just as the cosmic Jupiter forbids illegal canvassing for Roman magistracies (*non ambitione nec perfidia*, 76), so too he demands a fair actors' competition, and instigators of any such action are subject to whipping and costume-shredding (85)![25] The ethics of the theatre notably resemble those of corrupt Roman politics. There is trenchant irony in Mercury's claim that Jupiter, averred proponent of Roman *virtus* (75), so strongly disapproves of *perfidia*, that is, 'treachery' of the sort he employs to prevail over Amphitryon's household.[26] Mercury leavens this forceful persuasion towards gaining spectators' favourable reception of the play with a striking reminder that outside its fictionality he and Jupiter are a pair of Rome's low-to-no-status actors, gods-in-the-flesh and vulnerably human flesh that is subject to whipping for unsuccessful performance (26–31). This will not be the last time the gods draw attention to *Am*.'s multiple layers of construction. Such metatheatricality affects spectators' levels of detachment from, or sympathetic absorption in, events represented in the play: it's just a play – isn't it? Mercury's perplexing imbrication of identities in the prologue (Olympian audience-negotiator, god impersonating a human slave, Roman slave-actor) mirrors that of the play's generic affiliation: is it a tragedy, a comedy, a tragedy morphed into a comedy or a hybridized, sui generis *tragicomoedia* (51–63)?[27] Mercury's long-deferred indulgence turns out to be the audience's acceptance of the strange (*novom*, 89) appearance of gods as characters on the comic stage here in Rome. Mercury appropriately closes his prologue with a complete collapse of cosmic society's antipodes: it'll be worthwhile for spectators to watch gods ply the humble craft of acting (*facere histrioniam*, 152). The enormous gap between Olympian deities and the Roman actors impersonating them as they impersonate mortals has been opened up for consideration. From the start of *Am.*, boundaries are crossed, interrogated and problematized.

Mercury's manifold powers of deception are displayed in the first scene, where he goes toe-to-toe with a would-be *servus callidus* (in a different New Comedy Sosia might be an effective trickster). As an eavesdropper to Sosia's boisterous *canticum*, Mercury sings in asides (176–9, 185, 263–4) before joining Sosia in lively, musically accompanied ('recitative') trochaics for the long scene's remainder.[28] The god eventually confronts his double before Amphitryon's palace, so as to gaslight Sosia into believing he's no longer Amphitryon's slave of that name. Though driven by assertions and denials of identity coupled with onstage horseplay, the nocturnal scene is also framed in astronomical and cosmic terms. A frightful Sosia navigates the preternatural night with a lantern made of horn strips (149), which prompts Mercury's ominously paratragic address of his double, 'Where go you who carry Vulcan shut up in horn?' (341). Sosia ironically acknowledges, without rectification, his failure to thank the gods for his safe return from the war as legitimate ground for a thrashing of the sort he is about to receive at the hands of the eavesdropping god-in-disguise (180–4). After rehearsing his messenger's speech detailing Amphitryon's conquests (186–262), Sosia paints a comic picture of the sky at which he imaginatively gazes, a projection of his servile subjectivity and bibulous persona. In the slave's memory, this night's duration is matched only by that of an all-night beating he experienced while tortuously suspended from a beam. Ursa Major, Luna, Orion, Venus and the Pleiades are not budging, and the cause must be either Nocturnus' having passed out drunk or Sol's failure to rise for the same reason (271–6, 279–83).[29] Sosia of course cannot possibly imagine the real reason for the astronomical immobility: the ruler of the cosmos's protracted lust for a mortal woman. Mercury castigates Sosia for his anthropomorphizing in an aside: 'you think the gods are like you?' (284). Mercury's own human form is apparent to all in the theatre, and so Sosia scores a theological point. The irony of just having detailed his own assumption of Sosia's precise appearance and character (265–9) is entirely lost on Mercury, as also the fact that the raison d'être for the gods' appearance on the Plautine stage is a demystified Jupiter's all-too-human libido. The joke's on Mercury, as an apposite theological question is raised for spectators. Within a direct appeal to lonely spectators who hire prostitutes (*ubi sunt isti scortares qui soli inviti cubant?*), Sosia then jokes that such a night is perfect for 'working-out an expensive whore' (287–8). Mercury in another aside adds that Jupiter is 'indulging his desire' (*animo obsequens*, 290) in precisely this vein, thereby focalizing for spectators the lecherous god's disregard for Alcmena.

The bulk of the doubles' encounter is taken up with the assault on Sosia's unique identity by his divine simulacrum, an estrangement of self that has been likened to totalitarian-state brainwashing (Martin 1970) and hyper-aggressive police interrogation (Christenson 2000: 206). We might also consider Mercury's methods in light of modern 'disinformation' campaigns by states, media or unscrupulous politicians. Mercury begins by signposting his plan to befuddle Sosia in theatrical terms: *deludam* (295), 'I'll deceive him', that is, remove Sosia from the gods' *ludus*, their 'fun' or 'play'; *clare advorsum fabulor* (300), 'I'll speak loudly in his direction', i.e. create a miniature play-within-the-play, a *fabula* in which Sosia is made to overhear a theatricalizing Mercury plot violence against the next person he meets (302–41).[30] Spectators are invited to join the god in his role-playing, to vicariously share in Mercury's domination of his mortal counterpart. Terrorized by Mercury's staged threats, Sosia eventually faces the god directly. Mercury's divestment of the slave's personal identity begins with a swift series of repeated interrogations ('Who are you?', 'Where are you going?', 'What are you doing?', 'Whose slave are you?', 341–87), peppered with Mercury's impugning of, and physical reprisals for, Sosia's truthful answers. Sosia clings to his status as Amphitryon's slave ('I'm telling you, I'm this household's household-slave', 359), and even professes descent from his father Davus (365), a Plautine shtick whereby slaves claim personhood and a history outside their present enslavement.[31] Delivery of a powerful onstage blow leads Sosia to exclaim he's 'dead' (*perii*, 374) and momentarily acknowledge a transfer of ownership to Mercury's fists (by *usucapio*, 375; cf. p. 135 above). The more powerful brutally usurp as they please, Sosia concedes (396).

Sosia's attempt to secure a truce so he can reassert his status as Amphitryon's slave – sanctioned, in a double-speaking oath (392) – only results in further onstage violence (*vapula*, 395). Fresh tactics ensue as Sosia vows never to be silenced. The deracinated slave, already once removed from his natal self, clings to his normalized servile identity: 'you'll never strip me of being our house's Sosia' (*tu me alienabis numquam quin noster siem*, 399).[32] Mercury loudly counters that *he* is and will not cease to be Sosia, and charges the real Sosia with insanity (396–401). Sosia invokes his personal experience of the military campaign as evidence of who he is, but the omniscient god with a chorus of un-truths co-opts these same events as his own (404–22). Mercury expropriates even the most private of Sosia's memories when he recounts how at the height of battle Sosia went AWOL to drain a jug of wine in Amphitryon's tent (424–32; cf. 199, 253–5). Still unwilling to relinquish his entire sense of self, Sosia swears by Jupiter he's telling the truth, to which Mercury counter-swears by his own divinity that Jupiter won't accept Sosia's oath (435–7) – and metatheatrically adds that Sosia can be 'Sosia' when he no longer wants to be (439). Sosia considers physiology: he appears to be looking at his mirror image (*in speculum*, 442), someone with the same physical characteristics and costuming. Decisive proof of his cloning would be replication of his whip-scarred slave's back, he grimly jokes (446). Sosia makes a rush for the house, is violently rebuffed and concludes that Mercury has usurped his likeness (*imaginem*, 458). Playing on a technical meaning of *imago* ('death-mask'),[33] Sosia creatively responds to the theft of his unique identity by declaring his newfound eligibility to participate in Roman aristocratic funeral ritual (cf. Poly. 6.53) and fantasizes about manumission if Amphitryon fails to acknowledge him as his slave (457–62). Sosia's resilience, in contrast with the unenslaved characters' strong resistance to the 'alternative facts' posed by the gods in *Am.*, reflects his status, in that Sosia risks little, legally and socially, with estrangement from his servile identity. But Sosia's creative fluidity of self also promotes survival, self-refashioning even, if by forfeiting his appearance to Mercury he can shave his head and don the Roman cap of freedom (462).[34]

Is the theft of Sosia's subjective identity merely fun and games for spectators, as it is for Mercury? Judgement rests in the eye of the spectator. Readers of *Am.* today, while perhaps amused by this scene's extensive paronomasia, irony and confusion (Doppelgängers remain a popular sci-fi motif), may be affected by Sosia's gallows humour; his creative resilience amid extreme *aporia* (*ubi ego perii*?, 456); the pathos of his dependence on enslavement, torture even, as a primary mark of identity; the sinister Mercury's physical and psychological viciousness or the drastic power-differential between Sosia and his divine simulacrum; or simply by the god's head-spinning repetitions of falsehoods (familiar to us living in an age of advertising and political disinformation) in the service of Jupiter's desire. Can we insist with absolute surety that some in Plautus' audience weren't similarly affected (*mutatis mutandis*) or disoriented by oscillating emotions?

Mercury's work is not finished with Sosia's removal from the palace. He stays onstage to assess the play's progress and resume his function, established in the prologue, as Jupiter's apologist (463–98). Mercury expresses delight at the prospect of causing Amphitryon's household further *error* ('misunderstanding') and *dementia* ('madness'), terms evoking the sublime terror of tragedy, so that Jupiter can have his fill (*satietas*) of Alcmena (470–3). But spectators needn't worry: all the strange events in Amphitryon's household will ultimately be explained, and husband and wife will renew their established *concordia* (474–6) – this tragicomedy will end happily.[35] The reassurances here barely conceal Mercury's Schadenfreude at the bitter conflict (*turbas*, 476; *seditionem*, 478) and serious charges of adultery (*probi*, 477) about to ensue. Mercury's deal-brokering persona resurfaces from the prologue: Alcmena will bear twins (one son with Amphitryon, one with Jupiter (articulated in confusingly mercurial terms, 483–5). Her compensation for being the victim of Jupiter's libidinous deception is to consist of an efficient two-births-in-one with the fringe benefit of concealment of the secret affair from those not in the know (*clandestina ut celetur consuetio*, 490). Along with Mercury's smarminess here, the gods' taking credit for economization of Alcmena's labour smacks of solicitousness and sleight-of-hand. Omnipotent Jupiter can arrange for miraculously painless parturition commensurate with the supernatural conception of Hercules, as the god ultimately does, without publicly proclaiming this an act of benevolence. Mercury reiterates that Amphitryon will be apprised of all, since it wouldn't be just for Alcmena to bear responsibility for a god's offense (*delictum*, 494); still, despite Mercury's projection of harmonious, post-play bliss, he can't elide the fact that during the play Alcmena painfully absorbs the blame (*culpam*, 495) for Jupiter's caprice.

Mercury moves to the periphery in the following, musically accompanied scene that features the first appearance of Alcmena and Jupiter, cavalierly introduced by Mercury's announcement of the approach of 'counterfeit Amphitryon' and his commodified 'wife-on-loan' (*Amphitruo subditivos ... uxore usuraria*, 497–8). Speaking mostly in ironic asides, Mercury frames Jupiter's hoodwinking of Alcmena in low-comic terms for spectators: he's a 'first-rate con artist', a *sycophanta* (506), in Plautus a trickster (usually a slave) who specializes in deception by imposture.[36] Jupiter's expertise at blandishing a mortal woman is especially worth watching, he adds (508). Mercury then attempts to act as Jupiter's wingman, a comic parasite's duty for a patron (515), but his over-the-top, and highly ironic, pitch for Jupiter-Amphitryon's passionate devotion to his wife is angrily rebuked by his father (518–20, 539), a charismatic and skilled 'player' who resents the suggestion that he needs assistance in charming Alcmena. Like Roman elegy's lovesick lover (pp. 141–2 below), the play-acting Jupiter is 'savage because of love' (541), a rebuffed Mercury sardonically explains to the audience.

Mercury goes offstage for several scenes, reappearing at Jupiter's request as comedy's 'running slave' (*quam servolo in comoediis*, 987), conspicuously lacking the urgent news this stock character bears, and instead again justifies his own and his father's behaviour to spectators:

amanti supparasitor, hortor, adsto, admoneo, gaudeo.
si quid patri volup est, voluptas ea mi maxumast.
amat: sapit; recte facit, animo quando obsequitur suo,
quod omnis homines facere oportet, dum id modo fiat bono.

                                                                          993–6

I play the parasite for him when he's in love, I aid, abet, and advise him, share his joy. If some delight strikes father's fancy, the delight is all the more mine. He's in love: he strategizes, does the right thing by indulging his desire, as all men should do – as long as it's done in moderation.

Mercury offers himself as an internal model of how married men in the audience should regard Jupiter's performance in *Am*. Like Mercury, also subordinate to the god, they can identify with Jupiter's pursuit of sexual pleasure outside marriage. Roman boys will be boys, etc., though given the real-life politics of marriage (versus social and legal codification), the wives of men who emulate Jupiter might not necessarily agree,[37] even in a society where a *paterfamilias* enjoyed sexual omnipotence, provided he didn't adulterate another citizen's wife, commit rape (as narrowly defined in Roman law) or otherwise jeopardize his finances or public reputation, as Mercury's vague closing qualification about 'due measure' suggests. Despite Mercury's homophilic subterfuge ('we're all just guys'), this limitation in fact exists only for mortal men, as Jupiter towers imperiously above all restrictions and consequences. Mercury announces his final task in the play, mocking Amphitryon when he returns from his wild goose chase about Thebes by donning a garland (999, 1007–8) to signal he's drunk and, as Sosia, abusing his master from the palace's roof. All this mockery, the virtuoso comedian Mercury now solicitously suggests (*deludi* 997; *deludam*, 1005), isn't only intended to benefit Jupiter or estrange us, as the gods' co-conspirators, from the increasingly frustrated Amphitryon: it's actually for our pleasure, *iam hic deludetur, spectatores, vobis spectantibus* (998)! We should be grateful to the gods for their delightfully derisive performances.

An overpowering performance: Jupiter

Though they've heard much about Jupiter, spectators don't see him onstage until nearly halfway through the play (499–550), where they discover that he, like Amphitryon, is costumed as a *senex* (1032, 1071), in New Comedy's behavioural code an old(er) man who typically blocks a young man's pursuit of *amor*. Jupiter, however, is a *senex amator*, in Plautus a figure conspicuously lacking the social decorum and self-control demanded of a Roman *paterfamilias* and doomed to amorous failure. As Plautine comedy's only successful 'old man in love', Jupiter becomes an avatar of unaccountable phallic excess manifested in rape, uncontested power, control, manipulation and cruelty. His comic get-up aside, he is immediately distinguished from *Am*.'s other main characters by never singing a *canticum*, perhaps the definitive feature of Plautus' musical comedy (Fontaine 2014: 405–6). Jupiter, despite his considerable stage presence, in this formal sense is not fully comic. His musical distinctiveness, combined with his transcendent image as 'architect' of universal justice controlling human destiny introduced in Mercury's prologue (p. 135 above), suggest Jupiter's fitting role as a god of tragedy;[38] yet his performance in *Am*. dissonantly anchors him to coarsely comic and immanently human experience. Incongruous conceptions of Jupiter in cosmography, cult, myth and drama thus collide.

In a comic parody of epic departure scenes (e.g. Andromache's and Hector's in *Iliad* 6), Jupiter – apparently fatigued by the long night of sex, and at any rate needing to cede the stage to the approaching Amphitryon so that a confrontation between spouses can take place – in his first appearance is eager to leave Alcmena, on the pretext of returning to his (i.e. Amphitryon's) troops as dawn approaches (533). Military discipline breaks down when the *summus imperator* ('the supreme commander', 504) is absent, the god ironically notes.[39] To escape from his anxious faux-wife, Jupiter exploits Alcmena's pronounced patriotism by invoking the Roman elite's oft-avowed preference, e.g. Aeneas' in *Aeneid* 4, for duty over desire, self-abnegation in the service of country.[40] Even if Alcmena is comically depicted as a quasi-sensualist[41] in vigorously protesting her husband's departure, Jupiter's unctuous and expedient appropriation of imperialistic ideology (524–5, 527–8) bespeaks his self-serving manipulativeness. In so deftly twisting

Alcmena's patriotic deference to Roman-style militarism to his personal advantage, Jupiter here manifests Greenblatt's 'mobile sensibility' in an 'improvisation of power'.[42] In like vein, the scene casts the god as a narcissistic, proto-elegiac lover, or a comic parody of the type, since Jupiter is represented as passionately in love with his paramour-qua-wife (*efflictim amare . . . te efflictim deperit*, Mercury-as-wingman asserts, 518).[43] There's no mortal woman he loves more (509, 516) – true at this moment. Jupiter claims that he, as love's soldier, has stealthily deserted his command at night and for Alcmena stolen the service owed his army and Thebes (*clanculum abii: a legione operam hanc surrupi tibi*, 523). When Alcmena begins to cry, Jupiter's foremost concern is his male gaze: 'don't ruin your eyes' (*ne corrumpe oculos*, 530).[44] The god's devious appropriation of Roman martial virtue crests when he repurposes the defeated commander's golden bowl, a token of the rarest of public honours in Rome, the *spolia opima* Amphitryon is eligible for after killing his counterpart in battle, as a courting gift.[45] The compensatory gift works its magic. A consoled Alcmena's tears evaporate when she begs Jupiter to love her whether he's with her or apart, and to return soon (542–4). The scene concludes when the elegiac con artist, left alone onstage, instantaneously morphs into sky-god to majestically call forth the light of Day (546–50).[46] In this restoration of cosmic time and order, the day will be shortened proportionately to the night's extension; locally, however, further domestic disturbance awaits the Theban palace.

Jupiter next appears to deliver a monologue (861–81), in the full daylight, that strategically follows the contentious and confused meeting of the married couple (654–861). Despite Sosia's best efforts to preserve comic perspective as commentator there, the revelation of the pair's conflicting and mutually baffling accounts of the previous night crescendo into Amphitryon's reasonable fear that his wife has engaged in adultery and Alcmena's impassioned defence of her marital chastity. She is even made to swear by Juno that – technically not perjuriously – 'no mortal man except Amphitryon has touched her body to (hers')' (831–4). These tense matters unresolved, Amphitryon exits to find a neutral witness whose testimony about his activity the previous night will determine if divorce is warranted (848–52).

After Sosia and Alcmena enter the palace, Jupiter enters from a side-wing and immediately collapses his fluid identities – Olympian and cultic god, character impersonating Amphitryon, Roman actor – much as Mercury had done in the prologue (pp. 136–7 above). As Mercury becomes Sosia 'when it's useful' (*commodum*, 862), so the impulsive Jupiter becomes Amphitryon 'when (he) feels like it' (*quando lubet*, 864). 'I'm the one who inhabits the upper-story' (*in superiore qui habito cenaculo*, 863), he smartly quips to spectators, ambiguously evoking both Olympus (figuratively) and an attic-loft (literally) of one of Rome's hazardous wooden *insulae* that housed the low-status poor, such as actors. So any stage-performer with the will and proper costume can play either Jupiter or Amphitryon (864–6): stage-representation has spilled over into Rome's urban reality, all the world's truly a stage. Jupiter comes close to suggesting that we're all merely players in a humanly constructed cosmic drama ('this strange eventful history') stretching from earth to heaven and back again.[47] He seems worried that spectators may be weary of his deception of Alcmena. Speaking as a playwright-substitute, as Mercury before him (pp. 139–40 above), Jupiter insists he's only present for our benefit (*nunc huc honoris vostri venio gratia*), so as 'to bring this unfinished comedy to its conclusion' (867–8). We needn't worry about the disruption of domestic harmony in the Theban palace: he's come to help the falsely accused Alcmena, though we'll soon learn he's actually back for pre-parturition sex. Jupiter then smoothly glosses over his culpability in sowing the play's discord in hypothetical terms: 'It *would* be my fault (*culpa*) if what *I'd* stirred up *should* fall upon the innocent Alcmena' (870–2). It already has. Jupiter reveals a second, purely theatrical, motivation for returning: he can't resist playing Amphitryon again and inflicting an enhanced level of deception (*frustationem . . . maxumam*, 875) on the entire household. Gaslighting a virtuous woman into more extramarital sex and disorienting her husband's household to boot are most enjoyable to a comic sycophant and stage-performer like himself – we should enjoy being in on the divine prank as well. But Jupiter's game, as Alcmena's pregnancy, eventually must end. He repeats that he'll bring help to Alcmena and raises her compensation: the two-in-one birth will also be painless (*pariat sine doloribus*, 879).

A structurally intriguing scene ensues in which a human character has the opportunity, albeit unknowingly, to engage in critical discourse with a god, though Alcmena does not know the full extent of the injustice her disguised interlocutor has committed against her. A livid Alcmena bursts out of the palace and, not noticing Jupiter, addresses the audience (this most serious scene is in un-musical iambics): her husband must either disavow his accusation and apologize to her or she'll initiate a divorce (887–9). In an aside, Jupiter notes that he must accede to her demands, 'If I want her to take me as her lover again' (892).[48] We now know the real motivation behind his present solicitude: more sex! Jupiter admits his *amor* (894) has unjustly created trouble for Amphitryon, but adds, 'I'm an innocent victim too', since he now must bear the brunt of Amphitryon's accusations against his wife (*nunc autem insonti mihi / illius ira in hanc et maledicta expetent*, 895–6). His initial, 'hands-on' (903) effort to charm Alcmena, who now considers her husband her *inimicus* (900), is rejected. This time he won't be able to wheedle his way back into Alcmena's good graces with roses, chocolates or even a golden bowl after the bitter domestic dispute. Jupiter takes a new approach: he (i.e. the genuine Amphitryon) was only testing her reaction, for the fun of it (*ioco . . . ridiculi causa*, 916–17).[49] Moreover, since he intended the accusation of marital infidelity as a joke, she 'has no right to take it seriously' (920–1). Jupiter never explains why falsely accusing a woman devoted to chastity in marriage of adultery is funny but expects his authority (the identities of omnipotent god and *paterfamilias* overlap here) to trump Alcmena's subjective feelings. Alcmena responds that her pain was no joke (922), and Jupiter with more onstage, blandishing handsy-ness apologizes to no avail (923–4), as Alcmena utters, to a presumably hushed theatre (absent any music), the Roman divorce formula calling for a division of property (*tibi habeas res tuas, reddas meas*, 928).[50]

More effective manoeuvres are needed. Exploiting Alcmena's religious scrupulousness and assuming spectators' appreciation of the god's ironic wit, Jupiter swears by his own divinity (*summe Iuppiter*, 933) that he believes her to be chaste and calls down his own divine anger against Amphitryon if he's lying. Jupiter gets his desired reaction when the oath-respecting Alcmena averts his ill-omened words (*a, propitius sit potius!*, 935). He follows up with a still more cynical – and highly metatheatrical – ploy, co-opting for his present purposes Alcmena's earlier reflections (633–5) on the alternation of pleasure (*voluptas*) and sorrow (*maeror*) for mortals:

> nam in hominum aetate multa eveniunt huius modi:
> capiunt voluptates, capiunt rursum miserias;
> irae interveniunt, redeunt rursum in gratiam.
> verum irae si quae forte eveniunt huius modi
> inter eos, rursum si reventum in gratiam est,
> hic tanto amici sunt inter se quam prius.
>
> 938–43

In human life many things turn out like this: people experience pleasure, then they experience pain; anger arises, then they're reconciled. But whenever this sort of anger happens and they're reconciled again, then they're twice as much in love as they were before.

Jupiter's lofty-sounding gnomic reflections – he posits a tragicomic rhythm of human life,[51] as also a scene-structuring principle in *Am.* (Christenson 2000: 14) – hardly disguise his motivations. Given his expressed plans with Alcmena, the god is thinking less abstractly of the enhanced joys of 'make-up sex'.[52] Does it seem plausible to spectators that Alcmena and Amphitryon will be doubly in love when all the chaos is sorted out? Eloquent, self-dealing persuasion wins the day. Alcmena – an angry human placated by a god! – agrees to facilitate Jupiter-Amphitryon's thanksgiving sacrifice (to himself) to fulfil the genuine Amphitryon's prior vow to the god for military success (229–30). Meanwhile, Jupiter in an aside sadistically promises to cuff Amphitryon like a criminal (953) in their long-awaited, but mostly lost confrontation-scene.

Marital *pax* now seemingly restored, Sosia joins the counterfeit Amphitryon and his wife onstage. Sosia channels audience-response when he pushes back against Jupiter's characterization of the contentious encounter Sosia had earlier witnessed between the real Amphitryon and Alcmena, in which loomed the spectre of divorce, as a joke: 'I certainly took it as serious and sincere' (963). Sosia exits, Alcmena goes inside to prepare for the sacrifice and Jupiter again speaks directly to the audience. The pair who just left are duped (*errant probe*, 975), Jupiter gleefully announces, and there's further disruption to come. In summoning the offstage Mercury to return and drive off Amphitryon, Jupiter telepathically communicates with 'divine Sosia' (976); Plautus here scripts a demonstration that these are higher-order (immanent?) figures possessing their own supra-human communication system. Reprising now familiar and aggressively tragic language, Jupiter wants the latter 'deluded' (*deludi*), 'while I indulge myself with this borrowed wife of mine' (980–1) inside the palace. He sardonically frames Mercury's assistance here as sacral (*ut ministres mi, mihi quom sacruficem*, 983), extending the ridiculous conflation of sacrifice and sex he euphemistically suggested earlier in the scene ('I'll be doing the divine thing inside', 966)[53] and again placing his mobile sensibility (p. 142 above), this time in the religious sphere, on proud display.

Jupiter-Amphitryon only appears again for the regrettably fragmentary clash of the two Amphitryons before exiting into the palace to assist Alcmena in her labour (1039). Befuddled, abandoned and nearly stripped of his identity as *paterfamilias*, Amphitryon impiously pledges to burst into his home and kill whomever he meets – adulterer, wife, father, grandfather, et al. ('neither Jupiter nor all the gods will stop me!', 1051). Before this blaspheming Roman Campaneus (cf. Aesch. *Sept.* 427–9), in a fit of tragic madness prefiguring the intrafamilial violence of his yet to be born son (cf. Eur. *HF*), can commence eradicating his patriarchal line, Jupiter's cosmic thunderclap is heard and Amphitryon collapses onstage. The play's climax ensues with the Maenad-like Bromia's immediately following messenger's speech. In her brilliant *canticum*, Jupiter's cosmic status is restored in a narrative in which he, offstage, absurdly substitutes for Juno-Lucina in aiding Alcmena's parturition, and Hercules' birth seems almost appended as a provident afterthought to a play of disguise, deceit and seduction.[54] Bromia reports numinous phenomena accompanying Alcmena's painless parturition (*strepitus, crepitus, sonitus, tonitrus*, 1062), along with otherworldly light and the cosmic god's booming voice (Jupiter identifies himself as *caeli cultor*, 1065) to mark his offstage epiphany. The Jupiter Bromia describes is freed of human physiology, a disembodied voice, visible only as light, seemingly no longer the anthropomorphic lecher of myth. As she begins to relate the miraculous and terrifying first moments of Hercules' life (including a serpent-strangling!), the collapsed Amphitryon is revived from his death-like state (*quasi si ab Accherunte veniam*, 1078), his personal tragedy now apparently averted with a swiftly parodic self-anagnorisis (1082–3). Bromia brings him up to speed, including full revelation that Jupiter secretly slept with his wife on multiple occasions (1122) and that the snake-slaying twin is the god's son: so much for Mercury's claim that such matters would be kept tightly under wraps (pp. 139–40 above). Amphitryon declares his relief, in a sexual double-entendre (Christenson 2000: 314), 'at splitting half of his good fortune with Jupiter' (1125). Roman *pietas* implies some manner of reciprocity and interdependence (King 2003: 301–7), a mutual exchange between god and worshipping mortal, but Amphitryon's accounting is fuzzy: are matters with Jupiter so clearly all square? The Theban general calls for a propitiatory sacrifice to the god, co-father of the twins, and summons Tiresias.

Another thunderclap (*tonuit*, 1130), signalling that this Jupiter is the same as the one of the recent offstage epiphany, heralds the arrival of an actor re-costumed as the Olympian god. Jupiter is again his cosmic self, present for one last appearance in anthropomorphic form onstage, and in full control of *Am.*'s narrative. The god speaks grandiosely, if also tersely and impassively as *deus ex machina*, in confirming his role in the strange events at the palace, nixing the plan to summon Thebes' and tragedy's soothsayer (or any other human interpreters, 1132–3), and instructing Amphitryon to reconcile with Alcmena. In a swiftly bathetic turn, Jupiter blatantly emphasizes that he 'seized Alcmena's body' (*Alcumena usuram corporis / cepi*, 1134–5) and impregnated her in Amphitryon's absence.

As for mundane legalities, Jupiter nonchalantly adds that he forced Alcmena to engage in the sexual misconduct she fervently denied (882–3): *mea vi subactast facere* (1143). The verb *subigo* denotes violence (cf. Adams 1982: 155–6) and *vis* describes sexual assault (Adams 1982: 198). The *iniuria* Amphitryon has suffered clearly affords him legal redress (Treggiari 1991: 309–10). But absolute and capricious power prevails. Like future Roman emperors who crossed the boundary between humans and gods from the opposite side, almighty Jupiter eclipses and flouts human law.[55] Plautus provides a preview of what life for subjects of an artificially deified and fully licensed autocrat looks like[56] (for Nero's incarnation of such a terrorizing figure, see Wright's chapter in the volume).

Regarding compensation for the couple's (still unresolved) troubles, Jupiter again reminds us of the 'twofer' birth and assures Amphitryon that Hercules will bestow immortal fame on his mortal father (1138–40). All is presented conciliatorily, as if a reasonable exchange has taken place, even though the mortals never had a say in this unilateral 'agreement'. Amphitryon consents to all and urges spectators to applaud for 'mighty Jupiter', his former rival (*Iovis summi causa clare plaudite*, 1146), or at least the actor playing him, who is most deserving of their acclamation, if he, one of Roman society's disenfranchised *infames*, has in their eyes successfully impersonated their supreme deity.[57] This is no small task in that, as we've seen, the shape-shifting Jupiter in *Am.* uniquely subsumes so many New Comedy roles (*senex amator*, clever slave, sycophant, comic lover, braggart soldier) as he assumes absolute control of the theatre. Thanks to, probably, an artificial mechanical device, only now, for the first time onstage, Jupiter the divine character and theatrical construct transcends the stage, and Amphitryon now suggests we're obliged to clap for his performance. A cosmic Jupiter rises above Roman comedy's temporary stage to signal that, his glaring ethical flaws notwithstanding, he retains uncontested power and the universe's status quo has been restored. Jupiter achieves this grand transformation only because, as Aristotle observes (*Poet.* 1453a35), comedy prefers arbitrary, consequence-free endings, which we conventionally and sometimes inaptly deem 'happy'. The day is back on course, night is night again. The god most probably is off to do more of what spectators have just witnessed: 'I believe you all know how my father is' (104), Mercury had intimated in the prologue, referencing narratives of Jupiter's serial rapes with a nod and a wink – or perhaps a sympathetic shrug of resignation (an actor's choice).

Is *your* brow furrowed?

So Mercury asked spectators (*contraxistis frontem quia tragoediam / dixi futuram hanc?*, 52–3) when he coaxingly let it slip that *Am.* might be a tragedy. Unhappy fortunes ostensibly are reversed in *Am.*'s tidy ending: divorce no longer looms; Alcmena, absolved by Jupiter of her extramarital affair, is the mother of twins, one the glorious Hercules; the *paterfamilias* regains control of his household; Sosia will serve as Amphitryon's slave again. But do spectators so easily make the imaginative leap into post-play harmony as this neat closure suggests? Given especially that drama is fundamentally dialectical, nothing prevents us from asking impertinent questions extending beyond the boundaries of *Am.*'s fictional frame. Will Amphitryon apologize to Alcmena? Would Alcmena's renewed assertions of preserving her marital chastity bear any meaning in their confused, post-epiphanic household? Will Amphitryon perseverate on whether Alcmena found Jupiter to be a superior lover? What would Tiresias have said if he'd been brought onstage – what could he reasonably have said and would people have believed it? Was Hercules worth all that? Can this entire cosmic and comic mess simply be forgotten? Does Plautus' play escape audience censure for allowing gods of comedy and tragedy to conspire against defenceless mortals, precipitating ontological crises just for the fun of it, and to elide, or at least create fissures in, Roman theatre's previously well-defined generic boundaries? And what of that deal Mercury struck with spectators in the prologue: did a patriotic and beneficent Jupiter deliver to spectators the boons Virtus et al. might be expected to in wartime (p. 136 above), or were they fleeced by Mercury? The rest is silence.

Alcmena's and Amphitryon's anger, anguish and despair resonate with the audience at climactic moments, even if their characters at other times are portrayed farcically:[58] we seem strangely close to the cognitive realm of absurdist postmodern tragicomedy, where, as Ionesco insisted of his own work, 'the tragic feeling of a play can be underlined by farce' (1964: 25). The sublime in this instance is also the ridiculous.[59] Confronted with our moral complicity, are we proud of ourselves afterwards if we adopted the gods' Olympian and privileged theatrical perspective to laugh at their mortal dupes, whose plight – ignorance, vulnerability, distress and helplessness in the face of unaccountable power – also looms as our own dark human tragedy?[60] Even the most privileged members of Plautus' audience, high-status patriarchs, might feel insecure at the prospect of someone above them in Rome's complex vertical hierarchy exercising unrestrained power, with such a capacity for capricious arrogation.

For those who know the shape-shifting Jupiter's *modus operandi*,[61] there's a surplus of solipsistic malevolence still lurking in his universe, an unpredictable, mutable and hostile domain for his mortal victims. Doxastic conservatism embraces this universe's hierarchy as traditional, religiously and state-sanctioned, and so inevitable, but its grim ethos of autocratic domination, divine caprice and malignant hypocrisy undeniably has been exposed in *Am.*, a highly metatheatrical play that strongly suggests that deity – Jupiter's, at least – is a deeply fraught human construct. Plautus' transgressive *tragicomoedia* raises profound questions in clownish garb, and perhaps even encroaches on postmodern notions of the sublime that highlight the role of human misconception and reason's deficiency in the construction of 'reality' itself[62] (cf. this volume's Introduction, p. 7). Even so controlling a playwright as Plautus can't entirely prevent his fiction from leaking outside its frame, especially in a society divided into masters and slaves and so deeply entrenched in unjust privilege. It thus seems rash to altogether deny Plautus' audience any complexly fused seriocomic response to *Am.*, one that may range from laughter, glee or superciliousness to pity, compassion, fear, wonder, horror, awe, terror or simply confusion.[63]

Conclusion

Gnarly and unresolvable (historical) matters of authorial intent and audience reception notwithstanding,[64] *Am.* is a remarkable comedy in inviting its audiences, ancient and modern, to seriously ponder issues of cosmic order, justice, and human purpose and agency by having gods (tragi)comically descend to – or below – our level. The cocksure relocation of *Am.*'s deities also highlights the normalization of fascistic brutality, when this is unsentimentally made to seem tragicomically 'funny'. Any audience's (ancient or modern) accommodation of Jupiter only makes him more, rather than less frightening. Deeply flawed and slanted towards the privileged as representative Republican government and the Roman legal system were, there was an implict, abiding sense that some restraint against absolute power was needed, and concessions sometimes were granted to the lower classes, if only to ensure the privileged continue enjoying their privileges. While the vast majority of Roman citizens and subjects effectively were forced to grin and bear their oppression with resignation, they couldn't be prohibited from contemplating freedom and equality – certainly not as these might be only indirectly glimpsed in dramatic mythopoesis. Plautus' tragicomedy also challenges its audiences to consider why subjects play along with monstrous authoritarians. This complicated question lends itself to a myriad of responses across particular historical situations. Today, much of the world is fortunate to not live under a hereditary oligarchy such as the Roman Republic's, but despite advances in legal equality and most recently the #MeToo movement, 'Jupiters' (overwhelmingly, but not exclusively male) are still propped up in corporations, universities, churches and other institutional hierarchies, as also in sports and entertainment, where celebrity fetishizing resembles worship. The political ascendency of illiberal, clownish figures such as Donald Trump[65] within constitutional democracies is an alarming response to global tensions created by the quasi-religion of 'free marketism'.[66] There is grave potential for real-life tragicomedy and sublime horror when narcissistic and vicious personalities like Plautus' Jupiter assume active control over people's lives. The awesome power of Jupiter remains terrifyingly present today; still worse, the coerced or voluntary and self-interested participation of his subjects in it appears to be as potent as ever. *Amphitruo*'s emphasis on transgressive power (and its constructedness) ultimately suggests that we are not duty-bound to play along with it: the abruptness with which Plautus restores Jupiter's cosmic and religious authority after his ludicrous performance is all the more striking because of its patent arbitrariness.[67] However venerable its constructed tradition, unaccountable power casts an oppressive shadow; its origins lie in human social life and so it never is irrevocably fixed, but subject to scrutiny. Like Sosia, we can contemplate creative fantasies of freedom even in the face of overwhelming force.[68] Comedy's audiences, socially conditioned as they may be, don't have to mindlessly belly-laugh, and we can withhold our applause. Mercury in the prologue notes that the actor playing Jupiter faces a beating (even the lowly Roman theatre's hierarchy reflects the brutality of the gods' universe) if his performance is unsuccessful in winning spectators over (27–9), and in the play's final line Amphitryon leaves that determination to them (1146).[69] On today's geopolitical world stage we admire the inspiring example of the freedom-seeking people of Ukraine. It is, to Plautinists at least, exhilarating that Plautus can be made relevant in broad discussions of power today – and also deeply disheartening.[70]

Notes

1. This chapter is dedicated to the memory of Thom Worthen, whose ever-curious intellect often journeyed, as Lucretius might put it, 'beyond the fiery walls of the world' but never lost sight of its risible, if also terrifying lunacies.
2. For which see Papaioannou 2020.
3. For Plautine festival context see Franko 2014; more broadly in Rome, Padilla Peralta 2020: 131–50, e.g. 'The environment of festivals, games, and theater enabled community-bonding and building behaviors in part by unveiling and performing a vision of the *res publica* in which the gods were present and active; the gods were believed to be in attendance as citizens themselves—albeit uniquely powerful ones' (139).
4. The term preferred by Clark 2007, who demonstrates that '[divine] qualities were drawn on in the theatre to raise and to probe important questions about society' (20). Feeney 1998 writes of divine personifications more generally: 'part of a flexible and intelligent system, they may be apprehended as one of the specialized ways of conceptualizing and harnessing the power of divinity that was available to state, group, individual, and artist' (92).
5. All translations here are my own.
6. E.g. in *Trin.* the Sycophant claims to have navigated 'upstream' to Olympus in a fishing-boat, a dramatically tenuous scene and (temporary) comic catasterism that amounts to a meta-reflection on mimesis (Muecke 1985: 175–84). *Pseudolus*' confabulating cook claims to be Jupiter's private chef (842–6) within polemical discourse on cuisine-qua-comedy and Plautine (meta)poetics (Christenson 2020a: 85–8).
7. To which god we do not know. September's *Ludi Romani* in Jupiter's honour present an intriguing possibility. Our regrettable ignorance of Roman comedy's performance time(s) and setting(s) occludes consideration of celestial phenomena, such as the planets Jupiter and Mercury (cf. Van Steen's chapter in this volume), that might be visible to *Am*.'s spectators.
8. E.g. Gruen 2014: 606 (writing specifically of *Am*. 104–6): 'This light-hearted reference to divine amours delivered to a knowing audience has the delicious character of a mythological figure (i.e. Mercury) poking fun sympathetically at mythology – or, more probably, at those who swallow its sillier side'. Apropos of dismissing the gods' follies in *Am*. as festive fun, there is no evidence for a tradition in Roman theatre, akin to Athenian Old Comedy's, of bringing the gods onstage for ritually sanctioned ridicule (e.g. that of Zeus in Cratinus' *Nemesis,* with Bakola 2010: 168–73, 220–4). On the contrary, Mercury's prologue highlights *Am*.'s novelty in this regard.
9. Summary and assessment of the broad issues in Ando 2008: ix–vii. For the contested matter of 'belief' in Roman religion, see King 2003.
10. For the cognitive and social presence of belief in Roman religion (against previous scholarly denials of its existence), see Mackay 2017.
11. For its composition, see Manuwald 2011: 98–108.
12. Slater 2011, while refraining from discussion of *Am*., insightfully outlines a case for 'Plautus the Theologican reshaping Roman conceptions of the divine' (309). For my framing of

various issues, I am much indebted to Revermann's 2023 study of the representation of divinity on the Athenian stage.

13. In this chapter I sometimes collapse 'ancient audience', 'spectators' and 'we', and leave it to readers to draw distinctions among these equally hypothetical constructs. My views on *Am.* have evolved (γηράσκω δ' αἰεὶ πολλὰ διδασκόμενος) since I published a commentary on it in 2000, where overall I privileged its comic elements, sometimes at the expense of more nuanced reading of the play's polyphony. Here I focus on the more disquieting aspects – not entirely ignored in my previous work – of the gods' roles. I have benefitted from the criticisms of Gunderson 2015: 181–226, though I don't acknowledge the accuracy of them all (or condone their aggressive *ad hominem* tone).

14. It is unclear if this is Jupiter's first visit or a repeat performance: Christenson 2000: 47n.146

15. Chiu 2015 explores the mortal characters' reactions to Jupiter's distortion of cosmic time.

16. Parisi 2014 examines the contrasting semantic registers of epithets applied to Jupiter in arguing that *architectus* assumes broader programmatic significance in *Am.*, since it designates both (lofty) designer of the cosmos (e.g. Cic. *N.D.* 2.90) and (lowly) crafter of comic deception in Plautus (e.g. *Mil.* 901).

17. For the play she is, as Mercury puts it in financial terms, Jupiter's 'wife on loan' (*uxore usuraria*, 498).

18. Beard 2003 interprets Jupiter's role as an inversion of triumphal ritual, in which a *triumphator* imitates Jupiter, and concludes: 'The hermeneutic question that is at stake here (both in the drama and the procession) is: how *can* you ever tell the difference between "being", "playing", or "acting", god?' (43).

19. Visual evidence for early Roman theatrical spectacle is lacking, but the clever slave Pseudolus' features, for example, include a distended stomach, bulging eyes and an oversized head and feet (*Ps.* 1218–20, with Christenson 2020b: 329–30).

20. Mercury's superficial definition of the play's genre based on the cast's social class (after Aristotle's rigid distinctions between comedy and tragedy, *Poet.* 1448a) needn't circumscribe consideration of its hybridization of tragic and comic elements, especially as these may promote spectators' sympathetic identification with, and/or distance from, the human characters and thus provoke complex emotional responses. 'Tragicomedy' remains a slippery term, as it must have been for Plautus' audience, whether used as a broad descriptor reflecting incongruous social and biological rhythms of human life (Langer 1953: 362–3) or in attempts to define generic affiliation (historical overview in Foster 2016: 9–34; excellent historical account of tragicomic theory in Guthke 1966: 44–94). Hammond sensibly approaches classification of tragicomedy only in terms of 'family resemblance' (2021: 1–3). For 'tragic farce', see Charney 1987: 105–15.

21. Mercury, as if in colloquy with spectators, employs iambic trimeters more extensively than any other character (1–152, 463–98, 1006–8). Music also dramatically stops when Jupiter directly addresses spectators in iambics at 861–82 and 974–83, and he speaks thus as *deus ex machina* (1131–43); the play's only other spoken trimeters are contentiously exchanged between Jupiter and Alcmena (882–955; pp. 143–4 above) and in the corresponding (lost) scene between Amphitruo and Alcmena (frr. 7–10). For an illuminating account of *Am.*'s musical effects, see Moore 2021: 244–57.

22. Moodie makes a compelling case for Hermes/Mercury as 'a representative of the comic genres, an embodiment of that which is essentially comic' (2019: 117). For the astronomical implications of Hermes' revelry in 'perplexing' (περιτροπέων, *Hymn. Hom.* 4.452) mortals see Worthen 1991: 177–9.

23. Mercury's appeal to justice in a morally absolute sense had just (33-7) rhetorically sputtered into sophistic gibberish (Christenson 2000: 142-3).

24. Ovid apostrophizes Alcmena (*Tirynthia*, 112) in listing Jupiter's impersonation of Amphitryon among his mostly theriomorphic rapes just before transitioning to Neptune's similarly beastly assaults of mortal women.

25. Hiscock 2018: 58-61 analyses Mercury's acting edict (and *Am.*) in terms of 'aggressive' models of reception.

26. Leigh 2004: 37-56 explores the ideological contradictions of Plautine comedy's frequent association of the *servus callidus* with a triumphing Roman general against stereotypically alleged Carthaginian perfidy.

27. The gods ultimately settle on the 'brand' *comoedia* (88, 96, 868, 987). Mercury perhaps channels Plautine awareness that much depends on performance when he stresses that the play's script is set (*omnibus isdem vorsibus*, 55), whatever generic affiliation is affixed to it. Actors can play the serious comically, the comic seriously. How individual spectators emotionally process performance constitutes a further layer of a play's malleability; the truism that textual meaning takes place at the point of reception is all the more pertinent for live performance of a dramatic script.

28. In contrast to Jupiter, Mercury performs in all modalities of Plautine comedy (spoken, musically accompanied trochaics, polymetric song): cf. pp. 136-41 above.

29. Stewart 1960 identifies Nocturnus here with Dionysus, while Radif 2003 sees a reference to the notion of a nocturnal sun (still another doubling motif in *Am.*). Hannah 1993 elucidates technical astronomical aspects of Sosia's evocation of the evening (not dawn) sky.

30. For Mercury's typically Plautine 'faux monologue' here see further David 2015: 233-9.

31. By a legal fiction, Roman slaves have no parents (examples collected in Richlin 2017: 244-5; for metacomedy in Sosia's specific claim here see Wright 2013).

32. '[Sosia] grounds his identity in the objective condition of being a part of his master's property by incorporating the master's proprietary perspective' (Dressler 2016: 42).

33. The technical term for a theatrical mask is *persona*, while *imago* more generally refers to appearance, including a character's mask and costume.

34. Hints of Sosia's comic mobility, his ability to generate humour from, and even capitalize on, his ontological misfortune, can be glimpsed in his earlier interaction with Mercury, e.g. 304-7, 319-20, 331-2, 348-9, 380. Cf. his subsequent willingness to accept the (im)possibility of his own duality, 596-601.

35. If true, this doesn't necessarily make it a comedy. As Sophocles' *Philoctetes* and some extant plays of Euripides attest, tragedies can end happily (begrudgingly admitted by Aristotle, *Poet.* 1453a22-31). For the collapsing of generic boundaries in fifth-century drama, see Foley 2008.

36. A remarkable transfer of a stock comic role to a cosmic figure; so Dupont 2001: 181: 'The gods are thus in the position of ringmaster, a classic position in Roman comedy occupied by the parasite or principal slave, but they are ringmasters with powers infinitely superior to those of normal comic characters in the same position, a slave or a parasite, and it is this omnipotence that lends the comedy its tragic dimension, making of it so to speak a "supercomedy"'.

37. An elderly female slave protests the double standard in Roman marriage at *Merc.* 818-29.

38. Not in the literal sense that Dionysus presided over cultic theatre in Athens (it is unknown if Jupiter assumed a similar role in Rome).

39. Cf. Bromia's conventional designation of Jupiter as *summus imperator divom atque hominum*, 1121.

40. Jupiter here manifests a peculiarly Roman and Plautine figuration of epic's eristic/erotic dichotomy, for which see Shoshitaishvili, pp. 45–9, in this volume.

41. By matronly standards at least (Christenson 2000: 40–3).

42. I.e. the opportunistic Jupiter understands the belief system of his human other as a manipulable construct: see further Greenblatt 1980: 222–54. Slater 1993 analyses Plautus' improvising clever slaves as masters of mobile sensibility.

43. For elegiac elements, including the conflation of martial hero and solicitous lover, in the postclassical tradition of St Agnes literature, see White's chapter in the volume.

44. Cf. the Ovidian river god Anio's similar plea to Ilia as he is about to rape her: *quid fles et madidos lacrimis corrumpis ocellos?* (*Am*. 3.6.57).

45. For the *patera*'s expansive role as a prop in *Am*. see Polt 2013.

46. The actor playing Jupiter here demonstrates his mastery of Plautus' largely non-illusory drama by '(manipulating) the fictional temporality within the space of the theater' (Dixon and Garrison 2021: 85) through mere words and gestures. Ennius, Plautus' younger contemporary, verbally evokes an image of the sublime sky-god on the Roman stage: *aspice hoc sublime candens quem vocant omnes Iovem* ('behold this that glows aloft, which all call Jupiter', *scen*. 301 Jocelyn). Plautus similarly uses *sublimis* in this (physical) sense, 'raised up' (*As*. 868, *Men*. 992, 995, 1002, 1052), most evocatively (à la *Am*.'s Jupiter) at *Mil*. 1394, where slaves are fantastically ordered to seize and lift the soldier, his adulterous intentions exposed, so he can be grotesquely dismembered 'between heaven and earth' (1395).

47. In his colloquy with spectators, Jupiter anticipates not only Shakespearean metatheatre, but perhaps also the rudiments of Burke's 'dramatism' (1969), which emphasizes language's formative role in figuring human experience as theatrical.

48. Iurescia 2019: 437–8 discusses the pragmatics of the solicitous and deceptive Jupiter's 'overpoliteness' in the scene.

49. Feeney comments, 'The humour here is mordant, since ultimately Jupiter is telling the truth: in the end, it is all *iocus* to him, not *serium*' (1998: 107).

50. For this speech act see further Rosenmeyer 1995.

51. Gunderson perceptively comments, 'The *capiunt voluptates, capiunt miserias* clause would be at home in a tragedy. It offers the sort of reflection that someone might produce in reaction to a plot's reversal. Here, though, the sentiment expresses a tragicomic irony that arises from an unexpressed split between the subjects of the two verbs. Immortals dressed as mortals seize pleasure. And in return the merely mortal lay their hands upon woes. The mortals fought one another rancorously over a bitter truth. But amity is restored because the god showed up and told a lie' (2015: 223). For Jupiter's conflation of theatre and life see pp. 142–3 above.

52. Cf. the Ovidian 'love-doctor's' advocacy of strife in a relationship as a sure path to *concubitus foedera*, where '*Concordia* resides and *Gratia* is born' (*Ars*. 2. 462–4, perhaps with an intertextual nod to *Am*.; note also the Plautine use of divine qualities: p. 133 above).

53. For mortals, *res divina* means 'sacrifice'; Jupiter for his own amusement transforms it into a sexual euphemism (Christenson 2000: 287–8).

54. Though Hercules is a thematically relevant figure for *Am*., i.e. as a paradigm of a human who, after much personal toil (and infliction of violence on others), ultimately crosses over to the divine. For his heroic career as exemplary of the myth of replacement, see Worthen 1991: 98–120.

55. Roman law codified the emperor's exemption: *Dig.* 1.3.31 *princeps legibus solutus est*.
56. Caligula notoriously didn't wait for the senate's posthumous catasterism (Dio 59.26.5–10, 28.1–8).
57. Duncan 2006: 161 identifies the socially subversive potential posed by a successful actor like Roscius as suggestive of 'a deep Roman anxiety about acting as enabling a threatening social mobility, or even as exposing the fundamental arbitrariness of Roman social organization'.
58. Such as when the extremely pregnant Alcmena is made to seem sexually insatiable (Christenson 2001: 247–54) and Amphitryon behaves as a braggart soldier and general spoilsport (Christenson 2000: 30–1). De March 2019 applies Pirandello's theory of humour to account for the coexistence of serious and farcical elements in Alcmena's representation.
59. Longinus has little to say on comedy, but in a brief discussion of hyperbole concludes that 'laughter is an emotion (πάθος) based on pleasure' (*Subl.* 38.5). For the sublime in Greek Old Comedy see Porter 2016: 319–34.
60. We recognize that the human characters are tragically trapped in a divine comedy: '*Die Lust der Götter ist das Leid der Menschen. Die Tragödie der Menschen besteht darin, dass sie die Komödie der Götter ist*' (Schmidt 2003: 98). The notion of human beings as the gods' 'plaything' ('as flies to wanton boys') is presented as a commonplace at Pl. *Leg.* 644d7–9; cf. *Capt.* 22 *di nos quasi pilas homines habent*.
61. Cf. Ovid's *Metamorphoses*, with Hanses 2014.
62. For a survey of the vast and complex range of the postmodern sublime(s), see Shaw 2017: 167–207.
63. As the play's rich and differential reception indicates (survey in Lindberger 1956). Bond 1999 reports a fascinating array of audience reactions to his Perth production of *Am*.
64. We can easily imagine reactions to *Am*. mirroring the plurality and diverse experience of Roman comedy's heterogeneous audiences, differing as individuals did in legal and socio-economic status, gender, education, age, etc. 'The Romans' is a crude abstraction that arises from accepting our extant (elite) writers' perspectives as reliable indices of improbable cultural homogeneity. Tolliver, however, following a Christianizing scheme of Roman divinity's decline, clearly overreaches in generalizing that '(the) very fact that such a play (as *Am*.) could be produced suggests that popular respect for the Graeco-Roman gods was running low' (1952: 54). I am suggesting that *Am*., costumed as a Roman New Comedy, presented a – potentially, to some – frightening picture of power, without assuming any subversive intent on Plautus' part or that his sex farce had actual (and lasting) social impact on theological or other thinking in ancient Rome. Rey 2015 provides a survey of Plautine representation of Roman religious practice.
65. Apropos of Jupiter's expropriation of Alcmena's body while doing 'what he likes' (p. 135 above), Trump, a *vorsipellis* and tireless manufacturer of simulacra, was elected US president despite the emergence of videotape in which he boasts of his sexual omnipotence, 'I'm automatically attracted to beautiful . . . And when you're a star, they let you do it. You can do anything . . . Grab 'em by the pussy. You can do anything' (full transcript: https://www.nytimes.com/2016/10/08/us/donald-trump-tape-transcript.html, accessed 16 December 2022). À la Jupiter's immunity to human limitations, while campaigning Trump frequently claimed license to 'stand in the middle of Fifth Avenue and shoot somebody', and in his presidency habitually invoked an 'I was just joking' defence (cf. p. 143 above) when confronted with either his ignorance or cruelty: https://www.yahoo.com/video/trump-jokes-150223195.html, accessed 16 December 2022.
66. See the World Justice Project's most recent Rule of Law Index: https://worldjusticeproject.org/rule-of-law-index, accessed 16 December 2022.

67. 'And yet all of the furious action, in which Plautus confounds gods and mortals like long-lost twins, ends in setting two gods on high again – Mercury as god of comedy, of course, but also Jupiter who needs no prophets to speak his will, either to cast or audience – and it is Plautus who puts him back on high' (Slater 2014: 125).
68. Sosia's aspirations are not unique among Plautus' slaves (Richlin 2017: 417–77).
69. Cf. the comment of Bond 1999: 216: '(power) is key ... They, the audience, have the ability to make or mar the show by the quality of their attention and behaviour, have the power to ensure either a beating for the actors or the fruits of success.'
70. Special thanks are owed to Boris Shoshitaishvili for his helpful comments on the organization of an earlier draft of this chapter, as well as for his many insightful suggestions that have been incorporated into this volume's Introduction.

Works cited

Adams, J. N. (1982), *The Latin Sexual Vocabulary*, Baltimore: Johns Hopkins.
Ando, C., 2008, *The Matter of the Gods: Religion and Roman Empire*, Berkeley: The University of California Press.
Bakola, E. (2010), *Cratinus and the Art of Comedy*, Oxford: Oxford University Press.
Beard, M. (2003), 'The Triumph of the Absurd: Roman Street Theatre', in C. Edwards and G. Woolf (eds), *Rome the Cosmopolis*, 21–43, Cambridge: Cambridge University Press.
Bond, R. (1999), 'Plautus' *Amphitryo* as Tragi-comedy', *Greece & Rome*, 46: 203–20.
Burke, E. (1969), *A Grammar of Motives*, Berkeley: The University of California Press.
Charney, M. (1987), *Comedy High & Low*, New York: Peter Lang.
Chiu, A. (2015), 'The Longest Night: Time, Plot, and Characterization in Plautus's *Amphitruo*', *New England Classical Journal*, 42: 83–101.
Christenson, D. (2000), *Plautus: Amphitruo*, Cambridge: Cambridge University Press.
Christenson, D. (2001), 'Grotesque Realism in Plautus' *Amphitruo*', *Classical Journal*, 96: 243–60.
Christenson, D. (2016), 'All's Well That Ends Well? Old Fools, Morality, and Epilogues in Plautus', in S. Frangoulidis, S. J. Harrison and G. Manuwald (eds), *Roman Drama in its Contexts*, 215–29, Berlin: De Gruyter.
Christenson, D. (2020a), '*Nouo Modo Nouom Aliquid Inuentum*: Plautine Priorities', in G. F. Franko and D. Dutsch (eds), *A Companion to Plautus*, 77–91, Hoboken, NJ: Wiley Blackwell.
Christenson, D. (2020b), *Plautus: Pseudolus*, Cambridge: Cambridge University Press.
Clark, A. (2007), *Divine Qualities: Cult and Community in Republican Rome*, Oxford: Oxford University Press.
Connors, C. (2020), 'To Hell and Back: Comedy, Cult, and the House of the *Meretrix*', in G. F. Franko and D. Dutsch (eds), *A Companion to Plautus*, 151–63, Hoboken, NJ: Wiley Blackwell.
David, I. (2015), 'L'aparté chez Plaute à propos d'un passage d'Amphitryon (v. 153–340)', in P. Paré-Rey (ed.), *L'Aparté dans le théâtre antique. Un procédé dramatique à redécouvrir*, 228–47, Saint-Denis: Presses Universitaires de Vincennes.
De March, A. (2019), 'De tragikomische definities voorbij in Plautus' Amphitruo: Alcumena en Pirandello's humortheorie', *Lampas*, 52: 164–77.
Dixon, D. W. and J. S. Garrison (2021), *Performing Gods in Classical Antiquity and the Age of Shakespeare*, London: Bloomsbury.
Dressler, A. (2016), 'Plautus and the Poetics of Property: Reification, Recognition, and Utopia', *Materiali e discussioni per l'analisi dei testi classici*, 77: 9–56.
Duncan, A. (2006), *Performance and Identity in the Classical World*, Cambridge: Cambridge University Press.

Dupont, F. (2001), 'Duplication in Plautus' *Amphitruo*', in E. Segal (ed.), *Oxford Readings in Menander, Plautus, and Terence*, 176–202, Oxford: Oxford University Press.
Feeney, D. (1998), *Literature and Religion at Rome*, Cambridge: Cambridge University Press.
Foley, H. (2008), 'Generic Boundaries in Late Fifth-Century Athens', in M. Revermann and P. Wilson (eds), *Performance, Iconography, Reception: Studies in Honour of Oliver Taplin*, 15–36, Oxford: Oxford University Press.
Fontaine, M. (2014), 'The Reception of Greek Comedy in Rome', in M. Revermann (ed.), *The Cambridge Companion to Greek Comedy*, 404–23, Cambridge: Cambridge University Press.
Foster, V. A. (2016), *The Name and Nature of Tragicomedy*, London: Routledge.
Franko, G. F. (2014), 'Festivals, Producers, Theatrical Spaces, and Records', in M. Fontaine and A. C. Scafuro (eds), *Greek and Roman Comedy*, 409–23, Oxford: Oxford University Press.
Greenblatt, S. (1983), *Renaissance Self-Fashioning: from More to Shakespeare*, Chicago: The University of Chicago Press.
Gruen, E. S. (2014), 'Roman Comedy and the Social Scene', in M. Fontaine and A. C. Scafuro (eds), *Greek and Roman Comedy*, 601–14, Oxford: Oxford University Press.
Gunderson, E. (2015), *Laughing Awry: Plautus and Tragicomedy*, Oxford: Oxford University Press.
Guthke, K. S. (1966), *Modern Tragicomedy*, New York and Toronto: Random House.
Hammond, B. (2021), *Tragicomedy*, London: Methuen Drama/Bloomsbury.
Hannah, R. (1993), 'Alcumena's Long Night: Plautus, *Amphitruo* 273–276', *Latomus*, 52: 65–74.
Hanses, M. (2014), '*Plautinisches im Ovid*: The *Amphitruo* and the *Metamorphoses*', in I. N. Perysinakis and E. Karakasis (eds), *Plautine Trends: Studies in Plautine Comedy and its Reception*, 225–58, Berlin: De Gruyter.
Hiscock, M. (2018), 'Plautus, Rotrou, Molière: *Amphitryon* and the Violence of Reception', *Classical Receptions Journal*, 10: 40–69.
Ionesco, E. (1964), *Notes and Counternotes*, trans. D. Watson, London: John Calder.
Iurescia, F. (2019), 'How to Assess Politeness in Response to Impoliteness: Some Examples from Latin Comedy', in L. van Gils, C. Kroon and R. Risselada (eds), *Lemmata Linguistica Latina: Volume II: Clause and Discourse*, 431–47, Berlin: De Gruyter.
King, C. (2003), 'The Organization of Roman Religious Beliefs', *Classical Antiquity*, 22: 275–312.
Langer, S. K. (1953), *Feeling and Form: A Theory of Art*, New York: Scribner's.
Leigh, M. (2004), *Comedy and the Rise of Rome*, Oxford: Oxford University Press.
Lindberger, O. (1956), *The Transformations of Amphitryon*, Stockholm: Almquist & Wiksell.
Mackay, J. (2017), '*Das Erlöschen des Glaubens*: The Fate of Belief in the Study of Roman Religion', *Phasis*, 20: 83–150.
Manuwald, G. (2011), *Roman Republican Theatre: A History*, Cambridge: Cambridge University Press.
Martin, P. (1970), 'Plaute, *Amphitryon*, v. 292–462. Le dialogue Sosie-Mercure ou la destruction de l'homme par l'appareil tolitaire', *Caesarodunum*, 5: 171–7.
Moodie, E. (2019), 'Hermes/Mercury: God of Comedy?', in J. Miller and J. S. Clay (eds), *Tracking Hermes, Pursuing Mercury*, 107–18, Oxford: Oxford University Press.
Moore, T. J. (2021), 'Metre, Music, and Memory in Roman Comedy', in L. Curtis and N. Weiss (eds), *Music and Memory in the Ancient Greek and Roman Worlds*, 234–58, Cambridge: Cambridge University Press.
Muecke, F. (1985), 'The Sycophant Scene of the *Trinummus* (*Trin.* 4.2)', *Transactions of the American Philological Association*, 115: 167–86.
Papaioannou, S. (2020), 'Plautus and the Topography of His World', in G. F. Franko and D. Dutsch (eds), *A Companion to Plautus*, 287–300, Hoboken, NJ: Wiley Blackwell.
Parisi, S. (2014), '*Moechus* (e) *supremus*: gli epiteti di Giove nell' *Amphitruo* di Plauto', *Invigilata Lucernis*, 35–6: 255–69.
Padilla Peralta, D. (2020), *Divine Institutions: Religions and Communities in the Middle Roman Republic*, Princeton: Princeton University Press.

Polt, C. (2013), 'The Humour and Thematic Centrality of the *Patera* in Plautus' *Amphitruo*', *Greece & Rome*, 60: 232–45.
Porter, J. I. (2016), *The Sublime in Antiquity*, Cambridge: Cambridge University Press.
Radif, L. (2003), 'Il doppio notturno del sole: l'eclissi di Giove in *Amph.* 272', *Latomus*, 62: 789–93.
Revermann, M. (2023), 'Divinity on the Classical Greek Stage: Proposing a New Model', in S. D. Olsen, O. Taplan, and P. Tortaro (eds), *Page & Stage: Intersections of Text and Performance in Ancient Greek Drama*, 45–64, Berlin: de Gruyter.
Rey, S. (2015), 'Aperçus sur la religion romaine de l'époque républicaine, à travers les comédies de Plaute', *Archiv für Religionsgeschichte*, 16: 311–36.
Richlin, A. (2017), *Slave Theatre in the Roman Republic*, Cambridge: Cambridge University Press.
Rosenmeyer, P. A. (1995), 'Enacting the Law: Plautus' Use of the Divorce Formula on Stage', *Phoenix*, 49: 201–17.
Schmidt, E. A. (2003), 'Die Tragikomödie *Amphitruo* des Plautus als Komödie und Tragödie', *Museum Helveticum*, 60: 80–104.
Shaw, P. (2017), *The Sublime*, London: Routledge.
Slater, N. W. (1993), 'Improvisation in Plautus', in G. Vogt-Spira (ed.), *Beiträge zur mündlichen Kultur der Römer*, 113–24, Tübingen: Gunter Narr Verlag.
Slater, N. W. (2011), 'Plautus the Theologian', in A. Lardinois, J. Blok and M. G. M. van der Poel (eds), *Sacred Words: Orality, Literacy and Religion*, 297–310, Leiden: Brill.
Slater, N. W. (2014), 'Gods on High, Gods Down Low: Romanizing Epiphany', in I. N. Perysinakis and E. Karakasis (eds), *Plautine Trends: Studies in Plautine Comedy and its Reception*', 105–26, Berlin: De Gruyter.
Stewart, Z. (1960), 'The God Nocturnus in Plautus' *Amphitruo*', *Journal of Roman Studies*, 50: 37–43.
Tolliver, H. M. (1952), 'Plautus and the State Gods of Rome', *Classical Journal*, 48: 49–57.
Treggiari, S. (1991), *Roman Marriage*, Oxford: Oxford University Press.
Worthen, T. D. (1991), *The Myth of Replacement: Stars, Gods, and Order in the Universe*, Tucson: The University of Arizona Press.
Wright, M. (2013), 'Sosia's Ancestry and Plautus' Predecessors (*Amphitryo* 384–9)', *Latomus*, 72: 619–24.

PART III
HISTORY, HISTORIOGRAPHY AND THE COSMOS

CHAPTER 9
DAY SUDDENLY BECAME NIGHT: ECLIPSES AND THE SUBLIME IN GREEK HISTORIOGRAPHY
Philip Waddell

Introduction

The astronomical phenomena of eclipses were well-noted in classical historiography.[1] Since these events are now dated with precision, their inclusion in ancient historiography can aid modern scholars in establishing both specific and relative dating of historical events (e.g. Worthington 2004: 128–9). Further, modern scholars can use eclipse reports to check and correct historiographical timelines and narratives for accuracy. The question, however, of whether the date provided in an historical account appears to be accurate, and if so, when the relevant events surrounding it may have occurred, is only one aspect that informs our reading of these events in historiography. Eclipse episodes additionally serve a narrative purpose and may be employed or emphasized by the ancient historians to characterize actors through their interaction with the sublime.

Eclipses, as we will see in all the passages under discussion, are immediately felt as an inversion of the natural workings of the *cosmos*.[2] Regardless of leaders' eventual decisions in each crisis, the first reaction of the observer(s) is fear of divine manifestation of disordered nature.[3] The apparent disordering of nature through divine will, either as punishment in itself or as a communication of divine displeasure, might be especially intensified during the uncertainties of war. In his introduction, Thucydides describes eclipses as one of the prodigies that signalled the Peloponnesian War out for special consideration:[4]

τά τε πρότερον ἀκοῇ μὲν λεγόμενα, ἔργῳ δὲ σπανιώτερον βεβαιούμενα οὐκ ἄπιστα κατέστη, σεισμῶν τε πέρι, οἳ ἐπὶ πλεῖστον ἅμα μέρος γῆς καὶ ἰσχυρότατοι οἱ αὐτοὶ ἐπέσχον, ἡλίου τε ἐκλείψεις, αἳ πυκνότεραι παρὰ τὰ ἐκ τοῦ πρὶν χρόνου μνημονευόμενα ξυνέβησαν, αὐχμοί τε ἔστι παρ' οἷς μεγάλοι καὶ ἀπ' αὐτῶν καὶ λιμοὶ καὶ ἡ οὐχ ἥκιστα βλάψασα καὶ μέρος τι φθείρασα ἡ λοιμώδης νόσος· ταῦτα γὰρ πάντα μετὰ τοῦδε τοῦ πολέμου ἅμα ξυνεπέθετο.

1.23.3

And things formerly known from hearsay accounts, less often from factual confirmation, could now be believed, such as earthquakes, since these came without parallel in their wide distribution as well as severity, along with eclipses of the sun, which occurred more frequently than in any memories of the past, also droughts in some parts and the famines caused by them, and the disease that did the most damage and destroyed a large number: the plague. All these descended in conjunction with this war.

Thucydides, within a larger framework of comparing his war to the Graeco-Persian and Trojan Wars, describes omens that beset the Greek world, including earthquakes, eclipses, draughts, famines and plague. These portents, presented in crescendo culminating with plague, attest to the numinous nature of the Peloponnesian War. While it has been shown that, contrary to his assertions in this passage, Thucydides' narrative does not contain a greater number of eclipses than one would expect from such a period of time – he reports only two solar and one lunar eclipse – he clearly regards these phenomena as omens, and worthy of his reader's attention (Stephenson and Fatoohi 2001). In ancient historiography, generally speaking, omens and portents always come true, but are often misinterpreted or ignored (Mikalson 2002: 195–6, apropos of Herodotus). Even Thucydides, in his much-quoted opinion concerning the prophecy of the plague of Athens (2.54), critiques human credulity in seers, rather than in the omens themselves (Rustin 1990: 192–3) – otherwise, his statement at 1.23.3 concerning portents would have no force. Thus, the eclipse omen can be read at a cosmological level. No matter the action around it, the key political figure experiences a feeling of sublimity accompanying so sudden a disruption of cosmic laws portending earthly events, and must mediate that interaction on behalf of his army.

This chapter examines eclipses in historiography as three individuals deal with the apparent subversion and violation of the cosmological order through eclipses: Xerxes, Nicias and Alexander. The characterizations by Herodotus and Thucydides of Xerxes and Nicias, respectively, increase narrative tension and dramatic interest, to the doom of these characters as they engage with sudden astronomical disruptions. Both leaders, when faced with an eclipse, are too willing to entrust their armies to the interpretations of their advisors, and thereby proceed to their disastrous ends. By contrast, Arrian's representation of Alexander just before the battle of Gaugamela is much more complex, yet still operates within the framework of the first two cases. Arrian shows that, unlike Nicias, Alexander responds correctly to the eclipse and that, unlike Xerxes, he has divine favour. The deployment of eclipses in Greek historiography allows for an additional register of characterization as the historical figures mediate between sublime events and their military precarity.

Herodotus: Xerxes at Sardis

In book 7 of his *History*, Herodotus recounts the fateful invasion of Xerxes' great army from Persia. Herodotus colours and dramatizes this narrative with omens and portents warning Xerxes against pursuing his grandiose design. Among these is a dream that stopped Xerxes and Artabanus from halting the expedition (7.12–18), and another that

Day Suddenly Became Night: Eclipses and the Sublime in Greek Historiography

prophesied the king's crown would be taken from him (7.19). Herodotus clearly signals that Xerxes' expedition will be defeated, and also that the king is powerless to stop its failure. The last omen occurs as Xerxes is set to depart from Sardis, as Herodotus recounts a solar eclipse:

ὁρμημένῳ δέ οἱ ὁ ἥλιος ἐκλιπὼν τὴν ἐκ τοῦ οὐρανοῦ ἕδρην ἀφανὴς ἦν οὔτ᾽ ἐπινεφέλων ἐόντων αἰθρίης τε τὰ μάλιστα, ἀντὶ ἡμέρης τε νὺξ ἐγένετο. ἰδόντι δὲ καὶ μαθόντι τοῦτο τῷ Ξέρξῃ ἐπιμελὲς ἐγένετο, καὶ εἴρετο τοὺς Μάγους τὸ θέλει προφαίνειν τὸ φάσμα. οἱ δὲ ἔφραζον ὡς Ἕλλησι προδεικνύει ὁ θεὸς ἔκλειψιν τῶν πολίων, λέγοντες ἥλιον εἶναι Ἑλλήνων προδέκτορα, σελήνην δὲ σφέων. ταῦτα πυθόμενος ὁ Ξέρξης περιχαρὴς ἐὼν ἐποιέετο τὴν ἔλασιν.

7.37.2–3

As soon as the host set out, the sun left its seat in the heavens and disappeared, though the weather was clear and cloudless, and day turned into night. Troubled at the sight, Xerxes asked the *magi* what the portent meant. They declared that the god was warning the Greeks that their cities would be destroyed, since the sun prophesied for the Greeks, the moon for the Persians. Thus informed, Xerxes continued the march in high spirits.

Xerxes, struck by the ominous portent, attempts to discover its meaning by questioning his *magi*. Their response is that the omen was meant for the Greeks rather than the Persians, and so Xerxes need not worry. In terms of historical events, there is a problem with the story as Herodotus tells it: there was no eclipse in the spring of 480 BCE visible from Sardis (How and Wells 1912: 2.144–5, Glover 2014: 478). There was, however, an eclipse nearly a year earlier that was visible at Susa and another eclipse, visible from Sardis, in 478. This discrepancy has led some scholars to try to help Herodotus out of his dating error – either a clumsy mistake of source material or his confusion about details of time or location (e.g. Worthen 1997: 3, Glover 2014: 477–92).

Rather than wonder how Herodotus could be so wrong in his temporal presentation of events, let us focus on what is narratively gained by telling the story out of its proper chronological sequence. I argue, following the first of two possibilities given for the error in How and Wells (1912: 2.144–5), that the eclipse Herodotus references actually occurred at Susa in 481, as Xerxes' army was setting out from Persia.[5] The situations of the two events are roughly parallel – the army leaving Susa or Sardis – and dramatic tension is increased by postponing the eclipse until later in the narrative. Thus, the eclipse was transferred from Susa in 481 to Sardis in 480, when Xerxes commits, for Herodotus, his ultimate act of *hubris*, the bridging of the Hellespont. The omen then is pushed forward to a more dramatic historical moment: Xerxes' last opportunity to turn back before the plunge to his doom.

Xerxes is correct to be apprehensive in view of the eclipse, and his unspoken worry (i.e. that the expedition bodes ill for the Persian Empire) is realized in the following narrative. Herodotus characterizes Xerxes as a tragic figure who is blind to the signs that the gods give him, and so marches to his ruin. Xerxes thus joins the ranks of such figures as Croesus who are tragically unable to avoid their fate, although they have been repeatedly forewarned (e.g. Croesus' warnings at 1.13, 32, 34, 53, 55, 71, 85, explained at 1.90). The reader is reminded of the Croesus story explicitly when Xerxes encounters the Lydian king's boundary pillar at Cydrara (7.30) – the old boundaries are again being breached. In this case, Xerxes initially acts correctly: upon seeing the omen and recognizing its potential significance, he asks his advisors for guidance. He is, however, misled by their sanguine misreading of the omen. For the omen to be taken positively, from a Persian viewpoint, the sun must represent Greece while the moon represents Persia, which is the strategic interpretation of the *magi* for the king. Even more striking is the Helleno-centric identification of the Greeks with the sun, and the Persians with the subsidiary moon. The notion that the Greek city-states of the fifth century had a solar, rather than lunar, representative, especially when matched against the vast size and wealth of the Persian Empire, surely should have given Xerxes pause.[6]

Furthermore, even supposing the *magi* were aware of the probable inversion of roles, the truth would not likely be reported to Xerxes. By this point in the narrative, Herodotus' reader is well aware of the consequences of telling the King of Persia an unpalatable truth (e.g. 3.32, 34, 4.84, 7.11). Earlier in book 7, Herodotus introduced Onomacritus, an Athenian oracle-monger who gained favour from the Pisistratids by recounting to Xerxes select prophesies and omitting others that spoke of Persian destruction (7.6.3–4). In decoding this very clear omen, the Greek reader might share Xerxes' original dismay, but, unlike Xerxes, have good cause to doubt the veracity of the *magi*.

This episode also establishes a paradigm for this kind of interaction with the celestial sublime: the ruler/general sees the eclipse, enquires into its meaning and takes action accordingly. A narrative transformation occurs with the inquiry and subsequent action; the reader judges the behaviour of the king/general and predicts the eventual outcome based on his handling and processing of this portent. The historiographical deployment of eclipses characterizes the actors, especially since most readers were well aware of the eventual outcomes of all three historical incidents. The eclipse, as a powerful narrative device, enables the historian to hint at the result foreshadowed by the omen, and through this interaction with astronomical sublimity, to highlight the cunning or folly of the king/general.

Immediately following the eclipse and Xerxes' consultation of the *magi*, Herodotus recounts that Pythios the Lydian, one of Xerxes' nobles, was (correctly) apprehensive on account of the eclipse (7.38.1). Pythios asks that the eldest of his five sons serving in the king's army be left at home, just in case anything should befall the army (7.38.2).[7] An enraged Xerxes grants the request by executing the son and bisecting his body, and then marching his army through the gap. This story accomplishes several narrative tasks of Herodotean characterization. First, the true force of the omen is correctly understood by Pythios, who desires to avoid the total destruction of his family. The obvious meaning of the eclipse is now made manifest, since Xerxes' nobles are better able to interpret divine disfavour than their king. Secondly, Xerxes' intolerance for any voice at odds with his own is memorably showcased. The Greek reader is reminded that, under Persian rule, merely suggesting negative consequences to royal actions has disastrous outcomes. Thirdly, the scene recalls a previous incident in which Darius denied Oeobazus' request to leave his sons behind before the doomed expedition to Scythia (4.84). Darius killed all of Oeobazus' sons, and so, just as Xerxes would later do, left them behind. Herodotus' reader is thus given reason to anticipate a similar, ill-omened repetition of the Persian army's fate through this parallel action, especially as Xerxes emulates his father. If the meaning of the eclipse at Sardis was not sufficiently clear, Xerxes' actions immediately after aid our interpretation through his display of naked aggression and imperial power.

Herodotus uses the eclipse and its aftermath to suggest, rather than overtly predict, the imminent failure of Xerxes' expedition. The end is left in little doubt as Herodotus mobilizes the tragic story of Croesus and the largest mistake of Darius' reign at the outset of Xerxes' march of conquest. These two reminders from earlier in Herodotus' historiography provide a context for Xerxes' imminent failure to foresee the future. After the eclipse, Xerxes, rightly troubled and acting correctly, seeks an interpretation from the *magi* who, by implication, lie to their king. Herodotus, through the eclipse at Sardis, characterizes Xerxes as a tragic figure, reliant on his court and his own sense of invincibility as he inexorably retraces the footsteps of both his father and Croesus. Herodotus, however, is not alone in Greek historiography in his use of eclipses as events of cosmic consequence.

Thucydides: Nicias at Syracus

During the ill-fated Sicilian Expedition, everything possible had gone wrong: the overreach of the Athenian empire was coupled with the recall of Alcibiades (6.61), and the subsequent death of Lamachus (6.101). The expedition was left under the command of Nicias, who had opposed the idea from the beginning (6.9–14, 20–3). After months of siege and counter-siege, and the request and appearance of additional reinforcements from Athens, the Greek army was prepared to abandon their fortifications and escape. This process was halted in full force by an eclipse:

καὶ μελλόντων αὐτῶν, ἐπειδὴ ἑτοῖμα ἦν, ἀποπλεῖν ἡ σελήνη ἐκλείπει· ἐτύγχανε γὰρ πασσέληνος οὖσα. καὶ οἱ Ἀθηναῖοι οἵ τε πλείους ἐπισχεῖν ἐκέλευον τοὺς στρατηγοὺς ἐνθύμιον ποιούμενοι, καὶ ὁ Νικίας (ἦν γάρ τι καὶ ἄγαν θειασμῷ τε καὶ τῷ τοιούτῳ προσκείμενος) οὐδ' ἂν διαβουλεύσασθαι ἔτι ἔφη πρίν, ὡς οἱ μάντεις ἐξηγοῦντο, τρὶς ἐννέα ἡμέρας μεῖναι, ὅπως ἂν πρότερον κινηθείη. καὶ τοῖς μὲν Ἀθηναίοις μελλήσασι διὰ τοῦτο ἡ μονὴ ἐγεγένητο.

Thuc. 7.50.4

And when they were about to sail away, since everything was ready, there was an eclipse of the moon; for the moon happened to be full. Most of the Athenians, deeply impressed, urged the generals to stop, and besides Nicias (who was indeed somewhat over-credulous about divination and everything of the sort) said that until he had waited thrice nine days, as the seers dictated, he would not even deliberate about moving first. So after this reason for delay the Athenians stayed on.

In this passage, Thucydides makes a dual characterization, set up by the τε ... καὶ connection, implying a close coordination of subjects, of the Athenian soldiers and Nicias. The majority of the Athenians are disturbed by the eclipse and ask the generals to wait. The mob mentality of the Athenians, often noted by Thucydides, is here again put on display.[8] Orders and plans come from the soldiers rather than the generals. Further, the will of the Athenians is expressed as a voting majority (οἱ Ἀθηναῖοι οἵ τε πλείους), which recalls the Athenian democratic rule of the majority. The will of the *demos*, according to Thucydides, leads to disaster unless guided and controlled from above by politicians such as Pericles (e.g. 2.61.2, 65). Since Nicias, as Thucydides shows, repeatedly misreads the Athenian people, for example during the debate on the Sicilian Expedition and in his letter asking to be recalled (6.20-3, 7.11-15), it is impossible for him to exercise proper control over them.

Thucydides' use of the eclipse at Syracuse also serves to characterize Nicias and his religious/superstitious scruples. Thucydides in a parenthesis states that Nicias was devoted excessively (ἄγαν ... προσκείμενος) to 'divination and the like'. Thucydides does not critique Nicias' credulity, only his reliance on, or devotion to, the words of others concerning portents. Further, Thucydides tempers even this comment with τι, adding the amelioration of 'somewhat' to Nicias' excessive devotion.[9] In this way, while Thucydides might not have taken the omen of the eclipse as seriously as Nicias had, the historian signals that Nicias is not necessarily wrong to believe this occurrence to be a divine sign. Rather, Nicias is wrong in being overly reliant on divination, rather than on his own interpretations of what the omen might mean (Conner 1984: 194, Dover 1970: 428-9). Instead of thinking through the situation himself, Nicias consults the army's seers, and then, acquiescing to the majority, tables all discussion about the Athenian withdrawal for the specified twenty-seven days.[10] This delay proves disastrous for the Athenian expedition because the Syracusans, hearing the Athenian reaction to the eclipse, become more determined to maintain pressure on the Athenians and force a battle at sea (7.51). The paired reactions of the Sicilians and the Athenians to this cosmic occurrence is reminiscent of an earlier moment in the Sicilian expedition, when the Syracusans were terrified by lightning storms which the Athenians, in that instance acting rationally, knew were normal for that season of the year (6.70.1; Conner 1984: 194). Thus, through the Athenian and Nician (over)reaction to an eclipse, Thucydides shows that the tables have finally turned for the Sicilian expedition.

Centuries later, Plutarch in his *Nicias* presents a critique of the general's behaviour along similar lines to Thucydides'. Plutarch does not find fault with Nicias' religious behaviour, but with the interpretation put forth by the seers and accepted by Nicias:

τῷ μέντοι Νικίᾳ συνηνέχθη τότε μηδὲ μάντιν ἔχειν ἔμπειρον· ὁ γὰρ συνήθης αὐτοῦ καὶ τὸ πολὺ τῆς δεισιδαιμονίας ἀφαιρῶν Στιλβίδης ἐτεθνήκει μικρὸν ἔμπροσθεν.

Day Suddenly Became Night: Eclipses and the Sublime in Greek Historiography

ἐπεὶ τὸ σημεῖον, ὥς φησι Φιλόχορος, φεύγουσιν οὐκ ἦν πονηρόν, ἀλλὰ καὶ πάνυ χρηστόν: ἐπικρύψεως γὰρ αἱ σὺν φόβῳ πράξεις δέονται, τὸ δὲ φῶς πολέμιόν ἐστιν αὐταῖς. ἄλλως τε καὶ τῶν περὶ ἥλιον καὶ σελήνην ἐπὶ τρεῖς ἡμέρας ἐποιοῦντο φυλακήν, ὡς Αὐτοκλείδης διέγραψεν ἐν τοῖς ἐξηγητικοῖς: ὁ δὲ Νικίας ἄλλην ἔπεισε σελήνης ἀναμένειν περίοδον, ὥσπερ οὐκ εὐθὺς θεασάμενος αὐτὴν ἀποκαθαρθεῖσαν, ὅτε τὸν σκιερὸν τόπον καὶ ὑπὸ τῆς γῆς ἀντιφραττόμενον παρῆλθε.

Nic. 23.7–9

However, it was the lot of Nicias at this time to be without even a soothsayer who was expert. The one who had been his associate, and who used to set him free from most of his superstition, Stilbides, had died a short time before. For indeed the sign from Heaven, as Philochorus observed, was not an obnoxious one to fugitives, but rather very propitious; concealment is just what deeds of fear need, whereas light is an enemy to them. And besides, men were wont to be on their guard against portents of sun and moon for three days only, as Autocleides has remarked in his *Exegetics*; but Nicias persuaded the Athenians to wait for another full period of the moon, as if, forsooth, he did not see that the planet was restored to purity and splendor just as soon as she had passed beyond the region which was darkened and obscured by the earth.

There are many stories in Plutarch's *Lives* where a general calms his troops during an eclipse, including in the lives of Pericles (35.1–2) and Dion (24.1). Nicias, as portrayed in Plutarch's *Nicias*, was tragically unfortunate in that his seer, Stilbides, had recently died, and so he was without expert divination. Plutarch seems to echo Thucydides' judgment on Nicias' overreliance on diviners, since he notes that Stilbides usually calmed Nicias' religious feelings (Pelling 1992: 12–13). Further, Plutarch's *Nicias* paints the general as overly fearful and fawning towards the Athenian *demos*, who promote him for these qualities (2.4; Beck 2004: 109–10). Implicitly, the correct behaviour in Nicias' case would be to seek a professional opinion and make a command decision: either reveal the nature and cause of the eclipse (as Pericles and Dion did) or reinterpret the omen. Plutarch provides evidence from Philochorus, showing that an eclipse would be propitious for an escape, since darkness would be an aid to flight, and that Nicias need not have seen the omen as negative at all. Further, Plutarch, quoting Autokleides' *Exegetics*, states that the appropriate duration of time for propitiation of either solar or lunar phenomena was three days, rather than Nicias' twenty-seven.[11] Moreover, Nicias, as Plutarch points out, could plainly see that the moon was undamaged and still performed its celestial function immediately after the eclipse.

Nicias' reliance on diviners becomes disastrous in Plutarch's account when religious dread overcomes his knowledge, common sense and strategic leadership. For Plutarch, correct action should either mirror Pericles and Dion, who quickly explained to their troops what eclipses were and why they should not fear them, or Alexander, who made sure that interpretation of them fit his military plans.

Sublime Cosmos in Graeco-Roman Literature and Its Reception

Arrian: Alexander at Gaugamela

The behaviour of Alexander following the lunar eclipse before the battle of Gaugamela shows a marked contrast both to Nicias' and Xerxes', especially as he is represented by Arrian. Alexander was acutely aware of the power of his own image among his army and worked to maintain an awe-inspiring persona throughout his campaigns. The rumours of his divine parentage began early, possibly originating with Olympias, his mother, and continued throughout his life (Plut. *Alex.* 2; Worthington 2004: 31, 278-9). Indeed, Alexander found support for these rumours during his visit to the oracle of Zeus-Ammon at Siwa (Arr. *Anab.* 3.3-4).[12]

According to Arrian's version, Alexander took the lengthy detour to Siwa after his conquest of Egypt in order find out whether Zeus was his father, and if he could make the claim. Arrian records that rain fell on Alexander's army during the march there, and either two serpents or birds guided the army to and from the oracle – signs which were interpreted by Alexander as direct aid and communication from Zeus (3.3). At the oracle itself, Alexander met with the priests and privately asked his questions, to which, as he reported, he received a favourable reply (3.4.5). Alexander from this point on claimed direct descent from Zeus, setting himself up as a hero in the Homeric mould. Throughout his reign, Alexander fostered belief in himself not only as a son of Zeus, with all that this implied, but also as superhuman in all respects. Alexander was well aware of psychological power, and likely able to control the effect that an event such as an eclipse would have on his army and his enemies.

In the autumn of 331, after he had defeated Darius III's armies at Granicus and Issus, Alexander was prepared for what would be the climactic battle between his forces and those of the Persian Empire. Hearing news that Darius would contest his crossing of the Tigris, Alexander hurried there, and made the crossing unhindered. Following a two-day period of rest, Alexander was about to resume the march eastward. On the eve of his departure, the night of 20 September 331 BCE, the moon was eclipsed:[13]

ἐνταῦθα ἀναπαύει τὸν στρατόν: καὶ τῆς σελήνης τὸ πολὺ ἐκλιπὲς ἐγένετο: καὶ Ἀλέξανδρος ἔθυε τῇ τε σελήνῃ καὶ τῷ ἡλίῳ καὶ τῇ γῇ, ὅτων τὸ ἔργον τοῦτο λόγος εἶναι κατέχει. καὶ ἐδόκει Ἀριστάνδρῳ πρὸς Μακεδόνων καὶ Ἀλεξάνδρου εἶναι τῆς σελήνης τὸ πάθημα καὶ ἐκείνου τοῦ μηνὸς ἔσεσθαι ἡ μάχη, καὶ ἐκ τῶν ἱερῶν νίκην σημαίνεσθαι Ἀλεξάνδρῳ.

Arr. Anab. 3.7.6

While the troops were resting, there was an almost total eclipse of the moon, and Alexander offered sacrifice to Moon, Sun, and Earth, the three deities supposed to be concerned in this phenomenon. The opinion of Aristander, the seer, was that the moon's failure was propitious for Alexander and the Macedonians, and that the coming battle would be fought before the month was out; he concluded, moreover, that the sacrifices portended victory.

Day Suddenly Became Night: Eclipses and the Sublime in Greek Historiography

This eclipse occurs at a most dramatic moment, when Alexander, with fewer than 40,000 hoplites, is racing to encounter Darius and his immense force from the eastern and northern regions of the Persian Empire (3.8, 13; Bosworth 1988: 75–8).[14] Alexander ingeniously combines religious observance with a knowledge of natural phenomena: he sacrifices to the sun, moon and earth as planetary deities, while at the same time using Aristander's prophecy of a coming victory to argue for a pitched battle. Further, Alexander's seer Aristander announces that the moon's eclipse was unfavourable to Persia and favourable to Macedon, represented by the moon and sun, respectively.

Unlike Nicias, Alexander had much better control of his seer, since the unfavourable omen might well have been interpreted to portend disaster for the dramatically smaller Macedonian army. Indeed, Squillace includes this omen as an example of Alexander's 'propaganda machine' (2018: 153) during his conquest of the Persian Empire. Instead, the interpretation of Xerxes' omen of an eclipse portending the fall of empire is repeated. The omen in this case is much more understandable since the Macedonians identified with the sun (cf. Curt. 4.10.6).[15] Thus, we would expect a foreboding lunar prophecy to be regarded as propitious by the sun-loving Macedonians. Alexander also would have informed Aristander when the battle was likely to be fought, and so Aristander is able to incorporate this into his interpretation by informing the troops that the battle would be fought within a month – a safe bet, since Darius is supposed to be massing near the Tigris crossing. Alexander again skilfully manages the outcome of this celestial portent with favourable sacrifices through Aristander's positive interpretation of the eclipse.

There may, however, be a further element to consider. A boundary crossing similar to that committed by Xerxes in Herodotus recurs in the case of Alexander, when a single ruler attempts to unite Greece and Persia. In the eclipses at both Sardis and at the Tigris, Herodotus and Arrian agree that the sun represents Greeks and the moon represents Persians. In his characterization of Alexander, Arrian repeatedly portrays him as a divinely blessed king and commander, whose transgressions of boundaries are not only licit, but heaven sanctioned. Arrian, in recounting the eclipse before Gaugamela, may have had Herodotus' story of a trans-liminal crossing occasioning divine/celestial commentary in mind, but now the omen is doubly reversed. Rather than a solar eclipse, Arrian reports a lunar eclipse, albeit with the celestial bodies still representing the same parties as in Herodotus. Arrian also characterizes the responses to the eclipse: Alexander's piety and blessed status as a son of Zeus are on display, rather than Xerxes' bewilderment and anxiety. Thus, following the examples of Herodotus and Thucydides, Arrian uses the language of eclipse to characterize Alexander.

Conclusion

The narratives of Herodotus, Thucydides and Arrian all employ eclipses in order to elevate dramatic tension into cosmic relevance and display the characteristics of their central figures. These sublime interactions with cosmic irregularity force the actors to choose how to interpret the will of their gods. Herodotus and Thucydides portray commanders doomed by misreadings of eclipses that occur during pivotal military engagements. In both instances, the dread of the commanders is prescient, and their subsequent actions betray not only what their eventual fates will be, but also give a clue as to the causes of their downfalls. Thucydides, in dooming Nicias, blames the uncontrolled Athenian people who are forever changing their intentions and the inability of Nicias to reign them in. Herodotus shows Xerxes to be properly religious, but too easily reassured by those close to him in echoing Darius' foolhardy invasion of Scythia. Once reassured, Xerxes returns to type by punishing any view opposed to his own. Alexander's correct and politically savvy reaction to the eclipse before Gaugamela is deployed in Arrian to showcase the calm piety of the Macedonian king and the veracity of his claims to be born from Zeus. When Alexander transgresses boundaries, as Xerxes had done when he bridged the Hellespont, Arrian characterizes him as overturning the wrongs inflicted by the Persians against the Greeks through a reversal of the omen of the eclipse. Thus, while eclipses in historiography can be studied, as they traditionally have been, to establish relative or absolute chronology, they also illustrate how, in keeping with a historiographer's narrative aims, each protagonist mediates his interaction with the cosmic sublime for his own worldly success.

Notes

1. The present work takes inspiration from Worthen 1997.
2. For a concise discussion of eclipses in antiquity and in the Herodotus passage discussed here (pp. 160–3 above), see Glover 2014: 472–5.
3. A partial collection of ancient episodes centring on fear of eclipses, and a much more recent coda from twentieth-century Russia, can be found in McCartney 1936. For some examples of twentieth-century English beliefs concerning eclipse-presaged harsh weather, see McCartney 1928: 35–6.
4. For Thucydides, I print Jones's Oxford Classical Text (1902) with Lattimore's Hackett translation (1998); for Herodotus, Wilson's Oxford Classical Text (2015) and Mench's Hackett translation (2014); for Plutarch, Ziegler's Teubner (1959) and Perrin's Harvard University Press translation (1916); for Arrian, Roos's Teubner (1967) and De Sélincourt's Penguin (1958).
5. *Contra* Glover 2014, who posits a lunar rather than solar eclipse of 25 March 480 BCE, thus explaining the religious mistake of Herodotus' attribution of Persia to the moon, the Greeks to the sun. While Glover's argument is attractive, I contend that Herodotus was not so concerned with accuracy of place and time as he was with forging a dramatic historiographical narrative, even if it ignored, misreported or misinterpreted omens.
6. For the moon's coincidence with human agency, see Austin's chapter in this volume.
7. Glover 2014: 482–4 sees this as reinforcing the lunar eclipse of 25 March, since this episode must occur soon after the eclipse itself. Herodotus, however, apparently had few scruples about shifting the time and place of the Pythios story to continue the thrust of his narrative.
8. For Nicias' lack of control over his own forces, see his comments at 7.14.2.
9. For a view of Thucydides' supposed atheism in this episode, see Powell 1979: 47–8.

10. For Nicias' possible motivations in agreeing with the divination, see Powell 1979: 26.
11. Powell 1979: 27–8, however, posits that Plutarch's change in the prophecy from 'thrice-nine' to 'three' and the comment that eclipses are beneficial to those attempting to escape are both made in hindsight well after-the-fact. Thus, Nicias' diviners are not mistaken from a religious point of view.
12. The story also appears at Diod. Sic. 17.49–51, Curt. 4.7.5–30 and Plut. *Alex.* 26–7.
13. The eclipse is also recorded at Plut. *Alex.* 31.4 and Curt. 4.10.6 but omitted in Diod. Sic.'s account. For a discussion of the date, see Burn 1952: 84–5. For a recent study of the ancient Babylonian Astrological Calendar for this event, see van der Spek 2003: 289, 294–5, 328.
14. For the size of Darius' army, Curt. 4.12.11 gives the figure of 200,000 infantry while Arr. *Anab.* 3.8 reports 1 million. Regardless of the exact numbers, Alexander's army unquestionably was outnumbered.
15. Atkinson 1980: 389 also notes the possibility of an intertext between Curtius' account of Gaugamela and Hdt. 7.37, with Curtius taking inspiration from Herodotus' narrative.

Works cited

Atkinson, E. (1980), *A Commentary on Quintius Curtius Rufus' Historiae Alexandri Magni Books III and IV*, Amsterdam: J. C. Geiben.
Beck, M. (2004), 'Plutarch on the Statesman's Independence of Action', in L. De Blois, J. Bons, T. Kessels and D. Schenkenveld (eds), *The Statesman in Plutarch's Works, vol 1: Plutarch's Statesman and his Aftermath: Political, Philosophical, and Literary Aspects*, 105–14, Leiden: Brill.
Bosworth, A. (1988), *Conquest and Empire: The Reign of Alexander the Great*, Cambridge: Cambridge University Press.
Burn, A. (1952), 'Notes on Alexander's Campaigns, 332–330', *Journal of Hellenic Studies*, 72: 81–91.
Conner, R. (1984), *Thucydides*, Princeton: Princeton University Press.
Dover, K. (1970), *A Historical Commentary on Thucydides, volume IV*, Oxford: Oxford University Press.
Glover, E. (2014), 'The Eclipse of Xerxes in Herodotus 7.37: *lux a non obscurando*', *Classical Quarterly*, 64: 471–92.
How, W. and J. Wells (1912), *A Commentary on Herodotus in Two Volumes*, Oxford: Oxford University Press.
McCartney, E. (1928), 'Greek and Roman Weather Lore of the Sun and the Moon (Concluded)', *Classical Weekly*, 22: 33–7.
McCartney, E. (1936), 'Methods of Dispelling Fear of Eclipses', *Classical Weekly*, 36: 6–7.
Mikalson, J. (2002), 'Religion in Herodotus', in E. Bakker, I. De Jong, and H. Van Wees (eds), *Brill's Companion to Herodotus*, 187–98, Leiden: Brill.
Pelling, C. (1992), 'Plutarch and Thucydides', in P. Stadter (ed.), *Plutarch and the Historical Tradition*, 10–40, London: Routledge.
Powell, A. (1979), 'Thucydides and Divination', *Bulletin of the Institute of Classical Studies*, 26: 45–50.
Powell, C. (1979), 'Religion and the Sicilian Expedition', *Historia*, 28: 15–31.
Rustin, J. (1990), *Thucydides: The Peloponnesian War Book II*, Cambridge: Cambridge University Press.
Squillace, G. (2018), 'Alexander and his "Propoganda Machine"', in K. Nawotka, R. Rollinger, J. Wiesehöfer and A. Wojciechowska (eds), *The Historiography of Alexander the Great*, 149–56, Wiesbaden: Harrassowitz Verlag.

Stephenson, F. and L. Fatoohi (2001), 'The Eclipses Recorded by Thucydides', *Historia*, 50: 245–53.
van der Spek, R. (2003), 'Darius III, Alexander the Great and Babylonian Scholarship', *Achaemenid History*, 13: 289–346.
Worthen, T. (1997), 'Herodotus' Report on Thales' Eclipse', *Electronic Antiquity*, 3.7: 1–7.
Worthington, I. (2004), *Alexander the Great: Man and God*, Harlow: Pearson Education, Ltd.

CHAPTER 10
THE COSMIC BARRIER: THE ISTHMUS OF CORINTH IN IMPERIAL LATIN POETRY
David J. Wright

Introduction[1]

The Isthmus of Corinth, the narrow strip of land that connects the Peloponnese to central Greece, is a frequent point of reference in the poetry of the early Roman Empire. Richard Tarrant remarks, 'Latin poets from Ovid onward ... felt an almost irresistible urge to mention the Isthmus of Corinth wherever possible' (1989: 141–2). In this chapter, I seek to explain *why* the Isthmus of Corinth is such a popular poetic locus. What specifically was it about the Isthmus that drew the attention of so many Latin poets of the first century CE? I propose that the frequency of allusions to the Isthmus is a nod to plans of Caligula and Nero to build a canal across it, a topic of considerable controversy and consternation. Many of these poetic references to the Isthmus feature the language of cosmic disaster, and various prose sources record that those who planned a canal at the Isthmus were warned of a great flood. This backdrop of flood warnings is critical to understanding the first-century poetic references to the Isthmus, in which the rhetoric of cosmic cataclysm may hint at the canal project's potential deleterious effects: the image of the Isthmus as a barrier whose removal precipitates catastrophic destruction particularly appealed to poets of these politically chaotic times in the Roman world. My study culminates in analysis of a simile in Lucan's *Pharsalia* that offers a particularly pointed description of the Isthmus. I argue that Lucan's representation of the Isthmus specifically alludes to Nero's plans to build the canal and the likely disaster that would ensue by suggestively figuring the project as both a monstruous monument to the emperor's ego and a climatic threat. This reference also serves to more broadly characterize Nero as a tyrannical, transgressive and sublimely terrifying figure whose excessive actions threaten the very order of the cosmos (for Plautus' Jupiter as a tragicomic prototype of such a figure, see Christenson's chapter in this volume).

Geographic and cultural significance of the Isthmus

Its central and strategic location within the Mediterranean world made the Isthmus of Corinth a place of great significance. Thucydides attributes Corinth's rise to power and wealth to its location on the Isthmus, and styles the Isthmus as a locus for communication inside and outside the Peloponnese (1.13.5). Strabo describes the Isthmus as a pivotal space for commerce, as well as the crossroads between Asia and Italy (8.6.20). Greek city-states frequently regarded the Isthmus as an ideal meeting-place, especially during the Persian Wars, i.e. conflicts in which Greeks often represented themselves as fighting for their freedom (Pettegrew 2016: 32–3). The biennial Isthmian Games further contributed to the idea that the Isthmus was a space for Greeks from all over Hellas to gather and celebrate aspects of their shared culture. The Isthmus became a space loaded with symbolic import, especially regarding the freedom or domination of Greece. Pettegrew's analysis (2016: 95–7) of Polybius' representations of the Isthmus demonstrates that control of this tiny land bridge was key to controlling Greece (Polyb. 2.43.2). Polybius refers to the Isthmus as one of the 'fetters of Greece' (πέδας Ἑλληνικάς, 18.11, 18.45). Flaminius, following the conclusion of the Second Macedonian War, elects to declare the freedom of Greece at the Isthmian Games (Plut. *Vit. Flam.* 13.8). With the Romans' sacking of Corinth in 146 BCE, the region became closely associated with Greece's subjugation. Cicero anthropomorphizes the Isthmus, calling it the 'neck of Greece' (*faucibus Graeciae*), and states that Rome *had* to destroy Corinth because its location on the Isthmus made it well suited for imperial ambitions that threatened Rome (*Leg. agr.* 2.87).[2] Through these cultural, political and historical lenses we can more fully appreciate the symbolic implications of building a canal across the Isthmus. Since the space was deeply associated with Greek conceptions of freedom and dominance, a canal might easily be seen to signify Nero's political domination of Greece, akin to his competing in, and appropriating for his own aggrandizement, the Panhellenic Games. Poets understandably might emblematically use the prospect of the canal project to highlight Nero's tyrannical ambitions more generally, as they simultaneously exploited the Isthmus' specific connections with the 'destruction' of Greece.

Nero and boundaries

Various literary accounts present Nero as a transgressive figure who violates natural and social boundaries of gender, sexuality and class, as well as the human/animal and human/god divides, as Roman writers constructed these. Paradigmatic of Neronian subversion of gender and sexuality[3] is Suetonius' representation of Nero's transformation of the enslaved boy Sporus:

> puerum Sporum exsectis testibus etiam in muliebrem naturam transfigurare conatus cum dote et flammeo per sollemnia nuptiarum celeberrimo officio deductum ad se pro uxore habuit.
>
> Ner. 28.1

He tried to change the nature of the boy Sporus into a woman's by castrating him. After marrying him in a well-attended ceremony, with a dowry and a veil and in accordance with all the sacred rights of nuptials, he treated him as a wife.[4]

The Cosmic Barrier: The Isthmus of Corinth in Imperial Latin Poetry

Unsurprisingly in a slave society, the violence against Sporus is glossed over and Suetonius' text instead focuses on the gendered aspects of Sporus' metamorphosis. Since Romans viewed gender as 'natural' and binary, Nero here violates natural law by altering Sporus' (male) *naturam*. While Nero's homoerotic attraction to the boy conforms with elite standards of sexuality, same-sex marriage was not legally or socially sanctioned, and Nero disrupts class lines by marrying an enslaved person – remarkably so in that the emperor is the most powerful man in the Roman world. Suetonius also writes that Nero himself defied traditional gender constructions:

> suam quidem pudicitiam usque adeo prostituit, ut contaminatis paene omnibus membris novissime quasi genus lusus excogitaret, quo ferae pelle contectus emitteretur e cavea virorumque ac feminarum ad stipitem deligatorum inguina invaderet et, cum affatim desaevisset, conficeretur a Doryphoro liberto; cui etiam, sicut ipsi Sporus, ita ipse denupsit, voces quoque et heiulatus vim patientium virginum imitatus.
>
> Ner. 29.1

Indeed he dishonoured his own virtue to such an extent that, with nearly all of his limbs contaminated, he thought up a type of game in which, covered in the skin of a wild beast, he was released from a cage and attacked the private parts of men and women tied to a stake, and when he had raged enough, he was 'finished off' by the freedman Doryphorus. He (Nero) even thus married this man, just as Sporus had married him, and imitated the voices and the wailing of violated virgins.

Nero subverts Roman conceptions of the natural in multiple ways. He assumes the skin of an animal and blurs the line between man and beast. He thoroughly confutes gender constructs by marrying a man, this time playing the role of the bride (*denupsit*), and even plays the passive role on his wedding night by allowing himself to be sexually penetrated by a social inferior, in violation of elite male standards of bodily integrity.[5] In a similar vein, the allegations that Nero slept with his mother suggest no less stark a transgression of Roman social and sexual norms (Ormand 2018: 334–42).

Nero elsewhere is described as crossing the line between mortal and god. There are Roman precedents for this, such as the cases of Julius Caesar and Augustus (formally deified after their deaths). Nero's other Julio-Claudian predecessor Caligula explicitly promoted his own divinity during his lifetime, much to the chagrin of the senatorial elite. Nero famously built a statue of himself in the likeness of Helios outside his *Domus Aurea* (Plin. *NH* 34.45; Dio 65.15), and also cultivated a relationship with Apollo – some sources record Nero being hailed as Apollo-Sol (Suet. *Ner.* 53; Dio 62.20.5), and Nero's coins depict him singing with a lyre in the guise of Apollo.[6] Tacitus writes that Nero declared his voice to be 'celestial' and demanded that he receive sacrificial honours (*Ann.* 16.22). This penchant for blurring the human and divine also lies behind negative characterizations of Nero's attempt to build a canal through the Isthmus: he, as a mortal, seeks to alter landscapes which the gods themselves created.

In Lucan's *Pharsalia*, Nero seemingly is represented as one of the mythic Giants, though the presentation is open to varying interpretation. At the very beginning of his epic (1.33–66), Lucan presents Nero with sufficient ambiguity and irony that this passage can be read as either (sincerely) apotheosizing the emperor or criticizing his aspirations for divinity.[7] Lucan claims that the civil wars of the late first century BCE were all worth it because they resulted in the formation of the Principate and Nero's rise to power. Ostensibly, Lucan may be praising Nero in asserting that he will assume the role of an Olympian:

> te, cum statione peracta
> **astra petes** serus, praelati regia caeli
> excipiet gaudente polo: seu sceptra tenere
> seu te **flammigeros** Phoebi conscendere currus
> telluremque nihil mutato sole timentem
> igne uago lustrare iuuet ...
>
> *1.45–50*

The kingdom of heaven you prefer will accept you, the sky's axis rejoicing, when you, late, will seek the stars after completing your watch: whether it please you to hold the scepter or to climb upon the flame-bearing chariot of Phoebus and with wandering fire survey the land, fearing nothing, even though the sun has been transformed ...

Lucan suggests that Nero will be like Jupiter (*sceptra tenere*) or Apollo (*Phoebi conscendere currus*). But at the same time, one may interpret the language of 'seeking the stars' (*astra petes*) as figuring Nero as one of the Giants who seeks to overthrow the rule of Zeus; *petere* can mean 'attack' (*OLD* 2), which is what the Giants are up to when they build a path to the stars: 'They say that the Giants strove to attain the kingdom of the heavens and to heap up and pile the mountains to the lofty stars' (*adfectasse ferunt regnum caeleste gigantas / altaque congestos struxisse* **ad sidera** *montis*, Ov. Met. 1.52–3). The beginning of Lucan's encomium similarly recalls the Gigantomachy:

> quod si non aliam uenturo fata Neroni
> inuenere uiam magnoque aeterna parantur
> regna deis caelumque suo seruire Tonanti
> **non nisi** saeuorum potuit **post bella gigantum,**
> iam nihil, o superi, querimur; scelera ipsa nefasque
> hac mercede placent.
>
> *1.33–8*

But if the fates could find no other way for Nero's arrival, and the eternal kingdoms are bought by the gods at a hefty price, and heaven was not prepared to serve its own Tonans except after the battles of the savage Giants, we do not complain at all, you above; the very crimes and the sacrilege are pleasing at this price.

Lucan's satiric import perhaps rings loudest when he suggests that crimes (*scelera*) and sacrilege (*nefas*) of civil war should be considered positive developments. Furthermore, the image of Nero embarking on the flame-bearing (*flammigeros*) chariot of Apollo also suggests Phaethon, the notorious son of Apollo who almost destroys the world in a great conflagration.[8] Later in this panegyric, Lucan remarks that the sky 'will feel (Nero's) weight' (*sentiet axis onus*, 57): this too adds to the Gigantomachic, and therefore transgressive, aspects of Nero's apotheosis, since the Giants are characterized by their massive bodily weight.[9] All these examples reveal a larger pattern of presenting Nero as a scorner of 'natural' boundaries whose upheaval bears dire, even cosmic consequences.

Human technological interventions in the waterscape

Ancient literary sources that describe large-scale construction projects vary in their assessment of them. Some treat these feats of engineering with great praise, others may condemn a very similar project. For example, Statius in *Silvae* 4.3 commends the construction of Domitian's *Via Domitiana*, and Suetonius dedicates entire sections of his biographies to praising the building projects of Julius Caesar (44) and Augustus (29). Some of these projects earn special praise because they are thought to demonstrate (super)human domination of the natural world (Purcell 1996). At the same time, such texts may impugn feats of engineering for their perceived excess and luxuriousness and, in some cases paradoxically, their violation of the natural world. During the late Republic, one topos involves criticism of the lavish seaside villas of Roman elites. Horace touches on this theme in multiple *Odes*, e.g.:

> contracta pisces aequora sentiunt
> iactis in altum molibus: huc frequens
>   caementa demittit redemptor
>   cum famulis dominusque terrae
> fastidiosus.

3.1.33–7

The fish feel the shrinking seas when the moles are thrown into the deep. Here the contractor, along with his slaves, and the owner, hateful of the earth, repeatedly cast down cement.

These projects come under moral scrutiny because they violate the natural separation of land and sea.[10] Reitz-Joosse 2021: 63–99 demonstrates that praise or censure of these projects usually has much to do with the authors' attitudes towards the person undertaking the projects. Endeavours by Julius Caesar or Augustus, for example, tend to garner more plaudits because sources are more favourably disposed towards them as rulers, whereas the projects of figures to whom our extant sources are overwhelmingly hostile, such as Nero, meet with disapproval. In the latter cases, the projects are depicted as infringing on the natural world, while economic or other public benefits of these structures are ignored.

Some descriptions of these projects express ambiguity towards them. One such example comes from the *Georgics*, where, within the *Laudes Italiae*, Vergil catalogues Italy's prominent bodies of water. The poet describes the Portus Julius, an artificial harbour Agrippa created by connecting Lake Avernus and the Lucrine Lake to the Tyrrhenian sea thus:

> an memorem portus Lucrinoque addita claustra
> atque **indignatum** magnis stridoribus aequor,
> Iulia qua ponto longe **sonat** unda **refuso**
> Tyrrhenusque fretis immittitur aestus Auernis?
>
> *2.161–4*

Or should I mention the harbors and the barriers added to the Lucrine, or the sea, angry with a great rumbling, where the Julian wave, as the sea pours in, roars far and wide and the Tyrrhenian sea is let into the channels of Avernus?

Some critics, e.g. Hardie 1986: 208–9, Armstrong 2009, have seen in these lines an entirely positive portrayal of Octavian's works: the construction of the harbour demonstrates Octavian's superhuman power over nature in its suppression of potential cosmic disturbance. Thomas 1988: 186–7, however, maintains that the verses suggest a violation of nature and allude to the troubling prodigies arising from the harbour's construction that Servius (*ad loc.*) and Dio 48.50 record. Vergil's description is also filled with the language of cosmic destruction. At the opening of the *Aeneid*, Vergil uses similar language to describe a cosmic, world-threatening storm (1.50–156). The *Georgics* account describes a personified sea that is angry (*indignatum*) and generating loud noises (*sonat*), much like the destructive winds in *Aen.* 1 (*indignantes*, 55; *sonoras*, 53). Furthermore, the sea in this *Georgics* passage 'flows back' (*refuso*), just as the stormy sea in *Aen.* 1 (*refusa*, 126). There is a subtle suggestion that any attempt to control and alter this body of water may lead to dire, unintended consequences.

The *Aeneid* features another aquatic construction project that expresses anxiety about cosmic destruction. In book 9, the falling warrior Bitias is compared to the throwing of a piece of masonry in the sea to build a pier or the foundations of a seaside villa:

> dat tellus gemitum et clipeum super intonat ingens.
> talis in Euboico Baiarum litore quondam
> saxea pila cadit, magnis quam molibus ante
> constructam ponto iaciunt, sic illa **ruinam**
> prona trahit penitusque vadis inlisa recumbit;
> **miscent** se maria et nigrae attolluntur harenae,
> tum **sonitu** Prochyta alta tremit durumque cubile
> Inarime Iovis imperiis imposta Typhoeo.
>
> *9.709–16*

The Cosmic Barrier: The Isthmus of Corinth in Imperial Latin Poetry

The earth lets out a groan and his mighty shield thunders, such as a stone mole, which, constructed beforehand with great piles and tossed onto the sea, sometimes falls on the Euboean shore of Baiae. Thus the mole brings with it headfirst destruction and, dashed against shoals, settles in the depths; the seas are thrown into confusion and black sands are lifted up. Then lofty Prochyta and Inarime, the stiff bed placed upon Typhoeus by the order of Jupiter, quake at the sound.

The language of cosmic upheaval in this passage is manifest, most notably in the mixing of elements and spheres of the world (*miscent*), as well as in the sound (*sonitu*) made by this disturbance of a placid maritime environment; the stones bring 'havoc' (*ruinam*). The setting of the simile and the reference to Typhoeus are also significant, as they both suggest a Gigantomachy or Titanomachy.[11] One of the reputed locations for the War with the Giants was the Bay of Naples region, and explicit reference to Typhoeus here suggests a Gigantomachy. As Hardie 1986: 86–156 demonstrates in his analysis of the *Aeneid*'s cosmic language, the warring Giants and Titans are often depicted as disrupters of the cosmos via their physical destruction of a local landscape. As noted above (pp. 174–5), the Giants are represented as quintessentially transgressive figures in that they breach natural divisions between earth and sky. In their combination of cosmic language and allusions to the Gigantomachy, Latin poets established a connection between extravagant works of engineering, human overreach and cosmic disaster.

Nero's building projects

In addition to the planned canal through the Isthmus, Nero undertook various large-scale building projects, many of which are represented by his critics as violations of the natural world: a plan to build a canal from Ostia to Avernus and to construct the *Domus Aurea* figure as decadent efforts to recreate nature itself. Tacitus juxtaposes the two projects in his *Annals* (15.42). Nero famously builds his Golden House after the fire of 64 CE in Rome. Tacitus presents Nero as personally taking advantage of this situation (*usus est patriae ruinis*). The historiographer suggests the house, and its architects in particular, boldly defy the will of nature personified (*ingenium et audacia erat etiam, quae natura denegavisset*). Tacitus' account moralistically deems the task 'intolerable' (*intolerandus*) and caps off the section by tagging Nero as 'a seeker of the unbelievable' (*incredibilium cupitor*). A similar, if no more subtle, evaluation of these again juxtaposed projects occurs in Suet., *Ner*. 31. Suetonius opens with general disapproval of Nero's building program: 'he was no more destructive in any other matter than building' (*non in alia re tamen damnosior quam in aedificando*). Furthermore, for the 'bad' emperors, Suetonius usually divides the segments of his biographies into a 'good' and a 'bad' half, which he signposts.[12] Here again censure of these projects is levelled at their aim to artificially create or efface the boundaries of the natural world. Given Nero's overall characterization as a 'bad emperor' by subsequent imperial dynasties, authors writing under these regimes, such as Tacitus and Suetonius, unsurprisingly represent his large-scale building projects as grandiose and ill-advised. The representation of Nero's projects as destructive, excessively luxurious and ultimately ill-conceived thus functions to further vilify the former emperor's character and legacy.[13] Such hostile representations usually ignore any political and social messaging, or potential economic benefits of these ventures. The projects could, for example, alternatively be made to convey the emperor's power over nature and legitimize his rule (and Roman imperialism generally).

Nero's plan for the Corinthian Canal and its potentially dire environmental consequences

Ancient sources record that Periander, Demetrius Poliorcetes, Julius Caesar, Caligula, Nero and Herodes Atticus all formulated plans to build a canal through the Isthmus of Corinth. The viability of digging the canal seems to have been a topic of *Suasoriae*, one that Quintilian includes among a list of especially challenging projects for debate (*Inst.* 3.8.16). A majority of sources depict the canal project as a negative endeavour (Plin. *HN*. 4.10.4, Stat. *Silv*. 4.3.59–60, Paus. 2.1.5). Cassius Dio 16 (63.16) reports that blood came up from the ground and groans were heard on one such attempt. Pliny the Elder tells us that the attempted construction of the canal clearly was a *nefas* because of the way Demetrius, Julius Caesar, Caligula and Nero died (*HN* 4.10.4).

Strabo records a tradition that forecasted destruction on a cosmic scale: the Hellenistic polymath Eratosthenes wrote that Demetrius was dissuaded from this project when engineers told him that if he joined the two bodies of water, a catastrophic flood would submerge the island of Aegina, because water levels were thought to be unequal at the opposite sides of the Isthmus (1.3.11). Philostratus notes a similar warning, this time made to Nero (*VA* 4.24; cf. Lucian (Philostr.?), *Ner*. 4). The idea that joining two bodies of unequal water levels could cause a flood appears in other scientific sources not directly concerned with the Isthmus as early as Aristotle. According to *Mete*. 1.14, both the Egyptian king Sesostris and later Darius considered constructing a canal from the Mediterranean to the Red Sea, but ceased building it after learning the water levels were higher in the Mediterranean, fearing that a canal would cause a deluge destructive to the waters of the Nile (cf. Diodorus 1.33.9–12). The reasoning behind this concern seems to be that the land and sea were perceived as being 'in balance' and so the building of a canal threatened to disrupt the harmonious natural configuration.

The Isthmus in imperial poetry

The Isthmus figures prominently in Seneca's dramatic works. In his *Thyestes*, when Tantalus is summoned from the underworld, the natural world around him reacts:

> pallescit omnis arbor ac nudus stetit
> fugiente pomo ramus, et qui fluctibus

The Cosmic Barrier: The Isthmus of Corinth in Imperial Latin Poetry

illinc propinquis Isthmos atque illinc **fremit**
uicina gracili diuidens terra uada,
longe remotos latus exaudit sonos.

110–14

Every tree grows pale and the branches stand bare with their fruit in flight, and the Isthmus, which roars with waves nearby on both sides as it divides neighbouring seas with a narrow strip of land, now wide, hears distant sounds from afar.

Expressed as an adynaton, an image of impossibility, the Isthmus, normally a narrow strip of land, widens because of the cosmic disturbance Tantalus creates by coming to the upper world. The Isthmus 'roars' (*fremit*), again echoing language used of the winds that cause the cosmic storm in *Aen.* 1 ('they roar about the barriers', *circum claustra **fremunt***, 56), as well as of the enchained *Furor impius*, the embodiment of civil strife ('he roars dreadfully with a bloody mouth', *fremet **horridus ore cruento***, 1.296). Tarrant 1985: 104 aptly remarks, 'the Isthmus reflects the disturbance of natural order'. In the subsequent verses of Seneca's *Thyestes*, more 'unnatural' images appear: bodies of water deserting their own stations, drought and darkness, all established motifs of cosmic disaster (115–21). This image of an unstable border looks forward to the transgressions that occur in the play. In *Thy.*'s opening, Tantalus had crossed the impassable boundary between the underworld and upperworld ('Who drags me out from the inauspicious seat of the dead?', *quis inferorum sede ab infausta extrahit?*, 1). Characters in the play attempt to cross the line between mortals and gods – Tantalus himself had tried to coopt divine status by feeding Pelops to the gods.[14] Atreus claims his own godhead after he has fed Thyestes his own children: 'I stride level with the stars, touching the high axis above them with my haughty top' (*aequalis astris gradior et cunctos super / altum superbo uertice attingens polum*, 885–6). The exultant Atreus here echoes the Gigantomachy.[15] Atreus' use of Gigantomachic language is underscored by the fact that there are further images of the Gigantomachy in the preceding choral ode (806–12). Just as Nero will destroy the boundary between land and sea with his canal, the characters in the *Thyestes* similarly cross nature's sacred boundaries.[16]

The Isthmus appears later in *Thy.*, where it is marked as a barrier. In the first choral ode, when the chorus asks the gods to give the people of Argos respite from the evils of the House of Tantalus, they start their prayer with a formulaic condition: *Isthmi si quis amat regna Corinthii, / et portus geminos et mare **dissidens*** ... ('If any (god) loves the kingdom of the Isthmus at Corinth and the twin ports and the sea that stands apart ...', 124–5). *dissidens* here is especially marked; as Tarrant 1985: 107 notes, the verb *dissidere* has a political connotation, in that it can signify civil strife. On an immediate level, *dissidens* reflects internal strife within the House of Atreus and its kingdom. At the same time, civil strife is often styled as a cosmic issue, as often in Lucan's *Pharsalia*, a poem rife with the language of cosmic dissolution (Lapidge 1979), and where Pompey and Caesar essentially rip apart the Roman state, a microcosm of the universe. The harbours surrounding the Isthmus are also described by the chorus as 'twins' (*geminos*). As we will see, this language is used to describe the Isthmus in other contexts in early imperial poetry where it is figured as a space freighted with potentially cosmic consequence.

The cosmic associations of the Isthmus resurface later in *Thy.*, when a messenger arrives to announce Atreus' heinous acts. The messenger is in a state of disarray and must get his bearings before he gets to the heart of the matter:

> quaenam ista regio est? Argos et Sparte, pios
> sortita fratres, et maris **gemini premens**
> fauces Corinthos.
>
> 627–9

What place is this? Is it Argos? Is it Sparta, which obtained dutiful brothers by lot? And Corinth, controlling the 'neck' of twin seas?

premens is especially significant: the verb is used of Aeolus twice in the *Aen.* 1 storm scene to indicate his control over the agents of cosmic destruction.[17] The seas surrounding the Isthmus are again described as 'twins' (*gemini*), following the pattern of showing the Isthmus' dual nature.

The Isthmus assumes a cosmic function as well at the beginning of Seneca's *Medea*. Medea, recently rejected by Jason, calls down curses upon him. Her curse culminates with the Isthmus:

> da, da per auras curribus patriis uehi,
> committe habenas, genitor, et flagrantibus
> ignifera loris tribue moderari iuga:
> **gemino** Corinthos litori opponens **moras**
> cremata flammis maria committat duo.
>
> 33–6

Grant, grant that I ride through the air in the chariot of my father. Entrust the reins to me, father, and allow me to drive the fire-bearing yokes with the blazing reins. Let Corinth, as it places delays on its twin shore, be scorched by flames and join its two seas.

As Medea's highly personal execration escalates to the point of massive destruction, she conjures up the obliteration of the Isthmus and the joining of the 'twin' Ionian and Aegean seas. Medea here powerfully evokes fire, water – and with the Isthmus-strip – earth: cosmic disasters are often represented as a battle of the elements. The passage also recalls Phaethon, who nearly destroys the world when he loses control of his father Apollo's chariot and crashes into the world below.[18] Like Medea, Phaethon asks his divine father if he can drive his chariot and disastrous consequences follow. This reference clearly foreshadows Medea's exit in her dragon chariot after she envelops Corinth in destructive conflagration at the play's end, and the allusion bears further significance in light of the implied connection between Nero and Phaethon in the opening section of the *Pharsalia* (pp. 174–5 above).[19]

The Senecan Isthmus thus is a locus perched on a precipice of singular destruction, even at a cosmic level. Disruption of the balance this narrow strip of land provides between the precariously opposed 'twin' seas – a particularly trenchant metaphor for Romans, given their history of civil strife extending back to the city's foundation by Romulus and Remus – portends cataclysmic disaster. Nero's plan for a canal, if it lurks in the background of the Senecan descriptions of the Isthmus, may be viewed as fraught with enormous negative consequence(s). Long before Seneca, Periander, Demetrius and Julius Caesar famously considered, but ultimately abandoned, this grandiose project. Seneca himself had barely survived the reign of Caligula, who also planned a canal and even sent an official to Corinth to take measurements for this project (Suet. *Cal.* 21). For Seneca's audience, the project's longstanding historical associations with autocratic aspirations, combined with the spectre of profound social disturbance and devastating flooding of cosmic proportions (cf. Trinacty's chapter, pp. 67–87, in this volume), inform their likely anxious reading of these Isthmian descriptions in the tragedies – anxiety which only increases through its immediate connection with Nero and his desire to yoke the twin seas.

The Isthmus makes a prominent appearance in Lucan's *Pharsalia*, in the second simile of the epic. The triumvir Crassus is compared to the narrow strip of land:

> nam sola futuri
> Crassus erat belli medius **mora**. qualiter undas
> qui secat et **geminum** gracilis mare separat Isthmos
> nec patitur conferre fretum, si terra recedat,
> Ionium Aegaeo frangat mare, sic, ubi saeua
> arma ducum dirimens miserando funere Crassus
> Assyrias Latio maculauit sanguine Carrhas,
> Parthica Romanos soluerunt damna furores.
>
> *1.99–106*

For Crassus between them alone was the delay of the future war, just as the thin Isthmus which cuts and separates the twin sea and does not allow their waters to come into contact; if the land should recede, it would dash the Ionian upon the Aegean. Thus, when Crassus, previously dividing the fierce arms of the leaders, spattered Assyrian Carrhae in pitiable death with Latin blood, the losses inflicted by the Parthians unleashed Roman madness.

In Lucan's conceptual metaphor, Caesar and Pompey correspond to the two bodies of water that flank the Isthmus. Once Crassus is removed, nothing blocks Pompey and Caesar from all-out war that threatens to tear asunder the social fabric of the Roman world. Lucan's audience, acutely aware of Crassus' death and the civil destruction it unleashed, might readily conceive of a canal through the Isthmus that allows the two hostile seas to clash as precipitating cosmic disaster: it would dash the Ionian Sea upon the Aegean (*Ionium Aegaeo frangat mare*), a poetic analogue of the scientific sources' warning about the dangers of the canal vis-à-vis water levels. This simile's cataclysmic implications are amplified by its placement immediately after *Pharsalia*'s first, a comparison that programmatically likens the breakdown of Roman civil society in the early 40s BCE to the collapse of the universe:

> sic, cum conpage solute
> saecula tot mundi suprema coegerit hora
> antiquum repetens iterum chaos, [omnia mixtis
> sidera sideribus concurrent,] ignea pontum
> astra petent, tellus extendere litora nolet
> excutietque fretum, fratri contraria Phoebe
> ibit et obliquum bigas agitare per orbem
> indignata diem poscet sibi, totaque discors
> machina diuolsi turbabit foedera mundi.

1.72–80

Thus, when the bonds of the world have been disbanded and the final hour will have collapsed so many ages, as it seeks once again original chaos, [all the stars will become enmeshed and dash against one another,] the fiery stars will seek the sea, the land will be unwilling to extend its shores and will cast out the sea, Phoebe will go head-to-head with her brother, and angry that she has to drive her chariot in a slanting orbit will demand the day for herself. And the entire disharmonious scaffold will throw into confusion the laws of the shattered universe.

The collapse of Rome brought on by the civil war of Caesar and Pompey apocalyptically mirrors the universe's collapse. All the elemental spheres of the world abandon their stations and mix together in an indistinguishable mess, a return to primeval chaos. Lapidge 1979: 360 notes that this simile calls to mind Stoic conceptions of the (periodic) end of the universe. It also builds a powerful framework for the Isthmus simile (just twenty lines later), whose own cosmic concerns it deepens. Moreover, both of the epic's opening similes grapple with concerns about the extent of humankind's power over the natural world, an idea that is central to both the Isthmus as a place and to Nero's plan to bend nature to his will there.

In Lucan's second simile, the sea around the Isthmus is again highlighted as 'twin' (*geminum*, 101), as it was in Seneca. Lucan, who indisputably is writing in a later phase of Nero's reign (i.e. before his forced suicide in 65 CE), also describes the Isthmus as a 'delay', just as his uncle Seneca does at *Med.* 35. I am not alone in linking Lucan's simile to the Neronian canal project. Wuilleumier and Le Bonniec 1962: 32–3 briefly remark that Lucan's simile may be an allusion to what Nero had already planned: to remove the barrier posed by the Isthmus and connect the two seas via a canal. Padron 2004: 193 and Myers 2011: 407 have also noted the image of cosmic disaster in these lines. I maintain that we should view these two sets of ideas in close conjunction: the language and imagery of cosmic disaster readily suggest the canal project. Lucan's and Seneca's shared status as courtiers made them especially privy to Nero's (or talk of Nero's) ambitious designs. Nero in fact is the only monarch to act upon his plans for the canal. According to Suetonius and Philostratus, the princeps was present at the Isthmus the first day on which digging took place and even deigned to take part in some of the labour himself (Suet. *Ner.* 19.2, 37; Lucian (Philostr.?) *Ner.* 3); even if the project did not commence until 67 CE, it seems plausible that Lucan and Seneca were aware of its conception and planning before their deaths.[20]

Conclusion

Through a network of allusions, Lucan's simile effectively suggests that Nero, by breaching the boundary between land and sea and unleashing a massive flood, is a superhuman destroyer of worlds. In the *Pharsalia*, once Crassus dies, Pompey and Caesar destroy the world by engaging in civil war. In the world outside Lucan's and Seneca's poetry, Nero repeatedly violates boundaries of mortality, gender, sexuality and class. According to his detractors, Nero lays waste to the natural world through his monstrous and inhuman building projects and other transgressive practices. These narcissistic projects may bear further consequences on a cosmic level: the poetic references to the Isthmus subtly express Nero's potential for terrifying destruction. In the ancient Mediterranean world, the Isthmus constitutes a global boundary in that it divides Italy from Asia, the Peloponnese from mainland Greece, two large bodies of water, and land and sea generally. In this light, Nero's proposed project is disruptively figured as exceeding various natural limits. The Isthmus canal would create a significant gap, topographically as well as culturally, not unlike the ultimate 'cosmic gap' Porter 2016: 163–5 identifies in his discussion of Longinus' sublime. The images of an Isthmus disrupted in Imperial Latin poetry thus precariously highlight the *potentiality* of larger scale devastation a canal might precipitate – behind them all looms the figure of Nero as a frightfully sublime transgressor of the cosmos itself.

Notes

1. I thank David Christenson for his edits and suggestions.
2. For the Isthmus as a symbol of freedom and domination, see further Pettegrew 2016: 90–106.
3. For a broad overview of Roman sexuality see Skinner 2005: 192–239.
4. All translations of Latin and Greek in this chapter are my own.
5. For the sexual protocols and power dynamics of homosexual relationships see Williams 2010: 17–29.
6. *RIC* (*Roman Imperial Coinage*) I² 73–81, 121–23, 205–12, 380–5, 414–17, 451–5.
7. I follow Roche 2009: 7–10, 129–31 in viewing these lines as satirical.
8. Cf. the suggestion (pp. 180–1) of a connection between Nero's attempts to build the canal and Phaethon's nearly destroying the earth with his father's chariot in Seneca's *Medea*. Phaethon figures prominently in the cosmic myth of replacement: Worthen 1991: 101–4, 120, *et passim*.

9. Cf. Ovid's treatment of the Gigantomachy: 'When their frightful bodies, overcome by their own mass lay in ruin ...' (*obruta mole sua cum corpora dira iacerent ...*, *Met*. 1.156). Cf. also Suet. *Ner*. 51 for Nero's reputation for obesity.

10. For similar examples in Horace, see *Carm*. 2.8, 16, 3.24. For more on the morality of seaside building, see Edwards 1993: 137–72.

11. By the fifth century BCE, the Gigtantomachy, Titanomachy and Typhonomachy are often conflated (e.g. Eur. *Hec*. 466-74, *IT* 222-4, *Ion* 989); cf. Vian and Moore 1988: 195–217 and Vian 2005.

12. Suetonius' programmatic statement in *Ner*. is clear:

> haec partim nulla reprehensione, partim etiam non mediocri laude digna in unum contuli, ut secernerem a probris ac sceleribus eius, de quibus dehinc dicam.
>
> *Ner. 19.3*

> I have compiled these things into a whole, some with no disapproval, others even worthy of no moderate praise, so that I might separate them from his depraved and the wicked acts, about which I will speak from this point on.

Cf. the similar programmatic statement in Suet. *Cal*. 21.1; on this feature, see further Hanson 2021: 44–6.

13. For this practice, see further Elsner 1994.

14. Pindar discounts the tradition that Tantalus fed Pelops to the gods but offers an alternative in which he steals nectar and ambrosia from the gods, in essence trying to become immortal (Pind. *Ol*. 1.37-65).

15. The ever-transgressive Giants (pp. 174–5), in addition to attempting to topple Olympian power structure by unseating Zeus, disrupt the landscape by moving mountains, most famously Otus and Ephialtes (Hom. *Od*. 11.305–31). Segal 2008: 151–6 elucidates *Thy*.'s monstrous violations of corporeal boundaries and the psychological self.

16. Though Seneca's tragedies cannot be dated with certainty, *Thy*. is usually dated to the middle of Nero's reign, *c*. 60-2 CE: Fitch 1981, Tarrant 1985: 10–13, Nisbet 2008.

17. *Aen*.1.53-6 (*luctantes ventos tempestatesque sonoras / imperio **premit**,* 'he controls the struggling winds and raucous storms with his power'), 1.63 (*premere ... **sciret**,* 'he knows how to control them').

18. Recounted most fully in Ov. *Met*. 2.1–343.

19. Any attempt to connect this passage with Nero's canal designs must remain provisional, given our ignorance of the play's date of composition. Critics (e.g. Nisbet 2008: 349–51) usually put *Med*. in Seneca's 'middle period', and so before the beginning of Nero's reign in 54 CE, whereas scholarly speculation (e.g. Calder 1976: 3) about the canal-plan places it late in Nero's rule.

20. For the dating of Nero's attempt to build the canal, see Bradley 1978: 66.

Works cited

Armstrong, R. (2009), 'Against Nature? Some Augustan Responses to Man-made Marvels', in P. Hardie (ed.), *Paradox and the Marvellous in Augustan Culture*, 75–94, Oxford: Oxford University Press.

Bradley, K. R. (1978), 'The Chronology of Nero's Visit to Greece A.D. 66/67', *Latomus*, 37: 61–72.

Calder, W. M. III (1976), 'Seneca: Tragedian of Imperial Rome', *Classical Journal*, 72: 1–11.

Edwards, C. (1993), *The Politics of Immorality*, Cambridge: Cambridge University Press.
Elsner, J. (1994), 'Constructing Decadence: The Representation of Nero as an Imperial Builder', in J. Elsner and J. Masters (eds), *Reflections of Nero: Culture, History, & Representation*, 112–27, Chapel Hill: The University of North Carolina Press.
Fitch, J. G. (1981), 'Sense-Pauses and Relative Dating in Seneca, Sophocles, and Shakespeare', *American Journal of Philology*, 102: 289–307.
Hanson, W. J. (2021), 'Suetonius' Organizational Craft', diss. The University of Pennsylvania: Philadelphia.
Hardie, P. R. (1986), *Virgil's Aeneid: Cosmos and Imperium*, Oxford: Clarendon Press.
Lapidge, M. (1979), 'Lucan's Imagery of Cosmic Dissolution', *Hermes*, 107: 344–70.
Myers, M. Y. (2011), 'Lucan's Poetic Geographies', in P. Asso (ed.), *Brill's Companion to Lucan*, 399–416, Leiden: Brill.
Nisbet, R. G. M. (2008), 'The Dating of Seneca's Tragedies, with Special Reference to *Thyestes*', in J. G. Fitch (ed.), *Seneca*, 348–71, Oxford: Oxford University Press.
Ormand, K. (2018), *Controlling Desires: Sexuality in Ancient Greece and Rome*, Austin: The University of Texas Press.
Padron, R. (2004), *The Spacious Word: Cartography, Literature, and Empire in Early Modern Spain*, Chicago: The University of Chicago Press.
Pettegrew, D. K. (2016), *The Isthmus of Corinth: Crossroads of the Mediterranean World*, Ann Arbor: The University of Michigan Press.
Porter, J. I. (2016), *The Sublime in Antiquity*, Cambridge: Cambridge University Press.
Purcell, N. (1996), 'Rome and the Management of Water: Environment, Culture and Power', in J. Salmon and G. Shipley (eds), *Human Landscapes in Classical Antiquity*, 180–212, London: Routledge.
Reitz-Joosse, B. (2021), *Building in Words: The Process of Construction in Latin Literature*, Oxford: Oxford University Press.
Roche, P. A. (2009), *Lucan: De Bello Civili, Book 1*, Oxford: Oxford University Press.
Segal, C. (2008), 'Boundary Violation and the Landscape of the Self in Senecan Tragedy', in J. G. Fitch (ed.), *Seneca*, 136–56, Oxford: Oxford University Press.
Skinner, M. (2005), *Sexuality in Greek and Roman Culture*, Malden, MA: Blackwell.
Tarrant, R. J. (1985), *Seneca's Thyestes*, Atlanta: Scholar's Press.
Tarrant, R. J. (1989), 'The Reader as Author: Collaborative Interpolation in Latin Poetry', in J. N. Grant (ed.), *Editing Greek and Latin Texts*, 121–62, New York: AMS Press.
Thomas, R. F. (1988), *Virgil: Georgics, vol. 1: Books I–II*, Cambridge: Cambridge University Press.
Vian, F. (2005), 'Le syncrétism et l'évolution de la Gigantomachie', in D. Accoriati (ed.), *L'épopée posthomerique: Recueil d'études*, 197–207, Alessandria: Edizioni dell'Orso.
Vian, F. and M. B. Moore (1988), 'Gigantes', *Lexicon Iconographicum Mythologiae Classicae*, 4.1: 191–270.
Williams, C. A. (2010), *Roman Homosexuality*, Oxford and New York: Oxford University Press.
Worthen, T. D. (1991), *The Myth of Replacement: Stars, Gods, and Order in the Universe*, Tucson: The University of Arizona Press.
Wuilleumier, P. and H. Le Bonniec (1962), *Lucain: Bellum civile: liber primus = La Pharsale: livre premier*, Érasme, collection de textes latins commentés, 8, Paris: Presses Universitaires de France.

PART IV
RECEPTION

CHAPTER 11
READING THE CLASSICS IN PLAGUE-RIDDEN ENGLAND, 1629–1722
Thomas Willard

Indeed terror is in all cases whatsoever, either more openly or latently, the ruling principle of the sublime.

Edmund Burke, *A Philosophical Inquiry into the Origin of Our Ideas of the Sublime and the Beautiful*, 1757

All changed, changed utterly:
A terrible beauty is born.

W. B. Yeats, 'Easter, 1916'

Introduction

A recent history of England during the century from 1588 to 1688 has the title *Devil-Land* (Jackson 2022). Many observers of the troubled island nation, both foreign and domestic, suggested that it was far from the 'land of angels', as the old pun on 'Angles' and 'angels' had it, but that it must be overrun by devils, so troubled was it by wars and other disasters including crop failures, fires, and plagues.[1] In 1588, the Spanish Armada threatened the rule of Queen Elizabeth I, whose government had outlawed Roman Catholics. In 1688, the Bloodless Revolution removed King James II, whose Catholicism threatened to put the country back under the influence of Rome and the Roman Empire. Early in the seventeenth century, the English had actually executed King Charles I, in 1649, and disestablished the Church of England. Small wonder its Dutch neighbours, on whom two English leaders had declared trade wars, said Englishmen had tails.

It was a perfect time for rhetoric and poetry on the topos that came to be called 'the sublime'. But while the *Peri hupsous* of pseudo-Longinus had been translated into Latin (Robortello 1547) and into English under a variant title (Hall 1651), it would not become widely known until Boileau gave birth to the 'concept' in his French translation of 1674 (Doran 2015: 124–40). Even then, the concept or topos of the sublime did not reach many English writers until the early eighteenth century (Ashfield and de Bolla 1996: 1–16). Only then did English critics discover that Milton's *Paradise Lost* was a sublime epic (Moore 1990); however, early admirers had already appreciated that quality under different descriptions. In my contribution, I explore the ways that classically educated

Sublime Cosmos in Graeco-Roman Literature and Its Reception

English writers responded to such potentially sublime topics as fire, plague, and warfare before Longinian sublimity was introduced in the Neo-Classical writing of the early eighteenth century in England. My chief examples come from the writing of Thomas Hobbes (1588–1679) in prose and John Dryden (1631–1700) in poetry, with a side glance at Dryden's contemporary Thomas Sprat (1635–1713). I conclude with the early novelist Daniel Defoe (1660–1731) as he returned to the first year of London's Great Plague after the sublime was an established element of English writing.

I first review the constituents of the sublime as Longinus understood it and the prominence of terror that the eighteenth-century essayist Edmund Burke (1729–97) recognized in Longinus' writing. I also suggest how John Milton (1608–74) responded as a professedly Christian poet to sublime elements in classical poetry.

The Longinian sublime

There are problems with the text of Longinus that survived into the early modern period. It has lacunae; it breaks off just after a remark that the author has treated emotions in another treatise, now lost. The author says only that emotions are important because 'they seem to me to form part of the general subject of literature and especially of sublimity' (1995: 304–5; 44.12). Meanwhile, he has already mentioned that 'vehement emotion' (ἐνθουσιαστικὸν πάθος) is second only to 'grand conceptions' (τὸ περὶ τὰς νοήσεις ἀδρεπήβολον) in producing sublimity (1995: 180–1; 8.1). These two are the chief sources of 'grandeur' in writing, the other three being more strictly verbal: figures (σχημάτων), diction (φράσις) and 'word-arrangement' (σύνθεσις).

The phrase that the Loeb edition renders 'vehement emotion' or, more fully, 'the inspiration of vehement emotion' has obvious similarities to 'enthusiastic pathos'. The *Oxford English Dictionary* shows that the last two words were both borrowed from Greek by learned writers of the sixteenth century. Indeed, the *OED* in its third edition still gives the earliest instance of English 'pathos' as a gloss on a line in *The Shepheardes Calender of* Edmund Spenser (1579), which cites the line as containing 'A very Poeticall πάθος' (Spenser 1912: 440). The first edition of the *OED* also traced the word 'enthusiasm' to a comment on another poem in the same book, which referred to the author's 'labours and learning ... poured into the witte by a certaine ἐνθουσιασμὸς, and celestiall inspiration' (1912: 456). Of course, the English nouns 'enthusiasm' and 'pathos' have taken on vastly different meanings, as have their adjectival counterparts 'enthusiastic' and 'pathetic'; 'enthusiasm' can now mean fanaticism or false inspiration as well as eagerness or an object of interest, while 'pathos' can refer to suffering or sorrow as often as it does to the evocation of sympathy or the feeling of tenderness.

The old sense of enthusiasm as divine inspiration helps to explain the choice of quotations that Longinus offers from the epics of Homer. Although he refers to approximately a dozen passages in the *Iliad* and a dozen more in the *Odyssey*, Longinus takes special interest in the *Iliad*, since the gods add their support alternately to the warring Greeks and Trojans, making the passions of the warriors all the greater. Of particular interest for Longinus is a passage from *Il.* 15, in which the Trojan army, led by Hector and cheered on by some of the gods, drives the invading Greeks back to their ships. Longinus cites these lines as an example of genuine physical terror:

> He fell on the host as a wave of the sea on a hurrying vessel,
> Rising up under the clouds, a boisterous son of the storm-wind.
> The good ship is lost in the shroud of the foam, and the breath of the tempest
> Terribly roars in the sails, and in their heart tremble the sailors,
> By the breadth of a hand swept out from under the jaws of destruction.
>
> Sub. *1995: 200–3;* Il. *15.624–8*

Longinus comments: 'instead of dismissing the danger once and for all, [Homer] depicts the sailors as being all the time, again and again, with every wave on the brink of death' (1995: 202–3; 10.6). Lang, another translator, offers: 'Homer does not give any fixed limit to the danger, but gives us a vivid picture of men a thousand times on the brink of destruction, every wave threatening them with instant death' (1890: 23–4). It is this limitlessness, this sense of innumerable dangers to life, this vastness of peril, that characterizes the sublime terror as Longinus presents it.

The classical Greek word for 'terror' is *phobos* (Φόβος). Moreover, Phobos or Fear was a Greek god; according to Hesiod, he was the son of Ares and Aphrodite and the brother of Deimos (Δεῖμος) or Panic (2018: 66–7; 933–7). Psychologists usually explain the relation of the two emotions as that of momentary panic (for example, with the sudden approach of a lion) and long-term fear (of lions perhaps, bolstered by memories of people they killed). The fears that Sigmund Freud saw in shell-shocked veterans of the First World War (1914–18) forced him to reconsider his earlier teaching that dreams serve mainly to reveal desires, often repressed desires. Men who dreamed compulsively about moments when they were wounded in battle and nearly died, as they watched their comrades die, forced him to formulate the theory of 'repetition compulsion' (*Wiederholungszwang*). In *Beyond the Pleasure Principle*, he posited the existence of a 'death drive' (*Todestrieb*). He indeed moved into the cosmic realm of mythology in suggesting that all life was a struggle between Eros and Thanatos, or love and death, the first unifying organisms into a larger whole, the other disjoining the unities (Freud [1920] 1928). Written at the same time as *Beyond the Pleasure Principle* and in many ways a continuation of it, Freud's shorter essay 'The Uncanny' (*Das Unheimliche*) became his contribution to modern and post-modern discussion of the sublime ([1919] 2003). I will say more about it in the conclusion.

Building on the work of Freud and Jung, Ernest Becker argued persuasively that 'heroism is first and foremost a reflex of the terror of death' (1973: 13). John Milton understood this principle well enough when he began his major epic *Paradise Lost* in 'the midst of things, *presenting* Satan *with his* Angels *now fallen into Hell*' ([1667] 1674: bk. 1, 'Argument'). Milton has Satan speak to his former lieutenant Beelzebub. Although 'in pain', Satan and the other rebel angels are immortal beings, and they can learn from their recent 'experience' of defeat. Satan tells his fallen friend:

> We may with more successful hope resolve
> To wage by force or guile eternal Warr
> Irreconcileable, to our grand Foe,
> Who now triumphs, and in th' excess of joy
> Sole reigning holds the Tyranny of Heav'n.
>
> *1.120-4*

Satan summons his fallen troops to a 'great consult' (1.798) that Milton models on the war council in *Iliad* 2.188-393. He invites his army to debate the relative claims of force or fraud, which he now calls 'open Warr or covert guile' (2.41). Moloch argues for war, while Belial argues for caution in the face of overwhelming odds and, in effect, for 'ignoble ease' (2.227). Mammon sides with Belial and argues that the defeated forces accept 'the settl'd State / Of Order' (2.279-80). Finally, Beelzebub proposes the fallen angels lower their sights somewhat and concentrate on the long-prophesied 'Race call'd *Man*, about this time / To be created like to us though less / In power and excellence' (2.348-50). The devils 'vote' in favour of Beelzebub's plan (2.389).

Thus Satan gets his way, as Agamemnon did in the *Iliad*. Moloch plays the role of Thersites, Belial and Mammon together play the role of Odysseus, while Beelzebub, instructed by Satan, plays the role of Nestor. Satan releases the devils to build their new city of Pandaemonium ('all devils'), while he navigates the chaos between Hell and the newly created world rather as Odysseus navigated the tricky waters between Scylla and Charybdis in Homer (*Od.* 12.222-59), to which Milton refers (2.660). Such details as the apparent heroism of Satan caused William Blake to remark that Milton was 'a true Poet and of the Devil's party without knowing it' (1966: 150). They really serve as what Northrop Frye called 'demonic parody', for they suggest that classical values were negligent in the light of Christian revelation. Milton's first readers would very likely have recognized the deadly sins in his devils, including anger in Moloch, sloth in Belial (named at 2.227), covetousness in Mammon and above all pride in Satan. The Christian allegory is elaborated further when Satan leaves Hell through its new gates, to which a 'Snakey Sorceress' holds the 'fatal Key' (2.724-5). This turns out to be Satan's daughter, Sin, on whom he has fathered his son, Death (2.760, 804). Just as all the glories of Greece, from the 'Olympian Games' to songs of 'Heroic deeds' have their origins in Hell, as do theological arguments about 'Providence' and 'free will' (2.559-60) and the 'false Philosophie' that considers the good life (2.530-65), so heroism itself is the invention of devils like Satan. The true hero in *Paradise Lost* is Christ as the faithful son who does his father's will.

Surely, the major English-language contribution to the understanding of the sublime was the long essay on 'the Idea of the Sublime and the Beautiful' written by the Irish politician Edmund Burke and first printed in 1757. The essay's second part begins by discussing 'the Passion caused by the Sublime'. After treating astonishment, described as 'that state of the soul, in which all its motions are suspended, with some degree of horror', it moves straight into a section on terror:

> No passion so effectually [effectively] robs the mind of all its powers of acting and reasoning as *fear*. For fear being an apprehension of pain or death, it operates in a manner that resembles actual pain. Whatever therefore is terrible, with regard to sight, is sublime too, whether this cause of terror be endued with greatness of dimensions or not; for it is impossible to look on anything as trifling, or contemptible, that may be dangerous. There are many animals, who, though far from being large, are yet capable of raising ideas of the sublime, because they are considered as objects of terror.
>
> 1838: 130

Here Burke links terror with fears great and small that have behind them 'an apprehension of pain or death'. Although he does not refer to Aristotle's theory of dramatic catharsis or purgation, being mainly concerned with Aristotle's view of mimesis or imitation, he comes very close to Aristotle's understanding of tragedy as being aimed at accomplishing catharsis:

> Tragedy, then, is mimesis of an action which is elevated, complete, and of magnitude; in language embellished by distinct forms in its sections, employing the mode of enactment, not narrative; and through pity and fear accomplishing the catharsis of such emotion.
>
> 1995: 46–7; 1449b

For Aristotle, catharsis is the final function of drama as it was performed at the annual festival of Dionysus in Athens: to make members of the audience feel the pity and terror of the gods and heroes whose stories were told in the tragedies of Sophocles, Aeschylus and Euripides, but in the end to purge or purify their souls of the emotions of pity and terror that arose through empathetic participation in the drama.

The Burkean sublime extends the reach of sublimity beyond the traditional view of aesthetics as the study of beauty in the arts, very much as James Porter has shown that the Longinian sublime did in antiquity (2016: 5–7; cf. also White's chapter on sublimity in Keats in this volume). Arguably, Burke's comments on terrifying works of art could be applied to teen slasher movies such as Wes Craven's *Scream* (1996) and its several sequels, whatever their aesthetic value. For the moment, we may note that pseudo-Longinus finds that the beauty of Homer's battle scenes lies in the language used to describe them. We might think forward to the 'terrible beauty' in Yeats's poem on the bloody Easter Rising of 1916, which preceded the Irish Revolution (1919–21). I shall return to the question of beautiful terror in the conclusion.

Thomas Hobbes translates Thucydides

Born on 5 April 1588, Thomas Hobbes regarded himself as an Armada baby. Pregnant women throughout England were said to have gone into early labour on hearing that the

Spanish Armada was approaching English shores that year. Hobbes always claimed that his mother feared a Spanish vessel would sail up the Bristol Channel near the family residence, even though he was born several weeks before the fleet set sail. He said he had been born with a twin brother, whom he called Fear. As a thoroughly trained classicist who wrote his life story in Latin, he called this shadow side of himself Timor (1839: 1:86).

Hobbes's biography suggests he avoided conflict whenever he could (Malcolm 2004). Like many of his contemporaries during a century of English revolutions, both bloody (1642–51) and bloodless (1688), he repeatedly fled to Paris, where he joined in debates about science rather than the religion and politics discussed in England. He spent much of his life, after graduating from Cambridge University, as a tutor of young men in the wealthy Cavendish family and their companion on the Grand Tour of western Europe. He also served as librarian for the family at its luxurious Chatsworth House in Yorkshire, where he was able to purchase the wide range of books that he read before writing his political masterpiece, *Leviathan* (1651). In old age he held a pension from King Charles II, whom he had tutored while the king was living in exile, again in Paris. Hobbes is often quoted as having said that life outside such elevated society was 'nasty, brutal and short'. That was certainly true for the majority of people during the English Civil Wars, which saw more civilian deaths than either the Great War of 1914–18 or the Second World War of 1940–5.

Hobbes first achieved recognition for his complete translation of the eight books that Thucydides wrote on the Peloponnesian War (1629). Though not the first English translation of Thucydides, it was the first one made from a Greek manuscript, adding extensive marginal notes on the text. Hobbes called Thucydides his favourite historian, both for his realistic reporting of events and for his careful analysis of political rhetoric (Malcolm 2004; Johnson 1993: 3–26 and *passim*). In the dedication of his translation to the son of his long-time employer, Hobbes wrote of Thucydides:

> For his own studie, it was bestowed, for the most part, in that kind of Learning, which best deserveth the paines and hours of Great Persons, *History*, and *Civil knowledge*, and directed not to the Ostentation of his reading, but to the Government of Life, and the Publike good.
>
> 1629: A1v

Hobbes shared the value expressed here of trying to balance one's personal life with work for the public good. He also admired Thucydides for recognizing the war between Athens and Sparta as 'the greatest Commotion that ever happened among the *Grecians*' and for writing about the commotion as it happened (1629: 2). Hobbes, however, much preferred to read and write about what he called 'the inanity of ancient times' than to observe the inanity of England in its Civil War (3). Presumably the man with the invisible twin named Fear had something like Woody Allen's 'low threshold of death' in *Casino Royale* (1967). He would have agreed with Friedrich von Schiller's remark that 'nothing is more unworthy of man than to suffer violence' (1966: 193).

Reading the Classics in Plague-Ridden England, 1629–1722

In his second book, Thucydides writes about the arrival of plague in the Athenian camp in 430 BCE: 'so great a plague, and mortality of men, as was never remembered to have hapned in any place before' (1629: 106). Physicians could not treat it, but died first themselves. Thucydides describes the disease as he saw its effects in others and experienced it himself, though he survived to write about it. Hobbes puts the text into the simplest English, with many marginal notes. But there is no doubt that the suffering was beyond imagining. 'For this was a kind of sicknesse which far exceeded all expression of words' (108). Here we meet the Longinian sublime, with its sense of limitlessness, though Hobbes seems to have known the sublime only as a literary trope and not as a term. He voiced no sentiments about the plague in Athens, though he had been at Oxford during the plague of 1603, which killed some 30,000 people in London. More recently, he had probably been in England during the plague of 1625, which killed still more Londoners. But he experienced the sublime personally among the dales of Yorkshire, near the house of his patron.

During the English Civil War, Hobbes completed a poem on what would become the Romantic sublime in England: a Latin poem for his friend and former student William Cavendish. Entitled *De mirabilibus pecci*, it was later translated into English as *Wonders of the Peak in Darby-Shire commonly called the Devil's Arse of Peak* (1683). Seventeenth-century England had in fact seen a succession of landscape poems that focused on the awe of nature in the wild. The chief example was 'Cooper's Hill' by John Denham ([1642] 1650). Such poems celebrated glories in places earlier poets had missed when they wrote about the views from famous spots like Windsor Castle. Denham found 'things of wonder' on land he inherited – a place any hiking poet might find, though no one had thought to write about it yet. The subject of Hobbes's poem, still known as the Devil's Arse, is a natural cavern near Buxton in the Peak District of Yorkshire, an area celebrated by the Brontës in the nineteenth century. It has the largest entry of any cave in Britain; hence the name, no doubt. It also has the deepest reach.

Hobbes wrote his political masterpiece, *Leviathan*, during the Civil Wars. In it he developed the idea of the social contract, an agreement among members of a society as to what powers individual members will grant to the sovereign authority and what benefits will accrue to them as a result.[2] Despite his royalist leanings, he did not specify that the sovereign must be a monarch, let alone a hereditary one. He wrote instead about the desirable 'commonwealth', which was only tactful in a book published when England was a commonwealth under Oliver Cromwell. Although he called the state Leviathan, he intended none of the negative associations found in the Bible (e.g. Psalm 74:14). He treated it rather as an 'artificial Man; though of greater stature and strength than the Natural [man], for whose protection and defence it was intended' (1651: 1). The famous title-page illustration, prepared to Hobbes's specifications (Brown 1978), showed a sovereign holding a king's sword in his right hand and a bishop's sceptre in his left. On his tunic, there were images of countless small people, as if to illustrate the theory of the king's two bodies, the physical body and the body politic (Kantorowicz 1957). For Hobbes, the sovereign *is* the country that he or she represents. When the contract fails for one reason or another, and the sovereign no longer represents the country as a whole,

Hobbes sees descent into tyranny or oligarchy (ch. 19). When the sovereign power cannot protect the people, there is a return to the state of nature, with every man for himself in what is sometimes called 'the war of all against all' (ch. 13; see Kavka 1983). Hobbes describes a 'Passion' that he calls 'Panique Terror', which 'happens to none but in a throng' (ch. 6), that is, in a mob of people who feel disenfranchised.

Thomas Sprat poeticizes plague

For a person living in England in the mid-seventeenth century, plague was a recurrent feature of life. Three of the largest bouts had occurred in 1563, 1603 and 1625 – each of them taking approximately one-fifth of London's population of more than 200,000, while spreading into various counties. There had been a lesser wave of plague during the Civil War, in 1647–9. Weekly Bills of Mortality were prepared by law in each of London's parishes, enumerating any deaths by plague. Such death was a natural subject for a writer in search of one. For the writer could claim, with Thucydides, that it was prudent for people to learn about this dangerous matter. Thus it happened in the uneasy period after the death of Oliver Cromwell in 1658 that the young Oxford graduate Thomas Sprat (1635–1713) composed a poem on 'The Plague of Athens'.

Sprat's debut poem, written in 1659, was a tribute to the older poet Abraham Cowley, who had introduced a sort of free verse that became known as Pindarics: stanzas of varied lengths and rhyme schemes where the only consistency was in the use of iambs. (There was no effort to keep to Pindar's specific measures in the three-part ode.) Sprat followed his ode to Cowley with several odes to the memory of Oliver Cromwell. These would prove embarrassing to him and to his mentor, John Wilkins, the President of Wadham College, Oxford, to whom they were dedicated. For despite the word 'usurper' in the title, which suggested that Cromwell had been an illegitimate ruler of England, the epideictic was one of praise rather than blame. Sprat's final stanza began by saying to Cromwell's ghost:

> Nor didst thou only for thy Age provide,
>   But for the years to come beside,
> Our after-times and late posterity
>   Shall pay unto thy Fame, as much as we;
>   They too, are made by thee.

1659: 23

Sprat needed to clarify his political position because he had 'turned around with the Restoration', as a popular phrase went, becoming a fervent royalist. He found a good topic in 'The Plague of Athens' as 'excellently Translated by Mr. *Hobbs*' [sic] ([1659] 1667: 1). After all, Thucydides referred to the Peloponnesian War as a calamitous struggle among Greeks and thus a sort of civil war. He also recognized that people ceased to consult oracles and implore the gods when they realized that religious ritual could do nothing against the powerful disease in Athens (1659: 110). Sprat thought he could use the story of Athens during the Peloponnesian War as an 'allegory' of the recent Civil War in England and the increase of 'irreligion' as England's sin (Morgan 2008; Anselment 1996). Of course, this strategy was illogical. It replaced the statement that Athenians turned from religious observation when it proved of no avail against plague with the old belief that the gods sent plague to punish those who abandoned religious practices. Nevertheless, it was an effective strategy for a preacher's son who sought preferment in the church. In time Sprat became a bishop in the Church of England, which had been disestablished under Cromwell.

To develop the allegory of England as a new Greece, Sprat referred to the Athenian speculation that plague came from Ethiopia by way of Egypt. He then placed Egypt in its biblical role as a house of bondage (stanza 5). All sympathy went to the Greeks, though they too got no aid from their gods, nor did they yet have the philosophy of Plato and Aristotle to instruct and console them. The future looked dim as the poem drew to a close:

> Vertue was now esteem'd an empty name,
> And honesty the foolish voice of fame;
> For having pass'd those tott'ring flames before,
> They thought the punishment already o'er,
> Thought Heaven no worse torments had in store;
> Here having felt one Hell, they thought there was no more.
>
> *stanza 31*

The flames mentioned here are the fires to which Athenians took the dead en masse. Because the survivors remain pagans, Sprat supposes they have nowhere to go but to Hell. 'Thick troops of Souls' have already entered the underworld. Nor is there any promise of salvation in the world of humans, where:

> Such guilt, such wickedness,
> Such irreligion did increase,
> That the few good who did survive,
> Were angry with the Plague for suffering them to live.
>
> *stanza 30*

Such poetry is not pathetic so much as 'bathetic', as Alexander Pope later described the anti-sublime that he called 'the art of sinking in poetry' ([1728] 1993).

In the dedication of the poem, Sprat commented on the quality of Thucydides' account: 'In *Greek Thucydides* so well and so lively expresses it, that I know not which is more a Poem, his description or that of Lucretius' (A2r). Lucretius had concluded *De rerum natura* with an account of the plague. Sprat followed Thucydides closely, as did Lucretius, and he probably mentioned the Latin poem as precedent for the sudden shifts within his own poem (Anselment 1996: 7–8).[3] In their descriptions of the plague's horrible toll on the body, Sprat's Pindarics substitute the formality and logic of rhymed couplets for the denser lines of Lucretius' dactylic hexameters, Where Lucretius writes (in the Loeb translation), 'First they felt the head burning with heat, the two eyes red with the fire diffused beneath' (2014: 578–9; 6.1145–6), Sprat offers:

> Upon the Head first the disease,
> As a bold Conqueror doth seize,
> Begins with Mans Metropolis,
> Secur'd the Capitol, and then it knew
> It could at pleasure weaker parts subdue.
> Blood started through each eye;
> The redness of that Skie.

1667: 16; stanza 11

Despite the clever pun on 'Capitol,' there is little wonder that this would be Sprat's last published poem. His other writing about plague appeared in his history of the Royal Society of London (1667: 120–3, 164, 192).

John Dryden and the year of terrors

A more satisfactory poetic perspective on disasters appeared in the first long poem by John Dryden (1631–1700). The future poet laureate was a versatile writer of poetry, plays, translations, and critical essays. As poet, he made extensive use of iambic pentameter verse in rhymed couplets, a form that Chaucer introduced into English poetry and Dryden was first to call the 'heroic couplet'. He even asked permission to add rhymes to *Paradise Lost*, which he thought would augment its elevated diction. (Milton gave him leave to 'tag my points', i.e. button up his clothes (Parker 1968: 1.634–5)). As a critic, Dryden wrote in defence of 'heroic poesy' and 'heroic drama', making use of recent French criticism to shore up his arguments. Here he was the exception to the rule that English authors did not refer to Longinus on the sublime before 1700, for he included some reference to Boileau in the late 1670s (Hume 1970: 210). He in fact proved the corollary that English poets like Milton recognized sublimity before they knew the name. Moreover, he reached sublime moments in *Annus Mirabilis*, a book-length poem of 304 numbered quatrains, subtitled 'the Year of Wonders, 1666' and including references to both the Great Fire of London in September of that year and the Great Plague of London, which began in 1665 and continued into 1667.[4]

Both of these disasters contributed to English losses during the Second Anglo-Dutch War of 1665–7 and to a treaty less advantageous than Charles II had sought when he started the trade war. By concentrating on the year 1666, Dryden emphasized English victories at sea while ignoring the war's beginning and its embarrassing end. He also praised the king as the chief power behind the naval victories and the chief mourner for the victims of London's plague and fire. He did all this knowing that he had much for which to make up with the king.

Like Sprat, Dryden had supported the Commonwealth under which he grew up and its Lord Protector, Oliver Cromwell. He had written the first ode in the volume to which Sprat contributed. He made such comments on Cromwell as appear in this quatrain:

> His *Grandeur* he derived from heaven alone,
>   For he was Great, e're Fortune made him so;
> And Wars, like mists that rise against the Sun,
>   Made him but greater seem, not greater grow.
>
> 1659: stanza 6

While Sprat used the Athenian plague to hint at the false religious views that fueled Cromwell's cause, Dryden used the victories that he celebrated as evidence of the king's strategic strength. While acknowledging that God had the power to bring plague and fire on the people of London, he used the occasion to admit his own past errors of judgment and to ask forgiveness. In lines addressed directly to God but indirectly to the king, he wrote:

> . . . if my heedless Youth has stept astray,
>   Too soon forgetful of thy gracious hand,
> On me alone thy just displeasure lay,
>   But take thy judgments from this mourning land.
>
> 1668: stanza 265

In an encomium of the 'yay team' variety, Dryden played down the terror of the recent plague. He first mentioned the 'contagion' to explain the shortage of British manpower during the war (stanza 244). Then he made a single late reference to the plague itself after it was past its prime in the summer of 1666 (stanza 292). He hinted at misconduct during the Interregnum before the monarchy was restored by suggesting that St. Paul's Church at the centre of London had been 'prophan'd by Civil War' before it was destroyed by fire (stanza 276).

Dryden introduced London quite suddenly before getting to the plague and fire with an apostrophe:

> Yet, *London*, Empress of the Northern Clime,
>   By a high fate thou greatly did expire;
> Great as the worlds [i.e. world's], which at the death of time
>   Must fall and rise a nobler frame by fire.
>
> 1668: stanza 212

The suggestion here is that London has suffered the same fate as other states – notably Rome, since Britons believed their island was colonized by a grandson of Aeneas named Brutus.[5] Dryden suggests that what has been lost to fire will be replaced by 'a nobler frame'. The 'prodigious fire' has taken out palaces and temples (stanza 215), the buildings of tradesmen and 'every nobler portion of the town' (stanza 235). The royal buildings in

Westminster have escaped. However, the king mourns for what has been lost, including families and children trapped in their tenements:

> No thought can ease them, but the Sovereign's care,
>   Whose Praise th'afflicted as their Comfort sing,
> E'en those whose Want might drive to just despair,
>   Think Life's a Blessing under such a King.
>
> 1668: stanza 260

Fortunately, the fleet of warships had been spared, as if by the hand of God. (It was not until 1667 that they were sunk when the Dutch sailed up the Thames.) Meanwhile, the threat to 'Trade' during the war is bygone. This allows the poem to end on a high note:

> And, while this fam'd Emporium we prepare,
>   The *British* Ocean shall such triumphs boast,
> That those, who now disdain our Trade to share,
>   Shall rob like Pyrats on our wealthy Coast.
>
> 1668: stanza 303

Dryden adds a few classical references to catch the learned reader's eye – for example: 'A Key [quai] of Fire ran all along the Shore, / And lighten'd all the River with the blaze'. Here he inserts a marginal note: 'Sigea igni freta lata relucent *Virg.*' (stanza 231). The reference is to *Aen.* 2.312, translated 'the broad Sigean straits reflect the flames' (Vergil 1999: 336–7). The Vergilian text certainly rises to the sublime, as a conflicted Aeneas, perched atop his father's house, tells how his 'heart burns to muster a force for action'. Because the Britons believed what they learned from Vergil and Geoffrey of Monmouth (p. 199 above) – that the Romans were descended from the Trojans – the allusion comparing the River Thames to the Scamander River surrounding Troy is sufficient to add a note of sublimity to the poem. Not only does this allusion add to the fire's terror; it also puts Charles II in the heroic role of Aeneas.

Dryden was a fine Latinist and produced a translation of the *Aeneid* that remains in press today (Vergil 1997). In the dedication of *Annus Mirabilis*, he included 'An account of the ensuing Poem' (1667: A5R-a2r). Here he compared the virtues of Ovid and Vergil. He especially admired the treatment of plague in the *Georgics* (Vergil 1999: 210–17; 3.478–566). Towards the end, he wrote: 'Before I leave *Virgil* I must own the vanity to tell you, and by you the world, that he has been my master in this Poem: I have followed him every where, I know not with what success, but I am sure with diligence enough: my images are copied from him, and the rest are imitations of him' (1667: a1r).

The Great Plague in retrospect

During the Great Plague of 1665–7, the young physician Nathaneal Hodges (MD Oxford 1659) discovered that there was an active competition between the licensed physicians who remained in London, as he did, and a group of self-made doctors who organized as the Society of Chymical Physicians and sought a royal charter (Thomas 1972). These unlicensed physicians published a broadsheet offering '*Antidotes* so by us prepared, at reasonable Rates, with *Directions* how to use them' (Goddard et al. 1665). As a candidate for admission to the London College of Physicians, which included some of the most eminent practitioners in the country, Hodges hoped to win support for his application by issuing a book on these 'illegal practitioners, wherein their positions are examined, their cheats discovered, and their danger to the nation asserted' (1665: title page). His main complaint was that they were alchemists who, having failed in their search for the philosophers' stone, found a ready market for their chemicals in the terrified and often grieving public of London (1665: 116). He warned prospective patients about the dangers of chemicals used in untested and unregulated medicines, including mercury and antimony, either of which could be lethal in the wrong dosage.

Five years after the plague ended, and still a candidate for admission to the College of Physicians, Hodges wrote a history of the plague in Latin rather than English because he directed this at fellow physicians rather than patients (1672). This book won him membership and proved so popular that it was eventually translated into English (1720). Hodges took account of all the sources of plague – 'Supernatural, Preternatural, and Natural'. He started with the natural ones, which he traced to cargo from Holland and ultimately to silks from Turkey. Not wanting to be considered an atheist, he added that God could use pestilence to punish the unrighteous, as the Bible spoke of diseases as God's 'arrows' (e.g. Psalm 7:13). When it came to the actual medical details, he was closer to the truth, identifying lymphatic fluid (chyle) as the bodily 'Matter where the Spirits are generated' (1720: 67).

When it came to treatments for plague and the prevention of a recurrence, Hodges tried to be quite practical. He advised against bloodletting and saw no universal cure other than prayer. Vomiting or sweating seemed better treatments than phlebotomy, as did cupping buboes to relieve pressure and promote blood flow to the areas. He had no use for the popular remedies, such as the powdered horn of a unicorn or the equally mythic bezoar, but preferred 'simples' such as could be made from flowers, vegetables and fruits. He would wash these down with wine or a cordial made from herbs. He advised following the official pharmacopoeia and especially recommended the concoctions used by the famous Dr Theodore Mayerne. Finally, he recommended the purification of houses where the sick had lain or died and advised burning 'proper [personal] Things' (Hodges 1720: 127–8, 227).

No real treatments for Bubonic plague were known until the development of antibiotics in the twentieth century. Arguably, the real advances made in epidemiology in seventeenth-century England were mathematical, for as the monthly 'bills of mortality' were collected and analysed, there were major advances in statistics, leading to modern actuarial tables (Hacking 2006: 18–38). The chief innovator was John Graunt, a London haberdasher who all but created the study of demography (Lewin 2004; see Hacking 2006). Meanwhile, the real interest of many who read and wrote about mortality rates during plagues was often with the survivors, and it remains there. Especially in small towns that were quarantined from outside for months – notably the Yorkshire town of Eyam – the few people who survived have been of interest to historians and, most recently, to genetic researchers.

Plague history and the literary sublime

Daniel Defoe (1660?–1731) is the only author considered here who did not matriculate at Oxford or Cambridge. He had enough ambition for several men, but he came from a family of religious dissenters – people who would not assent to the Church of England's Articles of Religion. Being unable to subscribe to them, he was ineligible to matriculate. Nevertheless, he had a good education at a dissenting academy in Newington Green on London's east side, which remains a hotbed of religious evangelicals. Though the son of a candle maker, he became a leading newspaper man and best-selling novelist.

In 1722, Defoe released *The Journal of the Plague Year*, claiming that he only edited a journal kept by an ancestor during the year 1665. Its direct inspiration may have been the English translation of Hodges's book on the plague (1720). But it was presented as a journal kept by Defoe's ancestor, one H.F[oe], who closed his account with a quatrain:

> A *dreadful* Plague *in* London *was,*
> *In the Year Sixty Five,*
> *Which swept an Hundred Thousand Souls*
> *Away, yet I alive!*

Recent students of Defoe's work have found that it shows two contrary influences: the realism of the Enlightenment, by which he kept track of the numbers of plague casualties, and the religious enthusiasm of his early life. Distinct ambiguities arise in Defoe's narratives when Enlightenment precision combines with enthusiastic vastness. At least one scholar has suggested that the blend of rationalism and zeal in narrators like Robinson Crusoe and H.F. is 'best understood in relation to the contemporaneous conception of the sublime' (Hentzi 1993: 423). For it was precisely in the early years of the eighteenth century that English critics like Joseph Addison began writing about the sublime (Ashfield and de Boola 1996).

Thus, Defoe proceeds from tables of abortive births at different points of the year to horrid tales of mothers found dead with babies at their breasts who already show the 'tokens' of plague. After such stories, he says he could give more such examples (1968: 128–31). As the journal comes to a close in December 1665, H.F. generalizes about the growing indifference of Londoners:

> People had cast off all Apprehensions, and that too fast; indeed we were no more afraid now to pass by a Man with a white Cap upon his Head, or with a Cloth wrapt around his Neck, or with his Leg limping, occasion'd by the Sores in his Groyn, all

which were frightful to the last Degree, but [only] the week before; but now the Streets was [sic] full of them.

1968: 271

The plague would continue for more than a year before it reached the 100,000 victims in the quatrain. One may think of people who died from COVID-19 after their society wearied of continuing to take precautions and tried to normalize life during the pandemic.

Conclusion

I noted earlier the potential problem of separating discussion of the sublime from that of the beautiful, using the example of slasher films that target teenage audiences. This problem may be addressed by the late Harold Bloom, who professed to be a Longinian critic when he noted that 'the function of the Sublime was to persuade us to abandon easier for more difficult pleasures' (2010: xv). He was thinking back to Shelley and the Romantic sublime; however, the very sense of elevation in the word 'sublime', makes one look for something like Shelley's 'sacred chain of poets' with the intertextuality reaching across the centuries ([1840] 1891: 23). Shelley meanwhile could well have been thinking of Longinus on the inspiration that one writer receives from another (1995: 210–11; 13.2), even in treating terror like that which Hector inspired in the invading Greeks. Meanwhile, the 'terrible beauty' mentioned three times in Yeats's poem 'Easter, 1916' suggests that the terrors of modern life can become sublime when they are shown to be strangely beautiful in works of art.

I also noted that Yeats's contemporary Sigmund Freud contributed to discussion of the sublime in his essay on 'The Uncanny'. In the first sentence of that essay, Freud suggested that aesthetics could be considered beyond the theory of beauty to include 'the qualities of our feeling' (2003: 123). In thoughts parallel to Edmund Burke's, he identified an artistic device that 'belongs to the realm of the frightening, of what evokes fear and dread'. He added that the affective power of this device justified the use of a 'conceptual term': *das Unheimliche*, which he identified as the German equivalent of the English word 'uncanny' (125). He did not use the word 'sublime', but critics have applied his insights into the process of repression to the theory of the sublime (Bloom 1982). Freud's essay proceeded with a close if wandering analysis of E. T. A. Hoffmann's 1817 story 'The Sandman'. He found the uncanny elements there to be repressed memories of the protagonist's early home life (Haughton 2003: xli-liv; Royle 2003). Much of the fear in Hoffmann's story is the protagonist's fear of self-knowledge, even when his friends want and try to help him to it.

Freud's theory of the uncanny is perhaps the closest we come to a modern and post-modern sublime. Psychologists after Freud have realized what he suggested in *Civilization and Its Discontents* (1931): that repression not only causes neuroses but also allows society to function (Becker 1973: 47–66). The uncanny thus figures in much writing of the last century, when literary artists purposefully used techniques of 'defamiliarization' (the Russian *ostranenie* of Viktor Shlovsky) as well as 'alienation' (the German *Verfremdung* of Bertholt Brecht) (Cuddon 1998: 20–1, 191–2).

Notes

1. This paper grew out of thoughts exchanged with my old friend Thom Worthen after we found that we shared an interest in famous plagues. His work on the Plague of Athens included participation on a panel formed by physicians at the University of Arizona's College of Medicine (Iserson 1984).
2. Although Hobbes wrote a good deal about contracts in ch. 14, the term 'social contract' was coined in a book by his contemporary Jeremy Taylor (1660), who had served as chaplain to Charles I.
3. Kazantzidis 2021 analyses Lucretian aesthetics of disease and morbidity in terms of the terrifying sublime.
4. For the role of plague and conflagration in the cosmic myth of replacement see Worthen 1991: 54 *et passim*.
5. The standard source of this legend was the history of Britain prepared by a twelfth-century monk (Monmouth 2007: 4–5).

Works cited

Anselment, R. A. (1996), 'Thomas Sprat's *The Plague of Athens*: Thucydides, Lucretius, and the Pindaric Way', *Bulletin of the John Rylands Library*, 78: 3–20.
Aristotle (1995), *The Poetics*, trans. S. Halliwell, W. H. Fyfe, D. C. Innis, W. R. Roberts, revised D. A. Russell, Cambridge, MA: Harvard University Press.
Ashfield, A. and P. de Bolla (eds) (1996), *The Sublime: A Reader in British Eighteenth-Century Aesthetic Theory*, Cambridge: Cambridge University Press.
Becker, E. (1973), *The Denial of Death*, New York: Free Press.
Blake, W. (1966), 'The Marriage of Heaven and Hell', in G. Keynes (ed.), *The Complete Writings of William Blake with Variant Readings*, 148–58, Oxford: Oxford University Press.
Bloom, H. (1982), 'Freud and the Poetic Sublime', in H. Bloom (ed.), *Agon: Towards a Theory of Revisionism*, 91–118, New York: Oxford University Press.
Bloom, H. (ed.) (2010), *The Sublime*, New York: Infobase.
Brown, K. (1978), 'The Artist of the *Leviathan* Title Page', *The British Library Journal*, 4: 24–36.
Burke, E. ([1757] 1838), 'A Philosophical Inquiry into the Ideas of the Sublime and Beautiful', in *The Works of . . . Edmund Burke*, 12 vols, 1: 67–262, London: John C. Nimmo.
Casino Royale (1967), [Film] Dir. K. Hughes and J. Huston, USA: Columbia Pictures.
Coates, J. (1989), Review of P. Gay (ed.), *A Freud Reader*, Chicago Tribune, June 3.
Cowley, A. (1656), *Pindarique Odes, Written in Imitation of the Stile & Maner of the Odes of Pindar* bound with Abraham Cowley, *Poems*, London: Humphrey Moseley.
Cuddon, J. A. (ed.) (1998), *Dictionary of Literary Terms and Literary Theory*, 4th edn, revised C. A. Preston, Oxford: Blackwell.
Defoe, D. ([1722] 1968), *Journal of the Plague Year*, New York: Heritage Press.
Denham, J. ([1642] 1650), *Cooper's Hill: A Poeme. The Second Edition with Additions*, London: Humphrey Moseley.

Doran, R. (2015), *The Theory of the Sublime: From Longinus to Kant*, Cambridge: Cambridge University Press.

Dryden, J. (1659), 'Heroique Stanza's on the Late Usurper Oliver Cromwel. Written after his Funeral', in *Three Poems on the Death of the Late Usurper Oliver Cromwel*, 1–7, London: William Wilson.

Dryden, J. (1667), *Annus Mirabilis: The Year of Wonders, 1666. An Historical Poem, Containing The Progress and various Successes of our Naval War with Holland . . . and describing the Fire of London*, London: Henry Herringman.

Fowler, A. (ed.) (1971), *Milton: Paradise Lost*, revised edn, London and New York: Longman.

Freud, S. ([1919] 2003), *The Uncanny*, trans. D. McLintock, Introduction by A. Phillips, New York and London: Penguin.

Freud, S. ([1920] 1928), *Beyond the Pleasure Principle*, trans. J. Strachey, New York: Liveright.

Freud, S. (1931), *Civilization and Its Discontents*, trans. J. Strachey, London: Hogarth Press.

Frye, N. (1965), *The Return of Eden: Five Essays on Milton's Epics*, Toronto: University of Toronto Press.

Goddard, W., M. Needham, E. Bolnest, T. Williams, G. Thompson, T. O. Down and R. Barker (1665), *An Advertisement from the Society of Chymical Physitians, touching Medicines by them Prepared, in Pursuance of His Majesties Command, for the Prevention, and for the Cure of the Plague*, London: John Starkey.

Hacking, I. (2006), *The Emergence of Probability: A Philosophical Study of Early Ideas about Probability, Induction, and Statistical Inference*, 2nd edn, Cambridge: Cambridge University Press.

Hall, J. (1651), *Dionysius Longinus of the Height of Eloquence*, London: Roger Daniel.

Haughton, H. (2003), 'Introduction', in S. Freud, *The Uncanny*, trans. D. McLintock, vii–lx, London and New York: Penguin.

Hentzi, Gary. (1993), 'Sublime Moments and Social Authority in *Robinson Crusoe* and *A Journal of the Plague Year*', *Eighteenth Century Studies*, 26: 419–36.

Hesiod (2018), *Theogony*, in *Theogony, Works and Days, Testimonia*, trans. G. W. Most, Cambridge, MA: Harvard University Press.

Hobbes, T. (1651), *Leviathan: Or the Matter, Forme, and Power of a Common-wealth Eclesiasticall and Civill*, London: Andrew Crooke.

Hobbes, T. (1683), *De mirabilibus pecci, being Wonders of the Peak in Darby-Shire commonly called the Devil's Arse of Peak, in English and Latine*, 5th edn, London: William Cook.

Hobbes, T. (1839), *The English Works of Thomas Hobbes of Malmesbury*, ed. Sir William Molesworth (1839–45), 11 vols, London: Bohn.

Hodges, N. (1665), *Vindiciae Medicinae & Medicorum, or, An Apology for the Profession and Professors of Physick*, London: Henry Brome.

Hodges, N. (1672), *Loimologia, sive, Pestis nuperae apud Populum Londinensem grassantis Narratio Historica*, London: Joseph Nevill.

Hodges, N. (1720), *Loimologia: Or, An Historical Account of the Plague in London in 1665*, trans. J. Quincy, London: E. Bell and J. Osborne.

Hoffmann, E. T. A. (1982), *Tales of Hoffmann*, ed. and trans. J. R. Hollingdale, Penguin: London and New York.

The Holy Bible: King James Version ([1611] 1912), London: Oxford University Press.

Homer (2001), *Iliad*, trans. A. T. Murray, rev. T. F. Wyatt, Cambridge, MA: Harvard University Press.

Hume, R. (1970), *Dryden's Criticism*, Ithaca, NY: Cornell University Press.

Iserson, K. V. (1984), *Death in Athens: The Plague of 430 B.C.*, Tucson: Biomedical Communications.

Jackson, C. (2022), *Devil-Land: England Under Siege, 1588–1688*, London: Allen Lane.

Johnson, L. M. (1993), *Thucydides, Hobbes, and the Interpretation of Realism*, DeKalb: Northern Illinois University Press.

Jung, C. G. (1953), 'The Psychology of the Unconscious', in *Two Essays on Analytical Psychology*, trans. R. F. C. Hull, 3–117, New York: Pantheon.
Kantorowicz, E. H. (1957), *The King's Two Bodies: A Study in Medieval Political Theory*, Princeton: Princeton University Press.
Kazantzidis, G. (2021), *Lucretius on Disease: The Poetics of Morbidity in De Rerum Natura*, Berlin: De Gruyter.
Kavka, G. S. (1983), 'Hobbes's War of All Against All', *Ethics*, 93: 291–310.
Lewin, C. G. (2004), 'John Graunt', *Dictionary of National Biography*, www-oxfordDNB-com.
Longinus (1890), *On the Sublime*, trans. A. Lang, London and New York: Macmillan.
Longinus (1995), *On the Sublime*, trans. S. Halliwell, W. H. Fyfe, D. C. Innis, W. R. Roberts, rev. D. A. Russell, Cambridge, MA: Harvard University Press.
Lucretius (2014), *De Rerum Natura*, trans. W. H. D. Rouse, rev. M. F. Smith, Cambridge, MA: Harvard University Press.
Malcolm, N. (2004), 'Hobbes, Thomas', *Dictionary of National Biography*, www-oxfordDNB-com.
Milton, John ([1667] 1674) *Paradise Lost: A Poem in Twelve Books*, 2nd edn, London: T. Helder.
Monmouth, G. of (2007), *The History of the Kings of Britain: An Edition and Translation of the De gestis Britonum*, ed. M. D. Reeve, trans. N. Wright, Woodbridge, Suffolk: Boydel Press.
Moore, L. E. (1990), *Beautiful Sublime: The Making of Paradise Lost 1701–1734*, Stanford, CA: Stanford University Press.
Morgan, J. (2008), 'Sprat, Thomas', *Dictionary of National Biography*, www-oxfordDNB-com.
Parker, W. R. (1968), *Milton: A Biography*, 2nd edn, 2 vols, Oxford and New York: Oxford University Press.
Pope, A. ([1728] 1993), 'Peri Bathous, or The Art of Sinking in Poetry', in P. Rogers (ed.), *Alexander Pope, The Major Works*, 195–238, Oxford and New York: Oxford University Press.
Porter, J. I. (2016), *The Sublime in Antiquity*, Cambridge: Cambridge University Press.
Robortello, F. (trans.) (1554), *Dionysii Longini rhetoris praestantissimi liber de grandi sive sublimi orationis genere*, Basel: Oporinus.
Royle, N. (2003), 'Supplement: "The Sandman"', in N. Royle (ed.), *The Uncanny*, 39–50, Manchester and New York: Manchester University Press.
Schiller, F. von ([1792] 1966), *On the Sublime*, in J. A. Elias (ed.), *Naive and Sentimental Poetry and On the Sublime*, 193–212, New York: Frederick Ungar.
Scream (1996), [Film] Dir. W. Craven, USA: Miramax.
Shelley, P. B. ([1840] 1891), *A Defence of Poetry*, ed. A. S. Cook. Boston: Ginn.
Spenser, E. (1912), *The Poetical Works of Edmund Spenser*, ed. J. C. Smith and E. de Selincourt, London: Oxford University Press.
Sprat, T. (1659), 'To the Memory of the Late Usurper Oliver Cromwell: Pyndarick Odes', in *Three Poems upon the Death of the Late Usurper Oliver Cromwel*, 9–23, London: William Wilson.
Sprat, T. ([1659] 1665), *The Plague of Athens, Which hapned in the Second Year of the Peloponnesian Warre. First described in Greek by Thucydides; Then in Latin by Lucretius. Now attempted in English*, London: Henry Brome.
Sprat, T. (1667), *The History of the Royal Society of London*, London: T. R. for J. Martyn and J. Allestry.
Taylor, J. (1660), *Ductor dubitantium, or, The Rule of Conscience*, London: Richard Royston.
Thomas, H. (1972), 'The Society of Chymical Physitians: An Echo of the Great Plague of London, 1665', in A. G. Debus (ed.), *Science Medicine and Society in the Renaissance: Essays to Honor W. Pagel*, 2: 56–71, New York: Science History Publications.
Thucydides (1629), *Eight Bookes of the Peloponnesian Warre*, trans. T. Hobbes, London: Henry Seile.
Vergil (1997), *Virgil's Aeneid*, trans. J. Dryden, London and New York: Penguin Books.
Vergil (1999), *Eclogues, Georgics, Aeneid 1–6*, trans. H. R. Fairclough, rev. G. P. Gould, Cambridge, MA: Harvard University Press.
Worthen, T. D. (1991), *The Myth of Replacement: Stars, Gods, and Order in the Universe*, Tucson: The University of Arizona Press.

CHAPTER 12
'SOLUTION SWEET' AND KEATS'S POETIC IDEAL: EROTIC AND NUPTIAL IMAGERY IN *THE EVE OF ST. AGNES*
Cynthia White

Introduction

In a letter to his friend John Hamilton Reynolds, dated 3 May 1818,[1] John Keats (1795–1821) discusses poetry in general, and wonders whether Wordsworth as a poet 'has an extended vision or a circumscribed grandeur – whether he is an eagle in his nest, or on the wing'. Several months later, still exploring his own ideas about 'poetical Character', he writes to Richard Woodhouse, the attorney for his publisher, also a close friend.[2] In this important letter, dated 27 October 1818, Keats distinguishes his poetics from Wordsworth's, whose he terms the 'egotistical sublime', a style of writing that adheres to a single overriding truth, the 'circumscribed grandeur' he writes of in the letter to Reynolds. His own 'poetical Character', on the other hand, 'is not itself – it has no self – it is everything and nothing'. For Keats, the poet should assert no identity and 'is certainly the most unpoetical of all God's Creatures', that is, a 'camelion Poet'. Keats's comments on his poetic persona allow us to appreciate the multivalency of his *The Eve of St. Agnes*, one of the three medieval romances[3] published together with several odes and a fragment of *Hyperion* in July 1820. In the letter to Reynolds, the narrative poem is figured as a 'Mansion of Many Apartments', another metaphor for ever-widening knowledge that fuels his poetic expansiveness.

In his 'Mansion of Many Apartments', Keats conjures a chamber that intoxicates with its light and atmosphere and is so pleasant there is no thought of leaving; yet that very delight paradoxically leads to an encroaching awareness of the many doors into darkness where the world's miseries reside. That contrast, between the sublime and the mundanely human, or, perhaps, the space between, constitutes the mystery into which the thickly woven poetic texture of *The Eve of St. Agnes* takes readers. Indeed, it seems that as many interpretations as readers reside in the mansion the poet envisions as his poetry's aesthetic. Stillinger (1999), for example, isolates fifty-nine interpretations, many with multiple subheadings,[4] and since his study more recent scholarship has tended to concentrate upon the influence of Keats's medical training and other realia on his poems.[5] My chapter will develop the source narrative behind the ritual performed on the eve of St Agnes as a reception of poetic conceits common to Roman love elegy and nuptial epithalamia as they have been transmitted through early Christian poems, treatises and martyr acts of St Agnes. From the first account of her martyrdom (*c.* 350 CE) through fifth- and sixth-century accounts, the literary *acta* of St Agnes show a steady accretion of nuptial imagery. But it is her unique status as bride of Christ as received in early fourteenth-century media – paintings and manuscript illuminations, devotional literature, ritual and liturgy – in a circumscribed area of the northern Rhine that informs Agnes's ability to deliver a portentous dream of a young girl's future husband to her. The first part of the chapter examines this accretion of nuptial imagery in the Agnes literature and its clear correspondences with classical elegy and epithalamia. Nuptial imagery in the very earth(l)y passions of classical love poetry is transformed into a sacred marriage in the martyrdom texts of St Agnes, and into a mystic marriage in later images and literature. In the climactic dream stanzas of Keats's poem, the influence of classical and late antique nuptial literature powerfully blends with the poet's aesthetic principles concerning the sublime and the beautiful. It is this 'solution sweet' that the final section of my chapter will elucidate, when Agnes's dream oscillates between a divinely sublime love and the drear and dear beauty of quotidian experience.

The sources of the eve of St Agnes ritual

There is a scholarly consensus that the impetus for *The Eve of St. Agnes* was a reference to the symptoms of lovers in Robert Burton's *Anatomy of Melancholy*, which, as Keats tells us in his letter of 17–27 September 1819 to his brother George and his sister-in-law Georgina, he was reading.[6] In the section on symptoms of love, Burton connects music and poetry with love: 'For as Erasmus hath it, Musicam docet Amor & Poesin ('love inspires music and poetry'). Love will make them Musitians, and to compose ditties, Madrigals, Elegies, Love Sonnets, and sing them to several pretty tunes ...' (1994: 188). Following this description of young people singing and dancing comes a section detailing the behaviour of lovers and a divination ritual which combines the calendrical alignment of the eve of St Agnes (January 20) with faery superstition. This passage is assumed to be the source of the St Agnes's Eve divination ritual:

> They will in all places be doing thus, young folks
> Especially, reading love stories ... singing, telling
> or hearing lascivious tales ... hence it is, they can thinke,
> discourse willingly, or speake almost of no other subject.
> Tis their only desire if it may be done by art, to see their
> husbands picture in a glasse, they'le give any thing to
> know when they shall be married, how many husbands
> they shall have ... by fasting on S. Annes Eve[7] or night,
> to know who shall be their first husband.[8]

191

But Burton's reference does not explain how it comes to be that the young Christian martyr Agnes who rejects marriage in order to preserve her virginity for her bridegroom Christ becomes a patron saint of marriage, capable of bestowing dream visions of their future husbands upon virgins. How does the nuptial imagery in the legend of St Agnes's martyrdom, as it develops over time and texts, shape and deepen the dream stanzas of Keats's *The Eve of St. Agnes*?

St Agnes, martyr and bride of Christ

From the time of her martyrdom (*c.* 350 CE), the legends, stories, texts and images of St Agnes expand geographically as they assume literary accretions.[9] Agnes is one of only four female saints whose martyrdom and burial place, first recorded in the calendar called the *Depositio Martyrum*, is commemorated in the Chronography of 354, and the only one whose feast has remained in the liturgical cycle.[10] Coming as early in the year as it does (January 21), the feast day of St Agnes marks the new annual cycle of Christian liturgical celebrations. Such cosmic recurrences, as Worthen 1991 has argued, conflate myth and ritual to impose regularity and to 'defend a culture in all its regularity from unpredictable ... phenomena (234–5)'.[11] His grand theory of the 'myth of replacement', writ small and applied to the particular cosmic configuration of St Agnes's annual feast day, suggests that the predictability of marriage ensures replacement. Regularity of the seasons, celestial order and ritual time are not rooted in any single event but, like marriage, conspire to control disorder and ensure the regeneration of society.[12]

The *elogium* of Damasus

The *elogium* that Pope Damasus (366–84) composed for Agnes and the famed calligrapher Furius Dionysius Filocalus inscribed on a large marble slab still rests near her burial in the church of *S. Agnese* in Rome, on the *Via Nomentana* (Ferrua 1942: 175–8, no. 37).[13] This earliest written account of the martyrdom of St Agnes of Rome – Damasus' ten lines of dactylic hexameter – highlights Agnes's youth when she left her nurse's lap (*nutricis gremium subito liquisse puellam*) to face the threats of her cruel persecutor; so too her noble comportment, small stature, willingness to face torture by fire and that she covered her nudity with her hair, perhaps in modesty. Sághy 2000: 274 convincingly argues that Agnes's suffering is narrated without sentiment as a ploy by Damasus to control the martyr cult for the papacy. Nonetheless, Agnes's sudden leap from her nurse's lap may be the first anticipation of the nuptial imagery that will dominate her cult.

In Catullus' epithalamium, poem 61, Hymenaeus gives the blooming (*floridam*) bride to her wild (*fero*) groom from her mother's lap (*a gremio suae matris*) (56–8).[14] Marriage by force has a long history in Greek and Latin literature and myth, beginning with Hades' paradigmatic rape/marriage of Persephone; here, it is Agnes's youth and inexperience that make her reluctant. Agnes's sacrificial encounter with death may be considered an inversion of Vibia's (Catullus' bride's) sexual encounter because one was willing and one was not, but they both seek to evade marriage, and both encounters will be traumatic.[15] Marriage is figured as a kind of sacrifice (Feeney 2013: 77) in the poem's initial lines

(61.3–4), when the poet apostrophizes Hymenaeus, 'who snatches away a tender virgin for her groom' (*qui rapis teneram ad virum*).[16] Evident as early as the nuptial poetry of Sappho and Alcaeus, bridal reluctance[17] is a *topos* of the genre, one that further highlights Agnes's eagerness to face her persecutor in her martyrdom/marriage to Christ.

The Agnes legend in St Ambrose and Ps.-Ambrose

In his *De virginibus* (377 CE),[18] Ambrose, bishop of Milan (374–80), wrote the next extant account of Agnes's martyrdom: there her youth, frailty and courage echo Damasus' *elogium*, but Ambrose places her squarely in a nuptial context and contrasts her eagerness to approach her death with the reluctance of a bride to step out of her home to attend her wedding: 'A bride would not hurry to her bridal bed as joyfully as she went as a virgin to her punishment; not adorned with her hair bound like a bride, but (adorned) with Christ' (*non sic ad thalamum nupta properaret, ut ad supplici locum laeta successu, gradu festina virgo processit, non intorto crine caput compta, sed Christo*, 1.2.8). We also learn that the executioner attempted to persuade her to change her mind with alluring gifts (*blanditiis*), which she refused (1.2.9). A similar exchange reappears in St Agnes's *passio* (pp. 212–13 below), which frames Agnes as an elegiac *puella* wooed by her lover. Blandishments of all sorts are pervasive in Roman elegy, e.g. Ovid, *Am.* 3.1, where Ovid listens to the muses of elegy and tragedy competing for his verses. While tragedy invites him to 'undertake a greater work' and 'sing the deeds of heroes' (*incipe maius opus ... cane facta virorum*, 24), elegy chastises tragedy for her heavy themes: 'Can't you lighten up?' (*an numquam non gravis esse potes?*, 36). Such heaviness, she continues, prevents tragedy from entering the door[19] that opens at her charming words (*est blanditiis ianua laxa*, 46).

In a second text treating St Agnes's martyrdom, the Ps.-Ambrosian hymn, *Agnes beatae virginis* (Walpole 1922: 72–6[20]), the poet emphasizes her youth, that she is 'not yet ready for marriage' (*matura nondum nuptiis*, 6), even though, as also recorded by Damasus, she is strong enough to break through the guarded doorway (*solvit fores custodiae*, 11) that her terrified parents double-bolted to safeguard her chastity (*parentes territi / claustrum pudoris auxerant*, 9–10). The hymn again compares young Agnes led to her persecution with a bride going to her wedding: 'she seems so happy being led away (to her execution), you might think she were proceeding to her wedding, bearing new wealth to her husband, a dowry measured in blood' (*prodire quis nuptum putet / sic laeta vultu ducitur / novas viro ferens opes / dotata censu sanguinis*, 13–16). When ordered to light the sacrificial fire on the altar of the pagan god with 'torches' (*taedis*, 18), she responds, 'virgins of Christ do not raise up such torches' (*haud tales faces / sumpsere Christi virgines*, 19–20).[21] Here we see for the first time in the legend of St Agnes a conflation of marriage and death: her approach to her martyrdom as a nuptial *deductio*, with a reference to the torches that usually herald the approaching bride, and the blood of its consummation as a dowry.

In eroticized defiance, Agnes refuses to worship the Roman gods and demands the executioner strike: 'Here! Here! so I can put out the fires with my flowing blood' (*hic, hic ferite! ut profluo / cruore retinguam focos*, 23–4). Finally, in a new detail, as she fell Agnes 'covered her body with her robe, her face with her hand; she sought to find the ground with a bent knee, and glide into her fall modestly' (*nam ueste se totam tegens / uultumque texerat manu, / terram genu flexo petit / lapsu verecundo cadens*, 30–3).[22]

Prudentius, *Peristephanon* 14: *passio Agnetis*

In Prudentius' martyr-lyric, *Peristephanon* 14,[23] Agnes is highly sexualized, more an elegiac *puella* than a young bride.[24] A titillating addition here is the story of Agnes in the brothel. Realizing that threatening her virginity is more frightening to Agnes than torture, the tyrant orders her into a public brothel. In sympathy, most people look away as she is publicly paraded through the streets naked;[25] but the person who looks is blinded. Agnes's refusal to sacrifice to Minerva so incites the anger of her persecutor that he orders a soldier to take a sword and carry out the death sentence commanded by the emperor. Agnes insults her executioner and delivers, as a defiant response, a graphic image of the violent sexual penetration that she welcomes. She couches the encounter in erotic language, even calling her executioner a 'lover', while rejecting the poet-lover of Roman elegy: 'I'm thrilled that someone like you came, a wild, dark, violent executioner (*uaesanus, atrox, turbidus, armiger*, 70) rather than some drooping, tender and soft young man bathed in cologne (*languidus ac tener mollisque ephebus tinctus aromate*, 71–2), who might kill me at the cost of my honor. This one, this lover (*amator*, 74), I confess, is pleasing.' Prudentius here casts Agnes in the role of a *domina puella* who prefers a soldier to a lover, a Christianized elegiac mistress.[26] This triangle of characters – the mistress and a soldier or poet-lover analogizes (and embodies) programmatic statements about the nature of elegiac poetry.[27] Roman elegists often map the physical characteristics of the poet/elegist to the text: in Tib. 1.2., for example, the contrast between the martial hero and the elegiac lover is most pronounced. The soldier is *ferreus*, like iron: 'That man was *iron* who, when he could have had you, foolishly preferred to chase after war loot' (67–8); and the lover is characteristically described in soft, effeminate terms: 'And while I can hold you in my tender arms let me enjoy a soft slumber in the coarse grass' (*et te, dum liceat, teneris retinere lacertis / mollis et inculta sit mihi somnus humo*, 75–6). In Ov., Am. 1.6.3–6 we see this contrast in the context of Ovid's *paraclausithyron*, as the elegiac lover, conflating literal and figurative, describes his enfeebled physical condition in a protracted state of unrequited love to analogize the light, attenuated, delicate features of elegiac poetry and his long service to its muse Amor: 'I just need a small opening in the door to squeeze in. My long pining has diminished my size (*corpus tenuavit*, 5) so my slender limbs can fit' (*subducto pondere membra*, 6). This reflective subtext on the nature of elegiac poetry is an important component of the stanzas we will consider below in Keats's poem. There, as the poet-lover sheds and reassumes his persona, the metapoetics of Roman elegy shape our appreciation of Keats's 'poetical Character'.

To this point, we have seen Agnes in a multiplicity of representations: as a *virago*, virgin, prostitute and elegiac *puella*. Whereas Agnes is commemorated in the *elogia* of

Damasus as a tender, young girl who escapes from her nurse's lap (i.e. marriage) to face her execution with religious zeal, in Ambrose's and Ps.-Ambrose's accounts we meet an Agnes facing her execution as happily as if she were processing in her wedding. Nuptial imagery is compounded in *Peristephanon* 14, where Agnes is condemned to a brothel for refusing an offer of marriage to the prefect's son. While these nuptial accretions enhance the story's relatability, they also serve a social function by mitigating the societal disruption virginity and/or martyrdom instantiate. Replacing marriage to a man with marriage (or dedicated virginity) to God, young women complete the cycle of transitions from bride to wife to mother that reintegrates them into society and restores the natural order predicated upon marriage. This, too, has two clear parallels in Keats's poem: in the first, Angela, the old beldame who conspires with Porphyro to 'enliven' Madeline's St Agnes dream, will only cooperate in his scheme on one condition, that he marry her (179); the second occurs in the dream stanzas when Porphyro corrects Madeline's impression that their lovemaking is a dream ('This is no dream, my bride, my Madeline!', 326), and Madeline immediately fears the social stigma of abandonment: 'No dream, alas! alas! and woe is mine! / Porphyro will leave me here to fade and pine' (328–9).

The narrative elaboration in the next text, the *passio S. Agnetis*, introduces romance and an amplified relatability in new, decidedly nuptial details. Sanctity, eroticized sexuality and marriage are aspects of the legend the *passio S. Agnetis* further develops, and these become the *acta* that spread beyond Italy into Europe.[28]

The anonymous *Gesta Martyrum: passio Agnetis*

The *Passio S. Agnetis* appears in the late fifth- and sixth-century *Gesta Martyrum Romanorum*, erroneously attributed to Ambrose (Lanéry 2014), an anonymous compilation of the *acta* and *passiones* of the martyrs.[29] A creative synthesis of the earlier literature of Damasus, Ambrose and Prudentius, the *passio* further develops the *sponsa Christi* theme, a role that Madeline reprises: she is throughout *The Eve of St. Agnes* characterized as a 'missioned spirit' (193), 'a saint' (222), 'a splendid angel' (223), and 'so pure a thing, so free from mortal taint' (225).

The core narratives of Damasus, Ambrose, Ps.-Ambrose and Prudentius remain in the *passio*, with romantic explication: Agnes is still a young girl, but she is now 'beautiful in appearance, more beautiful in faith and scrupulously chaste' (*pulchra facie, sed pulchrior fide, et elegantior castitate*, 1). The lively *passio* account begins with Agnes attracting the attention of the prefect's son, Sempronius, when she is returning from school. He courts her with precious jewellery and the promise of wealth, a home, possessions, servants and every earthly delight, 'if only she would consent to marry him' (2). To this point, the common elements inherited and amalgamated in her developing hagiography have portrayed Agnes as a young aristocratic woman asserting her faith. They reference her marriageability without focusing upon it. Like the unobtainable *domina* of elegy, the eroticism of Agnes's virginity and her sexualized martyrdom thwart the social construct of marriage.[30]

Conversely, marriage is the centrepiece of Agnes's *passio*. The entire community is on stage in a local soap opera less about Agnes's faith than flouting societal expectations to marry and become integrated into her community as a wife and mother. In an animated rejection of Sempronius' offer, Agnes taunts him with the attributes of her other lover: 'he has offered me much better jewelry, and has already become engaged to me with a ring of his fidelity, adorned my right arm with an invaluable bracelet, and surrounded my neck with precious gems, given me priceless pearls for my ears, and covered me with shimmering and flashing gems' (3). As Agnes sensually enumerates her lover's gifts, she simultaneously accentuates her neck and arms and ears in drawing special attention to her body, as if intimately known to her beloved but forbidden to his rival. In an oxymoronic strip tease, Agnes rejects marriage to a man and consecrates her virginity to Christ, a virginal *sponsa Christi*. Keats's description of Madeline synaesthetically disrobing in a beautiful imbrication of sound, sight and touch in a moonlit twilight (227–31),[31] discussed below (p. 217), clearly recalls the paradoxically eroticized *sponsa Christi*.

Agnes continues to both torture and arouse her suitor, insisting that hers is no ephemeral courtship but a wedding preparation – the decoration of the bower and bed and the music of harmonious voices:[32] 'He has already prepared the marriage bed and his musical instruments sing to me in harmonious voices' (3). At the culmination of her stinging rejection of Sempronius, Agnes reveals that she and her lover have already consummated their union (*iam corpus eius corpori meo sociatum est*, 3). She tells Sempronius that she is completely devoted to her lover and, most paradoxically of all, explains their spiritual relationship in the deeply subjective language of Roman elegy: 'When I have made love, I remain chase; when I have touched him, I remain clean; when I have received him, I remain a virgin' (3). At the delivery of this news, Sempronius falls ill. Like the thwarted lover of Latin elegy, Sempronius is both out of his mind with blind love (*insanissimus . . . amore caeco*, 3) and pines for Agnes with deep sighs (*alta suspiria*, 4); even the prefect gets involved and tries to persuade Agnes with the alluring blandishments of elegy (*blandis sermonibus*). But the prefect's primary concern lies with the identity of the man to whom she claims to have been previously engaged. He presses her relentlessly for details, demanding to know the identity of this fiancé, of whose holy power Agnes boasts. As Cooper 1996 argues, this is a love triangle more concerned with the status and power of the two men, their authority and the social order: one attempts to persuade Agnes 'to accept the conjugal bed and her place in the social order' (54), while the other is a superior whose goals do not promote the social order. Cooper concludes: 'Thus we move from a celebration of sexuality in the service of social continuity to a denigration of sexuality in the service of a challenge to the establishment' (55). For Agnes, the choice is to challenge the establishment by refusing to participate in state religion and by rejecting a marriage proposal that affirms community priorities as well as her own place in an aristocratic circle of Roman elites. A similar social conflict in Keats's poem appears at the onset. In the Shakespearean feud between the young lovers' families, marriage is impossible. Like Romeo, Porphyro, whose 'house and land' (102) are at odds with Madeline's family's, crosses into enemy territory on the night of a grand celebration, where an aghast Angela urges him to run for his life: 'Hie thee from this place / they are all here to-night, the whole blood-thirsty race!' (98–9).

The *Gesta Martyrum* narrative unfolds as in Prudentius' poem, and Agnes is sent to a public brothel, though the *passio* fills in many details: the prefect cannot convince Agnes to abandon her faith (*superstitio*) and demands that she make sacrifice to the goddess Vesta if she insists upon remaining a virgin. When she mocks the gods and delivers an eloquent defence of her faith, the exasperated prefect orders her to be sent to a brothel. Undaunted by his threats, Agnes trusts that Christ will protect her virginity as an 'impregnable wall and guard' (*murus inexpugnabilis et custos*, 5).

The similar theme of the elegiac lover protected from all dangers appears in Tibullus 1.2, though in a subversive context, since here it is the lover rather than the beloved who is protected. In his *paraclausithryon*, Tibullus seeks to dupe his girlfriend's husband by sneaking into her house through a locked door. As he begs the door behind which his *amica* Delia is locked to open for him, and then begs Delia to unfasten it herself, Tibullus assures her that Venus will assist her, as she assists all lovers. He then offers the example of his own inviolable nocturnal wandering protected by Venus: 'Whoever's possessed by love goes wherever he wants safe and sacrosanct' (*quisquis amore tenetur eat tutusque sacerque / qualibet*, 28–9). As Agnes is led naked through the streets to the brothel, her unbound hair (*crine soluta*, 8) thickens and covers her. The spectacle of Agnes naked and eroticized by her unbound hair echoes another conceit of elegiac intimacies. In Ovid's description of Apollo in pursuit of a fleeing Daphne, he is so uncomfortably close that he breathes on strands of her hair falling onto her neck (*crinem sparsum cervicibus adflat*, *Met.* 1.542). And in the crepuscular light of the late afternoon sun, Ovid's beloved Corinna visits him with her 'hair parted' (*dividua ... coma*, *Am*. 1.5.10) on her gleaming neck, like an ancient queen entering her wedding chamber (*thalamus*).[33] In a parodic *deductio*, Agnes is being led to her first sexual encounter; a brothel is her *thalamus*. Agnes's nakedness, partly visible through her loose hair, recalls the eroticism of elegy; and though her flowing hair also marks her as anti-social, as a sign that she is defying the conventions of Roman *mores* and *cultus*,[34] through a Christian lens Agnes is sacrosanct in her miraculously thickened hair.

A second miracle occurs in the brothel when an angel surrounds Agnes with a light so splendid that anyone who glances at her suffers a diminution of vision that magnifies in proportion to the time spent looking at her. Though they enter the brothel in heated and raging desire (*ferventes et turpiter saevientes*, 9), a common descriptor of elegiac lovers, Sempronius' companions are chastened and reverent when they exit, to the ridicule of Sempronius, who deplores them as 'impotent, useless, soft, and pitiable' (*impotentes ... vanos et molles ac miseros*, 9), i.e. physically incapable of the task at hand. While Agnes's tormentors are turned from their raging desire into the *impotentes* of unconsummated desire, Porphyro's restrained desire (to the awakened Madeline, 'pallid, chill, and drear', 311) is dreamily transformed into that of a passionate lover, 'Ethereal, flushed, and like a throbbing star' (318). In Porphyro's own reckoning, his 'many hours of toil and quest' (338) transform him from the elegiac lover, an avatar of desire, into Madeline's possessor, her 'vassal blest' (335). That this was Keats's intended interpretation is still a matter of scholarly debate, but consideration of the revision he proposed to these lines of stanza 36 leaves little doubt.

When Keats was revising *The Eve of St. Agnes* in September 1819, he sensed that Porphyro, 'Ethereal, flushed, and like a throbbing star', did not explicitly enough convey the passionate sexual union that followed. In his revision of verses 314–22, Porphyro's 'arms, encroaching slow / Have zoned her, heart to heart', and while she sleeps, 'in serene repose / With her wild dream he mingled, as a rose / Marrieth its odour to a violet'. And so there could be no misunderstanding, the revised stanza 36 concludes, 'Still, still she dreams, louder the frost wind blows'. In the correspondence between his literary advisor Woodhouse and his publisher Taylor, the consternation the revision caused is evident. In his heated letter to Taylor,[35] Woodhouse directs his reviling censure at the revisions. He maintains that 'Porphyro, when acquainted with Madelaine's [sic] love for him, and arose, ethereal, flush'd, etc., etc.', intended to persuade Madeline to go off with him, succeeded, and they left to be married. But in the revised stanza, he continues, when Porphyro 'winds by degrees his arm round her, presses breast to breast, and acts all the acts of a *bona fide* husband, she fancies she is only playing the part of a wife in a dream'. In sum, Woodhouse concludes, the revisions will 'render the poem unfit for ladies'.[36] In the end, the revisions are rejected.[37] In my reading, the stanza as we have it richly implicates the mystic union of Agnes with Madeline to animate a metapoetic reading central to Keats's poetic principles.

One more image from the *passio* may enrich our discussion of the dream stanzas. When the fire that was to burn Agnes alive is magically turned back onto her persecutors, she prays in gratitude to her divine lover in language that is both reminiscent of an elegiac lover and sensually evocative of the lovers in the Song of Songs:[38] 'Now I see what I already believed; what I already hoped, I hold; what I desired, I embrace. I confess you with my lips and my heart, and I desire you with all my being' (*ecce iam quod credidi, video, quod speravi, iam teneo, quod concupivi, complector. te confiteor labiis et corde, et totis visceribus concupisco*, 13). Although the *passio* asserts that Agnes died as a consecrated bride of Christ (14), her final prayer is couched not in the language of epithalamia but in the sensuous language of elegy. Yet within decades of her death, Agnes's violently erotic martyrdom had been reshaped as a joyful marriage, paradigmatic of cosmic order, the 'right running'[39] of a man and woman, fertility in the right season,[40] prosperity and replacement.[41] In the late fourth-century episcopal milieu of Ambrose, that transition to consecrated virginity becomes associated with the ritual drama of the *velatio*, a central ritual of the Roman wedding.[42] Ambrose (as other Church Fathers) encouraged young girls of noble rank to become brides of Christ in his works on virgins and virginity (*De virginibus, De virginitate*) and in his preaching. As the virgins are understood to be 'married' to Christ and in that way to have transitioned to their appropriate status as wives, resistance to the model of virgins of Christ began to slacken. No longer martyrs of Christ, and no longer virgins of Christ, they were reintegrated into society as virgins and brides. In this new family, the *sponsa Christi* served God, her bishop,[43] and religious communities in the same way that wives served their husbands and families, without loss of her elite place in society. In classical nuptial texts as in St

Agnes's martyr legends, the boundaries within and between the literary and social constructs of love and marriage are always shifting. For Keats, love and marriage are opposing forces. In his letter of October 1818 to George and Georgina Keats (Rollins 1988, I: 403), he attempts to explain why he will never marry. Poetry is his love and demands solitude: solitude is sublime. Domestic happiness – 'an amiable wife and sweet children' – belong to his 'mighty abstract idea' of beauty: marriage is beauty. In poetic terms, elegy is the poetry of solitude, of impossible desire and impossible fulfilment; epithalamium is the poetry of marriage, the 'minute domestic happiness' that undergirds social order.[44] Keats speaks of marriage in terms of beauty again in a letter of July 1819 (Rollins 1988, II: 127) to Fanny Brawne, to whom he was engaged: 'I cannot conceive any beginning of such love as I have for you but Beauty'. With this he contrasts a different sort of love for which he has 'the highest respect', but which, he writes, 'has not the richness, the bloom, the full form, the enchantment of love after my own heart'. Rather than a means of harmonizing the ideal and real, elegy and epithalamia, love and marriage, Keats sees poetry as a means of comprehending the sublime.[45]

Agnes at Chichester

The 'dream' on St Agnes's Eve is widely attested in literature (n. 8 below) and is the ambient source of Keats's poem:[46]

> They (old dames) told her how, upon St. Agnes's Eve,
> Young virgins might have visions of delight,
> And soft adorings from their loves receive
> Upon the honey'd middle of the night,
> If ceremonies due they did aright;
> As, supperless to bed they must retire,
> And couch supine their beauties, lily white;
> Nor look behind, nor sideways, but require
> Of Heaven with upward eyes for all that they desire.
>
> *46–54*

Keats wrote *The Eve of St. Agnes* in January 1819 while staying in Chichester. Written in the epithalamic metres of Spenser,[47] the poem tells the love story of Madeline and Porphyro[48] in pictorial, seductive and intensely sensual language. The narrative is simple: it is the eve of St Agnes and Porphyro arrives at Madeline's castle on the moor where a celebration is already in progress. Though their relationship is complicated by their feuding families, the pair know each other. Porphyro contrives a transgressive plan to hide in her room, a nuptial *thalamus*, seduces her, perhaps as she is asleep dreaming the dream of St Agnes's Eve, and then in the morning they flee the castle together.[49]

The narrative begins when Porphyro appears from across the moor (to the south (351), in a place perhaps a little less frigid than this sleety wasteland), his heart on fire for

Madeline. Like an elegiac lover at the door of his unattainable beloved, Porphyro implores the saints to grant him sight of her, while an otherworldly focused Madeline, 'hoodwink'd with faery fancy' (70),[50] is indifferent to her immediate surroundings. To Madeline, as to Agnes, 'Came many a tip-toe amorous cavalier' that 'she saw not: her heart was otherwhere' as 'She sighed for Agnes's dreams, the sweetest of the year' (60–3). Unlike his counterpart in Roman elegy locked outside his mistress's door, Porphyro (surreptitiously) enters the castle amid celebration of the feast and quickly finds a friend and ally in the beldame Angela, 'weak in body and soul (90)'. This 'aged creature' (91), a mix of sibyl and crone, recalls a stock character in elegy (the *lena*, 'procuress'), ever protective of her mistress, who advises the *puella* to refuse the *pauper amator*, understood to be the poet. In Prop. 4.5, for example, we overhear this advice: 'Let the doorman be on the lookout only for those who bring gifts; if someone empty-handed knocks, let him sleep out there ignored against the closed bolt ... Look to the gold, not to the hand that brings it. After you've heard his verses, what will you have but words?' (47–54). Ovid's poet lover in *Am* 1.8 similarly overhears a conversation between such a bawd and her mistress, 'Look, what does that poet of yours give you besides new poems? (*ecce, quid iste tuus praeter nova carmina vates / donat?*) ... And if he should ask for a night without paying because he is handsome, let him press a lover of his own for something to give' (57–68). Keats's young lover is lucky in his intermediary agent; the significantly named Angela is willing to be complicit in his plan to see Madeline. She leads him, safe from danger to 'a little moonlit room / Pale, lattic'd, chill, and silent as a tomb', where was 'the holy loom / Which none but secret sisterhood may see / When they St. Agnes' wool are weaving piously' (112–17). When Porphyro learns that Madeline plans to conjure her future husband in her sleep, he 'scarce could brook / Tears, at the thought of those enchantments cold / And Madeline asleep in lap of legends old' (133–5). He hatches a 'stratagem' (139) to hide in Madeline's room, 'that he might see her beauty unespied / And win perhaps that night a peerless bride' (166–7), thus stepping out of her dream-vision as a physical presence. In a convoluted *deductio*, Angela leads Porphyro through many a dusky gallery to reach Madeline's room. There the reader experiences the sensuous vision of the poet's voyeuristic gaze upon Madeline, the saintlike twin of Agnes 'As down she knelt for heaven's grace and boon' (219).

As Porphyro spectates from his closet hideaway, Madeline slowly disrobes in cinematic mode:[51] her hair's pearls, her jewels, her bodice, individually detached from a moonlit body readers are seduced into imagining (227–30), seem to hang suspended in the air as her dress rustles to her knees, leaving her half hidden in the 'warm gules' of the 'wintry moon' (217–18). We recall Agnes's taunting of the prefect as she accentuated the delicate beauty of her neck, arm, and hand in enumerating the jewels her beloved gave to her, or imagine her similarly enclosed in a luminous aura and subjected to men's gazes – all at once sacred, profane and untouchable, both Virgin Mary and Magdalen – when she is naked in the brothel, covered only by her loose hair and the divine light that surrounds her. St Agnes's erotic martyrdom and sacred marriage adumbrate the sensual portrayal of Madeline. Madeline herself metapoetically feels Agnes's presence and 'sees / In fancy fair St. Agnes in her bed' (232–3).

Keats includes an ekphrastic digression (262–75) upon the bridal chamber and feast (*cena nuptialis*), a stock feature of epithalamia.[52] But when he was revising the poem in September 1819, he apparently felt the narrative digression was too vague and added a stanza between verses 54 and 55 (stanzas 6 and 7). The added stanza details what will transpire in the dream, and at the same time anticipates the real *cena nuptialis* and seduction:

> 'Twas said her future lord would there appear
> Offering as sacrifice – all in a dream –
> Delicious food even to her lips brought near;
> Viands and wine and fruit and sugar'd cream
> To touch her palate with the fine extreme
> Of relish: then soft music heard; and then
> More pleasure followed in a dizzy stream
> Palpable almost: then to wake again
> Warm in the virgin morn, no weeping Magdalen.
>
> *55–63, additional stanza*

His publishers excised this addition in the same letter and for the same reasons they had rejected the revised stanza. In that letter to Taylor, Woodhouse recognizes that the new stanza was 'to make the legend more clearly intelligible, and correspondent with what afterwards takes place, particularly with respect to the supper and the playing on the lute' but concludes that the sexual inference will inappropriately heighten readers' prurient curiosity. Keats's excised lines (esp. 57–60) recall the extravagant ekphrases of ancient epithalamia, while simultaneously making explicit the sensuous events following the feast that Porphyro produces (in spite of Madeline's prescribed fasting) from his hiding place. Even more lush, exotic and tactilely evocative are the images of the ekphrasis in stanzas 30 and 31:

> ...a heap
> Of candied apple quince and plum and gourd
> With jellies soother than the creamy curd
> And lucent syrups tinct with cinnamon
> Manna and dates in argosy transferred
> From Fez and spiced dainties everyone
> From silken Samarkand to cedared Lebanon.
> ...
> On golden dishes and in baskets bright
> Of wreathed silver: sumptuous they stand
> In the retired quiet of the night,
> Filling the chilly room with perfume light.
>
> *265–75*

The opulent and fanciful *cena* of Porphyro remarkably recalls another conventional epithalamic ekphrasis, the decoration of the bridal bower, as found in Claudian's epithalamium to Honorius and Maria:[53] Similarly lavish in its descriptive detail and evocative of exoticized excess, Claudian summons wedding gods (Hymenaeus, Grace, Concord) along with a band of flitting putti to hang lamps and garlands liberally, sprinkle the palace with nectar and burn a grove of Sabaean incense; then, to decorate the marriage bed with yellow silk coverlets from China and Sidonian tapestries canopied on carved columns. Dripping with exoticized, 'eastern' excess, both scenes are titillating, complicated, seductively erotic and, most significantly, richly epithalamic. In *The Eve of St. Agnes* we have arrived to where the poem's tension has been building, when Madeline's dream becomes conscious reality and Porphyro materializes before her eyes, 'no dream' (326).

Conclusion

We quickly revert from the epithalamic setting Keats has established in this ekphrasis to Porphyro, who resumes his role as elegiac lover as 'he took her hollow lute / Tumultuous, and, in chords that tenderest be / He play'd an ancient ditty, long since mute / In Provence call'd, "La belle dame sans mercy"' (289–92).[54] Madeline is startled awake by the song and when she opens her eyes, Porphyro sinks to his knees, 'pale as smooth-sculptured stone' (297). She unexpectedly begins to weep at the 'painful change that nigh expelled / The blisses of her dream so pure and deep' (300–1) as Porphyro watches, 'Fearing to move or speak' (306). It is music, the 'sweet tremble' (308) in her ear that gives resonance to her dream, 'spiritual and clear' (310); it is the music and its plaintive lyrics of frustrated desire, 'those complainings dear' (313), that lift her to the sublime mystic romance of St Agnes's dream. When it stops, Porphyro is 'pallid, chill, and drear' (311), like some statue of stone.[55] 'Give me that voice again' (313), she implores, but not so that she can re-enter a dream of transcendent love, of unfilled elegiac yearning. When she entreats Porphyro to resume that song, he returns to life, 'Beyond a mortal man impassion'd far ... Ethereal, flush'd, and like a throbbing star' (316–18).[56] He melts into Madeline's dream, which is no longer tragically and elusively sublime or mystically divine, but human and beautiful, no longer the unrealizable eroticism of elegy but the fecund and earthy love of epithalamia, a 'solution sweet' (322), beautifully rendered more beautiful than sublime in the unique elixir of the camelion poet.

Keats's 'solution sweet' takes us far beyond the plot of two young lovers. When Keats explained his ideas about the sublime and the beautiful in terms of the highest love or marriage in his letters to George and Georgina (October 1818) and to Fanny Brawne (July 1819), they were distinct ideas. And, just as he described his own dream of married love in his letters, his lovers in *The Eve of St. Agnes* experience the 'enchantment of love after their own hearts'. But in the poem, the sublime and the beautiful have melded, however evanescently, rather than remained distinct – for lovers and readers alike.

Notes

1. Rollins 1958, I: 275–83.
2. Rollins 1958, I: 386–8.
3. For a recent reading of Keats's *The Eve of St. Agnes* and the other medieval romances as overly concerned with the public reception of his poetry, in response to the criticism he endured for his Cockneyism, see Ulmer 2017: 111–46. See also Cox 2001, who likewise considers the romances of the 1820 volume to 'reflect the ideological vision and poetic practices of the Cockney School' (55).
4. He begins with two seminal extremes in Keatsian criticism: Wasserman 1953: 97–137, who views the poem as a metaphysical allegory, a romantic spiritual pilgrimage that leads to beauty and truth; and his own article (1961), an anti-romantic view of erotic love and the rape of Madeline by the stratagem of Porphyro, known as the 'dirty-minded reading' (38).
5. E.g. Ghosh 2020 and White 2020, who reads the 1820 collection as an extended meditation upon melancholy, under the influence of Robert Burton's *Anatomy of Melancholy*. White's commentary on the *The Eve of St. Agnes* begins by quoting Burton's allusion to a love-divination performed by young women on St Anne's eve or night, to determine who will become their husband, which he deems a 'brief stimulus, if not full-blown source, for *The Eve of St. Agnes*' (163).
6. Or, as many scholars and biographers of Keats propose, his friend (or lover) Isabella Jones who was in Chichester when Keats wrote the poem, suggested the theme: see Rollins 1958, I: 402 with n.5.
7. St Agnes's Eve is sometimes called St Anne's.
8. Literary references to the ritual locate it in faery religion by invoking Ben Johnson's Fairy queen Mab, who is considered to be the source of the St Agnes's Eve dreams in Johnson's *Entertainment at Althorp*, performed in 1603: 'And on sweet St. Anna's night (Mab can) / feed them with a promised sight / some of husband, some of lovers / which an empty dream discovers' (74–7). Multiple compilations of seventeenth- and eighteenth-century calendar customs and superstitions include the ritual performed on the eve of St Agnes in Keats's poem: Brand [1848] 1970: 34–8 collects examples of short poems from various locations in Great Britain; see also, Gomme 1885: 11–13, 30; Wright 1938: 106–10.
9. Cavalieri 1962 remains among the most comprehensive overviews of the Agnes legends, including the Greek passion narratives; Denomy 1938 is still relevant for the texts.
10. On the calendar, see Salzman 1990 (with excellent illustrations) and Burgess 2012; Lewis 2020 discusses the martyr feasts that were added to the calendar of 354 and what it means that time 'came to be performed through the destruction of human flesh' (167).
11. A dear and formidable (in a good way) colleague, Thom has continued in his *Myth of Replacement* to inspire me with new ways of approaching ancient literary texts about love and marriage.
12. On calendrical and cosmic time/timing and the regeneration of society, see Austin's chapter in this volume.
13. See Trout 2015: 150–1 and Appendix II: 645–6 for text, translation and commentary, and Trout 2014a for an account of all the verse inscriptions at the cemetery of St Agnes.
14. Feeney 2013 studies these sorts of comparisons, here of the bride and the groom, in hymenaeal literature to argue that they establish boundaries between nature and culture or beasts and gods, and that human life falls somewhere between these realms.

15. Clark 2006 considers epithalamic themes in the martyrdom of Eulalia (*Perisephanon* 3) 'inverted or distorted' (91).
16. Panoussi 2019: 23–8 argues that reluctance as a characterization is euphemistic and that the wedding texts of Catullus conceal sexual violence. All translations of Latin are my own.
17. For examples of bridal reluctance in the Roman wedding, see Hersch 2010: 144–8; Sourvinou-Inwood 1987 studies a series of images of erotic pursuits in a nuptial context.
18. *PL* 16.190–1, with Cazzaniga 1948.
19. A reference to the *paraclausithyron*, a sub-theme of Roman elegy, if a misnomer: '... an incorrect rendering of παρακλαυσίθυρον is pervasive in classical scholarship' (Cairns 2020: 1). *paraclausithyron*, a *hapax legomenon* in antiquity, has been used to refer to the poetry encompassing a lover's approach, vigil and lament outside his beloved's door, the result of its misapplication in Copley's seminal study (1956). It is the *kōmos* ('revelry') that encompasses all the events that lead to the lover's lament, which is properly the *paraclausithyron*. Nonetheless, following the term's widespread use in the field, here I also consider *paraclausithyron* to refer to any poetry connected to the lament.
20. With Fontaine 1992.
21. Though Agnes seems to be making a distinction here, both *taedae* and *faces* describe 'wedding torches', e.g. Catullus 61.117 (*tollite . . . faces*) and 66.79 (*cum iunxit lumine taeda*).
22. Friesen 2016 analyses this gesture in Polyxena and in Perpetua's theatricalized echo; Wilkinson, 2015: 28–57 considers the performance of modesty and dress in the context of self-determined agency.
23. For Prudentius' text, see the critical edition of Cunningham 1966.
24. Cf. Burrus 1995: 45, who reads Agnes through the lens of tragedy as a 'manly woman', a *virago* of ambiguous gender.
25. Grig 2005: 115 emphasizes the dual nature – virgin and martyr – of the female saint as an alignment of sexuality and sanctity: 'The body of the female saint is exposed and sexualized, and at the same time sacralized and forbidden to us.'
26. Tsartsidis 2020 reads Agnes through the lens of Roman elegy, a *domina puella* who assumes the active, dominant role of a man, but whose death by beheading rather than penetration relocates her to a Christian milieu. Uden 2009 sees a conflation of the elegiac *puella* and virgin martyr imagery in Maximianus' sixth-century elegy (3), with incidental references to St Agnes (esp. 211–12). See also Greene 2012 for the inversion of gender roles in elegy.
27. For the congruence of the elegist's body and his elegiac poetry, see Keith 1999. For the delicate themes of elegiac poetry as orally and politically subversive in reaction to Augustan ideology: Harrison 2013; Gibson 2005, 162–5 on the 'alienation' of the elegist; cf. Miller 2003.
28. The *Passio S. Agnetis* (*BHL* 156) appears in numerous editions, listed in the CPL (https://clavis.brepols.net/clacla/OA/link.aspx?clavis=CPL&number=2159, accessed 21 December 2022). For the Latin text, I use PL 17.735–42, which does not differ appreciably from the text in the *Acta Sanctorum* Ian. 2.715–18. Lapidge 2018 has compiled the first English translation and commentary of the forty *passiones*; *passio Agnetis*, 348–62.
29. There are two subsequent accounts that closely follow the *passio Agnetis*: the thirteenth-century *Golden Legend* of Jacobus de Voragine (Graesse 1890; for the English, Ryan 1993); and *Butler's Lives of the Saints* (Thurston and Attwater 1990, with a bibliography of Agnes's early *acta*, 136–7). Keats would have had ready access to the second.
30. For comic confusions of human and divine marriage, chastity and adultery, *et passim*, see Christenson's chapter in this volume.

31. Arsenau 1997 sees Madeline as an agent in her own seduction.
32. Common *topoi* of epithalamia are the decorating of the bridal bower and the hymning of the bride: see Menander Rhetor (Russell and Wilson 1981; Keydell 1962) for the outline of the genre's formula. Julius Caesar Scalinger recapitulates six remarkably similar *topoi* of epithalamia in his Renaissance (1561) poetic manual (Deitz and Vogt-Spira 1994). For Renaissance love poetry, especially the ways genre conceits of elegy and epithalamia overlap, with detailed examples of classical influences, see Parker 2012.
33. Hälikkä 2001 finds evidence for loose and bound hair 'representing Romanness and Roman ideals' (24), though in general 'loose hair asserts male dominance over the female' (34).
34. Prop. 1.2.1 is typically subversive when it undermines a Roman sense of *cultus* by asking Cynthia why she comes around with her 'hair done' (*ornato capillo*, 1) rather than leaving it natural. His argument is that 'if she pleases one man (him) she is well enough adorned' (*uni si qua placet, culta puella sat est*, 26).
35. Rollins 1958, II.161–5, 19 September 1819.
36. In the same letter, Woodhouse reports that Keats told him he did not want 'ladies to read his poetry, that he writes for men and that if there was an opening for doubt what took place, it was his fault for not writing clearly and comprehensibly, that she'd despise a man who would be such an eunuch in sentiment as to leave a maid, with that character about her, in such a situation'.
37. Stillinger 1961 (cf. n.4 above) famously argues for the restoration of the revised stanza, which makes graphically clear that sexual consummation occurs while Madeline is in her dreamlike trance, without her consent. See now Chen 2020, who also argues for a reconsideration of the discarded stanza as an example of 'Keats's erotic appropriation of a Christian image, namely Mary Magdalene', which adumbrates a religious sacredness.
38. Shuve 2021.
39. Worthen 1991: 19–37 does not write of marriage, but like other rituals the myths of replacement explicate, marriage can have both 'cosmic and ordinary significance' (37).
40. Cf. Cat. 62.56: 'when in ripe season (*maturo tempore*) she assumes her place in an equal marriage'; in Claud. *Nupt. Hon.*, Venus appears to Maria to persuade her to marry, 'so that she does not maintain a private home any longer . . . but assumes the appropriate fortune of her rank and the diadem, to pass it on to (her) children' (256–60).
41. A stock feature of epithalamium is the anticipation of children, e.g. Cat. 61.207, Stat. *Silv.* 1.2.268, Claud. *Nupt. Hon.* 340–1.
42. The *velatio* of Christian virgins has as its source the *flammeum* of the Roman wedding ceremony (Hersch 2010: 94–106). For the *velatio*'s liturgical formalization, see Hunter 2000: 288n.24 and Hotchin 2009: 193n.8. Muir 2004–5 studies the ceremony's elaboration and depictions of Agnes from the tenth to the fourteenth centuries to reflect 'dreams of a wedding with Christ, and visions of seeing Christ's heart and hearing his voice' (152); Muir 2008: 144n.69 includes antiphons added to the ceremony drawn directly from the *passio Agnetis*.
43. Walker 2020: 67–71, argues that Church Fathers appropriated the rights of secular husbands to use dedicated virgins to support their authority.
44. The essential solitude of *erōs* is richly explored in Shoshitaishvili's chapter in this volume.
45. On the 'romantic sublime' generally, see Shaw 2017: 116–44.
46. Quotes from *The Eve of St. Agnes* are from Barnard 1977.
47. Edgecombe 1994: 'the gestalt of Spenser's poem is there to be glimpsed through the interstices of Keats's . . . "extra-marital" epithalamion' (78).

48. On the significance of their names, see Gilbreath 1988, who associates Porphyro with the impious giant Porphyrion for challenging the 'moral authority that imposes chastity on young lovers' (24). A less recherchée etymology derives his name from the Greek adjective πορφύρεος/*porphureos*, which describes a range of deep colour(s) ('crimson', 'purple'), e.g. of gushing blood and, more subjectively, 'rosy' or 'glowing' passion, such as Aphrodite's (cf. LSJ and *The Cambridge Greek Lexicon* s.v.), and so tags Porphyro as erotically hyper-charged. Gibson 1977: 49 conflates Madeline and Mary Magdalen in reading the poem as an Annunciation parody.

49. Keats's reluctance to close with a 'happily ever after' or with a new adventure into a dark (stormy) room in the 'mansion of many apartments' reflects his theory of 'negative capability', where his *readers* (Falke 2019) may be expected to be 'capable of being in uncertainties, mysteries, doubts, without any irritable reaching after fact and reason' (Rollins 1958, I: 193–4).

50. Although not explored in the essay, the thread of images related to faery religion are studied as a persistent subtext in Arcana 1987.

51. Ostas 2011: 343–4 and n.15 does not address this passage but writes in general of Keats's cinematic point of view.

52. The highly wrought verbal and pictorializing work of a poetic ekphrasis can surpass its textual location to situate marriage in a larger cosmic context. On Achilles' shield (Hom. *Il.* 18.478–608), European literature's first extant ekphrasis, Vulcan engraves our full mortal existence in a telescopic view of the cosmos. Marriage is the first of the cyclical human rituals celebrated on the shield: as the nuptial *deductio* with its torches, flutes and dancing revellers passes through town, women exit their homes and stand at their doorways to observe. The women's view of the procession is thus monumentalized in Homer's ekphrasis, capturing their fleetingly sublime remove from the mundane into the cosmically regenerative promise of that *deductio*. Epithalamic descriptions of a wedding's decorative and culinary ephemerality sacralize nuptial settings and invite readers into the broader sublime cosmos.

53. Claud. *Nupt. Hon.* 202–1; cf. Stat. *Silv.* 1.2.19–23.

54. This song (of complaint) within a song, too, has precedent in Roman elegy. Propertius 2.1 references his song to his hard-hearted mistress in claiming her, rather than Calliope or Apollo, as his muse (*ingenium nobis ipsa puella facit*, 4), and concludes by pronouncing his own epitaph: 'a hard-hearted girl was the cause of death for this wretched man' (*huic misero fatum dura puella fuit*, 78).

55. See Bewell 1986 on the 'life and death of sculptural forms' in Keats.

56. Cf. Shoshitaishvili's chapter in this volume, p. 48n.14, where Andromache's robe of 'deep purple' (πορφυρέην) and Helen's of 'white marble' (μαρμαρέην) offer analogues of Porphyro's impassioned regenerative love versus the blissful eroticism of Madeline's dream.

Works cited

Arcana, J. (1987), 'Midwinter Night's Dream: *The Eve of St. Agnes* as Sacred Ritual in the Old Religion of the Britons', *Journal of Ritual Studies*, 1: 43–57.

Arsenau, M. (1997), 'Madeline, Mermaids, and Medusas in *The Eve of St. Agnes*', *Papers on Language & Literature*, 33: 227–33.

Barnard, J. (ed.) ([1973] 1977), *John Keats: The Complete Poems*, New York: Penguin.

Bewell, A. J. (1986), 'The Political Implication of Keats's Classicist Aesthetics', *Studies in Romanticism*, 25: 220–9.

Brand, J. ([1848–9] 1970), *Observations on the Popular Antiquities of Great Britain*, vol 1, New York: AMS Press.
Burgess, R. W. (2012), 'The Chronograph of 354: Its Manuscripts, Contents, and History', *Journal of Late Antiquity*, 5: 345–96.
Burrus, V. (1995), 'Reading Agnes: The Rhetoric of Gender in Ambrose and Prudentius', *Journal of Early Christian Studies*, 3: 25–46.
Burton, R. (1994), *Robert Burton: The Anatomy of Melancholy*, vol. III, T. C. Faulkner, N. K. Kiessling, R. L. Blair (eds), Oxford: Clarendon Press.
Cairns, F. (2020), 'The Terms *komos* and *paraclausithryon*', *Greek, Roman, and Byzantine Studies*, 60: 262–71.
Cavalieri, P. Franchi de' (1962), 'Sant' Agnese nella tradizione e nella leggenda', in P. Franchi de' Cavalieri (ed.), *Scritti agiografici (Studi e testi* 22), 293–379, Vatican City: Biblioteca apostolica vaticana.
Cazzaniga, E. (ed.) (1948), *Ambrosius Mediolanensis, De virginibus libri tres*, Corpus Scriptorum Latinorum Paravianum, Turin: In Aedibus I.B. Paraviae.
Chen, K.-po (2020), '"Of Heaven with Upward Eyes for All That They Desire": Sacredness and Eroticism in Keats's *The Eve of St. Agnes*', *Wenshaw Review of Literature and Culture*, 13: 153–81.
Clarke, J. (2006), 'Bridal Songs: Catullan Epithalamia and Prudentius, *Peristephanon 3*', *Antichthon*, 40: 89–103.
Cooper, K. (1996), *The Virgin and the Bride: Idealized Womanhood in Late Antiquity*, Cambridge, MA: Harvard University Press.
Copley, F. (1956), *Exclusus Amator: A Study in Latin Love Poetry*, Monographs of the American Philological Society 17, Madison: American Philological Association.
Cox, J. N. (2001), '*Lamia, Isabella*, and *The Eve of St. Agnes*', in S. J. Wolfson (ed.), *The Cambridge Companion to Keats*, 53–68, Cambridge: Cambridge University Press.
Cunningham, M. P. (1966), *Aurelii Prudentii Clementis Carmina*, Corpus Christianorum, Series Latina, cxxvi, Turnhout: Brepols.
Deitz, L. and G. Vogt-Spira (eds) (1994), *Julius Caesar Scaliger, Poetices Libri Septem*, Stuttgart: Frommann-Holzboog.
Denomy, A. J. (ed.) (1938), *The Old French Lives of Saint Agnes and Other Vernacular Versions of the Middle Ages*, Cambridge, MA: Harvard University Press.
Edgecombe, R. S. (1994), 'Keats's *The Eve of St. Agnes*', *Explicator*, 52: 77–9.
Falke, C. (2019), 'Negatively Capable Reading', in B. Rejack and M. Theun (eds), *Keats's Negative Capability: New Origins and Afterlives*, 79–92, Liverpool: Liverpool University Press.
Feeney, D. (2013), 'Catullus 61: Epithalamium and Comparison', *Cambridge Classical Journal*, 59: 70–97.
Ferrua, A. (1942), *Epigrammata Damasiana*, Rome: Pontificio Istituto di Archeologia Cristiana.
Fontaine, J. (1992), *Ambroise de Milan: Hymnes, texte établi, traduit et annoté*, Paris: Editions du Cerf.
Friesen, C. (2016), 'Dying Like a Woman: Euripides' Polyxena as *Exemplum* between Philo and Clement of Alexandria', *Greek, Roman, and Byzantine Studies*, 56: 623–45.
Ghosh, H. (2020), *John Keats' Medical Notebook: Text, Context and Poems*, Liverpool: Liverpool University Press.
Gibson, G. M. (1977), 'Ave Madeline: Ironic Annunciation in Keats's *The Eve of St. Agnes*', *Keats-Shelley Journal*, 26: 39–50.
Gibson, R. (2005), 'Love Elegy', in S. Harrison (ed.), *A Companion to Latin Literature*, 159–73, Malden, MA: Blackwell Publishing.
Gilbreath, M. (1988), 'The Etymology of Porphyro's Name in Keats's *The Eve of St. Agnes*', *Keats-Shelley Journal*, 37: 20–5.
Gomme, G. L. (ed.) (1885), *Mother Bunch's Closet Newly Broke Open and the History of Mother Bunch of the West*, London: Kessinger Publishing.

Graesse, Th. (1890), *Jacobi A Voragine Legenda Aurea Vulgo Historia Lombardica Dicat*, 3rd edn, Vratislaviae: Guilelmum Koebner.
Green, E. (2012), 'Gender and Elegy', in B. Gold (ed.), *A Companion to Roman Love Elegy*, 357–71, Chichester: Blackwell Publishing.
Grig, L. (2005), 'The Paradoxical Body of St. Agnes', in A. Hopkins and M. Wyke (eds), *Roman Bodies: Antiquity to the Eighteenth Century*, 111–22, Rome: British School at Rome.
Hälikkä, R. (2001), '*Sparsis Comis, Solutis Capillis*: "Loose" Hair in Ovid's Elegiac Poetry', *Arctos*, 35: 23–34.
Harrison, S. (2013), 'Time, Place and Political Background', in T. Thorsen (ed.), *The Cambridge Companion to Latin Love Elegy*, 133–50, Cambridge: Cambridge University Press.
Hersch, K. K. (2010), *The Roman Wedding: Ritual and Meaning in Antiquity*, Cambridge: Cambridge University Press.
Hotchin, J. (2009), 'The Nun's Crown', *Early Modern Women*, 4: 187–94.
Hunter, D. G. (2000), 'The Virgin, the Bride, and the Church: Reading Psalm 45 in Ambrose, Jerome, and Augustine', *Church History*, 69: 281–303.
Jones, H. (2007), 'Agnes and Constantia: Domesticity and Cult Patronage in the *Passion of Agnes*', in C. F. Cooper and J. Hillner (eds), *Religion, Dynasty, and Patronage in Early Christian Rome, 300–900*, 115–39, Cambridge: Cambridge University Press.
Keith, A. M. (1999), 'Slender Verse: Roman Elegy and Ancient Rhetorical Theory', *Mnemosyne*, 52: 41–62.
Keydell, R. (1962), 'Epithalamium', *Reallexikon für Antike und Christentum*, 5.927–43.
Lanéry, C. (2014), 'La légende de sainte Agnès: quelques réflexions sur la genèse d'un dossier hagiographique (IVe–VIe s.)', *Mélanges de l'École française de Rome – Moyen Âge*, 126.
Lapidge, M. (2018), *The Roman Martyrs: Introduction, Translation, and Commentary*, Oxford: Oxford University Press.
Lewis, N. D. (2020), '(En)Gendering Christian Time: Female Saints and Roman Martyrological Calendars', in E. Eidinow and L. Maurizio (eds), *Narratives of Time and Gender in Antiquity*, 166–80, New York: Routledge.
Miller, P. A. (2003), *Subjecting Verses: Latin Love Elegy and the Emergence of the Real*, Princeton: Princeton University Press.
Muir, C. D. (2004–5), 'St. Agnes of Rome as a Bride of Christ: A Northern European Phenomenon, c. 1450–1520', *Simiolus: Netherlands Quarterly for the History of Art*, 31: 134–55.
Muir, C. D. (2008), 'Love and Courtship in the Convent: St. Agnes and the Adult Christ in Two Upper Rhine Manuscripts', *Gesta*, 47: 123–45.
Ostas, M. (2011), 'Reading Keats, Thinking Politics', *Studies in Romanticism*, 50: 335–50.
Panoussi, V. (2019), *Brides, Mourners, Bacchae: Women's Rituals in Roman Literature*, Baltimore: Johns Hopkins University Press.
Parker, H. N. (2012), 'Renaissance Elegy', in B. Gold (ed.), *A Companion to Roman Love Elegy*, 476–90, Chichester: Blackwell Publishing.
Rollins, H. E. (1958), *The Letters of John Keats 1814–1821*, 2 vols, Cambridge, MA: Harvard University Press.
Russell, D. A. and N. G. Wilson (eds) (1981), *Menander Rhetor*, Oxford: Oxford University Press.
Ryan, W. G., Jr. (1993), *Jacobus de Voragine, the Golden Legend: Readings on the Saints*, 2 vols, Princeton: Princeton University Press.
Sághy, M. (2000), '*Scinditur in partes populus*: Pope Damasus and the Martyrs of Rome', *Early Medieval Europe*, 9: 273–87.
Salzman, M. R. (1990), *On Roman Time: The Codex-Calendar of 354 and the Rhythms of Urban Life in Late Antiquity*, Berkeley: University of California Press.
Shaw, Philip (2017), *The Sublime*, New York: Routledge.

Shuve, K. (2021), 'A Garden Enclosed, a Fountain Sealed: The Song of Songs and Ritual Purity in Early Latin Christianity', in T. Robinson (ed.), *A Companion to the Song of Songs in the History of Spirituality*, Brill's Companions to the Christian Tradition 98, 42–69, Leiden: Brill.

Sourvinou-Inwood, C. (1987), 'A Series of Erotic Pursuits: Images and Meanings', *Journal of Hellenic Studies*, 107: 131–53.

Stillinger, J. (1961), 'The Hoodwinking of Madeline: Scepticism in *The Eve of St. Agnes*', *Studies in Philology*, 58: 533–55.

Stillinger, J. (1971), *The Hoodwinking of Madeline and Other Essays on Keats' Poems*, Urbana: University of Illinois Press.

Stillinger, J. (1999), *Reading The Eve of St. Agnes: The Multiples of Complex Literary Transaction*, New York: Oxford University Press.

Thurston, H. J. and D. Attwater (eds) ([1981] 1990), *Butler's Lives of the Saints*, 4 vols, Westminster, MD: Christian Classics.

Trout, D. (2014a), '"Being Female": Verse Commemoration at the *Coemeterium S. Agnetis* (Via Nomentana)', in C. Harrison, C. Humfress, and I. Sandwell (eds), *Being Christian in Late Antiquity: Festschrift for Gillian Clark*, 215–34, Oxford: Oxford University Press.

Trout, D. (2014b), 'From the *Elogia* of Damasus to the *Acta* of the *Gesta Martyrum*: Re-staging Roman History', in B. Alroth and C. Scheffer (eds), *Attitudes Towards the Past in Antiquity: Creating Identities*, Proceedings of an International Conference held at Stockholm University, 15–17 May 2009, 311–20, Stockholm: Stockholm University Press.

Trout, D. (2015), *Damasus of Rome: The Epigraphic Poetry*, Oxford: Oxford University Press.

Tsartsidis, T. (2020), 'Prudentius' Agnes and the Elegiac *puella*', *Mnemosyne*, 74: 1034–54.

Uden, J. (2009), 'The Elegiac *puella* as Virgin Martyr', *Transactions of the American Philological Association*, 139: 207–22.

Ulmer, W. A. (2017), *John Keats: Reimagining History*, Camden: Palgrave Macmillan.

Walker, A. L. (2020), *Bride of Hades to Bride of Christ: The Virgin and the Otherworldly Bridegroom in Ancient Greece and Early Christian Rome*, New York: Routledge.

Walpole, A. S. (1922), *Early Latin Hymns with Introduction and Notes by the Late A. S. Walpole*, Cambridge: Cambridge University Press.

Wasserman, E. R. (1953), *The Finer Tone: Keats' Major Poems*, Baltimore: Johns Hopkins University Press.

White, R. S. (2020), *Keats's Anatomy of Melancholy: Lamia, Isabella, The Eve of St Agnes, and Other Poems (1820)*, Edinburgh: Edinburgh University Press.

Wilkinson, K. (2015), *Women and Modesty in Late Antiquity*, Cambridge: Cambridge University Press.

Worthen, T. D. (1991), *The Myth of Replacement: Stars, Gods, and Order in the Universe*, Tucson: The University of Arizona Press.

Wright, A. R. (1938), *British Calendar Customs: England*, vol. II: Fixed Festivals January–May, London: William Glaisher.

INDEX

Achilles 31, 33, 35, 38, 46
aevum/aiōn 13–14
Agamemnon 31–2, 46, 192
Aithōn 3, 18
Alcmena 134–5, 138–9, 140–7, 150 n.21, 153 n.65
Alexander 6, 160, 165–8
Ambrose, Bp./Ps.-Ambrose 210, 212, 215
Amphitruo 5, 134–48
amor 141, 143, 208, 211, 213–14; *see also* love
Andromache 35, 48 n.14, 141, 223 n.56
animus 71, 74, 84 n.65
anthropocentric 7, 60
anthropopathic 52, 55, 57, 60, 134
Antigonus of Carystus 92–3
Aphrodite 4, 29, 31–3, 35, 39–40, 51–61
apiculture 4, 89, 93, 98; *see also* bees
apis/Apis 92–3, 100 n.24, 101 n.30
apocalypse 72, 182; *see also* destruction
Apollo
    Nero as 173–5
    sun-god 19, 96, 114, 119, 133, 180
aporia 7, 23 n.8, 139
Ares 32, 59, 112, 117, 191
Aristaeus 4, 89–90, 96–8, 99 n.1, 100 n.18, 102 nn.49, 51
Aristophanes
    Acharnians 108–11, 114–15
    Birds 111
    Clouds 108–10, 117–22, 125 n.6, 128 nn.24, 25
    Ecclesiazusae 107, 109–11, 114–15
    Frogs 111
    Knights 109, 111
    Lysistrata 108–11, 113–14
    Peace 110–12, 116–18, 127–8 n.22
    Plutus 111, 114, 122
    Thesmophoriazusae 111, 113–15, 127 n.16
    Wasps 108–10, 115–16, 122
Aristotle
    bougonia 91–3
    comedy 146, 150 n.20
    Nichomachean Ethics 38–9
    tragedy 108, 150 n.20, 151 n.35, 193
Arrian 6, 160, 166–8
astronomy
    New Comedy 123, 128 n.25, 126–7 n.14, 127 n.22, 128 n.25
    phenomena 6, 21, 68, 122

Plautus 137, 150 n.22
precession 2
Athena/Athene 11, 15–16, 22, 35, 58–9, 97

barrier 6, 16, 171, 176, 179, 182; *see also* boundary
bees 89–98, 99 nn.4, 6, 100 nn.9, 13, 23; *see also* apiculture
bougonia 4, 89–99
boundary (*see also* barrier)
    crossing of 5, 6, 133, 135, 137, 146
    cultural 172, 183, 184 n.15, 216, 220 n.14
    generic 72, 147, 151 n.35
    land 70, 162
    natural 38, 167–8, 175, 177, 179, 183
bow
    bed 38
    contest 18–19, 21–2
    lyre 22, 25 n.35
Burton, Robert 208, 220 n.5

calendar
    Athenian 5, 19, 109, 117–18
    Babylonian 22, 169
    Chronography/Codex-Calendar of 354 CE 209, 220 n.10
    Depositio Martyrum 209
    Odyssey 16–20, 22
    solar and lunar 3, 22, 110, 119–20
Caligula 171, 173, 178, 181
Calypso 12–16, 20, 24 n.13
canal
    Isthmus 6, 171–3, 177–9, 181–3
    Ostia to Avernus 177
catasterism 112–13
cena nuptialis 218
Circe 12
City Dionysia 107–8, 110–11, 113, 115–16, 121
comedy
    Aristotle 146
    Athenian 5, 109–10, 13–15, 121–2, 149 n.8
    audience of 148, 153 n.64
    New 123, 128 n.27, 134–5, 137, 141, 146
    Old 5, 149 n.8
    Roman 134, 136, 141, 143, 146, 149 n.7
    slaves in 140, 151 nn.26, 36
commonality/συμφέρον 38–9, 45
constellation 5, 7, 14, 111–13, 115; *see also* star

Index

cosmogony 3–4, 51, 57, 60, 97, 99
cosmography/cosmology 3, 7, 8 n.4, 39, 41, 141
cosmos/κόσμος (*see also* universe)
    architect(us) of 135, 141, 150 n.16
    Hesiod 38, 51
    Homer 20
    Lucretius 67, 70
    physical 3, 7
    Plautus 5, 133
    Presocratics 37, 39–41
    Seneca 69–70, 73
    Shield of Achilles 97, 223 n.52
    threats to 159–60, 171–2, 183
creation myth 4, 89–90, 97–9, 102 n.56
cyclicality 2, 126 n.14, 223 n.52
Cyprus/Kypros 51, 54, 56–7, 61
Cyrene 90, 97

Damascus, Pope 209–10, 212
deductio 210, 214, 217, 223 n.52
Demeter 94
desire
    Aphrodite 39, 57, 59
    destructive 4, 214
    elegiac 214–16, 219
    Freud 191
    Homer 4, 18, 35–6, 46
    Jupiter 138–40, 143
    Lucretius 75–6
    Nero 181
    Plato 30, 43, 46
    Seneca 5, 69, 78–9
    Vergil 96, 141
destruction
    cosmic 6, 176–8, 180
    Isthmus 171–2, 181
    Presocratics 39
    Seneca 72, 78
    Vergil 176–8, 180
Dicaeopolis 114–15
didactic (poetry) 4, 68, 74, 89, 98, 102 n.49
dikē 11; *see also* justice
Dione 51, 56–7, 59
Dionysia 42, 108, 112, 115–17, 121, 125 n.4
Dionysus
    festival 193
    Osiris 93
    Theatre of 5, 111–12, 117, 123–4, 125 n.4
Diotima 31, 42–4
disorder 159, 209
domina puella 211, 221 n.26
Domus Aurea 173, 177
Dryden, John 6, 190, 198–200

earthquake
    Lucretius 68, 72–3

omens 7, 159–60
    Seneca 68, 73, 83 n.60
eclipse
    celestial phenomenon 75, 78, 121, 159
    lunar 6, 119, 127 n.22, 160, 166–7
    omen 159, 161–8
    penumbral 127 n.22
    solar 21, 118–19, 127 n.22, 160, 167
Egypt
    beekeeping 100 n.23
    bougonia 4, 92–4, 98, 99 n.5, 100 n.18
ekphrasis
    epithalamic 218–19
    Shield of Achilles 223 n.52
elegy, Roman 7, 141–2, 207–8, 210–14, 215–17, 222 n.32
Empedocles 4, 31, 37, 39, 40–5, 47
engineering 175, 177–8
England (*see also* plague)
    Chichester 216, 220 n.6
    Church of 189, 197, 202
    Civil War 194–7, 199
    Cockneyism 220 n.3
    Cromwell 195–7, 199
    eighteenth century 6, 189–90, 202
    Neo-Classical criticism 6, 190
    Romantic sublime 6, 195, 203
    seventeenth century 6, 189, 195–6, 201
Epicurus
    Lucretius 67–71, 73–6, 78
    physics 5, 67–8, 71, 74, 84 n.69
    Seneca 5, 67–9, 71, 73–6, 78–9
Epinomis 112–13, 127 n.14
epiphany
    Jupiter 135, 145
    Telemachus 11
epistemology 69, 73, 77–9
epithalamia 7, 207–9, 215–16, 218–19, 222 n.32
eris/ἔρις (*see also* strife)
    antipodal contact 31, 44–7, 47 n.6
    Homer 3–4, 29–38, 40–2, 45–7, 48 n.13
    Plato 4, 30, 42–3, 47
    Presocratics 31, 37, 39–42, 45, 47
erōs/ἔρως (*see also* love)
    antipodal contact 31, 44–7, 47 n.6
    Aphrodite 57, 59, 63 n.26
    Freud 191
    Homer 4, 30–6, 39–42, 44–6
    Plato 4, 30, 42–4, 46, 123
    Presocratics 31, 39–42, 45, 46

Fear/*Phobos* 191
flood
    Isthmus 6, 171, 178, 181, 183
    Seneca, in 68, 72, 81 nn.32, 36
Florentinus 4, 93–4,
Freud, Sigmund 191, 203

Index

Gaia 52–6, 62 n.14
Gaugamela, battle of 6, 160, 166–8
generation
    Aphrodite 4, 54, 56, 60, 61 n.3
    bee(s) 90–2, 94
    Olympian gods 4, 52
    ox- 4, 89
Geoponica 93
Georgics 95, 176, 200
Giants 174–5, 177

Hades 34, 209
hapax legomenon/-a 32, 221 n.19
harmony/ἁρμονία 4, 34–5, 38–9, 40–1, 43, 45
Hector/Hektor
    departure 141
    kleos 46
    speech of 29, 31–5, 40, 43
    warrior 191, 203
    Zeus 58
Helen (*see also* Paris)
    mystery 12
    robe 24 n.21, 36–7, 43
    teichoscopia 4, 34, 36
Hera 57–8, 61, 97
Heracles/Hercules 42, 135, 139, 145–7, 152
Heraclitus 4, 12, 21, 31, 37–45, 97
Hermes/Mercury 112–18, 116–17, 133–42, 144–8, 150 n.22, 154 n.67
Herodotus 6, 51, 100 n.16, 160–3, 167–8
Hesiod
    Aphrodite 51–2, 54–7, 60–1
    Theogony 4
    Works and Days 38–9
Hobbes, Thomas 190, 193–6
Homeric Hymn to Aphrodite 58–9, 62 n.15
Hostius Quadra 5, 73, 75–9, 82 n.47
Hymenaeus 209–10, 219
Hymettus, Mount 112, 115, 117, 123–5 n.4

imago 5, 74, 139, 151 n.33
immanence 1, 40, 134, 141, 144
initiation 11, 15
Ino 14, 24 n.14
intertextuality
    Seneca 5, 67–9, 71–3, 78
    Shelley 203
irregularity
    astronomical 1
    cosmic 1, 2, 117–18, 167
Isthmus of Corinth 6, 171–83
Ithaca 3, 15–16, 22, 127 n.15

Julius Caesar 173, 175, 178, 181
Jupiter
    architect(us) 135, 141, 150 n.16,
    planet 111–13, 116–17, 121
    Roman god 5, 133–48, 171, 174, 177
    Trump and 153 n.65
justice/*dikē*
    cosmic 134, 136, 148
    Jupiter 136, 141
    Odyssey 3, 11, 21, 38
    strife 38

kairos/Kairos 22, 23 n.8, 45–6, 48 n.22
Keats, John 7, 193, 207–9, 211–19
kleos 24 n.12, 46, 48 n.22
kronos/Kronos 51–2, 62 n.13

Lenaea 107, 110–12, 114, 116, 125 n.4
light
    moon 119, 213
    Odyssey 3, 11, 16–17, 19, 24 n.26
    otherworldly 145, 207, 214, 217
    Seneca 82 n.43
Longinus/Ps. Longinus 1
love (*see also amor, erōs*)
    death and 191
    elegiac 7, 140, 142, 207, 210–11, 213–19
    Iliad 31, 41
    Lucretius 76–7, 79
    Plato 30, 41–4
    Presocratics 37, 39, 41
    Roman comedy 141, 143–4, 146–7
    Seneca 73, 76–8
    strife and 4, 39–41
    sublime 208
Lucan
    Isthmus in 6, 171, 181–2
    Nero 174–5, 183
    Pharsalia 6, 171, 174, 179, 181–3
Lucretius
    Epicureanism 5, 68–71, 73–9
    plague 6, 197–8
    Seneca 67–79
    sublime 67, 72, 79 nn.1, 6, 81 n.37

Madeline
    bride of Christ 212–13
    dream 7, 212, 214, 218–19
    Porphyro and 214–17
    Saint Agnes and 215, 217
Mago 92, 100 n.22
*Manu and *Yemo: *see* twins
marriage
    Aphrodite 59
    bower 213, 219
    death and 210
    Homer 15, 17
    Keats 7, 216, 219
    mystic 208, 210, 217

Index

Nero 173
Penelope 12, 17
Roman comedy, in 140, 143
Saint Agnes 7, 208–10, 212–13, 215–19
sublime 223 n. 52
Mars 75, 112–13, 117, 136
martyr
    cult 7, 209, 220 n.10
    Gesta Martyrum 214
    Saint Agnes 207–17
Menelaos/Menelaus 12, 23 n.9, 31–2, 34–5
Mercury: *see* Hermes
metaphysics
    contact, of 31, 44–7
    erotic power 1, 41–2
    Helen 4, 36–7
    Presocratics 38–9
    sublime 3, 7, 72, 133
metapoetics 7, 133, 211, 215, 217
metatheatre
    Greek drama 5, 107, 109–10, 113, 115, 123–4
    Roman comedy 5, 137–8, 144, 147, 152 n.47
mill/milling 2, 20–1
Milton, John
    Paradise Lost 6, 189, 191–2
    sublime in 190, 198
miracle 4, 22, 52, 214
mirror
    Aristophanes 107, 120
    Hostius Quadra 5, 73, 75–8
    Lucretius 83 n.54
    Plautus 139
    Seneca 73, 75, 83 n.59
mobile sensibility 142, 145, 152
monster/*monstrum*
    bougonia 90, 95
    Lucretius 73
    Nero 171, 183
moon
    eclipse 161–3, 165–7
    Greek comedy 112, 116–21, 123, 127–8 n.22
    Keats 213, 217
    Odyssey 3, 19, 22
mountain 7, 53, 123–4, 174, 184 n.15
myth of replacement 2–3, 62 n.11, 72, 152 n.54, 183 n.8, 209
mythopoesis 3, 48 n.16, 134, 148

narcissism 64, 77, 142, 148, 183
Nausikaa 15–16
neikos/ νεῖκος 39–40, 47 n.6; *see also* strife
Nero 6, 146, 171–9, 181–3
Nicander 91, 103
Nicias 6, 117, 160, 163–8
nostos 18, 24 n.24, 135
nuptial 7, 172, 208–10, 212, 215–18

Odysseus 3, 11–22, 192
Olympian
    comedic actors as 137, 142, 145, 147
    genealogy 4, 52
    Nero 174
    pantheon 57–8, 60, 116–18
    planets 112, 126 n.14, 127 n.21
Olympus 15, 35, 117, 127 n.21, 133, 142
omen 20, 160–5, 167–8: *see also* prophecy
optics 69, 73, 75, 82 n.43, 84 n.61
oracle 114, 162, 166, 196
order
    celestial 126 n.14, 160, 209
    cosmic 1–2, 97, 142, 215
    divine 21, 58, 68
    natural 52, 60, 163, 179, 212
    Plautus 133, 148, 171
    social 60, 213, 216
Orion 112–13, 137
Orpheus 4, 89–90, 93, 95–6, 98, 99 n.1
Ouranos 4, 51–6, 60–1, 117, 127 n.21; *see also* sky/Sky
Ovid
    Amores 72, 210–11, 214, 217
    Fasti 94
    Metamorphoses 72–3, 91–2, 136, 214

Panhellenic
    Aphrodite 4, 52–4, 56–61
    Games 172
    gods 51–2
    myth 51, 56
paraclausithyron 211, 214, 221 n.19
Paris 3–4, 29–37, 40–6
parthenogenesis 53–6
passio Agnetis 209–15, 221 n.28
Peloponnese 171, 183
Peloponnesian War 115, 159–60, 194
Penelope 3, 11–13, 16–19, 21–2
Persia 118, 160–3, 166–8, 172
Phaethon 175, 180–1, 183 n.8
philia/φιλία; *philotēs*/φιλότης 30, 39–41, 43–4, 46, 47 n.6, 63 n.23
philommēdēs 4–5, 63 n.17, 64 n.35
plague
    Bubonic 201
    England 6, 189–90, 195–6, 198–9, 200–3
    Lucretius 6, 197
    Thucydides 6, 160, 195, 197, 199, 204 n.1
    Vergil 95–6, 200
planet
    deities 112, 115, 126–7 n.14, 167
    Jupiter (Zeus) 5, 21, 58–9, 97, 111–13, 116–17, 121
    Mars (Ares) 112–13, 117
    Mercury (Hermes) 112, 117

Saturn (Cronus) 112, 114, 117, 121
Venus (Aphrodite) 112–13
Plato
   Republic 29–30, 41
   Symposium 4, 31, 42–3, 61, 123
   themes 2, 37, 41, 44–7, 197
Pleiades 24, n.15, 112, 137
Plutarch 164–5
polemos 35, 38–9, 41, 47 n.6, 117; *see also* war
polis 29, 60
polymorphism 5, 134
Porphyro 7, 212–19, 220 n.5, 223 n.48
Porphyry 4, 97, 101 n.35
Porter, James 1–2, 72, 193
Poseidon 13, 58, 97
pregnancy 58, 135, 143, 193
Presocratics 31, 37, 42–4
procreation 43–4, 54, 56–8, 92
prologue
   Aristophanes 5, 7, 110–11, 113–16, 122–3
   Plautus 128 n.27, 134, 136–7, 139, 141–2, 146–8
prophecy 160, 167; *see also* omen
prosopopoeia 76
Proteus 90, 97
Prudentius 211–12, 214

rape 90, 134, 140–1, 146, 209, 220 n.4
ratio 5, 68–70, 73–4, 78–9, 82 n.44
replacement: *see* myth of replacement
right running 2, 215
ritual
   bougonia 4, 89–90, 92–3, 95, 97–9
   comedy/drama 133–4
   foundation 103 n.62
   initiation 23 n.3
   marriage/wedding 24 n.17, 215
   Saint Agnes eve 207–9
   separation 22 n.1
Romulus and Remus: *see* twins

Saint Agnes (*see also* marriage)
   Madeline and 217, 219
   martyr 207, 208–16
   mystic union 208, 215
   ritual 208, 216–17
Satan 191–2
Scheria 14–15
Seneca
   Epistulae Morales 80 n.10
   Isthmus in 6, 181, 183
   Medea 180, 182
   Naturales Quaestiones 5, 67–79
   Thyestes 6, 178–9
Shield of Achilles 97, 102 n.54, 127 n.15, 223 n.52
Sicilian Expedition 6, 163–4
simulacra 5, 74–9, 138–9, 153 n.65

sky/Sky (*see also* Ouranos)
   Aphrodite 53, 56
   Aristophanes 5, 109, 111–17, 122–4, 127, 128 n.27
   Homer 11, 14, 20–1
   Lucan 174–5
   Plato 44
   Plautus 133–4, 136–7, 142
Socrates
   Clouds 119–22, 128 n.25
   eris/*erōs* 29–31, 41–3, 46
   Seneca 67
'Solution sweet' 7, 208, 219
Sosia 135–9, 141–2, 144, 146, 148
sparagmos 90, 96, 98
Sparta 35–6, 114, 117, 180, 194
Sphairos 40–1, 43–4, 177, 182
sponsa Christi 212–13, 215
Sporus 172–3
Sprat, Thomas 6, 190, 196–9,
star (*see also* constellation)
   Aristophanes 5, 7, 14, 110–13, 116–17, 121–4
   chaos 182
   Dog- 96
   Odysseus and 14
   Porphyro and 214–15
   Seneca 74
   Socrates and 128 n.25
Stoicism 5, 67–9, 72–3, 78–9, 84 n.69, 182
sublime/sublimity 1–3 *et passim*
Succession Myth 52–3, 55, 58
Suetonius 172–3, 175, 177, 183
sun/Sun
   Athenian drama 107–10, 112–19, 121–4, 125 n.4, 127 n.22
   eclipse 160–2, 165–7
   light 114–15, 117, 121, 123–4, 128 n.26, 142
   Phoebus 174
   Seneca 73–5, 83 n.59
   time and 21–2
superstition 7, 70, 164–5, 208, 214, 220 n.8

Tantalus 178–9
Telemachus 11–13, 16–17, 21, 57
terror 139, 189–92
Theatre of Dionysus 111–12, 117, 124, 125 n.4
Thetis 58, 97
Thucydides 6, 159–60, 164–5, 167–8, 171, 193–7
timē/*moira* 53–8, 61, 62 n.1, 63 n.21
timing 3, 15–17, 19, 21–2, 23 n.8, 45
Titanomachy 38, 177, 184 n.11
Titans 52–6, 93
tragicomedy 115, 134, 136–7, 139, 147–8, 150 n.20
transgression (*see also* boundary)
   Alexander 167–8
   Giants 177, 184 n.15

Index

Homer 4, 38
Nero 171–5, 183
Plautus 135, 137, 148
Seneca 179
Trojan 31, 34–8, 43, 190, 200
Trojan War 30, 36–7, 40–1, 59, 160
Troy 13, 21, 34–6, 46, 58, 200
Trump, Donald 148, 153 n.65
twins/twinning
    Aegean and Ionian seas 179–82
    Amphitruo, in 135, 139, 145–6
    Aristaeus and Orpheus 96
    Castor and Pollux 114
    Hobbes 194
    Madeline and Saint Agnes 217
    *Manu and *Yemo 4, 98
    Romulus and Remus 4, 98

underworld 90, 95–6, 133, 178–9, 197
Ursa Major 112, 137
usucapio 135, 138

Varro 91, 93, 96, 101 n.26
Venus
    Aphrodite 112
    elegy 214
    images 77, 79
    marriage 222 n.40
    Mars and 75
    planet 113, 117, 137
Vergil
    Aeneid 176
    bougonia 4, 89–99
    Laudes Italiae 176

violence 38, 95, 138, 146, 173, 194
voluptas 75, 78–9, 140, 144

war (*see also polemos*)
    civil 89, 174–5, 181–3, 196
    Dryden 198–200
    English Civil 194–7
    Giants 177
    Heraclitus 38–9
    Homer 30–1, 35–7, 40–1, 43, 59, 160
    Peloponnesian 115, 159–60, 194, 196–7
warrior 13, 31–2, 34, 36–7, 43, 46
weaving
    Helen 36–7, 43, 48 n.14
    Penelope 12–13, 17, 24 n.21
    Saint Agnes 217
wedding
    chamber 214
    dedications 24 n.16
    Eros 43
    gods 219
    martyrdom 210, 212–13
    velatio 215, 222 n.42
Worthen, Thomas D. 2–3, 61 n.1, 84 n.71, 126 n.14, 127 n.21, 149 n.1, 204 n.1

Xerxes 6, 160–3, 166–8

Zeus
    Alexander, son of 166–8
    Athenian comedy 111–13, 116–17, 121
    Giants and 174, 184 n.15
    Homer 20–1, 51, 57–60, 97
    Titans and 53

www.ingramcontent.com/pod-product-compliance
Lightning Source LLC
Chambersburg PA
CBHW070724020526
44116CB00031B/1481